Enjoy tomorrow's Golden Age in the pages of today's Saturday Review

Stimulating, wide-ranging ideas... coverage of topics and people of particular interest to you... writing of rare quality...

These are the elements that make THE GOLDEN AGE an exciting reading adventure, an outstanding anthology.

They are the same elements that make up today's Saturday Review... and make it one of America's most widely-discussed, widely-quoted magazines.

Edited by Norman Cousins and a distinguished editorial team, SR covers world affairs... world peace... the environment... science... education... ideas... travel... literature... the arts... <u>the life of the mind.</u> It is written <u>by</u> and <u>for</u> people who think things through.

In addition to articles that make news, start conversation and action, Saturday Review publishes the most complete book review section of any general magazine. Plus scores of lively features that combine wit and wisdom...puzzles...cartoons...and more.

So when you finish the final pages of this book, you can begin an exciting new reading adventure...start enjoying a new golden age...by filling out and mailing the order form below, which starts Saturday Review coming your way regularly.

SUBSCRIPTION ORDER FORM

Please enter my subscription to Saturday Review as indicated below:

☐ **One year $12**
(\$7.50 under single-copy costs)

☐ **Two years $20**
(\$19.00 under single-copy costs)

☐ **Three years $25**
(\$33.50 under single-copy costs)

☐ New order　　　　☐ Renewal

Saturday Review is published 26 times a year. Above basic rates are good for U.S. and its possessions. Elsewhere add $2 per year.

☐ Payment enclosed
☐ Bill me
☐ Charge to: ☐ American Express ☐ Master Charge
　　　　　　　　　　　　　　　　　(Interbank No. _____)

My account No. _____

Valid through _____

Signature _____

Name _____
　　　　　　　　　(Please print)
Address _____

City _____ State _____ Zip _____

GUARANTEE: If not satisfied with Saturday Review at any time, for any reason, I may cancel my subscription and will receive a full refund on the unexpired portion.

EMA4L0503

Mail to: *Saturday Review/World*, INC.

PO BOX 2045 • ROCK ISLAND, ILL. 61206

PORTRAITS

What memories did Ford Madox Ford have of the superb writer, the tragic human being, Oscar Wilde? What family secrets does Laurence Housman reveal about his poet brother, A. E.? Can doctor-writer Oliver St. John Gogarty dare to understand his Dublin contemporary, James Joyce? Can Thomas Wolfe in his famous self-portrait convey to us a fraction of his agonizing struggles and his joys as he searches for the novelist's art to create *Of Time and the River?* All of these portraits in a gallery pour from the animated pages of the old *Saturday Review of Literature,* the more modern SR and the most recent *World.*

Memories of men who were and are famous, done by men who sometimes were famous and sometimes not, but who always possessed the talent to write about talent in a way that made it a golden time for the magazine in whose pages these pieces first appeared.

THE SOUND OF LAUGHTER

Finally, there is the leavening of laughter. From the first, *Saturday Review* knew that humor is essential to life. Goodman Ace and Cleveland Amory are proof that laughter civilizes, and are as much a part of the half-century tradition as the phoenix itself. Reader, a command and a benediction: read, laugh—and enjoy.

ABOUT THE EDITOR

RICHARD L. TOBIN, executive editor of *Saturday Review,* is a veteran newsman, broadcaster, and editor. In 1961, Mr. Tobin was managing editor of *Saturday Review,* and then became associate publisher in 1968.

THE
GOLDEN
AGE:
The Saturday Review
50th Anniversary Reader

Edited by Richard L. Tobin

THE GOLDEN AGE: THE SATURDAY REVIEW
50TH ANNIVERSARY READER
A Bantam Book published November 1974
2nd printing

All rights reserved.
Copyright © 1974 by Saturday Review/World, Inc.
This book may not be reproduced in whole or in part, by
mimeograph or any other means, without permission.
For information address: Bantam Books, Inc.

Published simultaneously in the United States and Canada

Bantam Books are published by Bantam Books, Inc. Its trade-
mark, consisting of the words "Bantam Books" and the
portrayal of a bantam, is registered in the United States
Patent Office and in other countries. Marca Registrada. Bantam
Books, Inc., 666 Fifth Avenue, New York, New York 10019.

PRINTED IN THE UNITED STATES OF AMERICA

Contents

PART I | First Impressions

PART II | Reflections

PART III | Portraits

PART IV | The Sound of Laughter

POSTSCRIPT

PART I
Part I

PART I
First Impressions

Timely and Timeless

By Henry Seidel Canby

August 2, 1924

A literary review without a program is like modern man without his clothes—healthy, agile, functioning in all his senses, but regarded as less than respectable, even by his friends. Yet what is a program but a reflection of temperament! A sanguine, full-blooded man thinks well of his universe, a melancholy man thinks ill of his, and each makes his program. There is more honest philosophizing in many a casual newspaper column, or blunt plain man's opinion, than in elaborate sets of principles chosen to fit a prevailing mood.

We cannot escape from our moods but we need not capitalize them for the supposed benefit of bored contemporaries. *The Saturday Review* is to have a guiding purpose, that must be drawn not from the temperament of the editorial staff but from things as they are in literature.

To my thinking, one of the most deceptive statements ever uttered is that life is more interesting than literature. Life is only rarely and by moments more interesting than literature; then, I grant, it is engrossing beyond all imagined experience. Vigorous writing is just an attempt to recapture the flavor and pulsation of such moments. But hour-by-hour living is dull beside good books, badly composed, badly selected, unrevealing. It is a fair question whether the shop girl going to work in the morning does not get more sensations of actual life from the book she is reading than through all the rest of her usual day. Men and women who do not find good books interesting are either too dull or too vivid. Either their imaginations cannot be kindled, or their real life is too intense to permit them even for a moment to step out of it.

That is why literature is one of the great subjects,

and, like all great subjects, to be taken with both good humor and utmost seriousness, to be loved and made fun of, to be pondered and fought for—

> How charming is divine Philosophy!
> Not harsh, and crabbed, as dull fools suppose.

The modern fashion, however, does not regard literature—or at least contemporary literature—as a harsh and crabbed female, but rather as a much advertised show girl, bought and paid for, and to be written about at so much a word. A great topic cannot be so approached. In the hearts of those who assess good writing as if it were pig iron or ladies' hose, good humor and sympathy are dead as soon as born. No affectation of wit or enthusiasm can take their place.

A critic of literature must be aware of his good fortune and unblushingly embrace his subject, leaving reticence and prejudice behind. The half-hearted intellectual, afraid of his enthusiasm, is as much of a charge upon criticism as the entranced sentimentalist. One suffers from too little love to give and the other from too little sense in loving.

But in pursuing literature, a literary review (which is a kind of literary personality with motives and character) must have two purposes, especially in America. There are two functions of literature that, so far as I am aware, have not been clearly distinguished in their modern aspects, although the general difference has been the cause of many a lively row. Literature can be timeless and literature can be timely.

There is a saving quality in the great authors which in every age has been a solace for the fine spirit lurking in man's complex of mechanism and mystery. Most of the superlatives applied by philosophic critics to good books refer to this essential quality of the great art of literature. It heartened Cicero when Caesar burst into Italy so roughly; exalted Milton in his blindness; came to many plain men in the King James version; kept Shelley afloat upon a sea of sex (and he drowned in its company); has been known to subdue even the growing pains of the undergraduate. I write lightly of what I in common with a multitude of others believe to be, like religion and hope, one of the few necessities men do not share with beasts. In a generation where size seems hopelessly confused with excellence, and civilization is written in terms of the advertising pages, the spiritual reserve in great books may not need defending, but must be constantly sought out and interpreted.

Every teacher and editor and scholar from Plato down has been a prophet of the religion of literature, until essayists and other preachers have come to praise books only because they can raise and solace the bedraggled soul. Yet this literature of the spirit to which belong mighty musings from the past, and recollected beauty, and all that deals with man not here and now but in his eternal aspects, whether as Prometheus or Falstaff, all this is a literature of retreat. Those who enjoy it are for the moment old. The drums have sounded for them; they have left the streets, left the battle, stepped out of the immediacies of life, are looking on, not into, experience. Now they understand, now they appreciate, now they think of race and family, love and truth, romance and beauty, all the attributes which we see in living only when we have time to meditate upon them.

Indeed a mild pessimism is necessary if literature in these classic aspects is to yield its best. The reader must be no Faust, but willing to leave the moment because memory is more fair. The dreamer has realized his incapacity, the vigorous have become weary, the efficient have learned a passive resignation before they read best in this aspect of literature. Good books in their eternal function are entrances into the life of the spirit, but they are also slow swinging doors leading from crowded corridors into seclusion.

It takes more than good reporting and skilled technique to make literature of this quality. We have had it in our century and a half of American literature—not often, but in greater proportion than has been supposed, except by inflamed patriots. Home-grown thought has advantages which sometimes compensate for other merits. Thoreau and Whitman knew more than Carlyle and Tennyson of the antidotes for *hysteria Americana*.

If *The Saturday Review,* in its purpose to uphold literature, can help to set right the curiously warped estimates of so-called American classics, it will earn a right to subsistence.

So much for the timeless literature of retreat, books in their noblest function of self-heal and illumination. But neither readers nor reviewers can live on mountain tops or in cloisters. New York keeps growing in spite of wise maxims in Plato's "Republic," and "Macbeth" and "Lear" stay true but remote, while the struggle for a million and blatant egoism involve the living. Every book, whatever its potentiality of lasting wisdom, exists in its own social complex and helps to explain it. Therefore, to search for eternal values only in literature and to disregard the rest, is inhuman and a little ridiculous, like trying to understand all ages without experiencing one's own. Good new books especially, whether they contain great art or little, are news of human nature as it is at the moment. We do not read a new book because we think it will live, we read it because it is alive—if it lives, it is because there was life enough to endure the change of seasons, but that is not our only, not even our chief concern, which is with to-day, not tomorrow. To paraphrase—

> If it be not good for me
> What care I how good it be.

This is the timely view of literature, and vigorous reviewers and active-minded readers cannot escape it, even by trying.

For an illustration, consider the literary aspects of this country, sprawling in its greatness. Just after the Revolution, the so-called Hartford wits, who should have been called the Yale Literati, celebrated in pompous heroics the leadership of the new United States. Freedom and Liberty and Opportunity and a half dozen other capitalizations were to conduct Europe and the World into a godlike Future, where man was to realize his glorious Destiny under a Universal Republic. No one writes that way now except in the bunkum of inferior statesmen. Nevertheless, the United States has become after all a model for the world— and I do not mean in virtue, wealth, kind of government, or mould of character. In the United States, that form of society which we still call democratic for want of a juster word, has reached its fullest development, and every civilized country is year by year borrowing, adapting, self-developing, with an equivalent society as an end almost in sight. England has Americanized in this sense almost unbelievably since 1900. The new countries of Eastern Europe are, one hears, more rapid still.

Of course, it is not properly speaking an Americanization, it is the results of the industrial revolution working out into a changed life for every individual. Politics are secondary; pure democracy is no nearer than before; but mass production, mass knowledge, mass communication have produced a society where every man can move, eat, read, hear with all the power that results, although wisdom is just as hard to attain as ever, and self-control much harder. A vulgar society of great energy, flexible, hysterical, confused, is the outcome: a society of infinite possibilities for slow good, or rapid evil. If you are optimistic you call it the emancipation of the common man; if pessimistic, you may quote Polybius on Rome—

The violent influx of prosperity will produce a more extravagant standard of living and an excessively keen competition between individuals. . . . As these tendencies develop, a process of deterioration will be initiated. . . . When they are inspired by a sense of injustice, by the material greed of some of their masters, and with a false conceit by the insincerity of others in pursuit of a political career, . . . the masses become so intensely exasperated and so completely guided by passion that they repudiate all subordination to or even equality with the upper classes and identify the interests of the community with their own. When this point is reached the commonwealth acquires the flattering appellations of Liberty and

Democracy, while it is subject to the appalling reality of the "despotism of the crowd."

And this society, for evident reasons, developed first and most fully in America. We alone had broken through our conventions to go pioneering in a strange environment; we alone had boundless physical opportunities open for a while to all; we alone had a political and social system with small resistance to mass control; we alone through immigration have a cosmopolitan population bound by no single tradition but the American which is liberal and elastic to an extreme.

I am neither praising the American mass civilization nor condemning it. Nor do I mean that having studied its blare and bustle one knows all, or even the most important, facts about the United States. My single point is that here is a type of civilization of obvious importance and therefore obvious interest, and that literature must and will report it. I say report it; literature will try to make art of it also, and may succeed; is certainly in some measure already succeeding. But we Americans who read, and we who edit, cannot remain indifferent to the mere reporting. Every attempt to present it in history, sociology, psychology, biology, as well as in pure literature, or pure comedy, must be interesting, must be for a reviewer as vital as the enduring values of literature.

This literature in its aspect of timeliness is active, not passive, which does not mean that it is better or truer than timeless literature but rather the reverse. It is a literature of men whose drums are still beating onward; it reports the turmoil, not meditation; admixture, not refinement; expectation, not memory; what is momentarily apparent rather than what is necessarily true. Not to read it is not to live now, however much one may dip into essential life. In extremes, the contrast is between the newspapers, the comic strips, the movies against Homer, Shakespeare, and Milton. But the means differ only as between to-day and yesterday—Ring Lardner, Hergesheimer, Robert Frost versus Cooper, Irving, Hawthorne; or between history in

literature and literature as art—Sinclair Lewis and
Edna St. Vincent Millay.

I shall drop then in conclusion those somewhat
formal terms, timeless and timely, and say that criticism,
which is part of the living fabric of contemporary
literature, must be keenly aware of both past and
present, and a partisan of both. It must be like a
modern university where one seeks Principles, but also
works in laboratories of immediate experience amidst
the vivid confusion of experiment. In one guise a gray-
beard philosopher searching for the Best, but also in
the mood of youth, watching the three-ringed show
under the great tent of To-day—yet discriminating in
both—that is the double function of criticism and this
REVIEW.

An Admirable Novel

THE GREAT GATSBY. By F. Scott Fitzgerald.
New York: Charles Scribner's Sons. 1925. $2.

Reviewed by William Rose Benét

May 9, 1925

The book finished, we find again, at the top of page
three, the introductory remark:

> No—Gatsby turned out all right at the end; it was
> what preyed on Gatsby, what foul dust floated in
> the wake of his dreams that temporarily closed out
> my interest in the abortive sorrows and short-winded
> elations of men.

Scott Fitzgerald's new novel is a remarkable analysis
of this "foul dust." And his analysis leads him at the

end of the book, to the conclusion that all of us "beat on, boats against the current, borne back ceaselessly into the past." There is depth of philosophy in this.

The writer—for the story is told in the first person, but in a first person who is not exactly the author, but rather one of the number of personalities that compose the actual author,—the hypothecated chronicler of Gatsby is one in whose tolerance all sorts and conditions of men confided. So he came to Gatsby, and the history of Gatsby, obscured by the "foul dust" aforementioned, "fair sickened" him of human nature.

"The Great Gatsby" is a disillusioned novel, and a mature novel. It is a novel with pace, from the first word to the last, and also a novel of admirable "control." Scott Fitzgerald started his literary career with enormous facility. His high spirits were infectious. The queer charm, color, wonder, and drama of a young and reckless world beat constantly upon his senses, stimulated a young and intensely romantic mind to a mixture of realism and extravaganza shaken up like a cocktail. Some people are born with a knack, whether for cutting figure eights, curving an in-sheet, picking out tunes on the piano, or revealing some peculiar charm of their intelligence on the typewritten page. Scott Fitzgerald was born with a knack for writing. What they call "a natural gift." And another gift of the fairies at his christening was a reckless confidence in himself. And he was quite intoxicated with the joy of life and rather engagingly savage toward an elder world. He was out "to get the world by the neck" and put words on paper in the patterns his exuberant fancy suggested. He didn't worry much about what had gone before Fitzgerald in literature. He dreamed gorgeously of what there was in Fitzgerald to "tell the world."

And all these elements contributed to the amazing performance of "This Side of Paradise," amazing in its excitement and gusto, amazing in phrase and epithet, amazing no less for all sorts of thoroughly bad writing pitched in with the good, for preposterous carelessness, and amazing as well as for the sheer pace of the narrative and the fresh quality of its oddly pervasive poetry. Short stories of flappers and philosophers displayed the same vitality and flourished much the same faults. "Tales of the Jazz Age" inhabited the same glamour. "The Beautiful and Damned," while still in the mirage, furnished a more valuable document concerning the younger generation of the first quarter of the Twentieth Century. But brilliant, irrefutably brilliant as were certain passages of the novels and tales of which the "boy wonder" of our time was so lavish, arresting as were certain gleams of insight, intensely promising as were certain observed facilities, there remained in general, glamour, glamour everywhere, and, after the glamour faded, little for the mind to hold except an impression of this kinetic glamour.

There ensued a play, in which the present writer found the first act (as read) excellent and the rest as satire somehow stricken with palsy, granted the cleverness of the original idea. There ensued a magazine phase in which, as was perfectly natural, most of the stories were negligible, though a few showed flashes. But one could discern the demands of the "market" blunting and dulling the blade of that bright sword wildly whirled. One began to believe that Fitzgerald was coming into line with the purveyors of the staple product. And suddenly one wanted him back in the phase when he was writing so well and, at the same time, writing so very badly. Today he was writing, for the most part, on an even level of magazine acceptability, and on an even level of what seemed perilously like absolute staleness of mind toward anything really creative.

But "The Great Gatsby" comes suddenly to knock all that surmise into a cocked hat. "The Great Gatsby" reveals thoroughly matured craftsmanship. It has structure. It has high occasions of felicitous, almost magic, phrase. And most of all, it is out of the mirage. For the first time Fitzgerald surveys the Babylonian captivity of this era unblinded by the bright lights. He gives you the bright lights in full measure, the affluence, the waste, but also the nakedness of the scaffolding that scrawls skeletons upon the sky when the gold and blue and red and green have faded, the ugly passion, the spiritual meagreness, the empty shell of luxury, the old irony of "fair-weather friends."

Gatsby remains. The mystery of Gatsby is a mystery saliently characteristic of this age in America. And Gatsby is only another modern instance of the eternal "fortunate youth." His actual age does not matter, in either sense. For all the cleverness of his hinted nefarious proceedings, he is the coney caught. For he is a man with a dream at the mercy of the foul dust that sometimes seems only to exist in order to swarm against the dream, whose midge-dance blots it from the sky. It is a strange dream, Gatsby's,—but he was a man who had hope. He was a child. He believed in a childish thing.

It is because Fitzgerald makes so acid on your tongue the taste of the defeat of Gatsby's childishness that his book, in our opinion, "acquires merit." And there are parts of the book, notably the second chapter, that, in our opinion, could not have been better written. There are astonishing feats that no one but Fitzgerald could have brought off, notably the catalogue of guests in Chapter IV. And Tom Buchanan, the "great, big hulking specimen," is an American university product of almost unbearable reality.

Yet one feels that, though irony has entered into Fitzgerald's soul, the sense of mere wonder is still stronger. And, of course, there is plenty of entertainment in the story. It arises in part from the almost photographic reproduction of the actions, gestures, speech of the types Fitzgerald has chosen in their moments of stress. Picayune souls for the most part, and Gatsby heroic among them only because he is partly a crazy man with a dream. But what does all that matter with the actual narration so vivid and graphic? As for the drama of the accident and Gatsby's end, it is the kind of thing newspapers carry every day, except that here is a novelist who has gone behind the curt paragraphs and made the real people live and breathe in all their sordidness. They are actual, rich and poor, cultivated and uncultivated, seen for a moment or two only or followed throughout the story. They are memorable individuals of today—not types.

Perhaps you have gathered that we like the book! We do. It has some miscues, but they seem to us negligible. It is written with concision and precision and mastery of material.

Manhattan at Last!

MANHATTAN TRANSFER. By John Dos Passos.
New York: Harper & Brothers. 1925. $2.

Reviewed by Sinclair Lewis

December 5, 1925

I didn't want to review the book: I was off for a vacation in Bermuda. Now that I've read it, still less do I want to because I am afraid that Mr. Dos Passos's "Manhattan Transfer" may veritably be a great book. And I have come to hate all the superlatives of book-boosting.

The professional executioners, like Mr. Canby, Mr. Sherman, Mr. Mencken—it is their official duty to jerk all the aesthetic criminals off into eternity. But we occasional guardians of spiritual peace, we are typical militiamen, we hate to quell literary strikes and arrest chronic offenders, we like only to parade with roses on our muskets, cheered by the flappers along the way. Yet violent strike duty is really less risky than being benevolent.

Nevertheless, I am going to take the risk.

I wonder whether it may not be true that "Manhattan Transfer" is a novel of the very first importance; a book which the idle reader can devour yet which the literary analyst must take as possibly inaugurating, at long last, the vast and blazing dawn we have awaited. It *may* be the foundation of a whole new school of novel-writing. Dos Passos *may* be, more than Dreiser, Cather, Hergesheimer, Cabell, or Anderson the father of humanized and living fiction . . . not merely for America but for the world!

Just to rub it in, I regard "Manhattan Transfer" as more important in every way than anything by Gertrude Stein or Marcel Proust or even the great white boar, Mr. Joyce's "Ulysses." For Mr. Dos Passos can use, and deftly does use, all their experimental psychology and style, all their revolt against the molds of classic fiction. But the difference! Dos Passos is *interesting!* Their novels are treatises on harmony, very scholarly, and confoundedly dull; "Manhattan Transfer" is the moving symphony itself.

True, no doubt, that without Joyce et Cie., Dreiser and Gesellschaft, Dos Passos might never have been able to devise this channel for the river of living life. Perhaps without a Belasco, even a Charley Hoyt, O'Neill might never have written as he does. But there is no "perhaps" in the question as to whether one prefers "Desire Under the Elms" to the glib falsities of "The Girl of the Golden West." And for one reader there is no question as to whether he prefers the breathless reality of "Manhattan Transfer" to the laboratory-reports of "Ulysses."

In "Manhattan Transfer," Mr. Dos Passos does, really does, what all of us have frequently proved could not be done; he presents the panorama, the sense, the smell, the sound, the soul, of New York. It is a long book—nearly two hundred thousand words, no doubt—but almost any other novelist would have had to take a million words to convey all the personalities and moods which here are quite completely expressed. The book covers some twenty-five years of the growth and decay of not only the hundred or more characters, but of the whole mass of the city—the other millions of characters whom you feel hauntingly behind the persons named and chronicled.

Mr. Dos Passos manages it by omitting the tedious transitions from which most of us can never escape. He flings the heart of a scene before you, ruthlessly casting away the "And so the months and seasons went by and Gertrudine realized that Augustus did not love her" sort of plodding whereby most journeymen novelists fatigue the soul. It is, indeed, the technique of the movie, in its flashes, its cut-backs, its speed.

Large numbers of persons are going to say that it is the technique of the movie. But it differs from the movie in two somewhat important details. It does not deal only with the outsides of human beings; and Dos Passos does not use the technique to acquire a jazz effect, but because, when he has given the complete inwardness of a situation, he will not, to make a tale easy to "drool out," go on with the unessentials.

Dickens, too, expressed the vast London of his day; Dickens, too, leapt from one set of characters to another; and I can hear (with all the classroom tedium returning, after these twenty years) some varnished pedagogue explaining to the four select young literary gentlemen and the hen-medic whom he always has in for tea on Sunday afternoon, that after all, one Mr. Dickens did in his untutored way manage to do everything that Mr. Dos Passos is alleged to have done.

Yet with all this, Dickens, who created characters more enduring than Dos Passos is likely to give us, like Mark Twain and O. Henry, doubted his own genius and, straightway after he had built immortal reality, apologized for such presumption by dragging in page on page of respectable and lying hypocrisy. That Dos Passos does not do, probably could not do, not for one phrase. There is nothing here which is not real, instinct with life as we all know it and all veil it; there is not one character without corpuscles; not one moment when Dos Passos is willing to emblazon his characters by the tricks of caricature, which, though they are considerably harder to achieve than is believed by the laymen, yet are pathetically easier than authentic revelation of genuine personality. And the classic method was —oh, it was rigged! By dismal coincidence, Mr. Jones had to be produced in the stage-coach at the same time with Mr. Smith, so that something very nasty and entertaining might happen. In "Manhattan Transfer," the thirty or forty characters either do not impinge at all or do so only naturally. Each thread of story is distinct yet all of them proceed together. Aunt Tessie McCabe of Benner's Falls may seem far from Croce of Naples, but Aunt Tessie's nephew Winthrop, who is a lawyer in Omaha, has for a client a spaghetti importer whose best friend is the nephew of Croce. And to just that natural degree does Dos Passos intertwine his stories.

But the thing that really distinguishes Dos Passos is not the mechanics of technique. It is his passion for the beauty and stir of life—of people, of rivers and little hills and tall towers by dawn and furnace-kindled dusk. Many wise persons will indicate that he is "sordid." He is not! Scarce Keats himself had a more passionate and sensitive reaction to beauty in her every guise. He does not always express it in breakfast food, easy for the moron to digest; no suave couplets are here, nor descriptions of sky-scrapers so neat that the Real Estate Sections of the Sunday newspapers will beg to reprint them. He deals not in photography but in broken color (though never, thank Heaven, in Picasso impressionism). But there is the City, smell of it, sound of it, harsh and stirring sight of it, the churn and crunch of littered water between ferry-boat and slip, the midnight of sky-scrapers where a dot of yellow betrays an illicit love or a weary accountant, insane clamor of subways in the dark, taste of spring in the law-haunted park; shriek of cabarets and howl of loneliness in hall bedrooms—a thousand divinations of beauty without one slobber of arty Beauty-mongering.

I am wondering again—I am wondering if this may not perhaps be the first book to catch Manhattan. What have we had before, what have we had? Whitman? That is not our Manhattan; it is a provincial city, near the frontier. Howells, Wharton, James? A provincial city near to Bath and the vicar's aunt. Hughes, Fitzgerald, Johnson, all the magazine reporters of the Jazz Age? Foam on the beer! O. Henry? Change Broadway to Market Street or State Street in his stories, and see whether any one perceives a change.

But, to return, the real discussion will be as to whether Mr. Dos Passos is Sordid and perhaps even Indecent. (Dear Lord, and is this to be but joking? Who was the mayor of Florence when Dante looked at Beatrice? Who was the master of the college which kicked out Shelley?)

Yes, Mr. Dos Passos will be slated as sordid. He alleges that the male persons, properly married, owning Buicks and bungalows, sometimes betray an interest in wenches who are not allied to them by matrimony. He hints that physiological processes continue much as they did in the days of Voltaire and M. le Père Rabelais. He maintains that bums on the Bowery often use expletives stronger than "By golly." He even has the nerve to imply that college bred journalists sometimes split infinitives and bottles of synthetic gin.

A low fellow! He does not see life as necessarily approaching the ideals of a Hartford insurance agent. He sees it as a roaring, thundering, incalculable, obscene, magnificent glory.

For whatever John Dos Passos does in this book, he finds life, our American life, our Manhattan life, not a pallid and improving affair, but the blood and meat of eternal humanity.

I have, fortunately, one complaint. I see no advantage in Mr. Dos Passos's trick of running words together as in a paralyzing German substantive; in using such barbarisms as "millionwindowed buildings" or "cabbageleaves." "Grimydark" does certainly give a closer knit impression than "Grimy, dark," but "pepperyfragrance," "tobaccosmoke" and "steamboatwhistles" are against God, who invented spacing and hyphenation to save the eyes. Mr. Dos Passos does not need to call attention to himself by thus wearing a red tie with his dinner clothes. That may be left to the vaudeville intellectuals who, having nothing to say and a genius for saying it badly, try to attract bourgeois notice—which they so much despise and so much desire —by omitting capitals, running words together, and using figures in place of letters. It is necessary to collate "Manhattan Transfer" with the book which introduced

Mr. Dos Passos; "Three Soldiers." To me it seemed
lively and authentic, to many it was arty and whining—
whine, whine, whine—the naughty brutal sergeant, oh,
the nasty fellow! I challenge those who felt so to read
"Manhattan Transfer." There is no whining here! There
is strength. There is the strong savor of very life. I met
Dos Passos once. I have a recollection of lanky vitality
and owlish spectacles. That was many years ago, and
it was not till now that I found the feather, the eagle's
feather—well, I forget the rest.

A New Novelist

IN OUR TIME. By Ernest Hemingway.
New York: Boni & Liveright. 1925. $2.

Reviewed by Louis Kronenberger

February 13, 1926

Ernest Hemingway's first book of short stories comes
fortified with the praise of men like Sherwood Anderson, Ford Madox Ford, Waldo Frank, and John Dos
Passos. The praise of such men fosters deduction. It
indicates that Mr. Hemingway must have merit; it implies that his work is experimental, original, modern-
istic; it may even suggest that his work stems in part
from the modes set by their own creation. All these
deductions are to some extent true, but only the first
is important. There are obvious traces of Sherwood
Anderson in Mr. Hemingway and there are subtler
traces of Gertrude Stein. His work is experimental and
very modern. But much more significantly, it has sound
merit of a personal, nonderivative nature; it shows no

important affinity with any other writer, and it represents the achievement of unique personal experience.

I think it should be emphasized that Mr. Hemingway's stories are as much an achievement as they are an experiment. Already he has succeeded in making some of them finished products, whose form is consonant with their substance and whose value is not an implication for the future but a realization in the present. It is true that he has no power of emotion or deep quality of cerebration, but the way he has observed people and things, speech, surroundings, atmosphere, the spirit of our times, constitutes sufficient accomplishment for the moment. When translated into words, this power of observation is doubly effective: it is precise and direct, it is also suggestive and illuminating. Almost wholly through his sense of observation, he gets life into these pages: life at any moment, life at a vivid moment, life at a high and crucial moment. At his best, getting it there for a moment's duration, he somehow sends it running backward and forward, so that whatever must be understood is comprehensible by a discerning reader.

For the rest, his stories are experiments demanding further discipline and art. Between each two he interposes a paragraph of bare incident which further suggests the spirit of our time. Unfortunately some of the stories themselves, in their form and meaning, are like these paragraphs. They imply significance but they do not attain it; their lacunæ are greater than their substance. They are not without life, but they lack meaning and intensity. Mr. Hemingway is in some respects an "intellectual" writer—in his culture, his humor, his implicit sophistication, his objectivity; but his work itself is finest when it portrays life, conversation, action. He is a synthetic observer, not an analyst.

Honest But Slap-Dash

SOLDIERS' PAY. By William Faulkner.
New York: Boni & Liveright. 1926. $2.

Reviewed by Thomas Boyd

April 24, 1926

William Faulkner's novel, "Soldiers' Pay," is not for people of prosaic minds. From the outset this story of strange humans in the spring of 1919, following the signing of the armistice, is pitched unnaturally high; and as the tale continues it seems as if the author were struggling to break all contacts with the normal world and to vault upward into a sort of esoteric sphere of his own making.

Shorn to its baldest, "Soldiers' Pay" tells of a young American aviator, given up for dead by his father, who returns to his north Georgia home badly mutilated and discovers that the girl to whom he is engaged has given herself to a youth who remained in the village during the war. This young aviator is described as having a face so scarred that even gin-drinking flappers faint when forced to gaze upon it. Discharged from an English hospital as incurable, he is on his way back to die on his native heath.

The story begins with three drunken soldiers riding westward in a parlor car after demobilization. One of the former doughboys nonchalantly tries to push another through the window. There is such talk as this: "You wrong me as ever man wronged. Accuse me of hiding mortgage on house? Take this soul and body; take all. Ravish me, big boy." The answer to that is given: "Hark, the sound of battle and the laughing horses draw near. But shall they dull this poor unworthy head? No! But I would like to of seen one of them laughing horses. Must of been lady horses all together. Your extreme highness . . . will you be kind enough to kindly condescend to honor these kind but unworthy strangers in a foreign land?"

At best such *non sequiturs* are amusing, suspiciously reminiscent of the mad dream of Leopold Bloom. They pave the way out of reality and place the action of the story on a shadowy horizon where vivid characterization is unnecessary and background not pertinent.

Thus "Soldiers' Pay" offers the reader a group of vague, abnormally behaving characters who waver uncertainly and fantastically through the story. Donald Mahon, the wounded hero, is described only by his scar. Mrs. Powers, the war widow, comes into the reader's consciousness as "the black woman." Januarius Jones seems like an offshoot of the personality of "stately plump Buck Mulligan" of "Ulysses."

These characters act with an almost delightful lack of responsibility. Meeting Donald Mahon on a train in New York State Mrs. Powers and Joe Gilligan, who evidently have other destinations, decide to accompany the wounded youth to his father's home in Georgia, a jaunt of only about a thousand miles. Staying over one night in a hotel the three live in a strange proximity. This sort of incident is capped only by the behavior of Januarius Jones. Jones, a fat satyr, appears from nowhere on the lawn of Donald Mahon's preacher father. He likes the place, and stays, hurling obscene words at Mahon's fiancée, whom he endeavors to seduce. But in this Jones fails, the girl preferring the village boy with an automobile.

Mr. Faulkner submits to very little government in writing. His impressionistic manner is honest but slapdash; often he sets down an extraordinarily vivid scene. The book has fervor and strength, but it would be more effective if it were better controlled. So far as the returned soldier is concerned, Larry Barreto made a much better job of him in "A Conqueror Passes."

Making of a Demagogue

MY BATTLE. By Adolf Hitler.
Abridged and translated by E. T. S. Dugdale.
Boston: Houghton Mifflin Company. 1933. $2.

Reviewed by Matthew Josephson

October 28, 1933

Adolf Hitler's impresarios would seem to have done him a disservice on the whole in pruning down his eight-hundred-page "autobiography" to the skeleton form in which it is now offered to an American audience. In its original dimensions this work had the abandon, the histrionic frenzy of one of Dostoievsky's garrulous sinners; it had, despite its turgid and atrocious German, literary qualities which were unconscious and all its own. These have been lost, and also such logical organization as existed in the original, which was never much. At the same time it has plainly been impossible to "tone down" the book, to amend all the things which would presumably be incomprehensible, alarming, or offensive to Americans. To do this it would have been necessary to amend all.

One's first impression of Hitler's memoirs—approximately nine-tenths propaganda—is apt to be of marked disappointment and incredulity. The author tells us little enough about himself; his tracts on Pan-Germanism are neither new nor apt to be favorably seen on this side of the Atlantic; his anti-Semitism, too, seems scarcely up-to-date, since he and his cohorts seem to have taken the upper hand over the Israelites so decisively that there is no more sporting excitement in the affair. Is this all, one asks? Is this the Word of the great captain of the Nazis, the bible of the party which has effected the most important political upheaval in Europe since 1919? One reads here scraps of world history intermingled with fairy tales, invocations to humanitarianism and to sadism, pæans to chivalry and to bullying, shots of international politics, modern publicity, and medieval superstition. Here shrewd, worldly observations are mingled with colossal nonsense, daring notions with beetling-browed ignorance and incitements to riot. When was there ever such a wonderful crazy-quilt of ideas gotten up by the "actual head of a great European State?" The writings and memoirs of a Churchill, a Clemenceau, a Lenin, and a Trotsky make Hitler's resemble nothing so much as the drivellings of an intoxicated schoolboy.

I have no wish to speak with impropriety; the new political dotage may gain over us here too. But before we become unhinged by the present state of the world and lose once for all our sense of proportion, let me record that in the period between 1919 and 1933, a modern dictator rose to triumph by choosing the mental age of ten or twelve as his frame of reference, the age at which "bogeys" and devils can be conjured up to terrify and enrage. Other German leaders thought that Hitler had pitched his key too low; but he has shown by his great lesson in politics that they were wrong.

The dogmas, the arguments in Hitler's book do not teach us anything about the social question or even the Nazi revolution—whose historic causes and implications have been widely discussed. They do tempt us to reflect specifically upon the nature and mechanism of a Fascist demagogue. By his confession of faith, world history to this successful demagogue is the affair of a few brilliant autocrats, Cæsar, Frederick the Great, and Bismarck. Behind the great autocrat is the great race from which he stems, and which he leads to glory: the Germans, for instance, *"the highest culture-race."* "But all the wisdom of this earth is as nothing unless served, covered, and protected by force." Hence Germany was at its apex under Bismarck and the rule of the Prussian army. The finest education for a man is German army life, and "the greatest and most unforgettable period" of Hitler's life was that of the World War. As compared with the "pure" Germans, the French are a race chiefly given to "bastardizing" the colored races which are under their dominion. The treaty of Brest-Litovsk forced upon the Russians by the victorious German army was a work of Christian mercy, "truly immense and humane," and in no way justified the harsh terms of Versailles. What caused the Germans finally to lose the war was not Allied and American power, or naval blockade and hunger, but the conspiracy of Jewish Marxists. Democracy and all representative forms of government are the inventions of international Jewish conspirators. Jews are possessed of superhuman cunning, and are devils who have long been plotting "the breakdown of human culture and the devastation of the world." To those who believe in socialism, lying is a daily necessity. If your enemies don't agree with you, or oppose you in print, wipe out their publications with a thirty centimeter grenade. Karl Marx was really working in the interests of international capitalism and stock exchanges. Trade-unionists who strike are also working for international capitalism. Further:

> On the one hand he (the Jew) is making use of his capitalist methods for exploiting humanity to the very full, and on the other he is getting ready to sacrifice his sway and very soon will come out as their leader in the fight against himself. "Against himself" is of course only a figurative expression, for the great master of lies knows very well how to emerge with apparently clean hands and burden others with the blame.
> We now see that Marxism is the enunciated form of the Jewish attempt to abolish the importance of personality in all departments of human life and to set the mass of numbers in its place. In politics the parliamentary form of government is its expression. . . .

In other words, the Jew is both exploiting and protecting humanity, and the Jew, to whom Hitler accords so much exceptional personal power, seeks to abolish the "importance of personality" and by having a majority rule relegate himself to a helpless minority!

Can such reasoning be answered? Hitler represents a revolt against reason. He himself urges an "intolerant fanaticism" as the answer to opposition. Does Adolf

Hitler believe all this weird farrago? One would think not, judging by his successful career. Hitler is far more intelligent than his enemies have estimated him to be. As a political strategist of the modern stripe he has shown a cynical boldness as well as resourcefulness. No, all this extravagance is purely propaganda after Hitler's fashion, the only propaganda he knows. For aside from his political strategy, he has won his chief fame as a platform demagogue, and is reputed to be one of the greatest natural orators of his kind. The unfortunate thing is that his genius is largely limited to the field of extemporaneous speech, before vast throngs, under torchlight and in the atmosphere of a revival camp; the hypnosis of those hours he cannot translate to the measured terms of the printed page. Where in a meeting he might shout down an opponent with an effect of thunderous magnificence, his "autobiography" expends itself in infantile abuse, in profanity, and in baseless calumny.

Those who doubt Hitler's cleverness, his capacity to be rational in the most worldly manner should note the passage where he explains his notion of propaganda:

> All propaganda . . . should adapt its intellectual level to the receptive ability of the least intellectual of those whom it is desired to address. Thus it must sink its mental elevation deeper in proportion to the numbers of the mass whom it has to grip. If . . . the object is to gather a whole nation within its circle of influence, there cannot be enough attention paid to avoidance of too high a level of intellectuality.

With this clue, we may understand better the expediency of his rantings, of his self-contradictions, of his diversified appeal to crowd passions, including those of blood-thirstiness or sadism. But for himself he holds other views, other beliefs in which he has been superbly consistent, however shifting his day-to-day tactics may have been.

We are familiar with the aspirations of Nazi as well as non-Nazi patriots to restore Germany's national self-respect, to render her self-sufficient and arm her against surrounding enemies, while unifying her people after years of internal dissension or class struggle. In these views, the officer caste, the Junkers, the Hugenberg industrialists as well as the Centrists of Bruning saw eye to eye with Hitler. But Hitler, from the very beginning, over a decade ago, as one of his German biographers relates, had more to offer than all the other parties.

What have you to give to the people in the way of Faith? he says to the other parties of the Right in 1923. "Nothing. For you no longer believe in your own formulas. That is the all powerful thing that our movement should create: for these vast, questing and bewildered masses a new, firm Faith, so that they may find at least one place that gives their hearts repose. And that we will bring about!"

This ruling idea of Hitler's—to conjure up faith in Race, or arms, or Wotan, or anything that might serve —drew the attention of the officer caste, the old-fashioned bureaucrats, police officials, and royalists who sheltered and nourished him in his early Munich days. Perhaps he seemed mad to them; but certainly "this unknown soldier who never died" seemed abler than all the Ludendorffs, Kapps, and even Hohenzollerns to rally the masses around himself by his evangelistic, and, indeed, "convulsionary" tactics.

This man exudes hate and passion, fascinates the crowd like the priest of some sinister cult. Look at him, speak to him in person, and he seems mediocre; but bring together a mob of ten thousand or a hundred thousand and he seems to magnify himself in proportion to the multitude he confronts. Tirelessly he speaks for one hour, two hours, three hours. He wrestles and fights, he jumps up and down, his gestures grow more and more extraordinary. A German observer of his great days of agitation relates:

The man on the platform no longer debates, but gives battle. The crowd does not see the enemy; this fighter has the enemy, the devil in himself. He fights against the disintegration of the nation, against the inertia of the people, the guilt of present and past rulers—against the very Marxist in himself, the bad student, the blunderer of 1922, 1923, and 1930, and 1932. He fights his own fear, his own devil, like an old anchorite —it is no longer agitation . . . but exorcism, revival. He can say whatever he wishes. . . . The walls shake. . . . The State trembles.

But Hitler, as his own autobiography reveals, was always one of those evangelists and dervishes, who immediately upon returning from trance or transport, inquired after the effect of the show upon the customers, the receipts in the box office. A born demagogue on the one side, on the other he was a shrewd hunter of political fortune, keeping his accounts, drawing money from all sides, utilizing his followers and lieutenants to the full as well as the chances presented by the times or by the mistakes of enemies. He himself was capable of growing and learning from misfortune. Around him the legend of an *instinktmench* was created, yet his impromptu appearances have often been fiascos. He is more likely, as it is claimed in certain quarters, a neurasthenic who in sleepless nights prepares his scenes. Thus he atoned for grievous blunders again and again. The march of the Brown Fascists of Germany has been a long one, so long that many experienced observers held that they had missed their hour of destiny by 1932. Hitler's successful bid for power in 1933 was the last of six desperate strokes during the course of eleven years.

Invested with power, Hitler will tend more and more to be a pure politician whose measures, under the surface at least, will appear to be dictated by the logic of events rather than by his nightmares. Yet the accidents of his personal orientation, as they have left their stamp upon his counter-revolutionary movement, are of the utmost significance for the Third Reich.

There are two signal facts about his early life which may be drawn from his own account. Adolf Hitler was born in 1889, a South German, in a small village of

Upper Austria, at the Bavarian frontier. In this region, the Germans on both sides of the border express their religious emotion still in the most primitive manner. If we are to accept anything of Hitler's doctrine of race heritage, the mystical or fanatical force in the man may be attributed, in part, at least, to his "hillbilly" environment.

The second significant fact that emerges from his autobiography is that Hitler *was a member of the middle class, the petite bourgeoisie, who was déclassé, but who refused all his life to become a proletarian.*

Hitler's father was a petty customs official, nationalistic and pious, who died when he was young and left his son in poverty. The family name had been Schicklgruber, according to reliable accounts, and had been changed by his parents. (In Germany it is: *Heil Hitler*; but in the United States we may say "Hail Schicklgruber" if we wish.) A "wayward son," as he confesses, a poor student who never matriculated as an architect, Hitler's studies were halted in Vienna toward 1910. Penniless, he worked at odd jobs connected with building, or house-painting. He was not happy nor of one mind with his fellow workers. In boyhood he had absorbed ideals of Pan-Germanism, he tells us, from an instructor at school as well as from his father. Siegfried and Frederick the Great were his idols. His comrades wanted him to join their union, and he refused. Their aspirations were not his; their socialist teachings which "repudiated" everything, the glory of war as of the Emperor, which held patriotism an instrument of capitalists, school a means of making slaves, and law the way of oppression for the working-class— all this was alien to him, though real enough to them.

In passages omitted from the present translation, he says: "My clothes were still in order, my speech scrupulous, my manner reserved. . ." He was, in short, a bourgeois, despite his ill-luck. And the supposition has been made that Hitler's "scabbing" brought his indignant comrades to drive him from his job. Here was the germ of his anti-Marxism. There seemed to be Jewish leaders among the socialist unions of Vienna, malodorous schemers, preachers of the class struggle, destroyers of himself and of the Fatherland, in his mind. "Then I became a fanatical anti-Semite . . ." he tells us in the unexpurgated German text. Hitler's mind was permanently colored in his Austrian youth; before he went to work in Munich in 1912, he was a Pan-Germanist, an anti-Semite, and a "Christian Socialist,"—for there were forerunners of Nazism long before the war both in Austria-Hungary and in Germany. In his intense nature the early convictions were unshaken and indeed strengthened by the events of the world war.

Among the idle veterans who hung about Munich in the winter of 1918–1919, and who with the Reichswehr put down Eisner's Red government in the bloodiest fashion, Hitler distinguished himself not only as a ferocious Red-hunter, but also as a *Hetzer*, a gifted agitator. His long and disordered readings as well as practice fitted him to be a skillful speaker; and soon he could spur the soldiers as none of the officers could. Among the prowling companies of veterans in regular guard service or free-lance corps which periodically disturbed the early years of the Republic with their clamor and their repeated insurrections, Hitler's band became a spearhead of terror and Hooliganism. These ex-soldiers, and also the high army officers who secretly or openly encouraged them, had appetite only for conquering the streets, for the beating, now of Jews, now of Reds. Recruits, such as the émigré Russian-German, Alfred von Rosenberg, brought the tactics of the Black Hundreds, or the notions of the rising Italian Fascism. At no time were the reactionary Guards or free-lance corps effectively put out of business in Bavaria. They were "murder organizations," it was protested; but nothing was done.

The day came when these ex-soldiers, ex-officers wanted a political movement, a party to represent the actual or potential force of arms they possessed. The leader, Hitler, emerged at first from a world of *franctireurs* and Hooligans. As his stage was broadened by making alliances with other elements of discontent, peasants and "Christian Socialists," his tactics changed; he became something of a politician as well as a Hooligan. There were fewer of the deliberate exhortations to murder or massacre or riot—though they were never missing. Gottfried Feder, Röhm, Gregor Strasser, and Goebbels, men of superior education, brought him new devices and ideas, and an improved dialectic for his credo, as they brought him recruits and money. There follow, then, all the picturesque and daring manœuvers, circus-meetings, provocations, street fighting, mass agitation, and press propaganda which were tolerated in Germany for a decade.

The Nazi movement made strange alliances as it groped toward power. Hitler took money from foreigners as well as from generals and capitalists. He promised much; to his followers, constantly trained for spectacular action, always secretly armed, he gave *panem et circenses*. But most of all, he showed a realistic political tendency to take people as they were, humoring their crudest fears or appetites, imposing upon them no self-denying, educational process such as the Communists attempted. Instead he professed to appeal to all their immediate, clashing interests. The class that wanted more dividends, the class that wanted higher farm prices or simply jobs, the elements that wanted action, or strengthening of the foreign policy—all those who wished their special interests served "without leaving the table"—he appealed to. And in the end, after the virtual break-down of the parliamentary system, he canalized the unrest which had gained over all Germany into his huge organization. The satisfactions and the dangers of futurity are now his. In the meantime, to effect union among fatally conflicting classes, Fascism must proceed with mounting violence.

In recent years our philosophers have often warned us of the dangers of exporting modern technical knowledge, with its telephones and machine guns, to the more savage races. Hitler, in his crusade against civilization, we must note, has used every modern instrument with daring: airplane, radio, press, the methods of American advertising, and those of Chicago gangsterism. He epitomizes our modern dilemma.

Adolf Hitler's autobiography, written in 1924, is already obsolete to him. What effect will it have upon American readers? Are they men of reason, or will the instigations, the monotonously repeated propaganda take sway over them? The test should be instructive to us, and the American version—even with its attacks on the church and on foreign powers "toned down"—was in my opinion worth publishing here. It is better for us to know soon whether Hitler's direct propaganda against the type of democratic political institutions we own here, and his incitements to riot will reach their mark, so that we may determine what part we must take.

In the terms of Adolf Hitler's unique dialectics, this review is only too patently "a shameful Jewish trick."

Ode to Liberty

IT CAN'T HAPPEN HERE. By Sinclair Lewis.
New York: Doubleday, Doran & Company. 1935. $2.50.

Reviewed by Elmer Davis

October 19, 1935

Suppose America went Fascist, what then? Mr. Lewis has supposed it, and the answer to the question makes a hair-raising story, once he gets into it. Granted that a Senator who, explicitly, is not Huey Long (still living when the book was written), with the support of a radio preacher who, explicitly, is not Father Coughlin, should win the next election on a program promising everything to everybody, except such Jews and Ne- groes as refused to be content with the station in life to which it has pleased God to appoint them; what would happen to the people of these states? Just about what happened in Germany, says Lewis; and (no doubt drawing a good deal of his information from his wife, Dorothy Thompson) he translates the present of Ger- many into the future of America with a skill and power that will give you insomnia for a couple of nights after you finish the book.

Unfortunately it takes him a hundred and fifty pages to really get going. The story of the campaign, the election, the first acts of the new administration, is done no better than it could be done by any one of fifty newspapermen on assignment from the city editor. Lewis is writing a missionary tract and a fervent prayer, and it is worth waiting for; but the first third of his book, mixing fiction with fact and real with imaginary characters, is the same type of story as Floyd Gibbons's "The Red Napoleon," or the preparedness-invasion stories that were so numerous in 1916. "The Red Napoleon" was tripe except for the purely military chapters and most of the war-time invasion stories were tripe without that exception; Lewis is far better than that, yet when he is writing about public affairs and their impact on private characters he gets into his story none of the unbearably vivid sense of a national crisis against which individuals play out their personal crises, that Rex Stout managed to put into "The President Vanishes." And Lewis's story creaks in the transition from self-government to dictatorship; it may be doubted if any President would be able to get away, at the very beginning of his administration, with the arrest of all members of Congress who refused to vote him absolute power.

But all that had to be got out of the way before Lewis could get down to his real business, and you are earnestly advised to push your way through it and give attention to what he has to say. Once he has all the works of German fascism going in America the story concentrates more and more on what happened in one small town in Vermont to the sort of people you know; and especially to Doremus Jessup, the easygoing, elderly liberal editor who saw his paper taken away from him, his son-in-law murdered, and his worthless and vicious hired man promoted to be fascist boss of the district. When Doremus Jessup, his daughter, his mistress, and a few of his friends become the local cell of the New Underground, the secret revolutionary organization in contact with the refugees in

Canada, the story becomes a thriller of the very first quality, and a thriller with as good a sermon behind it as Lewis has ever preached.

For essentially this is an ode to Liberty. Doremus Jessup was a liberal and he remained a liberal to the end; but a fighting liberal who found plenty of others like himself, men and women who believed that liberty not only is worth fighting for but can be fought for. Lewis writes like a man who has had to listen to communists; and the bigoted intolerance of communists who would rather continue as a persecuted sect, sustained only by the hope that some day they may do the persecuting, than admit any merit in people who fail to accept their theology, has never been more effectively blasted than by half a dozen scarifying paragraphs in this story. He pays his respects, too, to the gentlemen who talk about liberty, meaning only liberty for big money, and think that the Constitution consists of the due-process clause plus a few meaningless phrases. It may surprise some readers to find the author of "Babbitt" and "Elmer Gantry" appearing as a devotee of America, as fervent as Whitman; but the America he loves is Whitman's America, and Lincoln's, and Jefferson's. An America not to be restored, at this late date? Perhaps . . .

Steinbeck's Uncovered Wagon

THE GRAPES OF WRATH. By John Steinbeck.
New York: The Viking Press. 1939. $2.75.

Reviewed by George Stevens

April 15, 1939

It is exciting to watch the steady unfolding of a real writer's talent, to follow his development from promise to achievement, with the sense that he knows what he wants and knows what he is doing. It is particularly exciting because it is rare. Van Wyck Brooks pointed out long ago that the blighted career, the unfulfilled promise, is the rule in American writing, and his statement turned out to be as accurate in prophecy as in diagnosis. Writers who produced one or two good books; writers who abandoned literature to go to Hollywood, or to go to Spain, or to write plays, or to attend meetings, or simply to retire on their earnings; writers who exhausted their resources and kept doing the same book over and over—one after another they have left their over-excitable discoverers holding the bag: a bag full of words like "genius" and "masterpiece," to be taken three times a day, with meals.

Among the novelists of his generation, the most notable exception to this state of things is John Steinbeck. He has never yet flashed in the pan. According to his official biographer (Joseph H. Jackson in the S.R.L., September 25, 1937), Steinbeck tore up the manuscripts of his first two novels, and retired the third. Since his first published book, "The Cup of Gold," each successive one has revealed a new facet of his ability. "Tortilla Flat" was the humorous and sympathetic story of some attractive and disreputable Mexicans. "In Dubious Battle" was a serious labor novel, remarkable of its kind in presenting the issues in terms of animate characters, who had the vitality to take the story over for themselves. "Of Mice and Men" was a miniature tragedy which lost none of its effectiveness for being written with an eye on the stage, which was just as poignant whether you took it straight or symbolically. Different as these novels are (and Steinbeck's variety is further manifested in the stories in "The Long Valley"), there has been a constancy of flavor which is impossible to define: something deeper than the "personality" of the author, which never intrudes; something more impalpable than "ideas"; something in the style, but in a style of which one is almost never conscious.

For these reasons Steinbeck's reputation is unique. All our reviewers, and such critics as we have among us, are pretty consciously in the "watch Steinbeck" movement. If it is turning into a bandwagon, that is not Steinbeck's fault. He has already survived some fairly indiscriminate adulation. His activities, outside of writing novels, have managed to remain his own affairs, to a remarkable degree in the great American goldfish bowl; and nothing has interfered with his serious production. The lively curiosity which Steinbeck has inspired is a legitimate curiosity about his work. Because of his variety, nobody can put him in a pigeon-hole; nobody has been able to say, "Steinbeck has done it again," but rather, "What is Steinbeck going to do next?" Since it became known that Steinbeck had a new novel for spring publication, and that it was by far his longest and most ambitious production to date, it is safe to say (for whatever it may mean) that no other book on the current lists has been so eagerly looked forward to by the reviewers.

"The Grapes of Wrath" is worth it, worth all the talk, all the anticipation, all the enthusiasm. Here is the epitome of everything Steinbeck has so far given us. It has the humor and earthiness of "Tortilla Flat," the social consciousness of "In Dubious Battle," the passionate concern for the homeless and uprooted which made "Of Mice and Men" memorable. These elements, together with a narrative that moves with excitement for its own sake, are not mixed but fused, to produce the unique quality of "The Grapes of Wrath." That quality is an understanding of courage—courage seen with humor and bitterness and without a trace of sentimentality; courage that exists as the last affirmation of human dignity. To convey that understanding with passionate conviction, in human terms and also in terms of mature intelligence, so that we respond integrally and without reservation, is a very considerable thing for a novel to do. That is what "The Grapes of Wrath" does. It is by no means perfect, but possibly its faults (one of which is egregious) are a measure of its worth, in that it triumphantly lives them down.

"The Grapes of Wrath" is the story of the new American nomads, of the migrant farmers who have lost their few acres in the Oklahoma dust bowl to the onward march of tractors and foreclosures. It is in particular the story of one family, the Joads from a farm near Sallisaw. You have seen them going west through Texas and New Mexico on Route 66, or you have seen them in Resettlement Administration photographs: three generations in a second-hand truck, piled high with everything they own. Car after car, from Arkansas to California; people with no home but the road, no prospects but hope, no resources but courage: the thirty-niners in their uncovered wagons.

With this material Steinbeck has done what, according to at least one theory, cannot be done: he has made a living novel out of the news in the paper, out of contemporary social conditions. In "Land of the Free," Archibald MacLeish wrote a sound track to the Resettlement Administration's documentary stills. He looked at the pictures of the plowed-under farmers and wrote a poet's abstract statement, pared down to gaunt monosyllables, of a seemingly insoluble problem. Steinbeck has looked at the Oklahoma farmers themselves—the "Okies" in Salinas County, California, driven from camp to camp, finding no work, not allowed to settle. What he has written about them is a narrative: colorful, dramatic, subtle, coarse, comic, and tragic. For "The Grapes of Wrath" is not a social novel like most social novels. It is instead what a social novel ought to be. When you read it, you are in contact not with arguments, but with people.

I just said that Steinbeck has seen these people, which is a presumption, but is supported by the dedication: "To Carol, who willed it. To Tom, who lived it." Tom Joad comes out of State Prison on parole (he had killed a man in self-defense, and has nothing on his conscience) just in time to join his family, who had been forced off the land and were heading west, lured by rumors of a land of plenty where workers were wanted on the farms. Each of the Joads is alive and convincing: Pa and Ma, practical, wise with the tenant farmers' knowledge of the underside of life, accepting what came and making the best of it; Grampa, an obscene old goat, full of gusto, always throwing his hip out of joint when he laughed; Uncle John, who had to drink when his memories became unbearable; Casy, the preacher, who saw through and beyond his backwoods evangelism; Tom's younger brothers and sisters, Noah not quite right in the head, Rose of Sharon expecting a baby. A family out of "Tobacco Road"; but although Steinbeck never asks us to sympathize with them, although he makes them as funny as they are pitiful, they are human beings, not degenerates or freaks.

The laughter subsides as the uncovered wagon goes west; the comedy gives way to tragedy. Two of the family are left in unmarked graves along the roadside; and one burial scene is handled with the utmost skill and effectiveness. On to California and to disillusion, with the last of the money giving out, with rumors of work up the road (but no men wanted when they get there), with the California Gestapo burning the Okie's camps, arresting objectors as "dangerous reds," riding herd on those who do get work in the orchards at starvation wages. The Joads find a temporary haven in a government camp, and temporary work in a peach orchard, but always they have to move on—until Tom gets into trouble again, and Rose of Sharon's baby is born. From all their wanderings the Joads learn one thing: that the only people who will help them are others as down and out as themselves. It is out of this comradeship among the hopeless that courage is kept alive—the courage that is their last possession. In its affirmation of man's courage in desperation lie the human significance and value of "The Grapes of Wrath."

Others will see in it a different and more immediately sociological value. Unquestionably "The Grapes of Wrath" states the problem of the southwestern tenant farmer in a form that will bring it home to the imaginations of thousands who have hitherto looked on it with comparative unconcern. Unquestionably, also, Steinbeck sees his material both as a narrative and as a condition calling for action. At regular intervals in the book he inserts general chapters stating the problem in terms of pure non-fiction. For my own part, I found these chapters at best superfluous, occasionally sententious, and in one instance downright bad (this is a very windy passage indeed, in which the author coins the word "Manself," which I hope no one will ever use again). It is not these chapters, but the story of the Joads, that makes you want to do something about the migratory tenant farmers.

There remain one warning and one major criticism. It is only fair to say that there are conservative readers whom the language used by the Joad family will offend. In my opinion, all the dialogue is necessary and right; Steinbeck's ear is perfect, and he lets the Joads talk with uninhibited coarseness. I think this is vital in a serious book like "The Grapes of Wrath," and that it would be obscene to write the dialogue otherwise; but I realize that some readers will feel differently.

As for the criticism—a point on which another group of readers will disagree—I think that the last scene of the novel is bathos. It describes a physically possible but highly unusual event which even if palatable would be unconvincing; and even if Steinbeck had made it convincing, he would have added nothing to the story. The fact is that the story has no ending. We are left without knowing what happens to the characters. That is a necessary condition of writing about the immediate situation of the tenant farmers' odyssey, and we could put up with the absence of a satisfactory ending. But the final episode in the book seems to me a trick to jar the reader out of the realization that the story really does not end. It takes away a little of the effectiveness, and there will be many readers to wish Steinbeck hadn't done it.

But "The Grapes of Wrath" is good enough to live down more than this. Mrs. Roosevelt spoke recently of the need for a novelist who can interpret what is going on in this country among the kind of people of whom book readers in general know little—people like the Joads. John Steinbeck is the novelist. He knows what the country is doing to the Joads, and what goes on in their minds and emotions.

Dirty Weather

WILLIWAW. By Gore Vidal.
New York: E. P. Dutton & Co., Inc.
1946. 222 pp. $2.50.

Reviewed by Jonathan Daniels

July 6, 1946

The williwaw, as Gore Vidal explains in this strong,
simple book, is a big northern storm—a kind of hurricane with a lot of snow. And this particular williwaw
which he presents to his readers and his characters
on the voyage from Andrefoki Bay to Arunga in the
Aleutians is one not soon to be forgotten. It is so magnificent a storm, indeed, that it ought to be easy to
believe that Mr. Vidal is concerned with weather and
not with war and the picture of Americans in it.
Actually the war seems far off; his crew and his pas-
sengers—even the West Point major who recognized
his own resemblance to Wellington—seem very puny
in the wind. But there are few war books made of war
memories in which the picture of people in war seems
so clearly and so honestly drawn.

Mr. Vidal, of course, did not invent the device of
catastrophe as an aid to portraiture. Indeed, to the pattern of the stories of storm, he has added little more
than the word "williwaw." But he has not only used
a familiar device with the finest craftsmanship. More
important, he has brought to its use an understanding of character and a skill in portraying it which make
his voyagers seem almost the elemental figures of all
men at war.

Essentially it is a very simple and very masculine
book about very simple things. With the exception of
the brief stop at Big Harbour, where even old women
can profit on worn charms (and where young Olga's
greed can make a feud deadlier than the williwaw), it
is a wholly masculine story of hard drinking and hard
work, of all the varieties of fear, of homesickness,

vanity, and courage. Mr. Vidal writes no essays about the diverse male characteristics which his men at sea show before, after, and during the storm. Indeed, his characterization is as compact as ship construction and as sturdy as Warrant Officer Evans's ship. He may be a little too gentle with the terror of his chaplain. Perhaps he unduly enjoys the pompous stupidity and arrogance of his West Pointer. He is almost as casual about a murder which would take a lot of trouble and investigating to prove as his characters are. After all, the storm is over. The man is dead. The Army goes on. But throughout the book there is a basic faith in the courage and judgment of the very human officers and men of the storm-battered ship.

Indeed, for all Mr. Vidal's knowledge of the ways of the williwaw, I had a feeling that perhaps his report of the ship's escape from the storm was not quite so convincing as his portrayal of those who escaped. All in all, however, "Williwaw" can be read for the excitement. Mr. Vidal has written no creaking allegory or parable. His storm and his people are straight out of nature. Even his army men seen in storm seem even in a Diesel age at least as natural as the wind. But this is definitely not merely another book about war experiences. It is a novel of great promise by a young man whose skill as a craftsman is more important than his services as a soldier.

A Dixieland Stew

OTHER VOICES, OTHER ROOMS. By Truman Capote. New York: Random House. 1938. 231 pp. $2.75.

Reviewed by Richard McLaughlin

February 14, 1948

For years now we have had it drummed into us that the South is decaying. With the exception of the novels of Ellen Glasgow, Caroline Gordon, Stark Young, and Margaret Mitchell, we have a difficult time trying to visualize crinolines, magnolia blossoms, and barbecues ever having existed below the Mason and Dixon line. And certainly Truman Capote's novel does not suggest that young Southern novelists are inclined to look any more cheerfully on their sunny land this year than last.

Against the somewhat creaking, musty backdrop of the Louisiana swamplands, replete with rotting Spanish moss, toadstools, spider webs, crumbling, dilapidated old Southern mansions, and the pitter-patter of ghostly feet dancing on the dusty ballroom floor, Truman Capote unfolds his incredible little tale of Southern decay. Perhaps if we had not seen how skillfully and successfully Mr. Capote handled his frightening nightmare world of devil-children and escaped lunatics in his short stories, we would not be half so disappointed in the way he has put together various macabre elements for a full-length novel. Where the highly effective and carefully credited mood of terror and awful sense of evil in his short stories could hold a reader for a half hour's sitting, these same character creations in a novel appear more often like caricatures of nasty people whose actions and mannerisms fail to intrigue or terrify us.

It would appear that instead of writing a cohesive narrative of people who move in a region where the dream world exists side by side with the familiar and commonplace, Mr. Capote, for all his deftness in creating an image, has concocted a witch's brew which boils and boils to no avail. In fact, readers weary of reading about the South's decline are apt to accuse Mr. Capote of dishing up a Dixieland stew in which Faulkner, Caldwell, Welty, shades of the defunct *View* magazine, Charles Addams's weirdies, Proust's most celebrated passages, all seem to have gone. This is regrettable since Mr. Capote *does* have a remarkable facility with words; he can make perfectly normal horrors and shocks appear like enormities upon the senses. At times we can even hear a haunting, funereal music behind Mr. Capote's wayward language. If he had selected his material more carefully, shown more restraint, and had been less concerned with terrifying us out of our wits, he might have easily made a real and tenderly appealing story out of the experiences of thirteen-year-old Joel Knox and the people he meets during that long and lonely summer of his approaching maturity.

It is inevitable that comparisons will be made between Capote's book and Carson McCullers's "The Heart Is a Lonely Hunter." Unfortunately, though Capote's novel is also about the experiences and observations of an adolescent, he does not have the maturity or the all-pervading sense of humanity that Mrs. McCullers had when she was twenty-two. Besides, those other voices whispering in other rooms chill us without arousing our emotions.

Ordinarily we should be moved very deeply by a little boy thrown into the company of such queerly behaved folk as Mr. Capote writes about. But somehow— and it is one of the major flaws of Mr. Capote's book— we never feel sorry for little Joel Knox long enough to see him as a live, healthy, normal child. There are always too many disagreeable people crowding the scene. Or when that is not happening Mr. Capote's adolescent lets his morbid imagination lead him down those dark, unfathomable corridors of his nightmare world.

Capote might have stopped collecting his grotesques with Joel's father, who is paralyzed and is only a pair of eyes. But no—he creates a whole menagerie to terrify us. There is Miss Amy, Joel's stepmother, who traps bluejays in the house and breaks their backs with a poker; Randolph, who loves dressing up in ladies' clothes, and whose womanly fingers are extremely deft with fine handicraft work; Missouri, the Negro servant girl, whose frenzied incantations ask for nothing but revenge against the husband who once tried to slit her throat with a razor; Little Sunshine, the Negro hermit, who brews witch's potions for her; Idabel and Florabel, the twelve-year-old twins, one of whom talks right out of the ante-bellum South, the other an unnatural child whose tomboyish nature drives her to commit mayhem on her snaggletoothed twin; Miss Wisteria, the carnival

midget with whom Idabel falls in love, but whose lech-
erous hands seek to hold our little hero, Joel—who,
incidentally, has a rendezvous awaiting him with the
strange lady smiling at him from Randolph's window.

Nightmare on Anopopei

THE NAKED AND THE DEAD. By Norman Mailer.
New York: Rinehart & Co. 1948. 721 pp. $4.

Reviewed by Maxwell Geismar

May 8, 1948

Just when we have stopped talking about the new literary voices of the 1940's, they seem to be appearing.
Norman Mailer is a young American writer who grew
up in Brooklyn, went to Harvard, and found himself,
as a rifleman, in Leyte and Japan. His earlier work has
appeared in *Story* magazine and "Cross Section," but
"The Naked and the Dead" is his first novel. It is a
solid and interesting story of the capture of Anopopei,
a typical Japanese island in the Pacific, a nightmare in
short.

Mr. Mailer uses some of the technical devices which
John Dos Passos initiated in the American novel, while
there is also an influence of tone. But "Three Soldiers,"
like most of the typical stories of World War I, was
essentially a novel of individual protest. The military
organization was something to escape from, not to understand. The virtue of "The Naked and the Dead"—
and I think it will be the typical pattern of the new war
novels—is that it sees the individual within the military
organization, and attempts to evaluate the whole complex structure of the American Army in war and peace,
as a manifestation of contemporary society, as well as a
weapon of conquest and destruction. Or perhaps even,

in the Tolstoyan sense, as one-half of our "natural" existence.

That doesn't mean Mr. Mailer particularly approves of army life, or that the campaign on Anopopei was an idyll of human decency. The novel opens with an amphibious assault upon the island. The central group of characters are members of a reconnaissance squad; the slow, blundering, and tortured progress of the military action also marks their physical and moral disintegration as human beings. The plump and foul-mouthed Wilson, the superstitious and embittered Gallagher, the ambitious and servile Brown, the tough and rebellious Red Valsen, all are partially or completely destroyed by their ordeal; to live through it is not necessarily to have survived. Only the slow-thinking farm boy, Ridges, and the "intellectual" Brooklyn Jew, Goldstein, seem to have the necessary resources, whether of sheer animal vitality or of spiritual comprehension, to endure the impervious jungle, the sickening climate, the steady, demoralizing contact with filth, pain, and terror even more than the actual and paralyzing shock of combat.

Staff Sergeant Croft, too, an excellent soldier to begin with, becomes a rigid and implacable tyrant; if he has accepted the hatred of his men as part of his job, he soon begins to nourish it. As the novel moves up through the ranks of the military hierarchy, it is particularly good on the relationship of these men with the commissioned officers. There is an ironical episode in which Major Dalleson, a typical disciplinarian and drill-master, goes into panic because the Japs have given him a chance for a breakthrough, and he is forced to use his troops. Lieutenant Hearn is a social rebel who has broken away from the conventions and prejudices of the ruling class, financial or military. General Cummings, who has given up human relationships completely, for the sake of organization and efficiency, who believes that the only value of a human soul is the use it can be put to, also believes that, after the war with Russia, the next century will belong to the reactionaries and the capitalists. And why not?

The antagonism between these last two groups both

human and theoretical, gives Mr. Mailer a chance to build up, often very eloquently, the historical and philosophical connotations of the war. In the end Hearn is broken and killed. Perhaps this represents Mr. Mailer's own conclusion about the future, yet Hearn is a curiously vapid character, and the ordinary soldiers in "The Naked and the Dead" lack the vitality and originality of, say, the Britishers in "The Edge of the Night." Mr. Mailer leans rather heavily on the sexual experiences of his lower-class figures, too; these may be a solace for the common man, and even a source of strength, but they don't constitute his only achievement.

I think this is the main weakness of the novel, for there is no real balance of the dramatic forces in it, just as there is a final lack of emotional impact. The story ought to be more impressive than it is. Within these limits, however, "The Naked and the Dead" is a substantial work, and Mr. Mailer is a new novelist of consequence.

Community of Pride

GO TELL IT ON THE MOUNTAIN. By James Baldwin. New York: Alfred A. Knopf. 303 pp. $3.50.

Reviewed by Harvey Curtis Webster

May 16, 1953

Anyone who wants to cling firmly to his belief that Negroes are an inferior group should avoid knowledge of the Negro novel in our century. In the early 1900's most novels by Negroes probably were unpublished; those that were usually were cries of anger without measure or pleas for condescension. In the years between 1920 and 1950, the best novels by Negroes continued to emphasize either anger or compliance, but anyone who read could see the immense gain in craft the novels of Arna Bontemps, Langston Hughes, Chester Himes, and Richard Wright represented. In the Fifties—with Wright's "The Outsider," with Ralph Ellison's "Invisible Man," and now with James Baldwin's "Go Tell It on the Mountain"—the Negro novel has finally come of age. Sensibly, the protagonist is a Negro in all these books, but he is a Negro enmeshed in the human dilemma, not just a victim of underprivilege, segregation, and unreasoning violence.

Mr. Baldwin's first novel is about a day in the life of the leading members of the Temple of the Free Baptised in Harlem. This one day suggests the essence of all the days of Gabriel, Florence, Roy, Elizabeth, Elisha, and John. Gabriel, a minister from the Deep South who both lusts and represses unreasonably, is a god who punishes his own sins in others. His sister, Florence, hates his rigidity and hopes God is more merciful than he is. Elizabeth, Gabriel's second wife, hopes her illegitimate son John will experience "glory" before he accepts the rigors of salvation. Roy feels and acts damned. Elisha feels and acts saved. John, the central figure, is a fourteen-year-old boy who longs almost equally for salvation and damnation until the final scene when he descends into the pit (like Thomas Mann's Joseph) to rise again.

During the course of this day, with its simple events of home and church, each of the characters credibly recalls and relives his past in the North and South. The past of these representative, uneducated Negroes, includes rape, race violence, police beatings, suicide, white-hatred, and the hope of heaven. Their past, which differs from that of a comparable group of white people in degree rather than in kind, makes their present both believable and extraordinarily interesting. What happens on the one day that is the book's focus makes plausibly sympathetic the Holy Roller religion and, at the same time, reveals a good deal that is the mystical basis for even sophisticated religion.

Mr. Baldwin's first novel is written as skilfully as many a man's fifth essay in fiction. His handling of the flashbacks so that they show the past without interrupting the drama of the present is masterful. His penetration of the mind of John, especially in the scene of his conversion, is as valid as anything in William James's "Varieties of Religious Experience" and as moving as the interior monologues in Faulkner's "As I Lay Dying." Although Mr. Baldwin does not have either Wright's or Ellison's capacity to take all modern problems as his province, he never descends into the provincialism that has made so many Negro novels read like footnotes to Myrdal's "An American Dilemma." "Go Tell It on the Mountain" fulfils a great deal, promises more. Mr. Baldwin's readers will hope for the quick (but not too quick) completion of the second novel which he is writing at present.

Modern-Day Exodus

GOODBYE, COLUMBUS. By Philip Roth.
New York: Houghton Mifflin. 298 pp. $3.75.

Reviewed by Arnold Dolin

May 16, 1959

It's not far from Newark to Short Hills—or from the Bronx to Westchester—but the gap is sometimes unbridgeable, no matter how steep a toll one is prepared to pay. It is about the middle-class Jewish residents of both these worlds that Philip Roth writes in his first book, "Goodbye, Columbus," which contains a novella and five short stories.

Anyone who read these stories when they first appeared in *The New Yorker, Commentary,* and *The Paris Review* has probably not forgotten their passion and vitality. In awarding a Literary Fellowship to the twenty-six-year-old author, Houghton Mifflin has given deserved recognition to a brilliant new talent.

Philip Roth surveys the role of the Jew in modern American society with keen perception. Underlying his stories is the Jews' centuries-old tragic sense of life, leavened with warmth and humor, and with compassion. There are no excesses of sentimentality or bitterness: his characters cannot be typed as either Molly Goldbergs or Sammy Glicks.

If there is any doubt in my mind, it concerns the validity of these stories for the non-Jewish, or even the non-Eastern, reader. For so much depends on a familiarity with the peculiarly parochial surroundings and the subtle speech inflections. This is particularly true of the title novella, which chronicles the summer romance between Neil Klugman of Newark and Brenda Patimkin of Short Hills. Brenda's family has made the perilous jump to opulent suburbia, with its well-stocked basement freezers and its streets lined with "sporting-goods trees" (or so they appear, since golf and baseball equipment practically obscure the foliage). The bump in Brenda's nose has been fixed, and her father can heal any emotional crisis in her life with a new coat from Bonwit's.

Brenda and Neil meet in the golden sunlight of the Green Lane Country Club, surrounded by women "with their Cuban heels and boned-up breasts, their knuckle-sized rings, their straw hats, which resembled immense wicker pizza plates." The affair is ardently pursued through richly comic and deeply touching scenes— until Neil's dream of paradise is inevitably lost. But for the reader who lacks the proper frame of reference to recognize the deftness with which this milieu has been observed, there may be left only a sensitively rendered theme and some engaging characters that do not quite justify the story's length.

However, Roth's two finest stories do transcend this narrowly circumscribed area. Both are reminiscent of Bernard Malamud in their concern with the modern Jew's responsibility to his heritage and his guilt in ignoring it. Can he be assimilated into the American culture and still remain a Jew—or must there be either total acceptance or total denial?

"Eli, the Fanatic" sharply satirizes the embarrassment of self-consciously sophisticated Jewish commuters who suddenly find a Yeshivah school established in their progressive midst. There is both grotesque humor and sadness in the image of the bearded, black-coated Talmudic scholar walking the smart streets of their town. And the story achieves the level of almost ritualistic drama when Eli Peck, a successful young lawyer, trades his best tweed suit for the black raiment that will mark his Jewishness beyond his forgetting again.

In "Defender of the Faith," the hardened veteran of two years' fighting in Europe finds himself top sergeant in a Stateside training company. When three young Jewish recruits discover that Sergeant Marx, like Karl and Harpo, is also a Jew, they attempt to play on his sympathies. Unyielding at first, his infantryman's heart is soon divided and torn by echoes of his almost-forgotten Jewish past.

"The heart is half a prophet," says a Yiddish proverb. And Philip Roth has looked penetratingly into the heart of the American Jew who faces the loss of his identity. The conflict involved in this choice between two worlds provides the focal point of drama for a memorable collection of short stories.

PART II
Reflections

Must We Hate to Fight?

By Eleanor Roosevelt

July 4, 1942

Can we kill other human beings if we do not hate them? I suppose the answer must come from those in our fighting forces. Some young people will tell you that unless you hate the people of Germany and Japan, you cannot possibly win. On the other hand, many a young soldier going into the war will assure you that he cannot hate the individuals of any race. He can only hate the system which has made those individuals his enemies. If he must kill them in order to do away with the system, he will do so, but not because he hates them as individuals. If those who say that to win the war we must hate, are really expressing the beliefs of the majority of our people, I am afraid we have already lost the peace, because our main objective is to make a world in which all the people of the world may live with respect and good will for each other in peace.

If we allow the hate of other men as individuals to possess us, we cannot discard hate the day we have won and suddenly become understanding and co-operative neighbors.

There will be no victory if out of this war we simply develop armed camps again throughout the world. We may in the interests of self-preservation cut down the actual race to obtain guns, planes, and battleships because no people will survive if it goes on, nor will those who survive have the wherewithal for the decencies of life. Even if we cut out all weapons of force, there can exist armed camps in the minds of people, which express themselves through the economic systems which we set up and through all the barriers which we set up between peoples to keep them from real understanding. If we really do not mean that after this war we intend to see that people the world over have an opportunity to obtain a satisfactory life, then all we are doing is to prepare for a new war. There is no excuse for the bloodshed, the sacrifices, and the tears which the world as a whole is now enduring, unless we build a new worth-while world.

The saving grace for most of us is that hope does spring eternal in the human breast. We do believe that just around the corner is that solution to our problems which we have long been looking for and that human beings will never give up till they find the answers.

I believe that the solution will be easier to find when we work together, and when all the plans, all the abilities of people the world over, are concentrated on finding positive solutions, but if we hate each other then I despair of achieving any ultimate good results.

I will acknowledge that it is easier to urge upon our people that they hate those whom we now must fight as individuals, because it is always easier to build up contempt and dislike for that which is making us suffer than it is to force ourselves to analyze the reasons which have brought about these conditions and try to eliminate them.

In small ways we see over and over again that the child who is badgered and punished in youth grows up to treat anyone weaker than himself in much the same way. That is probably what we will do to the people of our nation as a whole when we tell them that in fighting to stamp out cruelty and hate, dominated by force, they must hate. Somehow as a whole the thousands in our fighting forces must preserve a belief and a respect for the individual and a hate only of the system, or else we will go down ourselves, victims of the very system which today we are striving to conquer.

Modern Man Is Obsolete

By Norman Cousins

August 18, 1945

Whatever elation there is in the world today because of final victory in the war is severely tempered by fear. It is a primitive fear, the fear of the unknown, the fear of forces man can neither channel nor comprehend. This fear is not new; in its classical form it is the fear of irrational death. But overnight it has become intensified, magnified. It has burst out of the subconscious and into the conscious, filling the mind with primordial apprehensions. It is thus that man stumbles fitfully into a new age of atomic energy for which he is as ill equipped to accept its potential blessings as he is to counteract or control its present dangers.

Where man can find no answer, he will find fear. While the dust was still settling over Hiroshima, he was asking himself questions and finding no answers. The biggest question of these concerns the nature of man. Is war in the nature of man? If so, how much time has he left before he employs the means he has already devised for the ultimate in self-destruction—extinction? And now that the science of warfare has reached the point where it threatens the planet itself, is it possible that man is destined to return the earth to its aboriginal incandescent mass blazing at fifty million degrees? If not—that is, if war is not in the nature of man—then how is he to interpret his own experience, which tells him that in all of recorded history there have been only 300 years in the aggregate during which he has been free of war?

Closely following upon these are other questions, flowing out endlessly from his fears and without prospect of definitive answer. Even assuming that he could hold destructive science in check, what changes would the new age bring or demand in his everyday life? What changes would it bring or demand in his culture, his education, his philosophy, his religion, his relationships with other human beings?

In speculating upon these questions, it should not be necessary to prove that on August 6, 1945, a new age was born. When on that day a parachute containing a small object floated to earth over Japan, it marked the violent death of one stage in man's history and the beginning of another. Nor should it be necessary to prove the saturating effect of the new age, permeating every aspect of man's activities, from machines to morals, from physics to philosophy, from politics to poetry; in sum, it is an effect creating a blanket of obsolescence not only over the methods and the products of man but over man himself.

It is a curious phenomenon of nature that only two species practise the art of war—men and ants, both of which, ironically, maintain complex social organizations. This does not mean that only men and ants engage in the murder of their own kind. Many animals of the same species kill each other, but only men and ants have practised the science of organized destruction, employing their massed numbers in violent combat and relying on strategy and tactics to meet developing situations or to capitalize on the weaknesses in the strategy and tactics of the other side. The longest continuous war ever fought between men lasted thirty years. The longest ant war ever recorded lasted six-and-a-half weeks, or whatever the corresponding units would be in ant reckoning.

It is encouraging to note that while all entomologists are agreed that war is instinctive with ants, not all anthropologists and biologists are agreed that war is instinctive with men. The strict empiricists, of course, find everything in man's history to indicate that war is locked up with his nature. But a broader and more generous, certainly more philosophical, view is held by those scientists who claim that the evidence to date is incomplete and misleading, and that man *does* have within him the power of abolishing war. Prominent among these is Julian Huxley, who draws a sharp distinction between human nature and the *expression* of human nature. Thus war is not a reflection but an expression of his nature. Moreover, the expression may change, as the factors which lead to war may change. "In man, as in ants, war in any serious sense is bound up with the existence of accumulations of property to fight about. . . . As for human nature, it contains no specific war instinct, as does the nature of harvester ants. There is in man's makeup a general aggressive tendency, but this, like all other human urges, is not a specific and unvarying instinct; it can be molded into the most varied forms."

But even if this gives us a reassuring answer to the question—is war inevitable because of man's nature?— it still leaves unanswered the question concerning the causes leading up to war. The expression of man's nature will continue to be warlike if the same conditions are continued that have provoked warlike expressions in him in the past. And since man's survival on earth is now absolutely dependent on his ability to avoid a new war, he is faced with the so-far insoluble problem of eliminating those causes.

In the most primitive sense, war in man is an expression of his competitive impulses. Like everything else in nature, he has had to fight for existence; but the battle against other animals, once won, gave way in his evolution to battle against his own kind. Darwin called it the survival of the fittest, and its most over-stretched interpretation is to be found in "Mein Kampf," with its naked glorification of brute force and the complete worship of might makes right. In the political and national sense, it has been the attempt of the "have-nots" to take from the "haves," or the attempt of the "haves" to add further to their lot at the expense of the "have-nots." Not always was property at stake; comparative advantages were measured in terms of power, and in terms of tribal or national superiority. The good luck of one nation became the hard luck of another. The good fortune of the Western powers in obtaining "concessions" in China at the turn of the century was the ill fortune of the Chinese. The power that Germany stripped from Austria, Czechoslovakia, Poland, and France at the beginning of World War II she added to her own.

What does it matter, then, if war is not in the nature of man so long as man continues through the expression of his nature to be a viciously competitive animal? The effect is the same, and therefore the result must be as conclusive—war being the effect, and complete obliteration of the human species being the result.

If this reasoning is correct, then modern man is obsolete, a self-made anachronism becoming more incongruous by the minute. He has exalted change in everything but himself. He has leaped centuries ahead in inventing a new world to live in, but he knows little or nothing about his own part in that world. He has surrounded and confounded himself with gaps—gaps between revolutionary science and evolutionary anthropology, between cosmic gadgets and human wisdom, between intellect and conscience. The struggle between science and morals that Henry Thomas Buckle foresaw a century ago has been all but won by science. Given time, man might be expected to bridge those gaps normally; but by his own hand, he is destroying even time. Communication, transportation, war no longer wait on time. Decision and execution in the modern world are becoming virtually synchronous. Thus, whatever bridges man has to build and cross he shall have to build and cross immediately.

This involves both biology and will. If he lacks the actual and potential biological equipment to build those bridges, then the birth certificate of the atomic age is in reality a *memento mori*. But even if he possesses the necessary biological equipment, he must still make the decision which says that he is to apply himself to the challenge. Capability without decision is inaction and inconsequence.

Man is left, then, with a crisis in decision. The main test before him involves his will to change rather than his ability to change. That he is capable of change is certain. For there is no more mutable or adaptable animal in the world. We have seen him migrate from one extreme clime to another. We have seen him step out of backward societies and join advanced groups. We have seen, within the space of a single generation, tribes of head-hunters spurn their acephalous pastimes and rituals and become purveyors of the Western arts. This is not to imply that the change was necessarily for the better; only that change was possible. Changeability with the head-hunters proceeded from external pressure and fear of punishment, true, and was only secondarily a matter of voluntary decision. But the stimulus was there; and mankind today need look no further for stimulus than its own desire to stay alive. The critical power of change, says Spengler, is directly linked to the survival drive. Once the instinct for survival is stimulated, the basic condition for change can be met.

That is why the quintessence of destruction as potentially represented by modern science must be dramatized and kept in the forefront of public opinion. The full dimensions of the peril must be seen and recognized. Then and only then will man realize that the first order of business is the question of continued existence. Then and only then will he be prepared to make the decisions necessary to assure that survival.

In making these decisions, there are two principal courses that are open to him. Both will keep him alive for an indefinite or at least a reasonably long period. These courses, however, are directly contradictory and represent polar extremes of approach.

The first course is the positive approach. It begins with a careful survey and appraisal of the obsolescences which constitute the afterbirth of the new age. The survey must begin with man himself. "The proper study of Mankind is Man," said Pope. No amount of tinkering with his institutions will be sufficient to insure his survival unless he can make the necessary adjustments in his own relationship to the world and to society.

The first adjustment or mutation needed in the expression of his nature, to use Huxley's words, is his savagely competitive impulses. In the pre-Atomic Age, those impulses were natural and occasionally justifiable, though they often led to war. But the rise of materialistic man had reasons behind it and must be viewed against its natural setting. Lyell, Spencer, Darwin,

Lamarck, Malthus, and others have concerned themselves with various aspects of this natural setting, but its dominant feature was an insufficiency of the goods and the needs of life. From Biblical history right up through the present, there was never time when starvation and economic suffering were not acute somewhere in the world.

This is only part of the story, of course, for it is dangerous to apply an economic interpretation indiscriminately to all history. Politics, religion, force for force's sake, jealousy, ambition, love of conquest, love of reform—all these and others have figured in the equations of history and war. But the economic factor was seldom if ever absent, even when it was not the prime mover. Populations frequently increased more rapidly than available land, goods, or wealth. Malthus believed that they increased so rapidly at times that war or plague became nature's safety valve. This interpretation has undergone some revision, but it is not the interpretation but the circumstances that raises the problem.

Yet all this has been—or can be—changed by the new age. Man now has it within his grasp to emancipate himself economically. If he wills it, he is in a position to refine his competitive impulse; he can take the step from competitive man to coöperative man. He has at last unlocked enough of the earth's secrets to provide for his needs on a world scale. The same atomic and electrical energy that can destroy a city can also usher in an age of economic sufficiency. It need no longer be a question as to which peoples shall prosper and which shall be deprived. There is power enough and resources enough for all.

It is here that man's survey of himself needs the severest scrutiny, for he is his own greatest obstacle to the achievement of those attainable and necessary goals. While he is willing to mobilize all his scientific and intellectual energies for purposes of death, he is unwilling to undertake any comparable mobilization for purposes of life. He has shattered the atom and harnessed its fabulous power to a bomb, but he balks—or allows himself to be balked—when it comes to harnessing that power for human progress. Already, many representatives of industry have counseled words of synthetic caution, informing a puzzled public that we shall not see the practical application of atomic energy for general use in our lifetime. If it works out this way, it will not be because of any lack of knowledge or skill, but only because of the fear in certain quarters that atomic energy will mean a complete revamping of the economic structure, with the probability that it would be operated as a government utility or public service.

This is not a matter of urging a change away from the present economic structure just for the sake of change; it is recognition of a hard new fact of life that has made that economic structure obsolete in an Atomic Age just as it has made practically all our other institutions obsolete.

The cry is certain to go up against further government experimentation with atomic energy for peacetime purposes, and industry will demand that government withdraw and give it the right to carry on its own experiments. These experiments, however, would most likely be no more consequential than the atomic bomb would have been if left to decentralized chance. Moreover, it takes enthusiasm to fertilize invention, and there is as yet little discernible enthusiasm for atomic energy in those quarters which are asking for the right to sponsor its peace-time uses. However understandable this lack of enthusiasm may be, it should not blind public opinion to the critical importance of having research for practical use carried on with the same urgency, the same fulness, the same scope and intensity as it has been for war ends thus far.

The size of the opportunity is exceeded only by the size of the promise. But even as man stands on the threshold of a new age, he is being pulled back by his coattails and told to look the other way, told that he must not allow his imagination to get out of hand—all this at a time when he should know almost instinctively that if he can put the same courage, daring, imagination, ingenuity, and skill that he demonstrated in winning the war into meeting the problems of the new age, he can win the peace as well.

He must believe, too, that mobilization of science and knowledge in peace should not be confined to cosmic forces, but must be extended to his other needs, principally health. What a fantastic irony that organized science knows the secret of the atom but as yet knows not a fig about the common cold! Who can tell what advances in medical knowledge might accrue to the welfare of mankind if as much mobilized effort were put into the study of man as there has been of matter! Cancer, heart disease, nephritis, leukemia, encephalitis, poliomyelitis, arteriosclerosis, aplastic anemia—all these are anomalies in the modern world; there is no reason why mobilized research should not be directed at their causes and cure. Nor is there any reason why even old age should not be regarded as a disease to be attacked by science in the same intensive fashion.

Surveying other adjustments he shall have to make if he chooses the positive course, man must consider himself in relation to his individual development. He can have the limitless opportunities that can come with time to think. The trend during the last fifty years towards shorter work weeks and shorter hours will not only be continued but sharply accelerated. Not more than half of each week will be spent earning a living. But a revolution is needed in his leisure-time activities—which so far have come to be associated almost entirely with the commodities of vended amusement. Once before, the world knew a Golden Age where the development of the individual—his mind and his body—was considered the first law of life. In Greece, it took the form of the revolution of awareness, the emancipation of the intellect from the limitations of corroding ignorance and prejudice.

Once again, if man wills it, he can be in a position to restore that first law of life. But he shall have to effect a radical transformation in his approach to and philosophy of education, which must prepare him for the opportunities and responsibilities not only of his chosen work but for the business of living itself. The primary aim should be the development of a critical intelligence. The futile war now going on between specialization and general study must be stopped. There need no longer be any conflict between the two. The individual will need both—specialization for the requirements of research, general knowledge for the requirements of living. As for the problem of time in which to accomplish these dual objectives, formalized education until the twenty-fifth or thirtieth year is doubtless indicated; but it should not abruptly end there. Education, like the capacity of the mind itself, has no rigid boundaries. Unlimited exploration should be the first imperative of any educational program.

We have saved for last the most crucial aspect of this general survey relating to the first course: the transformation or adjustment from national man to world man. Already he has become a world warrior; it is but one additional step—though a long one—for him to develop a world conscience. This is not vaporous idealism, but sheer driving necessity. It bears directly on the prospects of his own survival. He shall have to recognize the flat truth that the greatest obsolescence of all in the Atomic Age is national sovereignty. Even back in the old-fashioned rocket age before August 6, 1945, strict national sovereignty was an anomalous and preposterous hold-over from the tribal instinct in nations. If it was anomalous then, it is the quintessence of anomaly now. The world is a geographic entity. This is not only the basic requisite for world government but the basic reason behind the need. A common ground of destiny is not too large a site for the founding of any community.

Reject all other arguments for *real* world government —reject the economic, the ideological, the sociological, the humanitarian arguments, valid though they may be. Consider only the towering problem of policing the atom—the problem of keeping the smallest particle of matter from destroying all matter. We are building on soap bubbles if we expect this problem to be automatically solved by having America, Britain, and Canada keep the secret to themselves. That is not only highly improbable, but would in itself stimulate the other nations to undertake whatever additional research might be necessary over their present experimentation to yield the desired results. In all history, there is not a single instance of a new weapon being kept exclusively by any power or powers; sooner or later either the basic principles become generally known or parallel devices are invented. Before long, the atomic bomb will follow the jet plane, the rocket bomb, radar, and the flame thrower into general circulation. We must not forget that we were not the only horse in the atomic derby; we just happened to finish first. The others will be along in due time.

Nor can we rely on destructive atomic energy to take care of itself. Already there is the tempting but dangerous notion to the effect that the atomic bomb is so horrible and the terror of retaliation so great that we may have seen the last of war. This is quasi-logical, but war is no respecter of logic, relative or absolute. And if history teaches us anything, it is that the possibility of war increases in direct proportion to the effectiveness of the instruments of war.

Far from banishing war, the atomic bomb will in itself constitute a cause of war. In the absence of world control as part of world government, it will create universal fear and suspicion. Each nation will live nervously from one moment to the next, not knowing whether the designs or ambitions of other nations might prompt them to attempt a lightning blow of obliteration. The ordinary, the inevitable differences among nations which might in themselves be susceptible of solution might now become the signals for direct action, lest the other nation get in the first and decisive blow. Since the science of warfare will no longer be dependent upon armies but will be waged by push-buttons, releasing radio-controlled rocket planes carrying cargoes of atomic explosives, the slightest suspicion may start all the push-buttons going.

There is the argument, of course, that each nation will realize this; that is, that the first button might lead to universal catastrophe as all the other nations rush to their switchboards of annihilation. Here, too, there is the unwarranted presupposition of reason. In an atmosphere of high tension and suspicion, reason is an easy victim. Moreover, there will always be the feeling that one nation can escape though all the others may go down. What a temptation for the blitzkriegers!

No; there is no comfort to be derived from the war-is-now-too-horrible theory. There is one way and only one to achieve effective control of destructive atomic energy and that is through centralized world government. Not loose, informal organization. Not even through an international pool, or through an international policing agreement. A police force is no better than its laws, and there can be no laws without government. Finally, the potency of the weapon must dictate the potency of its control.

There is no need to discuss the historical reasons pointing to and arguing for world government. There is no need to talk of the difficulties in the way of world government. There is need only to ask whether we can afford to do without it. All other considerations become either secondary or inconsequential.

It would be comforting to know that the world had several generations in which it might be able to evolve naturally and progressively into a single governmental unit. In fact, even as late as August 5, 1945, it seemed that the Charter of the United Nations had made an adequate beginning in that direction, providing the machinery for revision which might lead within fifteen or twenty years to a real world structure. But the time factor has been shattered. We no longer have a leeway of fifteen or twenty years; whatever must be done must be done with an immediacy which is in keeping with the urgency. Once the basic peace settlements are arranged, the United Nations must convene again for an Atomic Age inventory, undertaking an overall examination of the revolutionary changes in the world since its conference in San Francisco in the long-ago spring of 1945.

If all this sounds like headlong argument, posing methods or solutions which seem above the reach of mortal man, the answer must be that mortal man's reach was long enough apparently to push science and invention ahead by at least five hundred years during five years of experimentation on atomic energy. His ability to do this not only indicates that he can extend or over-extend himself when pressed, but emphasizes the need to do the same with government.

In meeting this need, man need not be frightened by the enormity of the differences which shall have to be accommodated within the world structure. We can agree with Macneile Dixon in "The Human Situation," that "Many are the races and many the temperaments. There are vehement and hot-headed men, selfless and conciliatory men. They display, varying as they do in appearance, talents, behavior, every type of unpredictable reaction to their surroundings. There are sybarites and ascetics, dreamers and bustling active men of affairs, clever and stupid, worldly and religious, mockers and mystics, pugnacious, loyal, cunning, treacherous, cheerful and melancholy men. There are eagles among them, tigers, doves, and serpents. 'He was a comedian on the stage,' said the wife of a celebrated funny man, 'but a tragedian in the home.' " All these differences are in addition to those of ideology, politics, and geography.

And yet, it is not in spite of these variations but because of them that man is now in need of a general amalgam. If those variations did not exist, if man's actions were uniform and uniformly predictable, then man would be as free of war as the vegetable kingdom. The differences point up the problem, not the problem the differences. The important question is not how great an obstacle the differences may be to the setting up of a closely knit world structure, but whether man will be in a better position to reconcile those differences within world government than without it.

Man must decide, moreover, what is more important —his differences or his similarities. If he chooses the former, he embarks on a path that will, paradoxically, destroy the differences and himself as well. If he chooses the latter, he shows a willingness to meet the responsibilities that go with maturity and conscience. Though heterogeneity is the basic manifestation of nature, as

Spencer observed, a still greater manifestation is the ability of nature to create larger areas of homogeneity which act as a sort of rim to the spokes of the human wheel.

True, in making the jump to world government, man is taking a big chance. Not only does he have to create the first world authority, but he shall have to make sure that this authority is wisely used. The world institution must be compatible with—indeed, must promote —free institutions. This challenge is not less important than the challenge to establish world government itself, for all through history there has been too great a contradiction between ideals and institutions and the forces which have taken over those ideals and institutions. Another way of saying this is that we have too often allowed the best ideas to fall into the hands of the worst men. There has not been a great ideal or idea which has not been perverted or exploited at one time or another by those who were looking for means to an end—the end being seldom compatible with the idea itself. The greatest idea ever to be taken up by the mind of man— Christianity—was for centuries violated and corrupted by its very administrators. Alexander's vision of a brotherhood of man fell victim to its own force—force based on might makes right. Mohammed dreamed of a universal religion based on the noblest of ethics, and taught that conversion by the sword was no conversion at all; yet his followers built an empire largely at the point of the sword. Passing from religion to politics, we have only to consider the immediate past. It was in the name of socialism and social progress that Fascism came to Italy and Nazism to Germany.

That is the double nature of the challenge: to bring about world government and to keep it pure. It is a large order, perhaps the largest order man has had to meet in his 50,000-odd years on earth, but he himself has set up the conditions which have made the order necessary.

All these are the various mutations and adjustments needed in the expression of man's nature, in his way of life, his thinking, his economics, his education, his con-

ditioning and orientation, and his concept of government in an Atomic Age. But if he rejects this, the first
course, there is yet another way, an alternative to world
government. This is the second course. Preposterous as
this second course may seem, we describe it in all seriousness, for it is possible that through it man may find
a way to stay alive—which is the central problem under
consideration in this paper.

The second course is relatively simple. It requires that
man destroy, carefully and completely, everything relating to science and civilization. Let him destroy all
machines and the knowledge which can build or operate
those machines. Let him raze his cities, smash his laboratories, dismantle his factories, tear down his universities and schools, burn his libraries, rip apart his art.
Let him murder his scientists, his doctors, his teachers,
his lawmakers, his mechanics, his merchants, and anyone who has anything to do with the machinery of
knowledge or progress. Let him punish literacy by
death. Let him abolish nations and set up the tribe as
sovereign. In short, let him revert to his condition in
society in 10,000 B.C. Thus emancipated from science,
from progress, from government, from knowledge, from
thought, he can be reasonably certain of safe-guarding
his existence on this planet.

This is the alternative to world government—if
modern man wishes an alternative.

Is Our Common Man Too Common?

By Joseph Wood Krutch

January 10, 1953

The Age of the Common Man is not merely a phrase;
it is also a fact. Already we are definitely entered upon

it, and in all probability it is destined to continue for a long time to come, intensifying its characteristics as it develops in some of the directions which it has already begun to take.

Most people welcome the fact, but we have only begun to assess it or even to ask ourselves what choices are still open to us once the grand decision has been made, as by now it has. How common does the common man need to be? Does his dominance necessarily mean that the uncommon man will cease to be tolerated or that the world will become less suited to his needs, less favorable to the development of his talents, than it now is? Will excellence be looked upon as in itself unworthy or "undemocratic"? Can we have an Age of the Common Man without making it an Age of the Common Denominator? Do any dangers lie ahead?

One way to approach these questions is, of course, to ask what has happened already, what changes in attitudes have demonstrably taken place, how the culture of the first era of the Age of the Common Man differs from that which preceded it. What, in other words, is the culture of present-day America like, and are there aspects of it, directly traceable to the emphasis on the common man and his tastes, which are not wholly reassuring? And if there are, then to what extent are the defects corrigible, to what extent are they necessary consequences of the premises we have already accepted?

Unfortunately, but not surprisingly, there is no general agreement concerning the real nature of the situation at the present moment, though it does seem clear enough that most Americans judge both the present and the future a good deal more favorably than many observers from the Old World do.

Thus, in his recent book *The Big Change*, Frederick Lewis Allen summed up very cogently the case for contemporary American culture. Hundreds of thousands read the selections of the book club; hundreds of thousands more attend concerts of serious music; millions listen to debates, symphonies, and operas on the radio. Never before in the history of the world has so large a proportion of any population been so interested in and so alert to intellectual and artistic activities. Ours is the most cultured nation which ever existed.

Compare this with any one of the typical fulminations which proceed at regular intervals from European commentators and the result is both astonishing and disturbing. In Europe the prevalent opinion seems to be that this same civilization of ours constitutes a serious threat to the very existence of anything which can properly be called a culture.

We are told, in the first place, that for every American who does read the Book of the Month and attend a symphony concert there are a dozen who live in a vulgar dream-world induced by a perpetual diet of soap operas, comic books, torch songs, and "B" movies. Moreover, the material prosperity and political power of this majority of sick barbarians enable them to become, as no cultural proletariat ever was before, a threat to every civilized minority. They rule the roost, and they are becoming less and less tolerant of anyone or anything superior to them.

In the second place—and perhaps even more importantly—the culture of even the minority is described as largely an imitation. It consumes but does not produce art. The best of the books it reads and the music it listens to is imported. Its members are really only parasites feeding upon European culture, and their sterility will in time kill it completely. Even their power to "appreciate" is essentially shallow—the result of superficial education, propaganda, advertisement, and a general pro-cultural hoop-la, all of which produce something very different indeed from that deep, personal, demanding passion for Truth and Beauty which has always been the dynamic force in the production of any genuine culture.

Now it is easy enough to dismiss this European view as merely the product of ignorance, prejudice, and envy. But it is dangerous to do so. To look candidly at the two pictures is to perceive something recognizable in both of them. Nobody really knows what the American phenomenon means or what it portends. And the reason is that it is actually something genuinely new. Whether you call it the Dawn of the First Democratic Culture or call it the Triumph of Mediocrity, the fact remains that there is no obvious parallel in human history. Mr. Allen and those who agree with him are obviously right as far as they go. But the unique phenomenon which they describe can stand further analysis.

A college education for everybody and two cars in every garage are ideals not wholly unrelated. An even closer analogy can be drawn with the earlier, more modest ideal of universal literacy. America was the first country to teach nearly everybody to read. Whether we are quite aware of it or not, we are now embarked upon the pursuit of what is really an extension of the same ideal, namely, a minimum cultural literacy for all. There is a vast difference between being barely able to spell out a newspaper and being able to read in the full sense of what the term implies. There is a similar and probably no greater difference between, say, being able to get something out of the movie *The Great Caruso* or the latest volume dispatched to the members of a book club by editors who have trained themselves to understand the limitations of their average subscriber, and a genuine grasp of either music or literature. The term "literacy" covers a large area whether we are using it in its limited sense or extending it to include what I have called "cultural literacy." A few generations ago we pointed with pride to the fact that most Americans "could read"; we now point with pride to the fact that an astonishing proportion of them "read serious books" or "listen to serious music," and in both cases we take satisfaction in a mass capacity which exists only if we define it in minimum terms. In neither case does the phenomenon mean quite as much as those who celebrate it most enthusiastically sometimes seem to assume.

But, what, one may ask, is either disturbing or surprising about that? The minimum remains something more than any people as a whole ever before achieved. Is it likely that fewer people will read well just because a larger number can read a little? Is not, indeed, the opposite likely to be true? Is anything but good likely to come from the establishment of a broad base of even a minimum cultural literacy?

Any hesitation in answering "no" to the last question might seem at first sight to spring inevitably from nothing except arrogance, snobbishness, and a desire to preserve the privileges of an aristocracy. Yet a good many Europeans and an occasional American do seem inclined to take the negative position. The wide spread of our minimum culture does seem to them to constitute some sort of threat.

At least one fact or alleged fact they can cite as possible evidence on their side of the argument. So far, the number of recognized masterpieces produced by native-born Americans does seem disappointingly small when compared with the number of literate citizens we have produced. Is that because American art is inadequately recognized, or because we just haven't had time yet to mature? Or is it, perhaps, somehow connected—as some would say it is—with mass culture itself? Is the Good always the friend of the Best or is it sometimes and somehow the enemy? Is Excellence more likely to lose out to Mediocrity than it is to mere Ignorance or Nullity?

The line being taken in Europe today has a good deal in common with that of the American intellectual of the twenties. To some extent indeed it may have been learned from our post-World War I intellectuals; the disdainful European conception of American society is a good deal like Mencken's Boobocracy. At the present moment, however, the current of opinion at home is running in the opposite direction, and it is no longer unusual for the confessed intellectual to defend the culture which his predecessor of a generation ago despised and rejected. But complacency has its dangers too, and it may be worth while to examine a little further what can be said in support of the European's thesis.

This, he hears us say, is the Age of the Common Man. But we as well as he are not quite certain what we mean by that. In so far as we mean only the age of universal opportunity, what was once called simply "the career open to talents," nothing but good could seem to come of it. But many people do, sometimes without being entirely aware of it, mean something more. When we make ourselves the champion of any particular group we almost inevitably begin to idealize that group. From defending the common man we pass on to exalting him, and we find ourselves beginning to imply, not merely that he is as good as anybody else, but that he is actually better. Instead of demanding only that the common man be given an opportunity to become as uncommon as possible, we make his commonness a virtue and, even in the case of candidates for high office, we sometimes praise them for being nearly indistinguishable from the average man in the street. Secretly, no doubt, we hope that they are somehow superior, but we feel at the same time that a kind of decency requires them to conceal the fact as completely as possible.

The logical extreme of this opinion would be the conviction that any deviation in either direction from the statistical average is unadmirable; even, to take a concrete example, that the ideal man or woman could best be represented, not by an artist's dream, but by a composite photograph of the entire population. And though few would explicitly acknowledge their acceptance of this extreme position, there is a very strong tendency to emphasize quantitative rather than qualitative standards in estimating achievement. We are, for instance, more inclined to boast how many Americans go to college than to ask how much the average college education amounts to; how many people read books rather than how good the books are; how many listen to the radio rather than how good what they hear from it really is.

Argue, as I myself have argued, that more can be learned about almost any subject from ten minutes with a printed page than from half an hour with even one of the better educational programs and you will be met with the reply: "Perhaps. But so many *more* people will listen to the radio." In a democracy quantity is important. But when the stress upon it becomes too nearly exclusive, then democracy itself threatens to lose its promise of moving on to higher levels. Thus the Good really can become the enemy of the Best if one insists upon exclusively quantitative standards.

Certainly one of the striking—some would say one of the inevitable—characteristics of our society is its penchant for making widely and easily accessible either substitutes for, or inferior versions of, a vast number of good things, like the vile substitute for bread available at any grocer's. That bread can be come by without effort, and it may be true that fewer people are in want of bread of some kind than ever were in want of it in any society before. But that does not change the fact that it is a very inferior product.

Another and related tendency of this same society is its encouragement of passivity. A generation ago moralists viewed with alarm the popularity of "spectator sports": the fact that people gathered in stadia to watch others play games for them. But we have gone far beyond that and today the baseball fan who takes the trouble to make a journey to the Polo Grounds instead of watching the game on his TV set has almost earned the right to call himself an athlete. One wonders, sometimes, if the popularity of "discussion" programs does not mean very much the same thing; if most people have not now decided to let others hold remote conversations for them—as well as play remote games—even though the conversations are often no better than those they could hold for themselves.

As John Stuart Mill—certainly no anti-democrat—wrote a century ago: "Capacity for the nobler feeling is in most natures a very tender plant. . . . Men lose their high aspirations as they lose their intellectual tastes, because they have not time or opportunity for indulging them; and they addict themselves to inferior pleasures, not because they deliberately prefer them, but because they are either the only ones to which they have access, or the only ones which they are any longer capable of enjoying."

In the history books of the future this age of ours may come to be known as the Age of Statistics. In the biological and physical as well as the sociological sciences, statistics have become, as they never were before, the most important tool of investigation. But as every philosophical scientist knows, the conclusions drawn by a science depend to a considerable extent upon the tools used. And it is in the nature of statistics not only that they deal with quantity but that they emphasize the significance of averages and medians. What usually exists or usually happens establishes The Law, and The Law is soon thought of as identical with The Truth. In all the arts, nevertheless, it is the exceptional and the unpredictable which really count. It is the excellent, not the average, which is really important. And there is, therefore, one aspect of the cultural condition of a civilization to which statistical study is curiously inappropriate.

No one, it may be said, needs to accept the inferior substitute or hold himself down to the average level. But simple and complete as that answer may seem to be, there are facts and forces which do tend to encourage an almost unconscious acceptance of mediocrity. One, of course, is that the inferior substitute—whether it be baker's bread or the movie show playing at the neighborhood house—is so readily accessible and so forced upon one's attention by all the arts of advertising as well as by the very way in which our lives have been organized. Another and more serious one is the tendency of the mass media to force out of the field every enterprise which is not based upon mass appeal. Whatever the reason may be, it is a generally recognized fact that it is becoming increasingly difficult, economically, to publish a book which is not a best seller or produce a play which is not a smash hit. More and more, therefore, artistic enterprise must be abandoned to the movies and to television where the mass audience is sufficient to defray the staggering cost.

Besides these economic reasons why the new media tend to concern themselves only with mass appeals, there is the additional technical reason why the two newest of such media tend to confine themselves to it. Since TV and radio channels are limited in number, all the arguments in favor of democracy as it is sometimes defined justify the existing fact that these channels should be used to communicate what the greatest number of people seem to want. That is the argument of the great broadcasting chains, and on the premise assumed it is a valid one.

The only mechanical instrument of communication which can make a reasonable case for the claim that it has actually served to increase the popularity of the thing communicated on its highest level of excellence is the phonograph, and it is significant that the phonograph is the only such device for communication which —especially since the invention of tape recording and LP—has found it economically feasible to cater to relatively small minorities. The fact that it does not cost much to produce a record may well have an incalculably great effect upon American musical taste.

What the question comes down to in the simplest possible terms is one of those which we asked at the very beginning of this discussion: Can we have an Age of the Common Man without having also an Age of the Common Denominator? That question has not been answered, probably cannot be convincingly answered, at the present moment. But it is a fateful question and the one with which this discussion is concerned.

One must not, of course, idealize the past to the extent of assuming that the best works were always, inevitably, and immediately the most popular. Two years ago James D. Hart's thorough and amusing *The Popular Book* (Oxford University Press) demonstrated conclusively that since Colonial times there have always been absurd best sellers. The year that Hawthorne earned $144.09 royalty in six months was the year his own publisher paid Susan Warner $4,500 for the same period and another publisher sold 70,000 copies of one of Fanny Fern's several works.

Neither, I think, should it be supposed that any society ever has been or ever will be so organized as to favor exclusively the highest artistic excellence. As a system, aristocratic patronage is absurdly capricious; capitalistic democracy tends to favor vulgarity; socialism would probably favor official mediocrity. The question here is not whether contemporary America provides ideal conditions for cultural developments on the highest level, but whether it renders such development unusually difficult instead of making it, as the optimists insist, almost inevitable.

Of the unfavorable influences which I have mentioned, it seems to me that the most serious is the tendency to confuse the Common Denominator with a standard of excellence. The mechanical and economic facts which tend to give the purveyors of mediocrity a monopoly—highly developed in the case of radio and TV, probably growing in the publishing business—may possibly be changed by new developments, as they have already been changed in the case of the phonograph. But to confuse The Best with the most widely and the most generally acceptable is to reveal a spiritual confusion which is subtle and insidious as well as fundamental. It could easily nullify any solution of the mechanical and economic problems created by the age of mass production.

How real and how general does this confusion seem actually to be?

More than one sociologist has recently pointed out that as technology integrates larger and larger populations into tighter and tighter groups the members of these groups tend inevitably to work, live, and recreate themselves in the same way and in accordance with the standardized patterns which the facilities provided for these various activities lay down. For ill as well as for good, "community living" becomes more and more nearly inevitable and individual temperament or taste finds less and less opportunity to express itself.

One result of this is that the natural tendency of the adolescent to practice a desperate conformity is prolonged into adult life and the grown man continues to want what his neighbors have, to do what his neighbors do, to enjoy what his neighbors enjoy. This is one of the things which the European may have in mind when he calls us a nation of adolescents, and commercial interests take advantage of our adolescent characteristics by stressing, through all sorts of publicity, the fact that this is the kind of cigarette most people smoke, the kind of breakfast food most people eat, and the torch singer or crooner most people like. The best-selling book is not only the one easiest to buy, but it is also the one we must read unless we are willing to be made to seem somehow inferior. What is most popular must be best. As a broadcast official recently said, to call the most popular radio programs vulgar is to call the American people vulgar. And that, he seemed to imply, was not merely nonsense but pretty close to treason. The voice of the people is the voice of God. God loves the common man. If the common man loves Bob Hope then God must love Bob Hope also. In musical taste as in everything else the common man is divine.

It is this logic which, unfortunately, the purveyors to the mass audience are very prone to follow. Undoubtedly, it leads them to the line of least resistance at the same time that it provides them with a smug excuse for both inanity and vulgarity. They are, they say, servants of the public and have no right to doubt that the people know not only what they want but what is good for them. The age of the common man has no place for any holier-than-thou attitude. It believes in government "by" as well as "for" the people. Totalitarianism is what you get when you accept the "for" but not the "by," and the attitude of, for example, the British Broadcasting Company, with its notorious Third Program, merely demonstrates that England has not yet learned what democracy really means.

No doubt the questions involved are too complicated to be discussed here. A few years ago, Charles A. Siepmann in his *Radio, Television, and Society* fully and impartially reported on both the policies and the arguments as they affect the media with which he was dealing. But at least one conclusion seems obvious. If there is any such thing as responsibility on the part of those most powerful and best informed toward those whose appetites they feed, then no provider of movies or records or television programs can escape the minimal duty of giving his public the best rather than the worst it will stand for. Mr. Mencken once declared that no one had ever gone bankrupt by underestimating the taste of the American public, but there is an increasing tendency to believe that, by dint of long trying, certain commercial exploiters of the mass media have succeeded only too well in underestimating it considerably.

What is obviously called for is a public opinion less ready than it now is to excuse the failure to meet even minimal responsibilities; but that public opinion is not likely to arise unless those responsible for public thinking play their own parts, and there is a tendency for them to yield rather than protest. Unfortunately, the fanatical exaltation of the common denominator has been taken up not only by the common man himself and by those who hope to profit by his exploitation but also and increasingly by those who are supposed to be educators and intellectual leaders. Instead of asking "What would a good education consist of?" many professors of education are asking, "What do most college students want?"; instead of asking, "What books are wisest and best and most beautiful?", they conduct polls to determine which the largest number of students have read with least pain. Examination papers are marked, not in accordance with any fixed standard, but in accordance with a usual level of achievement; the amount of work required is fixed by the amount the average student does; even the words with which the average student is not familiar are edited out of the books he is given to read. How, granted such methods, is it other than inevitable both that the average will seldom be exceeded and that the average itself will gradually drop?

As David Reisman and his collaborators pointed out two years ago in their brilliant analysis called *The Lonely Crowd* (Yale University Press), the ideal now persistently held before the American citizen from the moment he enters kindergarten to the time when he is buried under auspices of a recognized funeral parlor is a kind of conformity more or less disguised under the term "adjustment." "Normality" has almost completely replaced "Excellence" as an ideal. It has also rendered all but obsolescent such terms as "Righteousness," "Integrity," and "Truth." The question is no longer how a boy ought to behave but how most boys do behave; not how honest a man ought to be but how honest men usually are. Even the Robber Baron, who represented an evil manifestation of the determination to excel, gives way to the moneymaker who wants only to be rich according to the accepted standards of his group. Or, as Mr. Reisman sums it up, the American who used to be conspicuously "inner-directed" is now conspicuously "outer-directed."

According to the anthropologists, many primitive societies are based almost exclusively upon the idea of conformity and generate what are, in the anthropologist's meaning of the term, remarkable cultures. It may, of course, be argued that America and the whole world which follows in America's wake is evolving in the direction of this kind of culture. But if by "culture" we mean something more narrowly defined, if we mean a culture which is continuous with that of the Western world since the Renaissance, then it is my contention that it cannot flourish where the stress is as nearly exclusively as it threatens to become upon "adjustment," "normality," or any of the other concepts which, in the end, come down to mean that the Common Denominator is identical with the Ideal. Especially, it cannot flourish under those conditions if the result which they tend to produce is intensified by the fact that ingenious methods of mass production and mass propaganda help impose upon all the tyranny of the average.

Salvation, if salvation is possible, may be made so by technological developments like those in the phonograph industry which tend to break monopoly and permit the individual to assert his preferences and his tastes. But the possible will not become the actual if in the meantime the desire for excellence has been lost and those who should be leaders have willingly become followers instead. If the Age of the Common Man is not to become the Age of the Common Denominator rather than what it was originally intended to be— namely an age in which every man had the opportunity to become as superior as he could—then the cultural as well as the political rights of minorities must somehow be acknowledged. There is not really anything undemocratic about either the desire for, or the recognition of, excellence. To prove that ours is the most cultured nation which ever existed will constitute only a barren victory if we must, to prove our point, use nothing but quantitative standards and reconcile ourselves to the common denominator as a measure of excellence.

One might sum up the situation in a series of propositions. (1) The Age of the Common Man has begun. (2) Despite all the gains that it may legitimately claim, they are threatened by those confusions which arise when the common denominator is consciously or unconsciously allowed to function as a standard of excellence. (3) The dominance of mass media almost exclusively under the control of those who are little concerned with anything except immediate financial gain does tend to debase taste. (4) Ultimate responsibility for the future rests with the thinkers and the educators whose most important social task at the moment is to define democratic culture in some fashion which will both reserve a place for uncommon excellence and, even in connection with the largest masses, emphasize the highest rather than the lowest common denominator.

The Problem of Ethics for Twentieth-Century Man

By Albert Schweitzer

June 13, 1953

The problem of ethics in the evolution of human thought cannot of course be dealt with exhaustively within the scope of the present article. By singling out the main features of this evolution, however, we can perhaps appreciate all the more clearly the nature of the role which ethics has played in the history of man's thinking.

What we call "ethics" and "morality"—which are terms borrowed from the Greek and the Latin respectively—may be broadly defined as our good behavior toward ourselves and other beings. We feel the obligation to concern ourselves not solely with our own well-being, but also with that of others and of human society. It is in the notion of the scope of this solidarity with others that the first evolution to be observed in the development of ethics occurs.

For the primitive the circle of solidarity is restricted. It is limited to those whom he can consider as in some way related to him by consanguinity, that is to say, to the members of his tribe, which he regards as a larger family. I speak from experience. In my hospital I have primitives. When I have occasion to ask a patient of this category to render some small services to a bed-ridden fellow-patient, he will oblige only if the latter belongs to his tribe. If this is not the case, he will reply quite candidly, "This not brother for me." No amount of persuasion and no kind of threat will budge him from his refusal to do that unimaginable thing: putting himself out for a stranger. I am the one who has to give in.

However, as man begins to reflect upon himself and his behavior toward others, he comes to realize that man as such is his fellow and his neighbor. In the course of a long evolutionary process he sees the circle of his responsibilities widen until it includes all the human beings with whom he has any association.

This clearer knowledge of ethics was achieved by the Chinese thinkers—Lao Tse, born in 604 B.C., Kung Tsu (Confucius), 551–479 B.C., Meng Tsu, 372–289 B.C., and Chuang Tsu, in the fourth century B.C.— and by the Hebrew prophets Amos, Hosea, and Isaiah of the eighth century B.C. The idea enounced by Jesus and Saint Paul that man owes himself to every human being is an integral part of Christian ethics.

For the great thinkers of India, whether they belong to Brahmanism, to Buddhism, or to Hinduism, the idea of brotherhood of all human beings is contained in their metaphysical notion of existence. But they encounter difficulties in incorporating it in their ethics. They are unable, in fact, to abolish the dividing walls between men erected by the existence of different castes and sanctioned by tradition. Zoroaster, who lived in the seventh century B.C., was prevented from arriving at the notion of the brotherhood of men because he had to make the distinction between those who believed in Ormuzd, the god of light and good, whom he heralded, and the unbelievers who remained under the sway of demons. He required believers, fighting for the coming of the reign of Ormuzd, to consider unbelievers as enemies and to treat them accordingly. To understand this position one must remember that the believers were the tribes of Bactrians who had become sedentary and aspired to live as honest and peaceful tillers of the soil, and that the unbelievers were the tribes which had remained nomadic, inhabiting the desert regions and living by pillage.

Plato and Aristotle, and with them the other thinkers of the classic period of Greek philosophy, consider only the Greek human being—a free man who is not under the necessity of earning his livelihood. Those who do not belong to this aristocracy are regarded by them as men of inferior quality in whom one need not be interested.

It was only in the course of the second period of Greek thought, that of the simultaneous flowering of Stoicism and Epicureanism, that the idea of the equality of men and of the interest attaching to the human being as such was recognized by the representatives of the two schools. The most remarkable proponent of this new conception is the Stoic Panaetius, who lived in the second century (180–110 B.C.). He is the prophet of humanism. The idea of the brotherhood of men does not become popular in antiquity. But the fact that philosophy should have proclaimed it as a conception dictated by reason is of great importance for its future.

It must be admitted, however, that the idea that the human being as such has a right to our interest has never enjoyed the full authority to which it might lay claim. Until our day it has been and continues to be constantly compromised by the importance assumed by differences of race, of religious belief, of nationality which cause us to regard our fellow-being as a stranger to whom we owe only indifference, if not contempt.

On undertaking to analyze the development of ethics one is led to give one's attention to the influence exerted upon ethics by the particular conception of the world to which it is related. There is, in fact, a fundamental difference between these various conceptions.

The difference stems from the manner in which the world itself is appraised. Some view it as inviting an affirmative attitude, which means interesting oneself in the things of this world and in the life we lead in it. Others, on the contrary, advocate an extraordinary negative attitude. They recommend that we dissociate ourselves from everything which concerns the world, including the existence which is ours upon this earth.

Affirmation is in conformity with our natural feeling; negation is opposed to it. Affirmation invites us to make a place for ourselves in the world and to engage in action; negation commits us to live in it as strangers and to choose nonactivity.

Ethics, by its very nature, is linked to the affirmation of the world. It is a response to the need to be active in order to serve the idea of good. It follows from this that the affirmation of the world favorably influences the development of ethics and that negation, on the contrary, impedes it. In the former case ethics can offer itself for what it is; in the latter it must relinquish its claims.

The negation of the world is professed by the thinkers of India and by the Christianity of antiquity and of the Middle Ages; affirmation by the Chinese thinkers, the Hebrew prophets, Zoroaster, and European thinkers of the Renaissance and of modern times.

Among the thinkers of India this negative conception of the world is the consequence of their conviction that true existence is immaterial, immutable, and eternal, and that the existence of the material world is unreal, deceptive, and transitory. The world which we are pleased to consider as real is for them but a mirage of the immaterial world in time and in space. It is wrong for man to interest himself in this phantasmagoria and in the role he plays in it. The only behavior compatible with a true knowledge of the nature of existence is nonactivity. In a certain measure nonactivity has an ethical character. In detaching himself from the things of this world man renounces the egoism which material interests and vulgar appetite inspire in him. Moreover, nonactivity means nonviolence. It preserves man from the danger of doing harm to others by acts of violence.

The philosophers of Brahmanism, of Sankhya, of Jainism, like Buddha, exalt nonviolence, which they call "ahimsa" and which they consider the sublime ethics. Nevertheless, it is imperfect and incomplete. It allows man the egoism of devoting himself entirely to the salvation which he hopes to gain by leading a kind of life which conforms to the true knowledge of the nature of existence; it does not command him in the name of compassion, but in the name of metaphysical theories; it demands only abstention from evil and not the activity which is inspired by the notion of good. Only the ethics which is allied to the affirmation of the world can be natural and complete. If, then, the ethics of the philosophers of India should venture to yield to the promptings of a more generous ethics than that of ahimsa, it will be able to do so only by making concessions to the affirmation of the world and to the principle of activity. Buddha, who takes a stand against the coldness of the Brahman doctrine by preaching pity, has difficulty in resisting the temptation of emancipating himself from the principle of nonactivity. He succumbs to it more than once, unable to help committing acts of charity or recommending them to his disciples. Under the cover of ethics the affirmation of the world wages a hidden struggle in India through the centuries against the principle of nonactivity. In Hinduism, which is a religious reaction from the exigencies of Brahamism, this affirmation succeeds in making itself recognized as the equal of nonactivity. The understanding between them is proclaimed and specified in the Bhagavad-Gita, a didactic poem incorporated in the great epic of the Mahabharata.

The Bhagavad-Gita admits Brahmanism's conception

of the world. It recognizes that the material world has only a deceptive reality and cannot lay claim to our interest. It is only a diverting show to which God treats himself. Man may, therefore, with good reason believe himself to be entitled to take part in this spectacle only in the capacity of a spectator. But by the same token he has the right to consider himself called upon to play his role as an actor in the play. Activity is thus justified by the spirit in which it operates. The man who practices it with the sole intention of fulfilling the will of God pursues the truth, even as does he who chooses nonactivity. On the other hand, ingenuous activity, which interests itself in this unreal world and undertakes to carry out in it any purpose whatever, is wrong and cannot be justified.

This theory which legitimizes activity by a logic resting on the idea that the world is but a show staged by God for his own enjoyment can in no way give satisfaction to true ethics, to that ethics which asserts the need to be active. The theory, nevertheless, enabled ethics to maintain itself in the Indies at a period when its existence was threatened by Brahmanism.

In our day the philosophers of India make great concessions to the principle of activity by invoking the fact that it is to be found also in the Upanishads. This is correct. The explanation is that the Aryans of India, in ancient times, as the Veda hymns tell us, led an existence filled with a naïve joy of living. The Brahman doctrine of the negation of the world makes its appearance, alongside of the affirmation, only in the Upanishads, sacred texts belonging to the beginning of the first millennium before Christ.

The Christianity of antiquity and of the Middle Ages professes the negation of the world, without however drawing from it the conclusion of nonactivity. This peculiarity stems from the fact that its negation of the world is of a different nature from that of the philosophers of India. According to its doctrine the world in which we live is not a phantasmagoria, but an imperfect world, destined to be transformed into the perfect world of the Kingdom of God. The idea of the Kingdom of

God was created by the Hebrew prophets of the eighth century B.C. It is this idea also which is at the center of the religion of Zoroaster in the seventh century.

Jesus announced the imminence of the transformation of the material world into the world of the Kingdom of God. He exhorted men to seek the perfection required for participation in the new existence in the new world. He asked man to detach himself from the things of this world in order to occupy himself solely with the practice of good. He allowed him to hold aloof from the world, but not from his duties toward men. In his ethics activity preserves all its rights and all its obligations. Herein is where it differs from that of Buddha, with which it has in common the idea of compassion. Because it is animated by the spirit of activity the ethics of Christianity maintains an affinity with affirmation of the world.

The transformation of the world into that of the Kingdom of God, which the first Christians regarded as near at hand, did not take place. During antiquity and the Middle Ages Christianity thus remains in the situation of having to despair of this world, without the hope of seeing the coming of the other—the hope which had sustained the first Christians. It would have been natural for Christianity then to come round to the affirmation of the world. Its active ethics made it possible for it to do so. But in antiquity and in the Middle Ages there did not exist a passionate affirmation of the world which alone would have served its purpose. This passionate affirmation came into being with the Renaissance. Christianity joined forces with it in the course of the sixteenth and seventeenth centuries. Its ethics, along with the ideal of self-perfection which it derived from Jesus, henceforth embraced also the other, which consists in creating new and better material and spiritual conditions for the existence of human society. From this time on Christian ethics was able to give an objective to its activity and thus achieved its full development. From the union of Christianity and the Renaissance's passionate affirmation of the world was born the civilization in which we live and which we have to maintain and to perfect. The ethical conceptions of the

Chinese philosophers and that of Zoroaster were from their origin linked with the affirmation of the world. They too bear within themselves the energies capable of producing an ethical civilization.

Having reached a certain level, ethics tends to develop depth. This tendency manifests itself in the need which it experiences to dedicate itself to the search for the fundamental principle of good.

Ethics no longer finds entire satisfaction in defining, enumerating, and recommending various virtues and various duties, but seeks to understand what they have in common in their diversity and how they flow from a single conception of good. It is thus that the great Chinese thinkers came to proclaim benevolence toward men as a fundamental virtue.

In Hebrew ethics, even before Jesus, emerges the question of the great commandment whose fulfillment is equivalent to that of the entire law. Jesus, in accord with the tradition of the Hebrew theologians, raises love to the rank of a supreme commandment.

In the first century of the Christian era philosophers of Stoicism following the path laid out by Panaetius, the creator of the idea of humanism, likewise came to consider love as the virtue of virtues; they are Seneca, Epictetus, and the Emperor Marcus Aurelius. Their ethics is essentially that of the great Chinese thinkers. They have in common with them not only the principle of love, but in addition—what is more important—the conviction that it stems from reason and is fundamentally reasonable.

In the course of the first and second centuries of the Christian era Graeco-Roman philosophy thus came to profess the same ethical ideal as Christianity. The possibility of an understanding between the ancient world and Christianity seemed to offer itself. No such development occurred. Ethical Stoicism did not become popular. Moreover, it also considered Christianity the worst of superstitions because it based itself on a divine revelation occurring in Jesus Christ, and because it awaited the miraculous coming of a new world. Christianity for its part despised philosophy as being merely the wisdom of this world. What separated the two also was the fact that philosophy adhered to the idea of the affirmation of the world, and Christianity to the idea of negation. No understanding was possible.

After a passage of centuries, however, such an understanding did occur. When in the sixteenth and seventeenth centuries Christianity began to familiarize itself with the passionate affirmation of the world which the Renaissance had bequeathed to European thought, it made acquaintance at the same time with ethical Stoicism and discovered with surprise that Jesus's principle of love had already been enunciated as a rational truth. It deduced from this that the fundamental ideas of religion must also be revealed truths subsequently confirmed by reason. Among the thinkers who at that time felt themselves to belong both to Christianity and to Stoicism the most remarkable were Erasmus of Rotterdam and Hugo Grotius.

Under the influence of Christianity the ethics of philosophy acquired an enthusiasm which it did not possess up to that time. Under the influence of philosophy the ethics of Christianity for its part began to reflect upon what it owed to itself and upon what it must accomplish in this world. Thus was born a spirit which could not permit the ethics of love to tolerate any longer the injustices, the cruelties, and the harmful superstitions which it had previously allowed. Torture was abolished, the scourge of sorcery trials came to an end, inhuman laws gave way to more human ones. A reform movement unprecedented in the history of humanity was undertaken and accomplished in the first enthusiasm of the discovery that the principle of love is taught also by reason.

To demonstrate the rationality of altruism, the love of others, eighteenth-century philosophers, including Hartley, the Baron d'Holbach, Helvetius, and Bentham, well-meaningly invoked the single argument of its utility. The Chinese thinkers and the representatives of ethical Stoicism had also brought forward this argument, but had advanced others as well. According to the thesis defended by these eighteenth-century thinkers, altruism could be regarded simply as enlightened self-interest, taking into account the fact that the well-being

of individuals and of society can be assured only by
the devotion men show toward their fellows. With this
superficial thesis Kant and the Scots philosopher David
Hume, among others, took sharp issue. Kant, in his
eagerness to defend the dignity of ethics, goes so far as
to claim that its utility must not be taken into consideration. However manifest it may be, it must not be allowed
as a motive of ethics. Ethics, according to the doctrine
of the categorical imperative, commands in an absolute
fashion. It is our conscience which reveals to us what
is right and what is wrong. We have merely to obey it.
The moral law which we bear within ourselves gives us
the certainty that we belong not only to the world as it
appears to us in time and space, but that we are at the
same time citizens of the world as such, the spiritual
world.

Hume, in order to refute the utilitarian thesis, proceeds empirically. He analyzes the motives of ethics and
reaches the conclusion that it is above all a matter of
feeling. Nature, he argues, has endowed us with the
faculty of sympathy. The latter enables us and obliges
us to experience the joy, the apprehensions, and the
sufferings of others as our own. We are, according to
an image used by Hume, like strings vibrating in unison
with those which are played. It is this sympathy which
leads us to devote ourselves to others and to wish to
contribute to their well-being and to that of society.
Philosophy since Hume—if we leave aside Nietzsche's
venture—has not dared seriously to question the concept that ethics is above all a matter of compassion.

But where does this leave ethics? Is it capable of
defining and of limiting the obligations of devotion to
others and thus reconciling egoism and altruism, as the
theory of utilitarianism attempted to do?

Hume hardly considers the question. Neither have
succeeding philosophers judged it necessary to take into
consideration the consequences of the principle of
devotion through compassion. It is as though they
sensed that these consequences might prove somewhat
troublesome. And so indeed they are. The ethics of
devotion through compassion no longer has the character of a law which we should like to continue to

attribute to it. It no longer involves clearly established and clearly formulated commandments. It is fundamentally subjective, because it leaves to each one of us the responsibility of deciding how far he shall go in devotion.

Not only does the ethics of devotion cease to prescribe in a precise fashion; it becomes by degrees less disposed to confine itself to the realm of the possible, as the law must do. It is constantly obliging us to attempt the impossible, to push devotion to the point of compromising our very existence. In the dreadful times which we have lived through many such situations arose, and many were those who sacrificed themselves for others. Even in everyday life the ethics of devotion, if it does not go to the length of demanding this ultimate sacrifice, often requires each one of us to abdicate interests, and to give up advantages out of regard for others. But too often we manage to silence our conscience, which is the guardian of our sense of responsibility. How many are the conflicts in which the ethics of devotion abandons us to ourselves. Those who manage enterprises rarely have occasion to congratulate themselves on having, out of compassion, given employment to someone who urgently needed it instead of entrusting it to the most qualified. But woe to them if they should believe themselves warranted by experiences of this kind never again to take heed of the argument of compassion.

There is a final consequence to be drawn from the principle of devotion: it no longer allows us to concern ourselves solely with human beings, but obliges us to act in the same way toward all living beings whose fate may be influenced by us. They too are our fellow-creatures by the fact they experience as we do an aspiration to happiness, as well as fear and suffering, and like us dread annihilation.

The man who has preserved his sensibility intact finds it altogether natural to have pity for all living beings. Why can philosophy not make up its mind to recognize that our behavior toward them must form an integral part of the ethics which it teaches? The reason is quite simple. Philosophy fears, and rightly so, that this immense enlargement of the circle of our responsibilities will deprive ethics of the slight hope it still has of being able to formulate commandments in a way that is at all reasonable and satisfying. Indeed, concern with the fate of all the beings with whom we have to deal creates even more numerous and more troublesome conflicts for us than those of devotion limited to human beings. In respect to creatures we find ourselves constantly in situations which oblige us to cause suffering and to impair life. The peasant cannot let all the animals born in his flock survive; he can keep only those he can feed and which it will pay him to raise. In many cases we even face the necessity of sacrificing lives to save others. A man who picks up a stray bird finds himself obliged to kill insects or fish to feed it. In acting thus he is completely in the realm of the arbitrary. By what right does he sacrifice many lives in order to save a single life? In exterminating animals which he regards as harmful in order to protect others he likewise falls into the realm of the arbitrary.

It is, therefore, incumbent upon each one of us to judge whether we find ourselves under the unavoidable necessity of inflicting suffering and of killing, and to resign ourselves to becoming guilty by necessity. As for forgiveness, we must seek it by missing no opportunity to succor living beings. How much better off we should be if men would reflect on the kindness which they owe to creatures and would abstain from all the harm they do them through heedlessness. The fight against the inhuman traditions and the inhuman feelings which are still current in our day is one which our civilization must wage, if we have any concern for our self-respect.

Among the inhuman customs which our civilization and our sentiment owe it to themselves no longer to tolerate I cannot refrain from naming two: bullfighting, with the kill, and stag-hunting. Thus it is the requirement of compassion toward all living beings which makes ethics as complete as it must be.

There has been another great change in the situation of ethics: it is today no longer able to count on the support of a conception of the world which can serve as its justification.

At all times it has been convinced that it was merely exacting the behavior conforming to the knowledge of the true nature of the universal will which manifests itself in creation. This is the conviction on which not only religion but also the rationalist philosophy of the seventeenth and eighteenth centuries are based. But it so happens that the conception of the world which ethics can invoke is the result of the interpretation of the very world to which ethics has offered, and still offers, itself. It attributes to the universal will qualities and intentions which give satisfaction to its own way of feeling and of judging. But in the course of the nineteenth century the research which allowed itself to be guided solely by concern for truth was bound to surrender to the evidence that ethics can expect nothing from a true knowledge of the world. The progress of science consists in an increasingly precise observation of the processes of nature. These allow us to harness the energies manifesting themselves in the universe to our own uses. But they oblige us at the same time increasingly to give up any attempt to understand its intentions. The world offers us the disconcerting spectacle of the will of life in conflict with itself. One existence maintains itself at the expense of another.

How can the ethics of devotion maintain itself without being sustained by a notion of the world which justifies it? It seems destined to founder in skepticism. This, however, is not the fate to which it is dedicated. In its beginnings ethics had to appeal to a conception of the world which would satisfy it. Having arrived at the knowledge that its fundamental principle is devotion, it becomes fully conscious of itself and thereby becomes autonomous.

We are in a position to understand its origins and its basis by meditating on the world and on ourselves.

We lack a complete and satisfying knowledge of the world. We are reduced to the simple observation that everything in it is life, like ourselves, and that all life is mystery. Our true knowledge of the world consists in being penetrated by the mystery of existence and of life. This mystery becomes only more mysterious as scientific research progresses. Being penetrated by the mystery of life corresponds to what in the language of mysticism is called "learned ignorance," which at least has knowledge of the essential.

The immediate datum of our consciousness, to which we come back each time we desire to achieve an understanding of ourselves and of our situation in the world, is: I am life which wants to live, surrounded by life which wants to live.

Being will-to-life, I feel the obligation to respect all will-to-life about me as equal to my own.

The fundamental idea of good is thus that it consists in preserving life, in favoring it, in wanting to bring it to its highest value, and evil consists in destroying life, doing it injury, hindering its development.

The principle of this veneration of life corresponds to that of love, as it has been discovered by religion and philosophy which sought to understand the fundamental notion of good.

The term "respect for life" is broader and because of this more colorless than that of love. But it bears the same energies within it.

This essentially philosophical notion of good has also the advantage of being more complete than that of love. Love includes only our obligation toward other beings, but not those toward ourselves. One cannot deduce from it, for example, the quality of veracity, a primordial quality of the ethical personality along with that of compassion. The respect which man owes to his own life imposes upon him that he be faithful to himself by renouncing every kind of dissimulation to which he might be tempted to resort in a given circumstance.

Through respect for life we enter into a spiritual relationship with the world. All the efforts undertaken by philosophy which built up grandiose systems to bring us into relation with the Absolute have remained vain. The Absolute is so abstract in character that we cannot communicate with it. It is not given to us to put ourselves at the disposal of the infinite and inscrutable creative will which is the basis of all existence, by having an understanding of its nature and its intentions.

But we enter into spiritual relationship with it by feeling ourselves under the impression of the mystery of life and by devoting ourselves to all the living beings whom we have the occasion and the power to serve. The ethics which obliges us solely to concern ourselves with men and society cannot have this meaning. Only that which is universal in obliging us to concern ourselves with all beings brings us truly into relationship with the Universe and the will which manifests itself in it.

In the world the will-to-life is in conflict with itself. In us, through a mystery which we do not understand, it wishes to be at peace with itself. In the world it manifests itself, in us it reveals itself. It reveals to us, among other things, that the world is our spiritual destiny. By conforming to it we live our existence instead of submitting to it. Through respect for life we become pious in an elementary, deep, and living sense.

What Is English?

By Archibald MacLeish

December 9, 1961

I do not put this question to be impertinent. I put it because I should like to know. I have been—officially at least—a teacher of English for the past twelve years and I have yet to hear myself defined. I will go further than that: I have yet to be told precisely what I'm doing.

The trouble in my case may be Harvard. Certainly the trouble at the beginning was Harvard. When I was notified in the early summer of 1949 that the President and Fellows of that University had approved my appointment to the Boylston Professorship of Rhetoric and Oratory I decided to drive down to Cambridge to find out what I was supposed to teach. It seemed like a good idea at the time: my last ten years or so had been in Washington and the years before that in journalism and my real profession throughout had been the writing of verse, not teaching. I say it seemed like a good idea. It didn't turn out that way.

My first call, logically, was at the Department of English since it was a Committee of the Department of English that had approached me—"approach" in the technical sense—the year before. It was an agreeable call but brief. Chairmen of Harvard departments, I was informed, do not tell their colleagues what to do: they merely circulate the memoranda. I was back on the wooden porch of Warren House in something under five minutes with the impression that Harvard would be an attractive place if one could get into it.

My second call was on the only member of the English Department I knew at all well, a displaced Yale man like myself. He listened, looked at the ceiling, and replied that I could teach his course in Shakespeare if I wanted. I left with the impression, later verified, that he was not entirely enthusiastic about my presence in Cambridge.

There remained the Provost of the University, the President being in Washington in those months. (By "the President" I mean, of course, the President of Harvard.) The Provost, when I found his office, was engaged but, being desperate, I decided to sit him out and that fetched him. He popped out of his office, listened mildly while I stated my business, and popped back in again with the remark, delivered over his shoulder as the door closed, that when Harvard appointed a man to a full professorship, to say nothing of the Boylston Professorship, it expected him to *know* what he wanted to teach.

It was an enlightening afternoon. I had been told in three different ways that freedom to teach at Harvard is literally freedom—with all the penalties attached. But it was not an *instructive* afternoon. I knew no more about my duties on the way back to the Franklin County Hills than I had known on the way down, and twelve years later I still know little more than I knew then.

I have taught the advanced writing course which all Boylston Professors since Barrett Wendell have offered and I have invented and annually reinvented a course in the nature of poetry; but though I take, or sometimes take, a proprietary satisfaction in both of them I am not at all sure that either is the course I should have taught or would have taught had I known what "English" is. It is not always English that turns up in the novels and poems and plays of the advanced writing course, nor does the course in poetry confine itself to poems in the English tongue. It can't very well since poetry recognizes no such limitation.

In those early days—my young days as a teacher of English when I was still in my late fifties—I used to assume that I was the only member of the profession who did not know what he was doing, but as time has passed I have begun to wonder. We have, at Harvard, an institution called the Visiting Committee, one to each department, which descends annually upon the appropriate classrooms to observe the progress of education. Our particular Visiting Committee in the Department of English ends its investigations, or always did when John Marquand was chairman, by offering a dinner to the permanent appointments. And the dinner always includes, or always included, a question which seems to stir the Departmental subconscious: Why are the graduates of Harvard University incapable of composing simple declarative sentences? Under ordinary circumstances a question such as this might be expected to serve as the gambit to a lively exchange involving, among other things, the truth of the fact asserted, but under the circumstances of our dinner, when the questioner is a distinguished alumnus who is also a member of the Committee to Visit the English Department, and when the effectiveness of the English Department in performing its duties is the subject of the Visitation, the innocent words take on a different aspect. They become charged with implications, the most challenging of which is the implication that if graduates of Harvard University are incapable of composing simple declarative sentences the Department of English is to blame. Which, in turn, implies that the teaching of English and the teaching of the composition of simple declarative sentences are one and the same thing. It is that last implication which spills the coffee on the tablecloth. Chairs are pushed back. Throats are cleared. And a strained voice, laboring under an emotion which an ignorant observer might think disproportionate to the cause, protests that teachers of English have better things to do than instruct the young in the composition of simple declarative sentences. Silence falls. Time passes. Someone suggests another drink all around. And there the issue reposes for another year. No member of the annual visitation has ever yet been rude enough to ask: What better things? And no member of the Department, within my memory, has ever said.

I suppose the reason for the persistence on one side and the passion on the other is historical. What our Visitors are remembering, consciously or not, is the importance of simple declarative sentences in the early days of the Republic, and the part played by Harvard College in the shaping of the minds of those who used them best. What my colleagues almost certainly remember is the importance to the growth of Harvard College of the liberation of their predecessors from such concerns. It was because the two Adamses and their contemporaries in Massachusetts and Virginia and Connecticut and Pennsylvania could write meaningful English that the American Revolution was not merely a defeat of England but a conquest of human liberty. But it is also true that it was not until that famous sailmaker's son, Francis J. Child, was relieved of his responsibility for the teaching of freshman composition that the Department of English at Harvard became an educational influence in the larger sense of that term.

It is, I think, this latter fact that explains the difficulty of defining "English" even today and even among those whose lives are devoted to its teaching, for the emancipation of Stubby Child took place less than a century ago. There was little "English," as we use the word, prior to 1876—at least in Cambridge. When letters were first taught in the Colonial colleges they were taught in Latin with Latin manuals and Latin and Greek examples. The teaching of composition in the vulgar tongue had begun, it is true, before the Revolution, but the extraordinary debate which preceded and accompanied that event was conducted with the classical modes and models in mind. Havard's historian, Samuel Eliot Morison, puts it with his usual pithiness: "The classical pseudonyms with which our Harvard signers of the great Declaration signed their early communications to the press were not pen-names chosen by chance, but represented a very definite point of view that every educated man recognized." And the same thing seems to have been true thirty years after the Revolution when the first chair in letters was established. John Quincy Adams, the first Boylston Professor, signalized his installation by delivering an inaugural address in which the word "English" never once occurs. It was not London to him, nor Stratford, from which the great tradition flowed but Athens and Rome. "Novelty," he told his audience, "will not be expected; nor is it perhaps to be desired. A subject which has exhausted the genius of Aristotle, Cicero, and Quintilian can neither require nor admit much additional illustration. . . ."

He was thinking, of course, of rhetoric and oratory, the two subjects attached by statute to his chair. *English* literature, in the year 1806, was something a gentleman read on his own time and for his own entertainment if he read it at all. Even a quarter of a century later instruction in this area seems to have been informal—and correspondingly pleasant. Mr. Morison quotes a member of the Harvard class of 1832 as remembering "our evenings with Chaucer and Spenser" in the study of John Quincy Adams's successor, Edward Tyrell Channing. The account hardly evokes the meeting of a course as we understand such things: "How his genial face shone in the light of the winter's fire and threw new meaning upon the rare gems of thought and humor and imagination of those kings of ancient song." It is a charming scene and one its author obviously relishes but even so he does not forget the serious business of his association with Professor Channing. It was not for those rare gems that he sat at the great man's feet. It was to learn to write. "Who of us," he reminds himself, "does not bless him every day that we write an English sentence for his pure taste and admirable simplicity!"

All of which would seem to support the conclusion that it was not until well along in Mr. Eliot's administration that "English" began at Harvard with the beginning of those laborious studies of Francis Child's in Anglo-Saxon and Middle English and Chaucer and Shakespeare and Dryden on which our modern literary scholarship is founded. But if this is so—if "English" is as new as this—then the difficulty of discussing it with members of Visiting Committees becomes understandable. Eighty years is a short time in which to fix the character and limits of a discipline. One can learn in so brief a time what "English" isn't—as, for example, that it isn't the thing it rebelled against at its beginnings. It isn't, that is to say, the "mere" teaching of the use of the English language. But one cannot learn so quickly what "English" is.

Literature? The teaching of literature in English? It sounds reasonable: if "English" isn't the teaching of the writing of the language it may well be the teaching of the reading of the language—the reading of what has already been written that deserves to be read again. But what do we mean by reading? Do we mean the reading of the words as words, the recognition of the structure, the interpretation of the references—in brief, the explication, as we put it, of the text? Or do we mean the reading of the substance of the words, what the words in their combination and their structure, their sounds and their significance, are *about?* But if we mean the latter, where does "English" end? The substance of the literature of our tongue is the whole substance of human experience as that experience has presented itself to the mind, the imagination, and the most sensitive of the users of that tongue. Nothing is foreign to it. Nothing is excluded. Everything has been touched, turned over, nuzzled, chewed, and much has been mastered, much has been perceived. If "English" has to do with the substance of English literature, where will we find faculties qualified to teach it? And how, if we found them, could they fit themselves into the academic order? What would be left for the other faculties —for the departments of philosophy and theology and biology and history and psychology?—above all for the departments of psychology?

Obviously "English" cannot claim so vast an empire. But what lesser kingdom is there then? The texts as texts? It was the teaching of the texts as texts that destroyed the classics in American education. When "The Odyssey" was assigned in the last century as so much Greek—so many lines a day and so many days in the year, leaving the poem to take care of itself— "The Odyssey" began to die and Greek with it. And when, later, the magnificent scholarship of Kittredge attached itself to English texts as texts, a generation of graduate students was produced which itched to teach anything else—biographies of poets, economic and sociological interpretations of novels, literary history— anything but the texts themselves. And when this revolution had set up its barricades, it in turn produced the counterrevolution of our own time. Back-to-the-text was the word with us—and the word became flesh in an army of brave new critics who carried everything before them only to leave us, when the counterrevolution subsided, where we are today: betwixt and between. We are agreed that it was a mistake to teach the poems of Shelley by way of the pitch of his voice and the bonfire on the beach but we are not yet entirely persuaded that *explication de texte* has told the truth about poetry either. "English," we think today, is something more than the teaching of the reading of words as words but something less also, surely less, than the teaching of the private life the words came out of, or the public life toward which they look.

Less and more—but how much less and how much more? That is the question we do not answer for our newly chosen colleagues knocking at our doors to ask us what they ought to teach. Can it be answered? I think for myself, overboldly perhaps, that it can. It can, that is, if we will look for the answer where answers are to be found in such cases: not in the theory but in the practice. Percy Bridgman once remarked of the language of physics that you can tell the meaning of a term far better by seeing what is done *with* it than by hearing what is said *about* it. The same thing is true of the language of education. The theoretical fences will all blow down, give them time enough and wind, but the actions will stand. A colleague working in an ungrateful corner of the curriculum brings the dust to air, raises the too long familiar from its accustomedness, calls Dr. Johnson from his sepulchre and makes him walk the College Yard. This is the teaching of "English," but what has this colleague taught? Or a lecturer somewhere else, struggling with an exhausted theme, renews a poem which had lost its voice and makes it cry like the first bird in Eden. This too is "English"—but what then is it?

Take the lecturer. Take Robert Penn Warren teaching "The Rime of the Ancient Mariner" in a lecture which has been widely published and much read: a lecture which gives voice to the poem. What *happens* in this lecture? The poem is "read," yes, but is it the "reading" that happens? There have been better "readings"—"readings" which place the poem more perfectly in its dramatic setting and better reveal the necessity that drives it. What truly happens here is something else. What happens is that the relation between the poem and the world of life in which the poem exists is discovered—discovered by a stroke as brief and brilliant as the blast of light which sometimes ties the earth and sky together. Every man, says Mr. Warren quietly, kills his own albatross . . . and there, with those words, the bird, the scene, the poem all come true— come real. The metaphysical talk about symbols and symbolism which usually fogs discussions of "The Rime"—is the albatross a symbol? Isn't it? But *is* it?— chokes on its own inanity and what is left is meaning, the only kind of meaning that truly means, personal meaning, immediate meaning. The world of ice and snow becomes the world of vision we all have glimpsed —we also. The murder of the bird becomes the murder of which we also are guilty, all of us: the destruction of life, the denial of love. The horror of thirst and windlessness, motionlessness, becomes the horror of stagnation we too have sensed when our rejection of love, of life, has stilled the winds of vision that should drive us. The salvation by wonder and pity becomes a salvation we could recognize if it came. Even the little precept at the end, those lines the overeducated read with titters of embarrassment, takes power to move our hearts:

> He prayeth best who loveth best
> All things both great and small.

One sees, looking back, what has happened. This myth of the poetic imagination which students in colleges are called on to admire as literature has become a myth of myself which I—student, teacher, man, woman, whoever—am called on to live as life. And one sees how this miracle has been accomplished. It has been accomplished not by squeezing the pips of the text but by a perception which has one foot in the text and the other in the world so that the two, text and world, are made to march together.

But is this what the teaching of "English," in its actions, is? Is this what happens in W. J. Bate's lectures on Johnson and in all the rest of the great achievements in the discipline? I think it is. I think "English" always stands with a foot in the text and a foot in the world, and that what it undertakes to teach is neither the one nor the other but the relation between them. The greatest poem, removed from the ground of our being, is an irrelevance. The ground of our being without the poem is a desert. "English," I think, is the teaching which attempts to minister between.

Why We Can't Wait

By Martin Luther King

May 30, 1964

It is the beginning of the year of our Lord 1963.

I see a young Negro boy. He is sitting on a stoop in front of a vermin-infested apartment house in Harlem. The stench of garbage is in the halls. The drunks, the jobless, the junkies are shadow-figures of his everyday world. The boy goes to a school attended mostly by Negro students, with a scattering of Puerto Ricans. His father is one of the jobless. His mother is a sleep-in domestic, working for a family on Long Island.

I see a young Negro girl. She is sitting on the stoop of a rickety wooden one-family house in Birmingham. Some visitors would call it a shack. It needs paint badly and the patched-up roof appears in danger of caving in. Half a dozen small children, in various stages of undress, are scampering about the house. The girl is forced to play the role of their mother. She can no longer attend the all-Negro school in her neighborhood because her mother died only recently after a car accident. Neighbors say if the ambulance hadn't come so late to take her to the all-Negro hospital, the mother might still be alive. The girl's father is a porter in a downtown department store. He will always be a porter, for there are no promotions for the Negro in this store, where every counter serves him except the one that sells hot dogs and orange juice.

This boy and this girl, separated by stretching miles, are wondering: Why does misery constantly haunt the Negro? In some distant past, had their forebears done some tragic injury to the nation, and was there a curse of punishment upon the black race? Had they shirked their duties as patriots, betrayed their country, denied their national birthright? Had they refused to defend their land against a foreign foe?

Not all of history is recorded in the books supplied to school children in Harlem or Birmingham. Yet this boy and this girl know something of the part of history that has been censored by the white writers and purchasers of board-of-education books. They know that Negroes were with George Washington at Valley Forge. They know that the first American to shed blood in the revolution that freed his country from British oppression was a black seaman named Crispus Attucks. The boy's Sunday-school teacher has told him that one of the team who designed the capital of their nation, Washington, D.C., was a Negro, Benjamin Banneker. Once the girl had heard a speaker, invited to her school during Negro History Week. This speaker told how, for two hundred years, without wages, black people, brought to this land in slave ships and in chains, had drained the swamps, built the homes, made cotton king, and helped, on whip-lashed backs, to lift this nation from colonial obscurity to commanding influence in domestic commerce and world trade.

Wherever there was hard work, duty work, dangerous work—in the mines, on the docks, in the blistering foundries—Negroes had done more than their share.

The pale history books in Harlem and Birmingham told how the nation had fought a war over slavery. Abraham Lincoln had signed a document that would come to be known as the Emancipation Proclamation. The war had been won, but not a just peace. Equality had never arrived. Equality was a hundred years late.

The boy and the girl knew more than history. They knew something about current events. They knew that African nations had burst the bonds of colonialism. They knew that a great-great-grandson of Crispus Attucks might be ruled out of some restricted, all-white restaurant in some restricted, all-white section of a Southern town, his United States Marines uniform notwithstanding. They knew that Negroes living in the capital of their own nation were confined to ghettos and could not always get a job for which they were qualified. They knew that white supremacists had defied the Supreme Court and that Southern governors had attempted to interpose themselves between the people and the highest law of the land. They knew that for years their own lawyers had won great victories in the courts that were not being translated into reality.

They were seeing on television, hearing from the radio, reading in the newspapers that this was the 100th birthday of their freedom.

But freedom had a dull ring, a mocking emptiness when, in their time—in the short life spans of this boy and girl—buses had stopped rolling in Montgomery; sit-inners were jailed and beaten: freedom riders were brutalized and murdered; dogs' fangs were bared in Birmingham; and in Brooklyn, New York, there were certain kinds of construction jobs for whites only.

It was the summer of 1963. Was emancipation a fact? Was freedom a force?

The boy in Harlem stood up. The girl in Birmingham arose. Separated by stretching miles, both of them squared their shoulders and lifted their eyes toward heaven. Across the miles they joined hands and took a firm, forward step. It was a step that rocked the richest, most powerful nation to its foundations.

The bitterly cold winter of 1962 lingered throughout the opening months of 1963, touching the land with chill and frost, and was then replaced by a placid spring. Americans awaited a quiet summer. That it would be pleasant they had no doubt. The worst of it would be the nightmare created by 60,000,000 cars, all apparently trying to reach the same destination at the same time. Fifty million families looked forward to the pleasure of two hundred million vacations in the American tradition of the frenetic hunt for relaxation.

It would be a pleasant summer because, in the mind of the average man, there was little cause for concern. The blithe outlook about the state of the nation was reflected from as high up as the White House. The Administration confidently readied a tax-reduction bill. Business and employment were at comfortable levels. Money was—for many Americans—plentiful.

Summer came, and the weather was beautiful. But the climate, the social climate of American life, erupted into lightning flashes, trembled with thunder, and vibrated to the relentless, growing rain of protest come to life through the land. Explosively, America's third revolution—the Negro revolution—had succeeded the American Revolution and the Civil War.

For the first time in the long and turbulent history of the nation, almost 1,000 cities were engulfed in civil turmoil, with violence trembling just below the surface. As in the French Revolution of 1789, the streets had become a battleground, just as they had become the battleground, in the 1830s, of England's tumultuous Chartist movement. As in these two revolutions, a submerged social group, propelled by a burning need for justice, lifting itself with sudden swiftness, moving with determination and a majestic scorn for risk and danger, created an uprising so powerful that it shook a huge society from its comfortable base.

Never in American history had a group seized the streets, the squares, the sacrosanct business thoroughfares, and the marbled halls of government to protest and proclaim the unendurability of their oppression. Had room-size machines turned human, burst from the plants that housed them, and stalked the land in revolt, the nation could not have been more amazed. Undeniably, the Negro had been an object of sympathy and wore the scars of deep grievances, but the nation had come to count on him as a creature who could quietly endure, silently suffer, and patiently wait. He was well trained in service and, whatever the provocation, he neither pushed back nor spoke back.

Just as lightning makes no sound until it strikes, the Negro Revolution generated quietly. But when it struck, the revealing flash of its power and the impact of its sincerity and fervor bespoke a force of frightening intensity. Three hundred years of humiliation, abuse, and deprivation cannot be expected to find voice in a whisper. The storm clouds did not release a "gentle rain from heaven" but a whirlwind, which has not yet spent its force or attained its full momentum.

Because there is more to come; because American society is bewildered by the spectacle of the Negro in revolt; because the dimensions are vast and the implications deep in a nation with 20,000,000 Negroes, it is important to understand the history that is being made today.

Some years ago I sat in a Harlem department store, surrounded by hundreds of people. I was autographing copies of *Stride Toward Freedom*, my book about the Montgomery bus boycott of 1955–56. As I signed my name to a page, I felt something sharp plunge forcefully into my chest. I had been stabbed with a letter opener, struck home by a woman who would later be judged insane. Rushed by ambulance to Harlem Hospital, I lay in a bed for hours while preparations were made to remove the keen-edged blade from my body. Days later, when I was well enough to talk with Dr. Aubrey Maynard, the chief of the surgeons who performed the delicate, dangerous operation, I learned the reason for the long delay that preceded surgery. He told me that the razor-sharp tip of the instrument had been touching my aorta and that my whole chest had to be opened to extract it.

"If you had sneezed during all those hours of waiting," Dr. Maynard said, "your aorta would have been punctured and you would have drowned in your own blood."

In the summer of 1963 the knife of violence was just that close to the nation's aorta. Hundreds of cities might now be mourning countless dead but for the operation of certain forces that gave political surgeons an opportunity to cut boldly and safely to remove the deadly peril.

What was it that gave us the second chance? To answer this we must answer another question. Why did this Revolution occur in 1963? Negroes had for decades endured evil. In the words of the poet, they had long asked: "Why must the blackness of nighttime collect in our mouth; why must we always taste grief in our blood?" Any time would seem to have been the right time. Why 1963?

Why did a thousand cities shudder almost simultaneously and why did the whole world—in gleaming capitals and mud-hut villages—hold its breath during those months? Why was it in this year that the American Negro, so long ignored, so long written out of the pages of history books, tramped a declaration of freedom with his marching feet across the pages of newspapers, the television screens, and the magazines? Sarah Turner closed the kitchen cupboard and went into the streets; John Wilkins shut down the elevator and enlisted in the nonviolent army; Bill Griggs slammed the brakes of his truck and slid to the sidewalk; the Reverend Arthur Jones led his flock into the streets and held church in jail. The words and actions of parliaments and statesmen, of kings and prime ministers, movie stars and athletes, were shifted from the front pages to make room for the history-making deeds of the servants, the drivers, the elevator operators, and the ministers. Why in 1963, and what has this to do with why the dark threat of violence did not erupt in blood?

The Negro had been deeply disappointed over the slow pace of school desegregation. He knew that in 1954 the highest court in the land had handed down a decree calling for desegregation of schools "with all deliberate speed." He knew that this edict from the Supreme Court had been heeded with all deliberate delay. At the beginning of 1963, nine years after this historic decision, approximately 9 per cent of Southern Negro students were attending integrated schools. If this pace were maintained, it would be the year 2054 before integration in Southern schools would be a reality.

In its wording the Supreme Court decision had revealed an awareness that attempts would be made to evade its intent. The phrase "all deliberate speed" did not mean that another century should be allowed to unfold before we released Negro children from the narrow pigeonhole of the segregated schools; it meant that, giving some courtesy and consideration to the need for softening old attitudes and outdated customs, democracy must press ahead, out of the past of ignorance and intolerance, and into the present of educational opportunity and moral freedom.

Yet the statistics make it abundantly clear that the segregationists of the South remained undefeated by the decision. From every section of Dixie, the announcement of the high court had been met with declarations of defiance. Once recovered from their initial outrage, these defenders of the status quo had seized the offensive to impose their own schedule of change. The progress that was supposed to have been achieved with deliberate speed had created change for less than 2 per cent of Negro children in most areas of the South, and not even one-tenth of 1 per cent in some parts of the deepest South.

There was another factor in the slow pace of progress, a factor of which few are aware and even fewer understand. It is an unadvertised fact that soon after the 1954 decision, the Supreme Court retreated from its own position by giving approval to the Pupil Placement Law. This law permitted the states themselves to determine where school children might be placed by virtue of family background, special ability, and other subjective criteria. The Pupil Placement Law was almost as far-reaching in modifying and limiting the integration of schools as the original decision had been in attempting to eliminate segregation. Without technically reversing itself, the court had granted legal sanction to tokenism and thereby guaranteed that segregation, in substance, would last for an indefinite period, though formally it was illegal.

To understand, then, the deep disillusion of the Negro in 1963, one must examine his contrasting emotions at the time of the decision and during the nine years that followed. One must understand the pendulum swing between the elation that arose when the edict was handed down and the despair that followed the failure to bring it to life.

A second reason for the outburst in 1963 was rooted in disappointment with both political parties. From the city of Los Angeles in 1960, the Democratic party had written an historic and sweeping civil rights pronouncement into its campaign platform. The Democratic standard bearer had repeated eloquently and often that the moral weight of the Presidency must be applied to this burning issue. From Chicago, the Republican party had been generous in its convention vows on civil rights, although its candidate had made no great effort in his campaign to convince the nation that he would redeem his party's promises.

Then 1961 and 1962 arrived, with both parties marking time in the cause of justice. In the Congress, reactionary Republicans were still doing business with the Dixiecrats. And the feeling was growing among Negroes that the Administration had oversimplified and underestimated the civil rights issue. President Kennedy, if not backing down, had backed away from the key pledge of his campaign—to wipe out housing discrimination immediately "with the stroke of a pen." When he had finally signed the housing order, two years after taking office, its terms, though praiseworthy, had revealed a serious weakness in its failure to attack the key problem of discrimination in financing by banks and other lending institutions.

While Negroes were being appointed to some significant jobs, and social hospitality was being extended at the White House to Negro leaders, the dreams of the masses remained in tatters. The Negro felt that he recognized the same old bone that had been tossed to him in the past—only now it was being handed to him on a platter, with courtesy.

The Administration had fashioned its primary approach to discrimination in the South around a series of lawsuits chiefly designed to protect the right to vote. Opposition toward action on other fronts had begun to harden. With each new Negro protest we were advised, sometimes privately and sometimes in public, to call off our efforts and channel all of our energies into registering voters. On each occasion we would agree with the importance of voting rights, but would patiently seek to explain that Negroes did not want to neglect all other rights while one was selected for concentrated attention.

It was necessary to conclude that our argument was not persuading the Administration any more than the government's logic was prevailing with us. Negroes had manifested their faith by giving a substantial majority of their votes to President Kennedy. They had expected more of him than of the previous Administration. In no sense had President Kennedy betrayed his promises.

Yet his Administration appeared to believe it was doing as much as was politically possible and had, by its positive deeds, earned enough credit to coast on civil rights. Politically, perhaps, this was not a surprising conclusion. How many people understood, during the first two years of the Kennedy Administration, that the Negroes' "Now" was becoming as militant as the segregationists' "Never"? Eventually, the President would set political considerations aside and rise to the level of his own unswerving moral commitment. But this was still in the future.

No discussion of the influences that bore on the thinking of the Negro in 1963 would be complete without some attention to the relationship of this revolution to international events. Throughout the upheavals of cold war politics, Negroes had seen their government go to the brink of nuclear conflict more than once. The justification for risking the annihilation of the human race was always expressed in terms of America's willingness to go to any lengths to preserve freedom. To the Negro, that readiness for heroic measures in the defense of liberty disappeared or became tragically weak when the threat was within our own borders and was concerned with the Negro's liberty. While the Negro is not so selfish as to stand isolated in concern for his own dilemma, ignoring the ebb and flow of events around the world, there is a certain bitter irony in the picture of his country championing freedom in foreign lands and failing to ensure that freedom to 20,000,000 of its own.

From beyond the borders of his own land, the Negro had been inspired by another powerful force. He had watched the decolonization and liberation of nations in Africa and Asia since World War II. He knew that yellow, black, and brown people had felt for years that the American Negro was too passive, unwilling to take strong measures to gain his freedom. He might have remembered the visit to this country of an African head of state, who was called upon by a delegation of prominent American Negroes. When they began reciting to him their long list of grievances, the visiting statesman had waved a weary hand and said:

"I am aware of current events. I know everything you are telling me about what the white man is doing to the Negro. Now tell me: What is the Negro doing for himself?"

The American Negro saw, in the land from which he had been snatched and thrown into slavery, a great pageant of political progress. He realized that just thirty years ago there were only three independent nations in the whole of Africa. He knew that by 1963 more than thirty-four African nations had risen from colonial bondage. The Negro saw black statesmen voting on vital issues in the United Nations—and knew that in many cities of his own land he was not permitted to take that significant walk to the ballot box. He saw black kings and potentates ruling from palaces—and knew he had been condemned to move from small ghettos to larger ones. Witnessing the drama of Negro progress elsewhere in the world, witnessing a level of conspicuous consumption at home exceeding anything in our history, it was natural that by 1963 Negroes would rise with resolution and demand a share of governing power and living conditions measured by current American standards rather than by the obsolete standards of colonial impoverishment.

An additional and decisive fact confronted the Negro and helped to bring him out of the houses into the streets, out of the trenches and into the front lines. This was his recognition that 100 years had passed since emancipation, with no profound effect on his plight.

With the dawn of 1963, plans were afoot all over the land to celebrate the Emancipation Proclamation, the 100th birthday of the Negro's liberation from bondage. In Washington, a federal commission had been established to mark the event. Governors of states and mayors of cities had utilized the date to enhance their political image by naming commissions, receiving committees, issuing statements, planning state pageants, sponsoring dinners, endorsing social activities. Champagne, this year, would bubble on countless tables. Appropriately attired, over thick cuts of roast beef, legions would listen as luminous phrases were spun to salute the great democratic landmark that 1963 represented.

But alas! All the talk and publicity accompanying the centennial only served to remind the Negro that he still wasn't free, that he still lived a form of slavery disguised by certain niceties of complexity. As the then Vice President, Lyndon B. Johnson, phrased it: "Emancipation was a proclamation but not a fact." The pen of the Great Emancipator had moved the Negro into the sunlight of physical freedom, but actual conditions had left him behind in the shadow of political, psychological, social, economic, and intellectual bondage. In the South, discrimination faced the Negro in its obvious and glaring forms. In the North, it confronted him in hidden and subtle disguise.

The Negro also had to recognize that 100 years after emancipation he lived on a lonely island of economic insecurity in the midst of a vast ocean of material prosperity. Negroes are still at the bottom of the economic ladder. They live within two concentric circles of segregation. One imprisons them on the basis of color; the other confines them within a separate culture of poverty. The average Negro is born into want and deprivation. His struggle to escape his circumstances is hindered by color discrimination. He is deprived of normal education and normal social and economic opportunities. When he seeks opportunity, he is told in effect to lift himself by his own bootstraps—advice that does not take into account the fact that he is barefoot.

By 1963 most of America's working population had forgotten the Great Depression or had never known it. The slow and steady growth of unemployment had touched some of the white working force, but the proportion was still not more than one in twenty. This was not true for the Negro. There were two and one-half times as many jobless Negroes as whites in 1963, and their median income was half that of the white man. Many white Americans of good will have never connected bigotry with economic exploitation. They have deplored prejudice but tolerated or ignored economic injustice. But the Negro knows that these two evils have a malignant kinship. He knows this because he has worked in shops that employ him exclusively because the pay is below a living standard. He knows it is not an accident of geography that wage rates in the South are significantly lower than those in the North. He knows that the growth in the number of women who work is not a phenomenon in Negro life. The average Negro woman has always had to work to help keep her family in food and clothes.

To the Negro, as 1963 approached, the economic structure of society appeared to be so ordered that a precise sifting of jobs took place. The lowest-paid employment and the most tentative jobs were reserved for him. If he sought to change his position, he was walled in by the tall barrier of discrimination. As summer came, more than ever the spread of unemployment had visible and tangible dimensions to the colored American. Equality meant dignity, and dignity demanded a job that was secure and a paycheck that lasted throughout the week.

The Negro's economic problem was compounded by the emergence and growth of automation. Since discrimination and lack of education confined him to unskilled and semi-skilled labor, the Negro was and remains the first to suffer in these days of great technological development. The Negro knew all too well that there was not in existence the kind of vigorous retraining program that could really help him to grapple with the magnitude of his problem.

The symbol of the job beyond the great wall was construction work. The Negro whose slave labor helped build a nation was being told by employers on the one hand and unions on the other that there was no place for him in this industry. Billions were being spent on city, state, and national building for which the Negro paid taxes but could draw no paycheck. No one who saw the spanning bridges, the grand mansions, the sturdy docks and stout factories of the South could question the Negro's ability to build if he were given a chance for apprenticeship training. It was plain, hard, raw discrimination that shut him out of decent employment.

In 1963 the Negro, who had realized for many years that he was not truly free, awoke from a stupor of inaction with the cold dash of realization that 1963 meant 100 years had passed since Lincoln gave his autograph to the cause of freedom.

The milestone of the centennial of emancipation gave the Negro a reason to act—a reason so simple and obvious that he almost had to step back to see it.

Simple logic made it painfully clear that if this centennial was to be meaningful, it must be observed not as a celebration, but rather as a commemoration of the one moment in the country's history when a bold, brave *start* had been made, and as a rededication to the obvious fact that urgent business was at hand—the resumption of that noble journey toward the goals reflected in the Preamble to the Constitution, the Constitution itself, the Bill of Rights and the Thirteenth, Fourteenth, and Fifteenth Amendments.

Yet not all of these forces conjoined could have brought about the massive and largely bloodless revolution of 1963 if there had not been at hand a philosophy and a method worthy of its goals. Nonviolent direct action did not originate in America, but it found its natural home in this land, where refusal to cooperate with injustice was an ancient and honorable tradition and where Christian forgiveness was written into the minds and hearts of good men. Tested in Montgomery during the winter of 1955–56 and toughened throughout the South in the eight ensuing years, nonviolent resistance had become, by 1963, the logical force in the greatest mass-action crusade for freedom that has ever occurred in American history.

Nonviolence is a powerful and just weapon. It is a weapon unique in history, which cuts without wounding and ennobles the man who wields it. It is a sword that heals. Both a practical and a moral answer to the Negro's cry for justice, nonviolent direct action proved that it could win victories without losing wars, and so became the triumphant tactic of the Negro Revolution of 1963.

The Age of Overwrite and Underthink

By Stephen Spender

March 12, 1966

In the famous controversy about the two cultures, one important point seems to have been overlooked: that if there truly is a gulf between the literary and the scientific culture, it cannot be bridged by science, but only by language. Language is the only means of communication between specialities as far apart as every individual's unique experience of his own life. Scientific specialization itself is human experience, and if it is to become part of the general culture it can only be so by communication through language. When there is a question of discussing and explaining our experiences of the other arts, music, or painting, we use words. If architecture aspires to the condition of music, all human experience aspires to words.

This very simple point, that we communicate by means of language, seems to be largely overlooked by our educators. Our own language is thought of as just one thing taught like all the others, not as an intermediary between all things taught. Before the end of the last century, English, I believe, was not a subject at English universities. There was no English school at Oxford and Cambridge. Everyone was supposed to know English literature, and apart from the grammar taught in one's childhood, how to write English was a benefit conferred by, or inferred from, a classical education. I suppose that some of those who hotly contested the introduction of the study of English literature must have argued, with reason, that if English becomes a subject, then reading and writing English literature becomes a specialization among other specializations. The main road of communication becomes a cellar occupied by people who make a profession of reading and writing. In our own time an attempt is being made to turn the tables on those who have made English one subject among other subjects by giving it the status of principal subject. Dr. Leavis and his followers argue that English should be the main study at the new universities. They argue that in the era of the breakdown of values, and in the absence of religion, our only connection with the past of the "organic community" is through the English books of the Great Tradition, as chosen by the Leavisite priesthood.

This seems an attempt to replace compulsory religious teaching with compulsory study of English literature. It seems an extreme position only serving to dramatize that it is a desperate one in the age of nuclear fission when the people who are studying either to reinvent us or to completely destroy us have no time for any other work than their frenetic pursuit of bigger and better means of doing one or the other.

What one may insist on, though, is that life attains significance through the consciousness of the individual who lives it and who is able to understand that significance through comparing his own experiences with those of other people. Language is the only means of communicating experiences, realizing consciousness. One cannot, I think, reasonably argue that everyone ought to be a New Critic, or a doctrinaire of the Great Tradition, but one can point out that it is urgent for people to be able to communicate, and that they can only do this through being able to read the works that illuminate their experiences. This means developing a capacity to speak, think, and write clearly.

It seems to be universally recognized that everyone should learn to read and write. Not to be able to do so is to be illiterate. Little importance, however, is attached to what you read and how you write. The idea that writing is not just a physical attainment, like using a knife and fork, but is communication, and that everyone should be concerned with it to the degree that he has experiences and ideas to express, seems to be regarded as eccentric. Yet it is doubtful whether you can carry on an intelligent conversation without being able to write down the ideas conversed about. Anyone can demonstrate this to himself by simply turning on the radio or TV and listening to the dismal attempts of experts in politics and government to communicate their expertise. What one witnesses again and again is the breakdown of language.

We groan over specialization, but we accept it as inevitable, reflecting that specialists are so specialized in matters of which we are so ignorant that even if they could tell us about the things they know, we would not understand. Yet there exist, especially in France and England, a few masters of exposition who show that the most specialized subject is often far more communicable than we would anticipate its being. Moreover, it is doubtful whether what we need or want to know from the specialist is really that which is highly technical and particular to his research. What we need to know from scientists is how their scientific picture of the world should affect and qualify our life. A good deal of this can be explained. And if—as Robert Oppenheimer seems to think—there is a highly important kind of scientific experience that cannot be communicated to the nonspecialist then the significance of noncommunicability is something that also needs to be explained, because it may be a factor, or, rather a blank, in the picture of life we need to allow for. In the past it was considered important to understand that there were incommunicable mysteries. But these were communicated as *experience of the incommunicable,* in that people realized there were mysteries of knowledge and priesthood. If there is a kind of scientific experience that is central to modern life and cannot be explained, then this is something different from mere "specialization," and it can and should be understood.

Whether what scientists have to explain to us is communicable, or whether they have to explain that it is incommunicable, the fact is that the present breakdown in communication is due at least partly to the neglect of English. It is slovenly to accept without question the cliché that we cannot communicate because we live in "an age of specialization." One only has to look at the essays of most sociologists to realize that language, the medium of communication, is often the last thing that people who have very important things to tell about the state of our society have taken trouble about. We enter the era of mass communication when the study of the traditional, and the ultimate, means of communication, the English language, is looked at as a matter concerning only literary specialists.

I do not see why an attempt should not be made at school through the widened study of writing and speaking English to break down some barriers of incommunicability. The basic condition for making such an attempt possible would be that everyone, in whatever discipline, wrote an essay on some general subject once a week or fortnight. Some of these essays might take the form of communications from members of one discipline to another. For example, students on the science side of the school might be asked to write essays directed to those studying history, explaining, in words that the science student hoped the historian would understand, what some aspect of his science was about, and vice versa. The historians, or the scientists, would then read the best essays from the science students, and perhaps both classes would meet to discuss the essays.

Another exercise that I have thought about (without being able to fire anyone else with my own enthusiasm) is that a day of a term or a year should be set aside for general academic exercise in which speakers from different specialized disciplines would explain before an audience what they thought was the meaning and importance of their work. A good classroom exercise might be to make students listen to TV interviews with Senators, ex-Presidents, etc., taking with them notebooks in which they would write down sentences in the interview that strike them as particularly good, or particularly bad, considered not for their content but as language—to be followed by a general discussion of these by the class. This might prove linguistically therapeutic.

I think, then, that we should regard English literature —fiction, nonfiction, poetry, etc.—primarily as teaching people to communicate with one another and in that way helping them to live their lives. We are not, even

in the university creative writing course, teaching them
to be writers. We are concerned only with teaching
them to read, to express themselves, to appreciate language, to discuss and talk better because they are trying
to read and write. Instead of giving them a specialist
view of writing, we should try to break this down, to
emphasize the importance of writing everything as well
as possible: a letter to a friend or to a member of the
family, a private journal. We should make them think
of reading and writing as two sides of the same medal.
One reads better because one writes better, one writes
better because one reads better.

That students often distinguish sharply between reading and writing is painfully evident. Some years ago,
after reading an essay by one of my students I suggested to her that she should read Samuel Butler's essays. "Oh, I don't read, Mr. Spender," she protested,
"I write."

As I suggested above, every student at school ought
to write a weekly essay. Students ought to be given a
wide choice of subjects, with a view, perhaps, to their
sometimes being very close to themselves and sometimes demanding that they should get away from their
self-absorption, their subjectivity, into their opposite,
the objective. But it is a mistake to produce the impression that this kind of belles-lettres is literature, or,
at any rate, more literary, than the subject I suggested
previously, of a scientist writing for a historian about
his scientific studies. Everything that is well written can
be literature, if literature is what we are concerned
with. One of the masterpieces of English literature is a
handbook on angling.

Feeling for language includes grammar, texture of
sentences, the difference between prose and poetry. The
important thing is to emphasize the sensuous aspects
of writing. For example, grammar is not just obeying
rules. It is the exercise of the power politics of language.
Words rule other words, subjects have objects. Prepositions are powerful indicators, instruments of authority,
traffic directors. All this suggests the visual and it seems
to me that grammar should be visualized as much as
possible, with parentheses enclosed in separating walls,

nouns elevated to kingship by verbs and ruling their objects, etc.

I hope that the following poem will illustrate what I am here trying to put forward:

Subject: Object: Sentence

A subject thought: because he had a verb
With several objects, that he ruled a sentence.
Has not Grammar willed him these substantives
Which he came into, as his just inheritance?

His objects were wine, women, fame and wealth,
And a subordinate clause—*all life can give.*
He grew so fond of having these, that, finally,
He found himself becoming quite subjective.
Subject, the dictionary warned, means *someone ruled by
Person or thing.* Was he not *having's* slave?
To achieve detachment, he must be *objective.*
Which means to free himself from the verb *have.*

Seeking detachment, he studies the context
Around his sentence, to place it in perspective:
Paraphrased, made a critical analysis,
and then reread it, feeling more *objective.*

Then, with a shock, he realized that *sentence*
Like subject-object, is treacherously double.
A sentence is condemned to stay as stated—
As in *life-sentence, death-sentence,* for example.*

Apart from one term teaching school in England, most of my experience of teaching is taking a creative writing course at Northwestern University—an "advanced composition course," as we call it there. Before discussing this I feel the need to make an apologia, to explain what my attitude is to such a course. Most writers feel, I gather, the same need to justify teaching "creative writing."

I do not think that the writer, taking such a course, thinks that he can provide a formula that will turn stu-

---

* Reprinted by permission of Random House, Inc., from *Selected Poems* by Stephen Spender. Copyright © 1964 by Stephen Spender.

dents into poets and novelists. A teaching course sets up a meeting place for students who are interested in writing. Here they exchange views and they come in contact with a vocational writer. The creative writing course is a Midwestern substitute for the Parisian café where young writers come and show one another their poems and stories, and where older writers are in the offing. The more students, with or without the official "writer," meet and continue their discussions outside the course, the better. I am very doubtful whether I have been of much help to the potential writers in my courses. I do think, though, that the atmosphere of a community has been created quite early in the course, and that this has been helpful.

The most difficult thing to teach writer-students is how to approach the problem of writing poetry. Obviously what one can do is give them an idea of the techniques of prosody, of the forms in which poems have been written, and of different metrical patterns. I understand that W. H. Auden, when he took a course at Ann Arbor, concentrated very much on technique. He would make his students write sonnets, sestinas, etc. (It is worth noting as a matter of literary history that the presence of Auden in America has—at any rate until quite recently—enormously stimulated the interest of young Americans in writing poems in traditional forms.)

To my mind, teaching poets to write in a wide variety of forms has its dangers. For a good many professional poets, especially among the moderns, have got on very well without knowing any more about form than was necessary to them for writing their own kind of poetry. A poet may not need to know more about form than suits his purposes at a particular stage of his development, and going beyond this stage he acquires new techniques and forms as they are needed. To a poet who has read a good deal of poetry by other poets, form— the kind of form that he needs for his own development —may come almost instinctively. When Auden was an undergraduate and started writing his own early poetry, he read a great deal but he had very little theoretical knowledge of form. The forms of his earlier work are more or less instinctive echoes of Anglo-Saxon, Hardy, *The Waste Land,* and *The Tower* of W. B. Yeats. Only about five years later did he seriously study a great many forms and become a virtuoso in them.

Another example that illustrates my doubt as to whether students should write exercises in traditional forms in poetry is from Robert Graves. Graves rarely if ever writes poems in which he shows interest in the virtuosity of form. Reading his poems, one has the impression that his stanza patterns "come" to him. I once asked him about this and he explained that the first lines of a poem nearly always come into his head in a certain pattern, and then, when writing the poem, he simply follows the stanza pattern throughout. I asked him what he did if he found that the accidental-seeming stanza pattern did not work—did he then begin again from the beginning of the poem, in a new pattern? He said no; if this happened he simply scrapped the poem.

Again, rereading recently T. S. Eliot's 1917 essay on the technique of Ezra Pound, it struck me that the young Eliot applies remarkably little formal analysis to the work of Pound, who, at that time, was open to such analysis, since he often wrote poems in conventional forms. Eliot writes not of "form" but of "technique," by which he means something different: the ability of the poet to create a language which is absolutely true to the music of his own ear, to the inner rhythms of his mind.

Another scruple of the same kind is my feeling that it might have been a positive disadvantage to Walt Whitman to have known how to write a sestina or a sonnet. Whitman was more made by what he did not know than by what he knew.

So I have doubts about teaching students to do exercises in a variety of conventional forms. Formal writing tends to become a habit that may not serve the interests of the writer's true development, and then it becomes difficult to shake off. Yet it may be argued that in teaching poetry—an unteachable subject about which nonetheless a lot can be learned—you have to make it an "academy," for it to be a subject at all. And some students gain from doing academic exercises.

Perhaps one should divide students into the group of those who can gain from using conventional forms, and of those who stand to lose. The imagists—within their narrow limits—were the only true modern poetic "schools" in English (in France, Mallarmé and Laforgue may have been another) in the sense of teaching poetry. What they taught was that the poet must create an image in language true to a "real" image, and realized with concreteness and the utmost economy, without regard for music and conventional form. Pound taught poetry by *reduction* of its aims to a minimum that can be taught.

There are, in general, a few learnable things about writing poetry—for example, to be careful about the consistency and concreteness of metaphors, to reduce adjectives to a minimum, to avoid archaisms, to realize that there is a certain literalness in poetry about the action of prepositions ("through" in a poem is like a line drawn through the diameter of a circle). Also the student can be taught to avoid being intoxicated by his emotions about other poets (*e.g.*, about Ginsberg) and to look carefully at those poems which, of their kind, are models (*e.g.*, Robert Graves and some of Auden).

If we instill a little discipline into some students, perhaps others can be taught something by an attempt to loosen up their imaginations through free-association, surrealist games. I have always thought that it would be a good idea to encourage each student to write for class at least one thoroughly erotic poem. Lastly, the teacher can use himself as a guinea pig for the benefit of the class, describing his own approach to writing poetry and illustrating the development of a poem from his own sketches.

I have heard that Auden made his students at Michigan learn by heart a canto of Dante in the Italian without regard to whether or not they knew the language. This sounds zany, but it might be inspired. Without knowing Italian, the student can get hang enough of the language to see the crystalline qualities of Dante, the greatest of all teachers of other poets. To look at a poem in another language is a way of seeing—projected as it were onto a screen—how the unfamiliar words work. One is too involved with one's language to have the same sense of the pure function of words as poetry in it, as one may get from the Italian, French, German, or Latin. Artistic effects appear more deliberated in a language not one's own. And deliberation is all that can be taught; spontaneity has to come of its own.

The most difficult thing in teaching an art is to make a student recognize his mistakes. This is no doubt partly due to the confusion of standards today, which may result in the student genuinely writing, or going through the act of writing, according to standards quite different from those that the teacher brings to bear on his work. But in America today there is a type of student who seems to write poems as though they were briefs to be defended in a court of law. He justifies what he has not expressed by explaining at length what he intended to express, and why he thinks it is there. This makes teaching extremely difficult because the most important of all things for an artist to know is where he has gone wrong. What the teacher really has to contest is the student's idea that writing is just a lottery: you put down something and maybe someone else will think it is marvelous. Or you wanted to say something and it is only ill will on the part of others that makes them refuse to see that you have said it. Once I received the following letter from a student: "Dear Mr. S.: I was just about to throw these poems away, when it occurred to me that you might like them." So he enclosed two hundred pages of manuscript.

Possibly these experiences of teaching creative writing will seem too advanced for schools. But they may suggest an attitude toward teaching English in school that could be helpful. This is to draw attention to language as an instrument, by comparing the different uses to which language is put in poetry and prose. Students are intrigued by questions such as: "What is poetry?" "What is the difference between poetry and prose?" One may point out to them that the answers to these questions are not absolute. There is no line completely dividing some poetry from some prose, some prose from some poetry. The difference between poetry and prose lies in the kind of use to which language is put, the direction in which it is being made to move. Prose directs language in one way, poetry in another. We get the feel of the difference between prose and poetry from the pull, the tug of language in one or the other direction, rather than from language arriving at a prose or a poetry goal. In the prose use of language the words used tend to disappear into the object, of nature, of events, of ideas, or persons conveyed, so that the reader is left with the object (scenery, a love affair, the categorical imperative, M. Charlus) without the particular verbal formula in which it was conveyed. With poetry there is the opposite tendency. The object tends to disappear into, to become replaced by, the words, which become verbal objects. We do not think of the nightingale in Keats's ode as something having a life independent of the words used by Keats. On the contrary, the function of the "dryad of the trees" is to bring us back perpetually to the words, so that we cannot even begin to think about anything in the poem without thinking of the words. The poet sets experiences and words chasing one another in a vicious circle.

Everybody does not have to like poetry. This is a truism but it is not obvious to some enthusiastic teachers who seem to regard poetry as a crusade. In order to write or read and enjoy poetry you have to take a sensuous pleasure in words for their own sake, and not regard them as mere conveyors of a sense that can be replaced by other words. Rather few people enjoy words for their own sake, and though something can be done to stimulate such enjoyment (perhaps discussion of words themselves, interest encouraged in dictionaries, the use of Roget's *Thesaurus,* etc.), some students will resist poetry. They may even do so because they have a passion for accurate prose, exact language disappearing into the objects described. It would be wrong to be snobbish about this and to risk putting the student off literature forever simply because he does not like poetry.

People who do like poetry find in it such significance that they are tempted to think that poetry nonlovers scarcely live their lives. For the poet, everything significant has poetic significance, and consequently whatever does not have poetic significance seems to him routine material, at best the potential stuff for a future poetry. The essentially cultist attitude is deplorable at all times, but it should especially be kept out of education. What is vitally important in education is that people should communicate, that they should develop to the greatest extent their awareness of themselves and of others, that they should learn to have contact with the life and the values of the past enclosed in masterpieces with the same freedom as they might speak to a wholly articulate and vividly alive friend or neighbor. Language is the lifeline between person and person, contemporaries and the past. Teachers of English therefore have an immense responsibility because they help a young generation make consciousness articulate.

The Historian's Opportunity

By Barbara W. Tuchman

February 25, 1967

Given the current decline of the novel and the parallel decline of poetry and the drama, public interest has turned toward the literature of actuality. It may be that in a time of widening uncertainty and chronic stress the historian's voice is the most needed, the more so as others seem inadequate, often absurd. While the reasons may be argued, the opportunity, I think, is plain for the historian to become the major interpreter in literary experience of man's role in society. The task is his to provide both the matter to satisfy the public interest and those insights into the human condition without which any reading matter is vapid.

Historians have performed this role before. Although we have no figures on readership in classical Greece and Rome, it is evident from their continuers and imitators and from later references that Herodotus, Thucydides and Xenophon, Tacitus, Polybius, Josephus, Plutarch, Livy, and the others were significant voices to their contemporaries. Since the outbreak of World War II the statistics of the book trade reflect the growing appetite of the public for biography, autobiography, science, sociology, and history—especially contemporary history.

The last category, as we have lately been made rather tiresomely aware, has its special problems, although in the long tradition of authorized biography a subject's family has usually found quieter means than legal recourse for retaining control over personal matters. The simple way to keep private affairs private is not to talk about them—to the authorized, or even the "hired," writer.

I do not cite as evidence of the public interest in the literature of actuality the fact that since 1964 nonfiction, so called, has outsold fiction by two to one, because that merely reflects the mass buying of cookbooks and peace-of-mind books (the two front runners), plus voyeur books—that is, the sex life of everybody else—cartoon books, and how-to books on baby care, home decorating, curing arthritis, counting calories, golf, etiquette, and that recent sleeper, avoiding probate. Nonbooks aside, by whatever criterion you use—number of titles published and book club choices, hardcovers and paperbacks, new titles and reprints—the categories concerned with reality all show greater increases than fiction.

People are turning to the books of reality for a truer image of man and society than is offered by contemporary novels. To look for the reason why fictional truth has gone askew is part of the historian's task. The novelists' failure is a consequence, I believe, of the historical experience of the twentieth century which, since the first World War, has been one of man's cumulative disillusionment in himself. The idea of progress was the greatest casualty of that war, and its aftermath was cynicism, confirmed by a second round of world conflict and by the implications of the Nazis' gas chambers. Then the advent into man's hands of unlimited lethal power has been topped by the frightening pressure of overpopulation so that now we live under the weight of a weird paradox which threatens us simultaneously with too many people in the world and too much power to destroy them. Finally, we are faced with mounting evidence—in pollution of air and water, in destruction of the balance of nature, in the coming ear-shattering boom of supersonic flight—that we cannot refrain from despoiling our environment.

The experience has produced what Van Wyck Brooks, discussing the literary scene of the 1920s and 1930s, already called "an eschatalogical despair of the world." Whereas "Whitman and Emerson," he wrote in *An Autobiography,* "had been impressed by the worth and good sense of the people, writers of the new time were similarly struck by their lusts, cupidity, violence, sinfulness, and evil . . . enough to destroy in them their inherited belief in human goodness." Gilbert Murray had found the same despair of the world overtaking the Greeks after their own period of prolonged internecine warfare and ascribed it to a sense of "the pressure of forces that man could not control or understand."

Man in the twentieth century is not a creature to be envied. Formerly he believed himself created by the divine spark. Now, bereft of that proud confidence, and contemplating his recent record and present problems, he can no longer, like the Psalmist, respect himself as "a little lower than the angels." He cannot picture himself today, as Michelangelo did on the Sistine ceiling, in the calm and noble image of Adam receiving the spark from the finger of God. Overtaken by doubt of human purpose and divine purpose, he doubts his capacity to be good or even to survive. He has lost certainty, including moral and ethical certainty, and is left with a sense of footloose purposelessness and self-disgust which literature naturally reflects. The result is what the *Times Literary Supplement* has named the "Ugh" school of fiction.

Writers who dislike their fellow men have taken over the literary world. The mainstream of their work is epitomized by the recent novel advertised as an "engrossing" treatment of "more or less random adventures touching on thievery, homosexuality, pimping, sadism, voyeurism, a gang bang." Unaccountably, drug addiction was missing. As we all know, this is not exceptional, but run-of-the-mill, and the drama, in the dreary examples that reach the stage today, does its best to keep pace. The preferred characters of current fiction are the drifters and derelicts of life in whose affairs or ultimate fate it is impossible to sustain interest. They do not excite the question that is the heart of narrative —"What happens next?"—because one cannot care what happens to them.

Perhaps the fault is not in the novelists but in the times that their characters are underlings; anti-heroes who reflect a general sense of man as victim. Perhaps the novelist today cannot honestly create a protagonist who is master of his fate and captain of his soul because man in the image of Henley seems obsolete. That man belonged to the self-confident nineteenth century, whereas the twentieth finds its exponent in losers, "beautiful losers" according to the title of a recent novel, although few seem to deserve the adjective. Oedipus was a loser and so was King Lear, but their losing was universal and profound, not pointless.

Since fiction and drama no longer present a true balance of human activity and motive, it is not to be wondered that they are losing their audience. According to a recent report from the capital, "Official Washington does not read contemporary novels" for the reason given by a sub-Cabinet officer in these words: "I try to read them and give up. Why should I spend my time on [books] . . . where the central character spends 350 pages quivering about whether to cross the street or go to the toilet?"

He has a point. Reading, which is to say writing, is the greatest gift with which man has endowed himself, by whose means we may soar on unlimited voyages. Are we to spend it picking through the garbage of humanity? Certainly the squalid and worthless, the mean and depraved are part of the human story just as dregs are part of wine, but the wine is what counts. Sexual perversion and hallucinatory drugs, as Eliot Fremont-Smith said of a recent novel, "are not what drive us, not what human history is about."

The task then devolves upon historians to tell what human history *is* about and what are the forces that *do* drive us. That is not to say that history excludes the squalid and depraved, but, being concerned as it is with reality and subject as it is to certain disciplines, it deals with these in proportion to the whole.

Historians start with a great advantage over fiction in that our characters, being public, are invested with power to affect destiny. They are the captains and kings, saints and fanatics, traitors, rogues and villains, pathfinders and explorers, thinkers and creators, even, occasionally, heroes. They are significant—if not necessarily admirable. They may be evil or corrupt or mad or stupid or even stuffed shirts, but at least, by virtue of circumstance or chance or office or character, they *matter*. They are the actors, not the acted upon, and are consequently that much more interesting.

Readers want to see man shaping his destiny or, at least, struggling with it, and this is the stuff of history. They want to know how things happened, why they happened, and particularly what they themselves have lived through, just as after a record heat or heavy snow the first thing one turns to in the morning paper is the account of yesterday's weather. And now more than ever, when man's place in the world has never been so subject to question, when alienation is the prevailing word, the public also hopes to find some guidelines to destiny, some pattern or meaning to our presence on this whirling globe. Whether or not, as individuals, historians believe in one pattern or another, or some of us in none, the evidence we have to present provides reassurance in showing that man has gone through his dark ages before.

When I was a young parent a series of books appeared on child behavior by Dr. Arnold Gesell and his associates of the Yale Clinic in which one discovered that the most aberrant, disturbing, or apparently psychotic behavior of one's own child turned out to be the common age pattern of the group innocently disporting itself behind Dr. Gesell's one-way observation screen. Nothing was ever so comforting. Historians provide a one-way screen on the past through which one can see man, at one time or another, committing every horror, indecency, or idiocy that he is capable of today. It is all already on his record, in kind if not in degree. I do not suggest that history can be as comforting as Gesell because the difference in degree that we face today is so great—in the speed and impact of the mechanisms we have created—that problems and dangers multiply faster than we can devise solutions. Henry Adams's law of acceleration is proving perilously true. Nevertheless, Adams's law is one of those guidelines historians have to offer. The story and study of the past, both recent and distant, will not reveal the future, but it flashes beacon lights along the way and it is a useful nostrum against despair.

Historians cannot expect to take over the leading role in literature without competition. Last summer Albert Rosenfeld, science editor of *Life,* wrote in an editorial that creative writers must turn to science to revive literature because "That is where the action is." There is a great and challenging truth in his statement. Science is formidably relevant and dynamic. "Great writing in any age," Rosenfeld continued, "casts some illumination on the major contemporary dilemmas." That is equally cogent. If science can evoke great creative writers who will do for space aeronautics or genetics or nuclear energy what Rachel Carson, for example, did for the sea around us, they will certainly win a large share of the public interest. The chief obstacle is language. Great writing in science must come from inside the discipline, and everything will depend on the rare talent which can break through the meshes of a technical vocabulary and express itself in words of common usage.

Here, too, we have a head start. Historians can—though not all do—make themselves understood in everyday English, the language in use from Chaucer to Churchill. Let us beware of the plight of our colleagues, the behavioral scientists, who by use of a proliferating jargon have painted themselves into a corner—or isolation ward—of unintelligibility. *They* know what they mean but no one else does. Psychologists and sociologists are the farthest gone in the disease and probably incurable. Their condition might be pitied if one did not suspect it was deliberate. Their retreat into the arcane is meant to set them apart from the great unlearned, to mark their possession of some unshared, unsharable expertise. No matter how illuminating their discoveries, if the behavioral scientists write only to be understood by one another, they must come to the end of the Mandarins.

Communication, after all, is what language was invented for. If history is to share its insights with a public in need of them it must practice communication as an art, as Gibbon did, or Parkman. History has, of course, other parts; like that other famous property it is divisible into three: the investigative or research, the didactic or theory, and the narrated or communication. The elements that enter into communication are what I want to discuss, because history, it seems to me, is nothing if not communicated. Research provides the material, and theory a pattern of thought, but it is through communication that history is heard and understood.

At the risk of stating the obvious, it is worth remarking that success of communication depends upon the charm (I use the word in its most serious sense) of the narrative. "Writings are useless," declared Theodore Roosevelt, speaking as president of the American Historical Association in 1912, "unless they are read, and they cannot be read unless they are readable."

The history most successfully communicated, as far as the public is concerned, can in one sense be determined by the annual lists of the top ten best sellers. Up to 1960 the all-time best seller in history was H. G. Wells's *Outline of History,* first published in 1921, which stayed among the top ten for three years in a row and reappeared on the list in a cheaper edition in 1930. It is the only book of history up to 1960 to have sold more than 2,000,000 copies—more, oddly enough, than *The Kinsey Report.* Since then the leading work in history has been William L. Shirer's *Rise and Fall of the Third Reich,* which had sold, at last report, close to 3,000,000 copies in the United States alone. These names suggest that the independent writer outside academic walls has had greater success in reaching the public than the academic.

The suggestion is borne out by the evidence. During the 1920s and 1930s, when serious books had a better chance of reaching the top ten, the best sellers in historical biography and straight history (as distinct from personal history and current events) included four academics, James Harvey Robinson, Charles Beard, Carl Van Doren, and James Truslow Adams three times over; and twelve nonacademics, Emil Ludwig with four books, Hendrick Van Loon with three, Lytton Strachey, Claude Bowers, Van Wyck Brooks, André Maurois, Francis Hackett, Stefan Zweig with two each, Will Durant, Frederick Lewis Allen, Margaret Leech, and Douglas Southall Freeman with one each. During the 1940s, when the war books took over, one academic, Arnold Toynbee (with his one-volume condensation) and one nonacademic, Catherine Drinker Bowen, made the top ten. After that, except for Shirer and Frederic Morton's *The Rothschilds,* the swamping effect of the nonbooks begins and one has to look just beneath the top ten to the books which have been best sellers during the course of the year without making the final list. Taking only the 1960s, these included three academics, Garrett Mattingly, Samuel Eliot Morison, Arthur Schlesinger, Jr., and nine independent writers, Winston Churchill, Bruce Catton, Alan Moorehead, Thomas Costain, Walter Lord, Cecil Woodham-Smith, and myself with two or more books each, Stewart Holbrook and George Kennan each with one.

To be a best seller is not necessarily a measure of quality but it *is* a measure of communication. That the independent writers have done better is hardly surprising, since communicating is their business; they know how. To capture and hold the interest of an audience is their object, as it has been that of every storyteller since Homer. Perhaps the academic historian suffers from having a captive audience, first in the supervisor of his dissertation, then in the lecture hall. Keeping the reader turning the page has not been his primary concern.

My intention is not to exacerbate the distinction between the professional historian and the so-called amateur but to clarify its terms. "Professional"—meaning someone who has had graduate training leading to a professional degree and who practices within a university—is a valid term, but "amateur"—used to mean someone outside the university without a graduate degree—is a misnomer. Graduate training certainly establishes a difference of which I, who did not have it, am deeply aware, sometimes regretfully, sometimes thankfully. But I would prefer to recognize the difference by distinguishing between academics and independents, or between scholars and writers, rather than between professionals and amateurs, because the question is not one of degree of professionalism but which profession. The faculty people are professional historians, we outside are professional writers. Insofar as they borrow our function and we borrow their subject, each of us has a great deal to learn from the other.

An objection often made to the independents is that they are insufficiently acquainted or careless with the facts. An extreme case is the Cortez of Keats, staring at the Pacific with a wild surmise, silent upon a peak in Darien. Keats, of course, got the name wrong but the idea right. Through the power of marvelous phrasing and the exercise of a poet's imagination he immortalized an historic moment. It is possible that his vision of the man on the peak is more important, for conveying history, than the name of the man. Poets aside, historians, of course, should offer both. There is no need to choose between accuracy and beauty; one should be clothed in the other.

In pockets of survival there may be some historians who still retain the old notion imposed by scientific history that, as another president of the American Historical Association, Walter Prescott Webb, put it, "There is something historically naughty about good writing," that "a great gulf exists between truth and beauty and the scholar who attempts to bridge it deserves to fall in and drown," and that "the real scholar must choose truth and somehow it is better if it is made so ugly that nobody could doubt its virginity." If some still believe this, communication is not for them.

For the first element in communication, Webb gave the perfect triple criterion: a writer's belief that he has something to say, that it is worth saying, and that he can say it better than anyone else—and, he added, "not for the few but for the many." For coupled with compulsion to write must go desire to be read. No writing comes alive unless the writer sees across his desk a reader, and searches constantly for the word or phrase which will carry the image he wants the reader to see and arouse the emotion he wants him to feel. Without consciousness of a live reader, what a man writes will die on his page. Macaulay was a master of this contact with the reader. His sister Hannah cried when he read the *History of England* aloud to her. What writer could ask for more?

When it comes to content, inspiration, what Webb calls the moment of synthesis—the revealing flash of a synthesizing idea—is obviously a help. Webb describes his own moment of insight when the idea came to him that the emergence of Americans from the life of the forests to the life of the plains was of dramatic significance. Admiral Mahan had his moment when, from the study of Hannibal's failure to control sea communication with Carthage, the idea flashed on him of the influence of sea power on history. The moment is exciting but not, I think, essential. A theme may do as well to begin with as a thesis and does not involve, like the overriding theory, a creeping temptation to adjust the facts. The integrating idea or insight then evolves from the internal logic of the material, in the course of putting it together. From the gathering of the particulars one arrives at the general, at that shining grail we are all in search of, the historical generalization. To state it in advance does not seem necessary to me. The process is more persuasive and the integrating idea more convincing if the reader discovers it for himself out of the evidence laid before him.

All theses run the risk of obsolescence. The pathways of history, said the great historian of the frontier, Frederick Jackson Turner, are "strewn with the wrecks" of once known and acknowledged truths, discarded by a later generation. Revision and counter-revision roll against the shores of history as rhythmically as waves. Even so, a true inspiration or integrating idea such as Mahan's or Turner's will be valid and enlightening for its time, regardless of subsequent fortune.

Though some will debate it, intuition, too, is an aid. The intuitive historian can reach an understanding of long past circumstance in much the same way as Democritus, the predecessor of Aristotle, arrived at the idea of the atom. His mind, mulling over observed phenomena, worked out a theory of matter as composed of an infinite number of mobile particles. The process may have been cerebral but its impetus was intuitive. Strict disciples of history as a science may scorn the intuitive process but that attitude comes from being more Catholic than the Pope. True scientists know its value. It is an arrow shot into the air, which will often pierce the same target that the scientific historian with his nose to the ground will take months to reach on foot.

Of all the historian's instruments, belief in the grandeur of his theme is the most compelling. Parkman, in his preface to *Montcalm and Wolfe*, describes his subject, the Seven Years War in the American theater, as "the most momentous and far-reaching question ever brought to issue on this continent." Its outcome determined that there would be an American Revolution. "With it began a new chapter in the annals of the world." That is the way an author should feel about his subject. It ensures that no reader can put the book down.

Enthusiasm, which is not quite the same thing, has a no less leavening effect. It was recognized by Admiral Mahan, who, in the course of studying Britain's contest with Napoleon, developed a particular admiration for Pitt. "His steadfast nature," Mahan wrote, "aroused in me an enthusiasm which I did not seek to check; for I believe enthusiasm no bad spirit in which to realize history to yourself and to others."

Mahan's prescription disposes of the myth of "pure objectivity" when used to mean "without bias." As John Gunther once said of journalism, "A reporter with no bias at all would be a vegetable." If such a thing as a "purely objective" historian could exist, his work would be unreadable—like eating sawdust. Bias is only misleading when it is concealed. After reading *The Proud Tower,* a one-time member of the Asquith government scolded me in a letter for misrepresenting, as he thought, his party. "Your bias against the Liberals sticks out," he wrote. I replied that it was better to have it stick out than be hidden. It can then be taken into account. I cannot deny that I acquired a distaste for Mr. Asquith as, for other reasons, I did for Henry Adams. There are some people in history one simply dislikes, and as long as they are not around to have their feelings hurt, I see no reason to conceal it. To take no sides in history would be as false as to take no sides in life.

A historian tries to be objective in the sense of learning as much as possible, and presenting as sympathetically as possible the motives and conditions of both sides, because to do so makes the drama more intense —and more believable. But let us not pretend that this is being without bias—as if historians were mere recorders who have given up the exercise of judgment. Bias means a *learning* which *is* the exercise of judgment as well as a source of insight. Admittedly, it is usually helped by emotional conditioning, but that is what makes for commitment. The great historians more often than not have been passionately committed to a cause or a protagonist, as Mommsen was to Julius Caesar or Michelet to the glorious power of the people.

How commitment can generate insight and heighten communication is nowhere better shown than in G. M. Trevelyan's *Garibaldi and the Thousand,* one of the finest works of history, I think, both for investigation and narrative, produced in this century. Trevelyan's commitment to his hero is explicit. Describing the footrack from the Villa Spinola down to the embarkation point in Genoa he writes in a footnote, "I had the honor of going down it" with a veteran of the Thousand. There is no doubt where he stands. His feeling of personal involvement led Trevelyan to visit every place connected with the Garibaldini, to walk in their footsteps, to interview those still living, until he knew the persons, terrain, view, sounds, smells, sights, distances, weather—in short, the feel—of every scene of action he was to write about.

As the Thousand marched to the battle of Calatafimi, Trevelyan writes, "Their hearts were light with the sense that they were enviable above all Italians, that their unique campaign was poetry made real." The quality of emotion here is not, as so often, created out of the historian's feelings and foisted onto his characters, but drawn from the evidence. A footnote gives the original from a letter of one of the Garibaldini to his mother, telling her, *"che questa spedizione è così poetica."* ("This expedition is a poetical thing.") Approaching the battle, they pass through a green valley at early morning. "In the bloom of the early Sicilian summer," Trevelyan writes, "the vale fresh from last night's rain, and sung over by the nightingale at dawn, lay ready to exhale its odors to the rising sun. Nature seemed in tune with the hearts of Garibaldi and his men." Here, too, he worked from evidence in diaries and letters that it had rained the night before and that the nightingale had sung. In these two passages he has conveyed the sense of miraculous freshness and noble enterprise which the Garibaldi expedition signalized for the liberal spirit of the nineteenth century. He could accomplish this, first, because of his quick sensitivity to source material, and, second, because he himself was in tune with the hearts of Garibaldi and his men.

Again, when Garibaldi's bugler blew reveille, "the unexpected music rang through the noonday stillness like a summons to the soul of Italy." In the verb of sound, "rang," the reader hears the bugle and in the phrase, "like a summons to the soul of Italy," feels the emotion of the listener. Without knowing that he is being told, he has learned the meaning to history of the Expedition.

To visit the scene before writing, even the scene of long dead adventures, is, as it were, to start business with money in the bank. It was said of Arthur Waley, the great Orientalist who died a few months ago, that he had never visited Asia, explaining that he was content with the ideal image of the East in his imagination. For a historian that would be a risky position. On the terrain motives become clear, reasons and explanations and origins of things emerge that might otherwise have remained obscure. As a source of understanding, not to mention as a corrective for fixed ideas and mistaken notions, nothing is more valuable than knowing the scene in person, and, even more so, living the life that belongs to it. Without that intimacy Francis Parkman would not have been the master he was.

Parkman's hero was really the forest. Through experience he learned passion for it, and fear, and understood both its savagery and beauty. In those long days of intermittent blindness when he was not allowed to write, his mind must have worked over remembered visions of the forest so that they come through on the page with extra clarity. As a scout paddles across the lake in autumn, "the mossed rocks double in the watery mirror" and "sumachs on the shore glow like rubies against the dark green spruce." Or the frontier settler, returning at evening, sees "a column of blue smoke rising quietly in the still evening air" and runs to find the smoldering logs of his cabin and the scalped bodies of his murdered wife and children.

Vision, knowledge, experience will not make a great

writer without that extra command of language which becomes their voice. This, too, was Parkman's. When the English are about to descend the rapids of the upper St. Lawrence, they look on the river whose "reckless surges dashed and bounded in the sun, beautiful and terrible as young tigers at play." In choice of verbs and nouns and images that is a masterpiece. It is only physical description, to be sure, not a great thought, but it takes perfect command of words to express great thoughts in the event one has them.

Steeped in the documents he spent his life collecting, as he was steeped in the forest, Parkman understood the hardship and endurance, grim energy, and implacable combat that underlay the founding of the American nation. He knew the different groups of combatants as if he had lived with each, and could write with equal sympathy of French or Indians, English or colonials. Consider his seventeenth-century French courtiers, "the butterflies of Versailles . . . facing death with careless gallantry, in their small three-cornered hats, powdered perukes, embroidered coats, and lace ruffles. Their valets served them with ices in the trenches, under the cannon of besieged towns." In this case the ices in the trenches is a specimen of the historian's selective insight at work. He has chosen a vivid item to represent a larger whole. It distills an era and a culture in a detail.

Distillation is selection, and selection, as I am hardly the first to affirm, is the essence of writing history. It is the cardinal process of composition, the most difficult, the most delicate, the most fraught with error as well as art. Ability to distinguish what is significant from what is insignificant is *sine qua non*. Failure to do so means that the point of the story, not to mention the reader's interest, becomes lost in a morass of undifferentiated matter. What it requires is simply the courage and self-confidence to make choices and, above all, to leave things out.

In history as in painting, wrote the great stylist Macaulay, to put in everything achieves a less, rather than a more, truthful result. The best picture and the best history, he said, are those "which exhibit such parts of the truth as most nearly produce the effect of the whole." This is such an obvious rule that it is puzzling why so many historians today seem to practice a reverse trend toward total inclusion. Perhaps the reason is timidity; fear of being criticized for having left something out, or, by injudicious selection, of not conforming to the dominant thesis of the moment. Here the independent writer has an advantage over the professional historian: He need not be afraid of the outstuck neck.

Finally, the historian cannot do without imagination. Parkman, intense as always in his effort to make the reader "feel the situation," chose to picture the land between the Hudson and Montreal as it would look to a wild goose flying northward in spring. He sees the blue line of the river, the dark mass of forests and shimmer of lakes, the geometric lines and mounds of manmade forts, "with the flag of the Bourbons like a flickering white speck" marking Ticonderoga, and the "mountain wilderness of the Adirondacks like a stormy sea congealed." On reading that passage I feel the excitement of the Count of Monte Cristo when he opened the treasure chest. It would not be remarkable for one of us who has traveled in airplanes to think of the device of the bird's eye view, but Parkman had never been off the ground. It was a pure effort of imagination to put himself behind the eye of the goose, to see the flag as a flickering white speck and the mountains, in that perfect phrase, as "a stormy sea congealed."

Great as this is, the more necessary use of imagination is in application to human behavior and to the action of circumstance on motive. It becomes a deliberate effort at empathy, essential if one is to understand and interpret the actions of historical figures. With antipathetic characters it is all the more necessary. The historian must put himself inside them, as Parkman put himself inside the wild goose, or as I tried to do inside Sir John French in an effort to understand the draining away of his will to fight. As soon as the effort was made the explanation offered itself. I could feel the oppression, the weight of responsibility, the consciousness of the absence of any trained reserves to take the place of the BEF if it were lost. The effort to get *in*side is, obviously enough, a path to insight. It is the *Einfühlung* that Herder demanded of historians: the effort to "feel oneself into everything." The interpreter of the Hebrew scriptures, as he put it, must be "a shepherd with shepherds, a peasant in the midst of an agricultural people, an oriental with the primitive dwellers of the East."

To describe the historian's task today in terms of narrative history and two romantic practitioners, Parkman and Trevelyan, will seem old-fashioned at a time when interdisciplinary techniques, and horizontal subjects such as demography, and the computerized mechanics of quantification are the areas of fresh endeavor. These are methods of research, not of communication, for one reason because the people who use them tend to lose contact with ordinary language; they have caught the jargon disease. Their efforts are directed, I take it, toward uncovering underlying patterns in history and human behavior which presumably might help in understanding the past and managing the future, or even the present. Whether quantification will reveal anything which could not have been discerned by deduction is not yet clear. What seems to be missing in the studies that I have seen is a certain element of common sense.

The new techniques will, I am sure, turn up suggestive material and open avenues of thought, but they will not, I think, transform history into a science and they can never make it literature. Events happen; but to become history they must be communicated and understood. For that, history needs writers—preferably great writers—a Trevelyan who can find and understand the *cosi poetica* in a soldier's letter and make the right use of it, a Parkman who can see and feel, and report with Shakespeare's gift of words; both, I need not add, assemblers of their own primary material. To be a really great historian, Macaulay said, "is the rarest of intellectual distinctions." For all who try, the opportunity is now and the audience awaits.

Lessons of the
Cuban Missile Crisis

By Robert F. Kennedy

October 26, 1968

On Tuesday morning, October 16, 1962, shortly after 9 o'clock, President Kennedy called and asked me to come to the White House. He said only that we were facing great trouble. Shortly afterward, in his office, he told me that a U-2 had just finished a photographic mission and that the intelligence community had become convinced that Russia was placing missiles and atomic weapons in Cuba.

That was the beginning of the Cuban missile crisis— a confrontation between the two giant atomic nations, the U.S. and the U.S.S.R., which brought the world to the abyss of nuclear destruction and the end of mankind. From that moment in President Kennedy's office until Sunday morning, October 28, that was my life— and for Americans and Russians, for the whole world, it was their life, as well.

The same group that met that first morning in the Cabinet Room met almost continuously through the next twelve days and almost daily for some six weeks thereafter. Others in the group, which was later to be called the "Ex-Comm" (the Executive Committee of the National Security Council), included Secretary of State Dean Rusk; Secretary of Defense Robert McNamara; Director of the Central Intelligence Agency, John McCone; Secretary of the Treasury Douglas Dillon; President Kennedy's adviser on national-security affairs, McGeorge Bundy; Presidential Counsel Theodore C. Sorensen; Under Secretary of State George Ball; Deputy Under Secretary of State U. Alexis Johnson; General Maxwell Taylor, Chairman of the Joint Chiefs of Staff; Edwin Martin, Assistant Secretary of State for Inter-American Affairs; originally, Charles Bohlen, who, after the first day, left to become Ambassador to France and was succeeded by Llewellyn Thompson as the adviser on Russian affairs; Roswell Gilpatric, Deputy Secretary of Defense; Paul Nitze, Assistant Secretary of Defense; and, intermittently at various meetings, Vice President Lyndon B. Johnson; Adlai Stevenson, Ambassador to the United Nations; Kenneth O'Donnell, Special Assistant to the President; and Donald Wilson, who was Deputy Director of USIA.

The general feeling in the beginning was that some form of action was required. There were those, although they were a small minority, who felt the missiles did not alter the balance of power and therefore necessitated no action. Most felt, at that stage, that an air strike against the missile sites could be the only course. Listening to the proposals, I passed a note to the President: "I now know how Tojo felt when he was planning Pearl Harbor."

It was during the afternoon and evening of that first day, Tuesday, that we began to discuss the idea of a quarantine or blockade. Secretary McNamara, by Wednesday, became the blockade's strongest advocate. He argued that it was limited pressure, which could be increased as the circumstances warranted. Further, it was dramatic and forceful pressure, which would be understood yet, most importantly, still leave us in control of events.

Those who argued for the military strike instead of a blockade pointed out that a blockade would not in fact remove the missiles and would not even stop the work from going ahead on the missile sites themselves. The missiles were already in Cuba, and all we would be doing with a blockade would be "closing the door after the horse had left the barn." Their most forceful argument was that our installation of a blockade around Cuba invited the Russians to do the same to Berlin. If we demanded the removal of missiles from Cuba as the price for lifting our blockade, they would demand the removal of missiles surrounding the Soviet Union as the reciprocal act.

The members of the Joint Chiefs of Staff were unanimous in calling for immediate military action. They forcefully presented their view that the blockade would not be effective. General Curtis LeMay, Air Force Chief of Staff, argued strongly with the President that a military attack was essential. When the President questioned what the response of the Russians might be, General LeMay assured him there would be no reaction. President Kennedy was skeptical. "They, no more than we, can let these things go by without doing something. They can't, after all their statements, permit us to take out their missiles, kill a lot of Russians, and then do nothing. If they don't take action in Cuba, they certainly will in Berlin."

I supported McNamara's position in favor of a blockade. This was not from a deep conviction that it would be a successful course of action, but a feeling that it had more flexibility and fewer liabilities than a military attack. Most importantly, like others, I could not accept the idea that the United States would rain bombs on Cuba, killing thousands and thousands of civilians in a surprise attack. With some trepidation, I argued that, whatever validity the military and political arguments were for an attack in preference to a blockade, America's traditions and history would not permit such a course of action. This, I said, could not be undertaken by the U.S. if we were to maintain our moral position at home and around the globe.

We spent more time on this moral question during the first five days than on any other single matter.

By Thursday night, there was a majority opinion in our group for a blockade. We explained our recommendations to the President. At the beginning, the meeting seemed to proceed in an orderly and satisfactory way. However, as people talked, as the President raised probing questions, minds and opinions began to change again, and not only on small points. For some, it was from one extreme to another—supporting an air attack at the beginning of the meeting and, by the time we left the White House, supporting no action at all.

The President, not at all satisfied, sent us back to our deliberations. Because any other step would arouse suspicion, he returned to his regular schedule and his campaign speaking engagements.

We met all day Friday and Friday night. Then again early Saturday morning we were back at the State Department. I talked to the President several times on Friday. Saturday morning at 10 o'clock I called him at the Blackstone Hotel in Chicago and told him we were ready to meet with him. He canceled his trip and returned to Washington. As he was returning to Washington, our Armed Forces across the world were put on alert.

At 2:30, we walked up to the Oval Room. The meeting went on until ten minutes after five. Bob McNamara presented the arguments for the blockade; others presented the arguments for the military attack.

The President made his decision that afternoon in favor of the blockade. There was one final meeting the next morning, with Walter C. Sweeney, Jr., Commanding General of the Tactical Air Command, who told the President that even a major surprise air attack could not be certain of destroying all the missile sites and nuclear weapons in Cuba. That ended the small, lingering doubt that might still have remained in his mind. It had worried him that a blockade would not remove the missiles—now it was clear that an attack could not accomplish that task completely, either.

The President's speech was now scheduled for Monday evening. Under the direction of George Ball, Alex Johnson, and Ed Martin, a detailed hour-to-hour program was arranged, to inform our allies, prepare for the meeting of the Organization of American States, inform the ambassadors stationed in Washington, and prepare for them and others, in written form, the legal justification on which our action was predicated.

The diplomatic effort was of great significance. We were able to establish a firm legal foundation for our action under the OAS Charter, and our position around the world was greatly strengthened when the Organization of American States unanimously supported the recommendation for a quarantine. Further, with the support of detailed photographs, former Secretary of State Dean Acheson—who obliged the President by once again being willing to help—was able to quickly convince President de Gaulle of the correctness of our response. General de Gaulle said, "It is exactly what I would have done," adding that it was not necessary to see the photographs, as "a great Government such as yours does not act without evidence." Chancellor Adenauer voiced his support, as well, and the Soviet Union was prevented from separating the U.S. from Europe. (Diefenbaker of Canada was the only NATO leader who expressed doubts as to our course.)

On that Monday afternoon, before his speech and after lunch with Jackie, the President . . . met with the members of the Cabinet and informed them for the first time of the crisis. Then, not long before the broadcast, he met with the leaders of Congress. This was the most difficult meeting. Many Congressional leaders were sharp in their criticism. Senator Russell said he could not live with himself if he did not say in the strongest possible terms how important it was that we act with greater strength than the President was contemplating. Senator Fulbright also strongly advised military action rather than such a weak step as the blockade. Others said they were skeptical but would remain publicly silent, only because it was such a dangerous hour for the country.

At 7 o'clock, the President went on television to the nation. He was calm and confident that he had selected the right course.

Our group met with the President at 10 o'clock in the morning at the White House. There was a certain spirit of lightness—not gaiety certainly, but a feeling of relaxation, perhaps. We had taken the first step, it wasn't so bad, and we were still alive.

We came back about 6 o'clock that evening. During this meeting, we learned that an extraordinary number of coded messages had been sent to all the Russian ships on their way to Cuba.

The President composed a letter to Khrushchev, asking him to observe the quarantine legally established by a vote of the OAS, making it clear that the U.S. did not wish to fire on any ships of the Soviet Union, and adding at the end: "I am concerned that we both show prudence and do nothing to allow events to make the situation more difficult to control than it is." We then discussed in detail the rules that were to be given to the Navy intercepting a merchant vessel in the quarantine zone.

The next morning, Wednesday, the quarantine went into effect, and the reports during the early hours told of the Russian ships coming steadily on toward Cuba. This Wednesday-morning meeting, along with that of the following Saturday, October 27, seemed the most trying, the most difficult, and the most filled with tension. The U-2s and low-flying planes had returned the previous day with their film, and through the evening it was analyzed. Comparisons with the pictures of a few days earlier made clear that . . . within a few days several of the launching pads would be ready for war.

A few minutes after 10 o'clock Secretary McNamara announced that two Russian ships, the *Gagarin* and the *Komiles,* were within a few miles of our quarantine barrier. Then it was 10:25—a messenger brought in a note to John McCone. "Mr. President, we have a preliminary report which seems to indicate that some of the Russian ships have stopped dead in the water."

Despite what had happened the danger was anything but over. We learned later in the day that fourteen of the twenty-two ships had stopped or had turned back to Russia. Most of those continuing were tankers. . . .

There were almost daily communications with Khrushchev. All our efforts and letters, however, seemed to be having little effect. On the contrary, as we waited for the reply to President Kennedy's latest communication with Khrushchev, reports came in that a greater number of Russian personnel were working to expedite the construction of the missile sites and to assemble the IL-28s. The President in response ordered a gradual increase in pressure, still attempting to avoid the alternative of direct military action. He increased the number of low-level flights over Cuba from twice a day to once every two hours. In the meantime, we awaited Khrushchev's answer.

At 6 o'clock that night the message came. There was no question that the letter had been written by him personally. It was very long and emotional. But it was not incoherent, and the emotion was directed at the death, destruction, and anarchy that nuclear war would bring to his people and all mankind.

We must not succumb to "petty passions" or to "transient things," he wrote, but should realize that "if indeed war should break out, then it would not be in our power to stop it, for such is the logic of war. I have participated in two wars and know that war ends when it has rolled through cities and villages, everywhere sowing death and destruction." The United States, he went on to say, should not be concerned about the missiles in Cuba; they would never be used to attack the United States and were there for defensive purposes only. "You can be calm in this regard, that we are of sound mind and understand perfectly well that if we attack you, you will respond the same way. But you too will receive the same that you hurl against us. And I think that you also understand this. . . . This indicates that we are normal people, that we correctly understand and correctly evaluate the situation. Consequently, how can we permit the incorrect actions which you ascribe to us? Only lunatics or suicides, who themselves want to perish and to destroy the whole world before they die, could do this."

But he went on: "We want something quite different . . . not to destroy your country . . . but despite our ideological differences, to compete peacefully, not by military means."

There was no purpose, he said, for us to interfere with any of his ships now bound for Cuba, for they contained no weapons. He then explained why they carried no missiles: all the shipments of weapons were already within Cuba. This was the first time he had acknowledged the presence of missiles in Cuba. He made reference to the landing at the Bay of Pigs and the fact that President Kennedy had told him in Vienna that this was a mistake. He valued such frankness, wrote Khrushchev, and he, too, had similar courage, for he had acknowledged "those mistakes which had been committed during the history of our state and I not only acknowledged but sharply condemned them."

The reason he had sent these weapons to Cuba was because the U.S. was interested in overthrowing the Cuban Government, as the U.S. had actively attempted to overthrow the Communist government in the Soviet Union after their revolution. But then he went on: "If assurances were given that the President of the United States would not participate in an attack on Cuba and the blockade lifted, then the question of the removal or the destruction of the missile sites in Cuba would then be an entirely different question. Armaments bring only disasters. When one accumulates them, this damages the economy, and if one puts them to use, then they destroy people on both sides. Consequently, only a madman can believe that armaments are the principal means in the life of society. No, they are an enforced loss of human energy, and what is more are for the destruction of man himself. If people do not show wisdom, then in the final analysis they will come to a clash, like blind moles, and then reciprocal extermination will begin."

I had a slight feeling of optimism as I drove home from the State Department that night. The letter, with all its rhetoric, had the beginnings perhaps of some accommodation, some agreement. The feeling was strengthened by the fact that John Scali, a very able and experienced reporter for ABC, had been approached by an important official of the Soviet Embassy with a proposal that the Soviet Union would remove the missiles under United Nations supervision and inspection, and the U.S. would lift the blockade and give a pledge not to invade Cuba as its part of the understanding.

On Saturday morning, October 27, I received a memorandum from J. Edgar Hoover of the FBI that gave me a feeling of considerable disquiet. He had received information the night before that instructions from Moscow had been received by certain Soviet personnel in New York, ordering them to prepare to destroy all sensitive documents on the basis that the U.S. would probably be taking military action against Cuba or Soviet ships, and this would mean war. I asked myself as I drove to the White House: If the Soviets were anxious to find an answer to the crisis, why were they giving these instructions to Soviet personnel? Did the Khrushchev letter really indicate a solution could be found?

It was therefore with some sense of foreboding that I went to the meeting of our Ex-Comm committee. My concern was justified. A new, this time very formal, letter had arrived from Khrushchev to President Kennedy. It was obviously no longer Mr. Khrushchev personally who was writing, but the Foreign Office of the Kremlin. The letter was quite different from the letter received twelve hours before. "We will remove our missiles from Cuba, you will remove yours from Turkey. . . . The Soviet Union will pledge not to invade or interfere with the internal affairs of Turkey; the U.S. to make the same pledge regarding Cuba."

The Joint Chiefs of Staff joined the meeting and recommended their solution. It had the attraction of being a very simple next step—an air strike on Monday, followed shortly afterward by an invasion. They were not at all surprised that nothing had been achieved by limited force, for this is exactly what they had predicted.

The State Department submitted a draft of a letter for response from President Kennedy to Khrushchev. It answered the arguments made in Khrushchev's latest letter, maintaining that we could not remove the missiles from Turkey and that no trade could be made.

I disagreed with the content and tenor of the letter. I suggested, and was supported by Ted Sorensen and others, that we ignore the latest Khrushchev letter and respond to his earlier letter's proposal, as refined in the offer made to John Scali. There were arguments back and forth. Everyone was tense; some were already near exhaustion; all were weighted down with concern and worry. President Kennedy was by far the calmest.

Finally, when we almost seemed unable to communicate with one another, he suggested with a note of some exasperation that—inasmuch as I felt so strongly that the State Department's various efforts to respond were not satisfactory—Ted Sorensen and I should leave the meeting and go into his office and compose an alternative response, so he could then decide between the two. Forty-five minutes later, we took it to him and to the whole group. He worked on it, refined it, had it typed, and signed it. It accepted Khrushchev's "offer."

I had promised my daughters for a long time that I would take them to the horse show, and early Sunday morning I went to the Washington Armory to watch the horses jump. In any case, there was nothing I could do but wait. Around 10 o'clock, I received a call at the horse show. It was Secretary Rusk. He said he had just received word from the Russians that they had agreed to withdraw the missiles from Cuba.

I often thought afterward of some of the things we learned from this confrontation. The time that was available to the President and his advisers to work secretly, quietly, privately, developing a course of action and recommendations for the President, was essential. If our deliberations had been publicized, if we had had to make a decision in twenty-four hours, I believe the course that we ultimately would have taken would have been quite different and filled with far greater risks. Such time is not always present, although, perhaps surprisingly, on most occasions of great crisis it is; but when it is, it should be utilized.

I believe our deliberations proved conclusively how important it is that the President have the recommendations and opinions of more than one individual, of more than one department, and of more than one point of view. Opinion, even fact itself, can best be judged by conflict, by debate. There is an important element missing when there is unanimity of viewpoint. Yet that not only can happen; it frequently does when the recommendations are being given to the President of the United States. His office creates such respect and awe that it has almost a cowering effect on men. Frequently, I saw advisers adapt their opinions to what they believed President Kennedy and, later, President Johnson wished to hear.

It is also important that different departments of government be represented. Thirty years ago, the world was a far, far different place. The Secretary of State and his department could handle all international problems. We could and did, in places we felt our national interests were involved (such as Latin America), impose our will by force if we believed it necessary. Thirty years ago, only the State Department was involved in international matters. But that is no longer true. A number of other agencies and departments have primary responsibilities and power in the foreign-relations field, including the Pentagon, the CIA, AID, and, to a lesser degree, the USIA, and other independent or semi-independent departments.

Individual representatives of at least the Pentagon, the CIA, and AID must be heard and listened to by the President of the United States in addition to the State Department. They have information, intelligence, opinions, and judgments which may be invaluable and quite different from those of the State Department. At the missile-crisis conferences, the President made certain there were experts and representatives of different points of view. He wanted to hear presented and challenged all the possible consequences of a particular course of action. The first step might appear sensible, but what would be the reaction of our adversaries, and would we actually stand to gain?

I remember an earlier meeting on Laos, in 1961, when the military unanimously recommended sending in substantial numbers of U.S. troops to stabilize the country. They were to be brought in through two airports with limited capability. Someone questioned what we would do if only a limited number landed and then the Communist Pathet Lao knocked out the airports and proceeded to attack our troops, limited in number and not completely equipped. The representatives of the military said we would then have to destroy Hanoi and possibly use nuclear weapons. President Kennedy did not send in the troops and concentrated on diplomatic steps to protect our interests.

One of the Joint Chiefs of Staff once said to me he believed in a preventive attack against the Soviet Union. On that fateful Sunday morning when the Russians answered they were withdrawing their missiles, it was suggested by one high military adviser that we attack Monday in any case. Another felt that we had in some way been betrayed. President Kennedy was disturbed by this inability to look beyond the limited military field. This experience pointed out for us all the importance of civilian direction and control and the importance of raising probing questions to military recommendations. His conduct of the missile crisis showed how important this kind of skeptical probing and questioning could be.

It also showed how important it was to be respected around the world, how vital it was to have allies and friends. Now, five years later, I discern a feeling of isolationism in Congress and through the country, a feeling that we are too involved with other nations, a resentment of the fact that we do not have greater support in Vietnam, an impression that our AID program is useless and that our alliances are dangerous. I think it would be well to think back to those days in October of 1962.

It was the vote of the Organization of American States that gave a legal basis for the quarantine. It had a major psychological and practical effect on the Russians and changed our position from that of an outlaw acting in violation of international law to a country acting in accordance with twenty allies legally protecting their position. Had our relationship of trust and mutual respect not been present, had our NATO allies been skeptical about what we were doing and its implications for them, and had Khrushchev thus been able to split off NATO or even one of our chief allies, our position would have been seriously undermined.

The final lesson of the Cuban missile crisis is the importance of placing ourselves in the other country's shoes. During the crisis, President Kennedy spent more time trying to determine the effect of a particular course of action on Khrushchev or the Russians than on any other phase of what he was doing. What guided all his deliberations was an effort not to disgrace Khrushchev, not to humiliate the Soviet Union, not to have them feel they would have to escalate their response because their national security or national interests so committed them.

President Kennedy understood that the Soviet Union did not want war, and they understood that we wished to avoid armed conflict. During our crisis talks, he kept stressing the fact that we would indeed have war if we placed the Soviet Union in a position she believed would adversely affect her national security, or such public humiliation that she lost the respect of her own people and countries around the globe. The missiles in Cuba, we felt, vitally concerned our national security, but not that of the U.S.S.R.

Even after it was all over, he permitted no crowing that would cause the Soviets to eat crow. He made no statement attempting to take credit for himself or his Administration for what had occurred. He instructed all members of the Ex-Comm and Government that no interview should be given, no statement made, which would claim any kind of victory. He respected Khrushchev for properly determining what was in his own country's interest and what was in the interest of mankind. If it was a triumph, it was a triumph for the next generation and not for any particular government or people.

Why and How I Work

By Arnold J. Toynbee

April 5, 1969

What has made me work? When I was a child at school, the spur that I was first conscious of was anxiety. I was anxious always to be well ahead in puzzling out the meaning of passages of Greek and Latin that I might be called on to construe in class. I am still anxious to arrive well in time for catching trains and planes. This has its disadvantages. It uses up a lot of nervous energy that might be put to more positive use; and sometimes I carry my beforehandness to a point at which it catches me out. When I arrive at the station forty minutes ahead of my train's departure time, the porter will not wait till the train comes into the station; so I have to put my luggage on board myself. Something like that happened to me once when I was called on to construe a difficult passage of Thucydides. I had prepared it carefully; but that had been several weeks ago; and I had now far outshot the point that we had reached in class, and my mastery of this passage had grown rusty.

Anxiety can be a bad thing if it goes to these extremes, and it is never a good thing in itself. It is, though, a powerful driving force; so its drawbacks may be outweighed by its results.

A second spur that has pricked me on has been, and still is, conscience. My grandfather on my father's side came off a farm within sight of the tower of St. Botolph's Church in Boston, England. The puritan conscience was perhaps part of my father's family's social heritage. In my attitude toward work I am American-minded, not Australian-minded. To be always working, and still at full stretch, has been laid upon me by my conscience as a duty. This enslavement to work for work's sake is, I suppose, irrational; but thinking so would not liberate me. If I slacked, or even just slackened, I should be conscience-stricken and therefore uneasy and unhappy, so this spur seems likely to continue to drive me on so long as I have any working power left in me.

Anxiety and conscience are a powerful pair of dynamos. Between them they have ensured that I shall work hard, but they cannot ensure that one shall work at anything worthwhile. They are blind forces, which drive but do not direct. Fortunately, I have also been moved by a third motive: the wish to see and understand. I did not become conscious of this motive till some time after I had become aware of the other two; but I think that, before I became conscious of it, it must have been moving me, and this since an early stage of my life. Curiosity is a positive motive for action. It is also one of the distinctive characteristics of human nature as contrasted with the natures of non-human animals. All human beings have curiosity in some degree; and we also all have it about things that are of no practical use—or that seem, at least, to be of no practical use at the time when one's curiosity is first excited by them. However, this universal human quality is stronger in some people than it is in others. This is one of the points in which human beings differ from each other markedly. The charge of curiosity with which I have been endowed happens to be high. This is a gift of the gods, and I am heartily grateful for it.

When I am asked, as I sometimes am, why I have spent my life on studying history, my answer is "for fun." I find this an adequate answer, and it is certainly a sincere one. If the questioner goes on to ask whether, if I could have my life over again, I would spend it in the same way again, I answer that I would, and I say this with conviction.

But why study history in particular? Curiosity is omnivorous. There are innumerable other things in the universe besides history that can and do arouse curiosity in human beings. Why has my curiosity focused itself on history? The answer to this question is one that I know for certain. I am an historian because my mother was one. I cannot remember a time when I had not already taken it for granted that I was going to follow my mother's bent. When I had turned four, my father said that they could no longer afford a nurse for me. My mother asked if she might keep the nurse for a year longer, supposing that she earned the nurse's twelve months' wage by writing a book, and my father agreed. I can remember vividly the excitement of seeing the proofs of *Tales from Scottish History* arrive. The fee was £20, and that was a nurse's wage for a year in England in 1893–94. When the year was up and the money was spent, the nurse went and my mother took over the job of putting me to bed. She kept me happy and good at bedtime by telling me the history of England, in installments, from the beginning to 1895.

Certainly it was my mother who inspired me to become an historian, but I have followed her bent in this rather general sense only. My mother, I think, loved the concrete facts of history for their own sake. I love them, too, of course. If one did not love them, one could never become an historian. Facts are an historian's stock in trade, and he has to acquire them in quantities that would be repellent if the facts did not fascinate him. I love the facts of history, but not for their own sake. I love them as clues to something beyond them—as clues to the nature and meaning of the mysterious universe in which every human being awakes to consciousness. We wish to understand the universe and our place in it. We know that our understanding of it will never be more than a glimmer, but this does not discourage us from seeking as much light as we can win.

Curiosity may be focused on anything in the universe; but the spiritual reality behind the phenomena is, I believe, the ultimate objective of all curiosity; and it is in virtue of this that curiosity has something divine in it. Thanks to my mother's bent, my approach to this ultimate objective happens to be through the study of human affairs. Physics, botany, geology, or any other study that one can think of, offer an alternative road toward the same human goal. However, in the Jewish-Christian-Muslim Weltanschauung, history is set in a framework of theology. This traditional Western vista of history has been rejected by many Western historians —and by their non-Western disciples—during the last two centuries and a half. Yet I believe that every student of human affairs does have a theology, whether he acknowledges this or not; and I believe that he is most at the mercy of his theology when he is most successful in keeping it repressed below the threshold of his consciousness.

Of course I can only speak for myself. I am sure that the reason why the study of human affairs has the hold on me that it has is because it is the window on the universe that is open for me. A geologist or a botanist, traveling through a landscape that has not been the scene of any important events in human history, will see in it the hand of God, as vividly as I see this at, say, Bodh Gaya or Jerusalem. But, since my own approach to the presence behind the phenomena happens to lie in the field of human affairs, unhumanized non-human nature does not speak to me movingly. I am moved by Mount Cynthus more than by Mount Everest, and by the Jordan more than by the Amazon.

Why work, and why at history? Because, for me, this is the pursuit that leads, however haltingly, toward the *Visio Beatifica*.

How do I work? Between the ages of ten and twenty-two, I was preparing, most of the time, for sitting for successive examinations. Such preparations are educative in some ways. They make one responsible for putting oneself to work. Though an able and sympathetic master can help one greatly to learn how to do that, he cannot do it for one; and no one in the world except oneself can help one when one has taken one's seat in the examination hall with an examination paper before one's eyes and three hours, but not a minute more, allowed to spend on answering the questions.

H. J. Haselfoot, the master at my preparatory school who gave me special coaching, was the best teacher that I have ever had. He taught me how to work, and I have been benefiting by his teaching ever since. Though I recognized, at the time, what an exceptionally good teacher he was, my gratitude to him has continually increased as I have found his advice holds good for tackling one intellectual job after another. Mr. Haselfoot's first and best piece of advice was: "Don't panic because the time given for answering the questions is limited. Don't plunge in without previous thought. The best-spent time out of your three hours will be the time before you put pen to paper, if only you give yourself this time at the beginning to think of your problem as a whole. This is the right method, whether the problem you are faced with is a subject for an essay or a piece of Greek or Latin to be translated into English or, conversely, a piece of English to be put into Greek or Latin prose or verse." Mr. Haselfoot taught me to try always to be articulate; to try always to see the wood, without letting oneself get lost among the trees; to proceed from the known to the unknown; and to take it for granted that a passage of Greek or Latin must make sense, and to recognize that, so long as it did not seem to make sense, one had certainly not yet got on the right track.

The three-hours' essay is a splendid education for journalism and for the civil service and for the law. If one has learned the art of essay writing at any early age, one will know how to write an article or a minute, or how to digest a brief, against time—and one is always working against time in practical life. Scholars who have not schooled themselves to work against time are putting themselves in danger of remaining unproductive, and they cannot vindicate their unpracticalness by contending that work done against time will be imperfect. It will, of course, be imperfect; all human work is imperfect, because human nature is; and this intrinsic imperfection of human affairs cannot be overcome by procrastination. In work of every kind, including intellectual work, there comes the right moment for taking action. There is no instrument that will tell one when the moment has arrived; one has to sense it by intuition, and the right timing will be different in each case. But to hit upon it is indispensable for success; and to delay too long can be just as fatal as to act precipitately can be. The effect of wrong timing, either way, will be to aggravate the imperfection that is inherent in any human activity.

Thus education through preparing for examinations, and through taking these when the time comes, can have some good effects. It can, however, also have the very bad effect of inducing a habit of passivity in one's attitude toward the acquisition of knowledge. The examination, in which one is going to have to take action eventually, is, for most of the time, apparently far off; and, when it does overtake one, the action is short and sharp. One is engaged in the preparation over far longer stretches of time, and this may therefore have a greater effect on one than the examinations themselves. In preparing for an examination, the prospective examinee does not have the initiative. The examiner has that. He dictates to the examinee, at the last minute, the action that the examinee has to take. During the long drawn-out preparatory period, all that the examinee can do is to accumulate as much knowledge as he can of the whole of the field in which he is going to have to stand fire. The examination system may thus put it into the examinee's head that the ideal objective in intellectual work is to acquire an exhaustive knowledge of a precisely delimited field.

In my own intellectual history, a danger arose from my having acquired the examinee's habit of mind. It was no wonder that I acquired this, considering how great a part successive examinations played in my intellectual life. It is true that I kept myself free from one of the examinee's occupational infirmities. I refused to allow myself to be cooped up within an arbitrarily delimited field of knowledge. Mr. Haselfoot had saved me from that by teaching me, once and for all, to look at a problem as a whole; and, since the problem that I had made mine was human affairs, nothing short of a study of human affairs as a whole would satisfy me. This was good in itself, but it did not combine well with another of the examinee's infirmities—one to which I had succumbed—and this was the bad habit of accumulating knowledge for passing examinations, and not for use.

In expanding the field of my curiosity to embrace all human affairs, I had been doing to myself what the giants in Jötenheim had once done to the god Thor when they had covertly connected up with the sea the drinking horn that they had challenged him to drain. Thor was a mighty drinker, and, in a long draught, he had swallowed one-third of the waters of the sea before he had been forced to confess himself beaten. Even a god could not drain the sea dry; and even a young man of twenty-two, with the whole of his working life still ahead of him, could not have mastered the whole of human affairs, however hard he might work and however long he might keep his wits. Without realizing it, I had pitted myself against infinity; and in a contest between a mortal and infinity the mortal is bound to lose, unless he can extricate himself in good time from this unequally matched duel.

To extricate myself, I developed a way of my own for banning infinity. Instead of going on acquiring knowledge ad infinitum, I started to do something with the knowledge that I already possessed, and this active use of knowledge gave direction, for the future, to my acquisition of knowledge. I refused to set limits to my acquisition of knowledge by confining it within an arbitrarily delimited field, but I found a better way of setting bounds to the boundless. I limited infinity by directing my acquisition of knowledge to meet the demands of action. The knowledge was there, at my disposal, stored on the shelves of libraries and in the galleries of museums. I need not, after all, be in such a hurry to master it, for it would not run away. I could and would take as much of it as I wanted, when I wanted it, for use in making something with it. In other words, I would acquire knowledge, henceforward, for use in projects of my own, not for the sake of satisfying an imaginary post-mortem examiner.

After I started to make something out of what I knew, the meaning of the word "work" underwent, for me, a significant change, which was also, I feel sure, a salutary one. Work now came, for me, to mean writing or making preparations to write. It no longer meant reading. Since 1911 I have allocated no working time for reading, and, in particular, I have reserved exclusively for writing the hours between breakfast and lunch —the time of day at which my mind is the most active. I have left my reading to take care of itself, and this policy has justified itself, to my mind, by its results. I have read what I have needed to read for use in my writing, though I have written far more than I had dreamed of writing at the start, and though I have interpreted my needs broadly. (I have always succeeded in reading a good deal more than has been strictly necessary for my successive practical purposes.)

This change in the purpose of my reading led me to make a corresponding change in my way of taking notes. I had begun by making notes on the margins of my Greek and Latin texts, and this scholiast's way of note-taking had been the most convenient so long as the interpretation and understanding of texts had been, for me, an end in itself. Now, however, I had learned to use texts as materials for making something of my own, and for this new purpose I needed to have my notes in some handier and more accessible repository. From about 1922 onward, I started to take notes in notebooks on points, in books that I was reading, which seemed likely to come in useful for something that I was going to write. Usefulness for writing had now become my criterion, so I took my notes of this new kind, not only on Greek or Latin texts, but on modern books as well. By 1968, I had more than thirty of these notebooks, full to the brim. They have long since become my most relevant immediate source of the information that I need for writing. From a note of a passage in some book that I have read, I can always refer back to the original.

In giving priority to writing, I have renounced any considerable further acquisition of knowledge in the field of languages. But there is another field of knowledge—the first-hand knowledge of countrysides—in which I have always been eagerly adding to my stock whenever I have had the opportunity. Till after my retirement, I was starved of travel, to some extent, by lack of time and funds. But since 1911 I have always traveled as often and as long and as far as I have been able. This is the one activity to which I have given precedence over my otherwise paramount activity of writing. Whenever I have had a chance of intellectually profitable travel, my writing has had to wait. As I see it, travel ought to come before everything else for a student of human affairs. Human beings and human societies cannot be understood apart from their environment, and their geographical environment cannot be apprehended at second hand. One may pore for years over descriptions and photographs and maps of a country without getting a true notion of its character; and, then, one glimpse of the landscape with one's own eyes will give the essential information which the secondary sources had failed to convey.

I would like to offer five pieces of advice to intellectual workers who agree with me that the right and healthy purpose of acquiring knowledge is to make out of it some work of one's own. First, there is Mr. Haselfoot's golden counsel: "Don't plunge in precipitately; think before you act; give yourself time to see your subject or your problem as a whole." I found that this counsel stood me in good stead when I was starting out on each of the two largest enterprises on which I have embarked so far: the Chatham House "Survey of International Affairs" and "A Study of History."

In the "Survey" (which I had the happiness of writing, from first to last, in partnership with my wife) our task was to carry on the story of international affairs from the points at which the Chatham House *History of the Peace Conference* (of 1919) had broken off. The field of the "Survey" was to be the whole world, and I was unwilling to farm out to specialists the surveying of the affairs of some allegedly "outlandish" regions. To take the whole world for one's province was an exciting task, but it was also a big one and a formidable one. Where to begin? I began by writing a small volume, *The World after the Peace Conference,* in which I tried to give a cross-section picture of the state of the world in or about the year 1920. This gave me a base line for starting a narrative that my wife and I eventually carried down to the year 1946.

In approaching "A Study of History," I began by making a false start. In the summer of 1920, when the idea of the book was already simmering in my mind, I tried to write it in the form of a commentary on the second chorus in Sophocles' *Antigone*. This Greek poem does convey, superbly, the strangeness, the grandeur, and the pathos of human life; but my medieval-minded approach to my subject by reference to a Greek masterpiece was too indirect to be practicable, as I soon discovered. Sophocles could not find my way into my subject for me. I had to find it for myself, and I did not find it till a year later, when I was on the train—somewhere in Western Bulgaria—en route from Istanbul to London after having been observing the Greco-Turkish War in Anatolia as The Manchester *Guardian's* special correspondent. I then found myself jotting down, on half a sheet of notepaper, a dozen headings which turned out to be the subjects of the principal divisions of my future book.

This time, I did not rush into action. My first considerable stretches of free time, after that, were the long summer vacations of 1927 and 1928, and I spent these, not on trying to start writing the first part of the book, but on expanding each of my headings into sets of detailed notes. I did not begin writing till the summer of 1930; and meanwhile, in 1929, I had taken the longest journey that I had made yet. I had traveled to China and Japan, going out overland to the head of the Persian Gulf and thence by sea, and coming back overland via the Trans-Siberian Railway. It was after this that I found myself ready to start writing the book.

My second piece of advice is: "Act promptly as soon as you feel that your mind is ripe for taking action. To wait too long may be even more untoward in its effects than to plunge in too precipitately."

When my wife and I were starting to write the "Survey," we were working under the direction of an older and more experienced scholar, Sir James Headlam-Morley, the historical adviser to the Foreign Office, who was also chairman of the Publications Committee of the Royal Institute of International Affairs. When, some time after our starting date, I produced my little volume on *The World after the Peace Conference*, Headlam-Morley became worried. "This piece that you have produced is all very well," he said; "but your real job is to write a narrative, recording what happened next. I recognize that the job is a vast one. What you need to do now is to make a start with some piece of it. When once you have done that, you will find that the rest will come. In starting, you will be feeling your way; for a survey of current history is a new genre of history writing. My advice is that, for your first piece, you should choose some topic that is not very large and also not very important. Probably you will not be satisfied with your first draft, and will find that you want to work over it again. Never mind; the point of getting down now to the writing of this first piece is that it will help you to get the whole thing moving." Headlam-Morley suggested that I should begin by writing the history of the postwar dispute between the Netherlands and Belgium over the navigation of the Scheldt. I followed his suggestion, and it all turned out as he had said that it would.

My third piece of advice is one that is good, I believe, not only for writers of historical works, but for writers in every field. "Write regularly, day in and day out, at whatever times of day you find that you write best. Don't wait till you feel that you are in the mood." Write, whether you are feeling inclined to write or not. What you write when you are feeling out of sorts will not be so good, of course, as what you write when you are in your best form. You will be dissatisfied with your first draft, as I was dissatisfied with my first draft on the dispute over the navigation of the Scheldt. However, you can revise your first draft, and, though, even after that, this piece will not be so good as a piece that you wrote originally with zest, it will nevertheless probably pass muster, and meanwhile you will have made progress with the carrying out of your project. If you were to wait till you had achieved perfection, you would be waiting for the rest of your working life; for nothing made by human hands or minds is perfect.

My fourth piece of advice is: "Don't waste odd pieces of time." Don't say to yourself: "There, I have finished that piece of work, and it is really not worth beginning this next piece till tomorrow morning or till after the weekend. So for the rest of today or for the rest of this week I might as well let myself relax and take things easy." The truth is that you might not as well do that; for the right moment for starting on your next job is not tomorrow or next week; it is *instanter,* or, in the American idiom, "right now." (It is significant that "right now" is an Americanism; for Americans are pre-eminently men of action.)

My fifth piece of advice is: "Always look ahead. Look far ahead, as a racing motorist looks, through his telescopic sight, at the horizon which he will have reached before he knows it."

Since before the outbreak of the First World War, I have had an agenda stretching ahead of me through an incalculable number of future years. In the autumn of 1965, for instance, I published a book called *Hannibal's Legacy* whose germ was a course of lectures that I had given at Oxford for the School of Literae Humaniores in the academic year 1913–14. While I was writing my notes for those lectures, I was planning to turn them into a book. Event after event, beginning with the First World War, then intervened between me and this particular objective. But I never lost sight of the subject, which was the effect of the First and Second Romano-Carthaginian Wars on Roman life. I always kept a lookout for relevant books and articles, and made notes on these, in my growing series of notebooks, for use when, some day or other, I should get down, at last, to carrying out this particular project. I did get down to it in the summer of 1957, and, in writing the book, I have used notes that I had taken five, ten, or twenty years before the opportunity came for using them.

My wife says that I have a peculiar faculty—a "sixth sense," she calls it—for scenting, years in advance, what I am going to need for carrying out some project which, on my agenda, is still a long way down the list. She also says that I have a gift for recording, in a brief note, just what I am going to want later on. The use that I have made of my notebooks certainly shows that this has been my way of working; but I am not sure that it indicates any special capacity. Probably any intellectual worker who thought of using this method could use it successfully. No doubt, it requires some ability, but, above all, it requires practice and persistence.

New Light on the Human Potential

By Herbert A. Otto

December 20, 1969

William James once estimated that the healthy human being is functioning at less than 10 per cent of his capacity. It took more than half a century before this idea found acceptance among a small proportion of behavioral scientists. In 1954, the highly respected and widely known psychologist Gardner Murphy published his pioneering volume *Human Potentialities*. The early Sixties saw the beginnings of the human potentialities research project at the University of Utah and the organization of Esalen Institute in California, the first of a series of "Growth Centers" that were later to be referred to as the Human Potentialities Movement.

Today, many well-known scientists such as Abraham Maslow, Margaret Mead, Gardner Murphy, O. Spurgeon English, and Carl Rogers subscribe to the hypothesis that man is using a very small fraction of his capacities. Margaret Mead quotes a 6 per cent figure, and my own estimate is 5 per cent or less. Commitment to the hypothesis is not restricted to the United States. Scientists in the U.S.S.R. and other countries are also at work. Surprisingly, the so-called human potentialities hypothesis is still largely unknown.

What are the dimensions of the human potential? The knowledge we do have about man is minimal and has not yet been brought together with the human potentialities hypothesis as an organizing force and synthesizing element. Of course, we know more about man today than we did fifty years ago, but this is like the very small part of the iceberg we see above the water. Man essentially remains a mystery. From the depths of this mystery there are numerous indicators of the human potential.

Certain indicators of man's potential are revealed to us in childhood. They become "lost" or submerged as we succumb to the imprinting of the cultural mold in the "growing up" process. Do you remember when you were a child and it rained after a dry spell and there was a very particular, intensive earthy smell in the air? Do you remember how people smelled when they hugged you? Do you recall the brilliant colors of leaves, flowers, grass, and even brick surfaces and lighted signs that you experienced as a child? Furthermore, do you recall that when father and mother stepped into the room you *knew* how they felt about themselves, about life, and about you—at that moment.

Today we know that man's sense of smell, one of the most powerful and primitive senses, is highly developed. In the average man this capacity has been suppressed except for very occasional use. Some scientists claim that man's sense of smell is almost as keen as a hunting dog's. Some connoisseurs of wines, for example, can tell by the bouquet not only the type of grape and locality where they were grown but even the vintage year and vineyard. Perfume mixers can often detect fantastically minute amounts in mixed essences; finally there are considerable data on odor discrimination from the laboratory. It is also clear that, since the air has become an overcrowded garbage dump for industrial wastes and the internal combustion engine, it is easier to turn off our sense of smell than to keep it functioning. The capacity to experience the environment more fully through our olfactory organs remains a potential.

It is possible to regain these capacities through training. In a similar manner, sensory and other capacities, including visual, kinesthetic, and tactile abilities, have become stunted and dulled. We perceive less clearly, and as a result we feel less—we use our dulled senses to close ourselves off from both our physical and interpersonal environments. Today we also dull our perceptions of how other people feel and we consistently shut off awareness of our own feelings. For many who put their senses to sleep it is a sleep that lasts unto death. Again, through sensory and other training the doors of perception can be cleansed (to use Blake's words) and our capacities reawakened. Anthropological research abounds with reports of primitive tribes that have developed exceptional sensory and perceptive abilities as a result of training. Utilization of these capacities by modern man for life-enrichment purposes awaits the future.

Neurological research has shed new light on man's potential. Work at the UCLA Brain Research Institute points to enormous abilities latent in everyone by suggesting an incredible hypothesis: The ultimate creative capacity of the human brain may be, for all practical purposes, infinite. To use the computer analogy, man is a vast storehouse of data, but we have not learned how to program ourselves to utilize these data for problem-solving purposes. Recall of experiential data is extremely spotty and selective for most adults. My own research has convinced me that the recall of experiences can be vastly improved by use of certain simple training techniques, provided sufficient motivation is present.

Under emergency conditions, man is capable of prodigious feats of physical strength. For example, a middle-aged California woman with various ailments lifted a car just enough to let her son roll out from under it after it had collapsed on him. According to newspaper reports the car weighed in excess of 2,000 pounds. There are numerous similar accounts indicating that every person has vast physical reserve capacities that can be tapped. Similarly, the extraordinary feats of athletes and acrobats—involving the conscious and specialized development of certain parts of the human organism as a result of consistent application and a high degree of motivation—point to the fantastic plasticity and capabilities of the human being.

Until World War II, the field of hypnosis was not regarded as respectable by many scientists and was associated with stage performances and charlatanism. Since that time hypnosis has attained a measure of scientific respectability. Medical and therapeutic applications of hypnosis include the use of this technique in surgery and anesthesiology (hypnoanesthesia for major and minor surgery), gynecology (infertility, frigidity, menopausal conditions), pediatrics (enuresis, tics, asthma in children, etc.), and in dentistry. Scores of texts on medical and dental hypnosis are available. Dr. William S. Kroger, one of the specialists in the field and author of the well-known text *Clinical and Experimental Hypnosis*, writes that hypnotherapy is "directed to the patient's needs and is a methodology to tap the 'forgotten assets' of the *hidden potentials* of behavior and response that so often lead to new learnings and understanding." (My italics.) As far as we know now, the possibilities opened by hypnosis for the potential functioning of the human organism are not brought about by the hypnotist. Changes are induced by the subject, utilizing his belief-structure, with the hypnotist operating as an "enabler," making it possible for the subject to tap some of his unrealized potential.

The whole area of parapsychology that deals with extrasensory perception (ESP), "mental telepathy," and other paranormal phenomena, and that owes much of its development to the work of Dr. J. B. Rhine and others is still regarded by much of the scientific establishment with the same measure of suspicion accorded hypnosis in the pre-World War II days. It is of interest that a number of laboratories in the U.S.S.R. are devoted to the study of telepathy as a physical phenomenon, with research conducted under the heading "cerebral radio-communication" and "bioelectronics." The work is supported by the Soviet government. The reluctance to accept findings from this field of research is perhaps best summarized by an observation of Carl C. Jung's in 1958:

> (Some) people deny the findings of parapsychology outright, either for philosophical reasons or from intellectual laziness. This can hardly be considered a scientifically responsible attitude, even though it is a popular way out of quite extraordinary intellectual difficulty.

Although the intensive study of creativity had its beginnings in fairly recent times, much of value has been discovered about man's creative potential. There is evidence that every person has creative abilities that can be developed. A considerable number of studies indicate that much in our educational system—including conformity pressures exerted by teachers, emphasis on memory development, and rote learning, plus the overcrowding of classrooms—militates against the development of creative capacities. Research has established that children between the ages of two and three can learn to read, tape record a story, and type it as it is played back. Hundreds of children between the ages of four and six have been taught by the Japanese pedagogue Suzuki to play violin concertos. Japanese research with infants and small children also suggests the value of early "maximum input" (music, color, verbal, tactile stimuli) in the personality development of infants. My own observations tend to confirm this. We have consistently underestimated the child's capacity to learn and his ability to realize his potential while *enjoying* both the play elements and the discipline involved in this process.

In contrast to the Japanese work, much recent Russian research appears to be concentrated in the area of mentation, with special emphasis on extending and enlarging man's mental processes and his capacity for learning. As early as 1964 the following appeared in *Soviet Life Today*, a U.S.S.R. English language magazine:

> The latest findings in anthropology, psychology, logic, and physiology show that the potential of the human

mind is very great indeed. "As soon as modern science gave us some understanding of the structure and work of the human brain, we were struck with its enormous reserve capacity," writes Yefremov (Ivan Yefremov, eminent Soviet scholar and writer). "Man, under average conditions of work and life, uses only a small part of his thinking equipment. . . . If we were able to force our brain to work at only half its capacity, we could, without any difficulty whatever, learn forty languages, memorize the large Soviet Encyclopedia from cover to cover, and complete the required courses of dozens of colleges."

The statement is hardly an exaggeration. It is the generally accepted theoretical view of man's mental potentialities.

How can we tap this gigantic potential? It is a big and very complex problem with many ramifications.

Another signpost of man's potential is what I have come to call the "Grandma Moses effect." This artist's experience indicates that artistic talents can be discovered and brought to full flowering in the latter part of the life cycle. In every retirement community there can be found similar examples of residents who did not use latent artistic abilities or other talents until after retirement. In many instances the presence of a talent is suspected or known but allowed to remain fallow for the best part of a lifetime.

Reasons why well-functioning mature adults do not use specific abilities are complex. Studies conducted at the University of Utah as a part of the Human Potentialities Research Project revealed that unconscious blocks are often present. In a number of instances a person with definite evidence that he has a specific talent (let's say he won a state-wide contest in sculpture while in high school) may not wish to realize this talent at a later time because he fears this would introduce a change in life-style. Sometimes fear of the passion of creation is another roadblock in self-actualization. On the basis of work at Utah it became clear that persons who live close to their capacity, who continue to activate their potential, have a pronounced sense of well-being and considerable energy and see themselves as leading purposeful and creative lives.

Most people are unaware of their strengths and potentialities. If a person with some college background is handed a form and asked to write out his personality strengths, he will list, on an average, five or six strengths. Asked to do the same thing for his weaknesses, the list will be two to three times as long. There are a number of reasons for this low self-assessment. Many participants in my classes and marathon group weekends have pointed out that "listing your strengths feels like bragging about yourself. It's something that just isn't done." Paradoxically, in a group, people feel more comfortable about sharing problem areas and hang-ups than they do about personality resources and latent abilities. This is traceable to the fact that we are members of a pathology-oriented culture. Psychological and psychiatric jargon dealing with emotional dysfunction and mental illness has become the parlance of the man in the street. In addition, from early childhood in our educational system we learn largely by our mistakes—by having them pointed out to us repeatedly. All this results in early "negative conditioning" and influences our attitude and perception of ourselves and other people. An attitudinal climate has become established which is continually fed and reinforced.

As a part of this negative conditioning there is the heavy emphasis by communications media on violence in television programs and motion pictures. The current American news format of radio, television, and newspapers—the widely prevalent idea of what constitutes news—results from a narrow, brutalizing concept thirty or forty years behind the times and is inimical to the development of human potential.

The news media give much time and prominent space to violence and consistently underplay "good" news. This gives the consumer the impression that important things that happen are various types of destructive activities. Consistent and repeated emphasis on bad news not only creates anxiety and tension but instills the belief that there is little except violence, disasters, accidents, and mayhem abroad in the world. As a consequence, the consumer of such news gradually experiences a shift in his outlook about the world leading to the formation of feelings of alienation and separation. The world is increasingly perceived as a threat, as the viewer becomes anxious that violence and mayhem may be perpetrated on him from somewhere out of the strange and unpredictable environment in which he lives. There slowly grows a conviction that it is safer to withdraw from such a world, to isolate himself from its struggles, and to let others make the decisions and become involved.

As a result of the steady diet of violence in the media, an even more fundamental and insidious erosion in man's self-system takes place. The erosion affects what I call the "trust factor." If we have been given a certain amount of affection, love, and understanding in our formative years, we are able to place a certain amount of trust in our fellow man. Trust is one of the most important elements in today's society although we tend to minimize its importance. *We basically trust people.* For example, we place an enormous amount of trust in our fellow man when driving on a freeway or in an express lane. We trust those with whom we are associated to fulfill their obligations and responsibilities. The element of trust is the basic rule in human relations. When we distrust people, they usually sense our attitude and reciprocate in kind.

The consistent emphasis in the news on criminal violence, burglarizing, and assault makes slow but pervasive inroads into our reservoir of trust. As we hear and read much about the acts of violence and injury men perpetrate upon one another, year after year, with so little emphasis placed on the loving, caring, and humanitarian acts of man, we begin to trust our fellow man less, and we thereby diminish ourselves. It is my conclusion the media's excessive emphasis on violence, like the drop of water on the stone, erodes and wears away the trust factor in man. By undermining the trust factor in man, media contribute to man's estrangement from man and prevent the full flourishing and deeper development of a sense of community and communion with all men.

Our self-concept, how we feel about ourselves and our fellow man and the world, is determined to a considerable extent by the inputs from the physical and interpersonal environment to which we are exposed. In the physical environment, there are the irritants in the air, i.e., air pollution plus the ugliness and noise of megapolis. Our interpersonal environment is characterized by estrangement and distance from others (and self), and by the artificiality and superficiality of our social encounters and the resultant violation of authenticity. Existing in a setting that provides as consistent inputs multiple irritants, ugliness and violence, and lack of close and meaningful relationships, man is in danger of becoming increasingly irritated, ugly, and violent.

As work in the area of human potentialities progressed, it has become ever clearer that personality, to a much greater degree than previously suspected, functions in response to the environment. This is additional confirmation of what field theorists and proponents of the holistic approach to the study of man have long suspected.

Perhaps the most important task facing us today is the regeneration of our environment and institutional structures such as school, government, church, etc. With increasing sophistication has come the recognition that institutions are not sacrosanct and that they have but one purpose and function—to serve as a framework for the actualization of human potential. It is possible to evaluate both the institution and the contribution of the institution by asking this question: "To what extent does the function of the institution foster the realization of human potential?"

Experimental groups consistently have found that the more a person's environment can be involved in the process of realizing potential, the greater the gains. It is understandable why scientists concerned with the study of personality have been reluctant to consider the importance of here-and-now inputs in relation to personality functioning. To do so would open a Pandora's box of possibilities and complex forces that until fairly recently were considered to be the exclusive domain of the social scientist. Many scientists and professionals, particularly psychotherapists, feel they have acquired a certain familiarity with the topography of "intra-psychic forces" and are reluctant to admit the reality of additional complex factors in the functioning of the personality.

It is significant that an increasing number of psychologists, psychiatrists, and social workers now realize that over and beyond keeping up with developments in their respective fields, the best way to acquire additional professional competence is through group experiences designed for personal growth and that focus on the unfolding of individual possibilities. From this group of aware professionals and others came much of the initial support and interest in Esalen Institute and similar "Growth Centers" later referred to as the Human Potentialities Movement.

Esalen Institute in Big Sur, California, was organized in 1962 by Michael Murphy and his partner, Dick Price. Under their imaginative management the institute experienced a phenomenal growth, established a branch in San Francisco, and is now famous for its seminars and weekend experiences offered by pioneering professionals. Since 1962 more than 100,000 persons have enrolled for one of these activities.

The past three years have seen a rapid mushrooming of Growth Centers. There are more than fifty such organizations ranging from Esalen and Kairos Institutes in California to Oasis in Chicago and Aureon Institute in New York. The experiences offered at these Growth Centers are based on several hypotheses: 1) that the average healthy person functions at a fraction of his capacity; 2) that man's most exciting life-long adventure is actualizing his potential; 3) that the group environment is one of the best settings in which to achieve growth; and 4) that personality growth can be achieved by anyone willing to invest himself in this process.

Human potentialities is rapidly emerging as a discrete field of scientific inquiry. Exploring the human potential can become the meeting ground for a wide range of disciplines, offering a dynamic synthesis for seemingly divergent areas of research. It is possible that the field of human potentialities offers an answer to the long search for a synthesizing and organizing principle which will unify the sciences. The explosive growth of the Human Potentialities Movement is indicative of a growing public interest. Although there exist a considerable number of methods—all designed to tap human potential—work on assessment or evaluation of these methods has in most instances not progressed beyond field testing and informal feedback of results. The need for research in the area of human potentialities has never been more pressing. The National Center for the Exploration of Human Potential in La Jolla, California, has recently been organized for this purpose. A nonprofit organization, the center will act as a clearing house of information for current and past approaches that have been successful in fostering personal growth. One of the main purposes of the center will be to conduct and coordinate basic and applied research concerning the expansion of human potential.

Among the many fascinating questions posed by researchers are some of the following: What is the relationship of body-rhythms, biorhythms, and the expansion of sensory awareness to the uncovering of human potential? What are the applications of methods and approaches from other cultures such as yoga techniques, Sulfi methods, types of meditation, etc.? What is the role of ecstasy and play vis-à-vis the realizing of human possibilities? The exploration of these and similar questions can help us create a society truly devoted to the full development of human capacities—particularly the capacities for love, joy, creativity, spiritual experiencing. This is the challenge and promise of our lifetime.

FDR: The Untold Story of His Last Year

By James MacGregor Burns

April 11, 1970

Late in March 1944, a young cardiologist at the United States Naval Hospital in Bethesda, Lt. Comdr. Howard G. Bruenn, had an emergency summons from his superiors. He was requested to conduct a heart examination the next day; his patient would be the President of the United States. The young Navy doctor was called in so hurriedly that he had no time to look over Franklin D. Roosevelt's medical records before greeting his eminent patient. He soon felt at ease, however, when the President came rolling down the corridor in his wheelchair, wisecracking with an old friend and waving genially to the nurses and patients who clustered in the hallways and peeked around corners. As the President was lifted to the examining table, he seemed to Dr. Bruenn neither disturbed by having to undergo examination nor annoyed by it—indeed, not especially interested.

Little could the young doctor know that he was about to examine a medical case that would become a political issue in later years. As the cold war deepened after World War II, it was charged that Roosevelt was too ill during his final year to carry the burden of the wartime Presidency; that he could not make tough strategic decisions; that he was, in Ambassador Patrick Hurley's words, "already a sick man at Yalta." Until now, the truth has been elusive. At Eleanor Roosevelt's request, there was no autopsy of the President; the official medical records disappeared; and the President's physicians, including Bruenn, chose not to publish their own recollections and records. This month, however, Bruenn is furnishing a full medical report on President Roosevelt's last year in the *Annals of Internal Medicine* (April 1970). How does the old allegation about the sick, incompetent President stand up in the light of what Bruenn discloses?

It was with mounting surprise and shock, Bruenn recently told me, that he had taken the President's blood pressure that day in March 1944; he also studied his lungs and heart, read the electrocardiogram, fluoroscopy, and X-rays, and checked the earlier records. The Commander-in-Chief was clearly an ill man. Not only was he tired and gray, slightly feverish, somewhat breathless, and coughing frequently—evidently suffering from bronchitis—but his basic condition was serious. His heart, Bruenn found, while regular in rhythm, was enlarged. At the apex, he found a blowing systolic murmur. The second aortic sound was loud and booming. Blood pressure was 186/108, compared with 136/78 in mid-1935, 162/98 two years later, and 188/105 in early 1941. Since 1941, there had been significant increase in the size of the cardiac shadow. The enlargement of the heart was evidently caused by a dilated and tortuous aorta; furthermore, the pulmonary vessels were engorged.

Bruenn's diagnosis was alarming: hypertension, hypertensive heart disease, cardiac failure.

It is not clear, though, as to just who was alarmed. Bruenn reported his findings to the Surgeon General, Adm. Ross T. McIntire, an ear, nose, and throat specialist, who was also the President's old friend and physician. Roosevelt's condition had been wholly unsuspected up to that time. Emergency conferences were now held among Admiral McIntire, Bruenn, and a half-dozen other specialists and consultants. It was evident that the President had to be put on a regimen, but how much could a President—especially *this* President —be expected to follow the ordinary heart patient's routine? One or two weeks of nursing care were suggested but rejected because of the demands on the office; the invasion of Normandy, for one thing, was only two months off. Bruenn urged that the President at least be digitalized; there was some resistance, but the young Navy officer insisted that, if that were not done, he could take no further responsibility for the case. The doctors finally agreed on a program: digitalis, less daily activity, fewer cigarettes, a one-hour rest after meals, a quiet dinner in the White House quarters, at least ten hours' sleep, no swimming in the pool, a diet of 2,600 calories moderately low in fat, and mild laxatives to avoid straining.

The crucial question during these worrisome days was who should tell the President about his condition, and how candidly. It was soon clear that Roosevelt would not raise the question himself; he did not seem curious as to why he had been examined or prescribed a new regimen. He simply followed the doctors' recommendations to the extent he could and let the matter rest there. Bruenn, a junior officer, did not feel it his right or duty to inform the President. Evidently, everyone assumed that McIntire had the responsibility and would exercise it, but there is no evidence that he did. Perhaps he lacked confidence in his own effectiveness in passing on such portentous findings to his chief, especially if he should be asked difficult questions. Perhaps he sensed that the President would neither accept the significance of the findings nor act on them —that in a fundamental sense the President did not want to know. Perhaps he realized how fatalistic the President was, or perhaps he realized that no matter how well grounded the findings, there was a heavy psychological and political element in the situation, and that a President—especially one with Roosevelt's fortitude and self-confidence—could not be advised as authoritatively as the ordinary patient. Or perhaps, after all his optimistic reports on the President in the past, he was simply too timid.

Conceivably, he *did* tell the President, but that probably would not have made much difference. For a quarter of a century Roosevelt's health had been a personal and political issue; meantime he had become one of the most active and effective political leaders of his era. He had an enormous self-confidence in his ability to carry on, to win out. With the doctors' help, he might have reasoned, he would overcome this health problem just as he had the effects of polio. In any event, as a soldier he would not quit while the war was still being waged.

On the face of it, Bruenn's findings would seem to support the charge that Roosevelt was an ill man at Yalta, and, indeed, during the last year or two of his life. Paradoxically, Bruenn's disclosures—which are as full and authoritative as anything we are likely to have on the matter—will force us to revise most interpretations of the significance of Roosevelt's medical condition during his final year.

For Bruenn's records indicate that during the last year the digitalis and the other ministrations seemed to work. To be sure, the President did have one heart attack—in the middle of a speech he was making at Bremerton upon return from his Pacific trip in August 1944—but he was able to finish the speech. He looked gaunt and haggard in that last year, but this was in large part because he wanted to carry out the doctors' recommendation that he lose weight. He conducted a brilliant re-election campaign against Governor Thomas E. Dewey; his "my dog Fala" speech was a virtuoso performance. If he erred later in the year in withdrawing Gen. Joseph Stilwell from China, it was not because Roosevelt lost contact with the Chinese tragedy; he was in close touch with the principals. He carefully laid the ground for American—and Soviet—acceptance of the new United Nations organization. His death on April 12, 1945, was not directly from a heart attack, but from a cerebral hemorrhage.

The crucial test of Roosevelt's last year, and of his health, was Yalta, where the great strategic questions of World War II converged. Bruenn's long-delayed report should effectively remove Roosevelt's health as a major historical factor. To be sure, the President's health was probably not good enough that last year to have enabled him to conduct a sweeping alteration of his foreign policy—for example, to shift to a hard-line strategy toward Moscow. But such a shift was virtually out of the question anyway; Roosevelt had made his commitment to a coalition strategy with Russia, and he was going to see it through, at least as long as the war lasted. In most respects, his final year was a culmination of the decisions reached earlier in the war, especially at Teheran.

But to remove Roosevelt's health as an issue in history is not to remove the historical issue. On the contrary, it is to sharpen the charge made by Roosevelt's critics after Yalta and ever since, the charge that in his last year in office Roosevelt knowingly sold his country out in a series of Munich-type appeasements of the Soviet Union. Most of the American official records are now open on this period. What today, a quarter of a century later, with all the advantages—and the humility—of hindsight, can we say about Roosevelt's decisions during that last year, especially at Yalta?

The two great assumptions made by Roosevelt's critics are that he was blind to the real history and nature of Soviet communism and hence was willing to trust it, and that as the commander of the greatest aggregation of balanced military power in history he was in a position to exact major concessions from Moscow about postwar arrangements but failed to do so.

The first assumption is not well founded. One cannot study Roosevelt's whole political and personal development without crediting him with the most realistic apperception of the ambitions and realpolitik of rival leaders and their constituencies. This was the man, after all, who had vanquished his domestic opponents, had early recognized the nature of Nazism, and had conducted a kind of cold war against the Soviet Union itself (largely because of its war on Finland) during the months before the German attack on Russia in June 1941. Roosevelt had few illusions about Soviet communism as it was. He was not totally defeatist, however, about Soviet foreign policy—as it might be. Since we still harbor some hope in the matter twenty-five years later (and about our own foreign policy, too), it would hardly seem unpatriotic for Roosevelt to have tried to make postwar arrangements that might serve to undergird a continued Anglo-American-Soviet coalition.

The second assumption compels us to look at Roosevelt's main decisions about postwar arrangements—decisions shaped throughout the war, but formalized at

Yalta. The question is: Did Roosevelt have the bargaining power to compel Russia to make greater concessions to the Anglo-American position than it did?

The cardinal issue during Roosevelt's last year was Poland. In fact, by 1945, Stalin had both moral and military control of the situation. By the time of Yalta, the Red Army had overrun Poland, after having suffered frightful losses. Stalin had possession of the real estate. It was understood, of course, that questions such as the shape and future government of Poland would be decided by the Big Three, but morally that expectation rested on the assumption that the Allies jointly had regained Poland—that they had fully shared in the sacrifices of the anti-Hitler effort. And of course they had not. From Stalin's point of view, the British and Americans were in no position to claim a share of the diplomatic spoils of Poland.

The issue cuts much deeper. For three solid years, Stalin had pleaded with Roosevelt and Churchill for a major cross-Channel invasion of France, in order to take the Nazis' pressure off his troops. For three long years, Roosevelt and Churchill had responded with promises. The cross-Channel invasion of June 1944 had come too late, from Moscow's standpoint, to make much difference in eastern Europe. The Red Army had had to go it alone. Far from getting major military aid from the Allies, Stalin contended, he had had to bail them out in the Battle of the Bulge.

At Yalta, Roosevelt was under no illusion about prospects for Poland. It had long been agreed by the Big Three that the war-racked nation would be picked up like a carpetbag and set down a few hundred miles to the west, satisfying Russia's appetite, penalizing Germany's, and taming Poland's. The cardinal issue was: Who would govern Poland, the Lublin Poles, a communist-dominated group nurtured by Moscow, or a genuine coalition of Lublin Poles and "London Poles," the non-communist leadership long sponsored by Churchill? A few weeks before Yalta, the Soviets recognized the Lublin Poles in the face of Roosevelt's and Churchill's urgent pleas for delay. Roosevelt decided to be relatively flexible at Yalta about Poland's new borders—which in any event had been essentially determined by the Red Army's advance, by understandings at Teheran, and by the position of Britain's Lord Curzon a generation before—but to insist on a democratic, independent, and viable Polish government.

From the start, Stalin was absolutely obdurate on Poland. When Roosevelt led off the discussion by saying that he had "six or seven million Poles in the United States" and that "the Poles, like the Chinese, wanted to save face," the Marshal shot back, "Who will save face —the Poles in Poland or the émigré Poles?" When Churchill at his most eloquent reminded the Marshal that Britain had gone to war with Germany so that Poland would be free and independent and that "this had nearly cost us our life as a nation," the Marshal asked for an intermission—and then came back well primed. His remarks suggest the absolute stone wall Churchill and Roosevelt were up against at Yalta. Said Stalin:

"The Prime Minister has said that for Great Britain the question of Poland is a question of honor. For Russia, it is not only a question of honor but of security. . . . During the past thirty years, our German enemy has passed through this corridor twice. This is because Poland was weak. It is in the Russian interest as well as that of Poland that Poland be strong and powerful. . . .

"The Prime Minister thinks we should make a gesture of magnanimity. But I must remind you that the Curzon line was invented not by Russia but by foreigners. The Curzon line was made by Curzon, Clemenceau, and the Americans in 1918 and 1919. Russia was not invited and did not participate. . . ." Stalin was speaking with more and more heat. "Some want us to be less Russian than Curzon and Clemenceau. What will the Russians say at Moscow, and the Ukrainians? They will say that Stalin and Molotov are far less defenders of Russia than Curzon and Clemenceau.

"I cannot take such a position and return to Moscow."

By now Stalin was standing. He preferred that the war continue and let Poland get more land at the ex-

pense of Germany. As for the government, how could
they set up a Polish government at Yalta without the
participation of Poles, who were not there? "They all
say that I am a dictator, but I have enough democratic
feeling not to set up a Polish government without
Poles." As a military man, he wanted peace and quiet
in the wake of the Red Army. The Lublin government
could maintain order, while the agents of the London
government had already killed 212 Russian soldiers.
The Red Army would support only the Lublin government, "and I cannot do otherwise. Such is the situation."

There was a pause, and Roosevelt suggested adjourn-
ment. During the next three days, he and Churchill and
their aides waged a tough and concerted campaign to
win concessions from Stalin on Polish independence.
Roosevelt warned the Marshal that unless the Big Three
could agree on Poland—which to the President meant
not recognizing the Lublin regime—they would "lose
the confidence of the world." Churchill warned that
150,000 Polish soldiers on the Italian and western fronts
would feel betrayed.

The pressure on Roosevelt during this period was
acute. He looked worse than ever; Churchill's physician
wrote him off as a dying man. One evening, after an
especially difficult discussion of Poland, the President's
blood pressure for the first time showed *pulsus alternans*. Although his lungs and heart were good, Bruenn
insisted on no visitors until noon and more rest. Within
two days his appetite was excellent and the *pulsus
alternans* had disappeared.

Step by step, Roosevelt and Churchill exacted paper
concessions from the Russians: that the Lublin government be "reorganized on a broader democratic basis"
with the inclusion of democratic leaders from within
Poland and from without; that free and unfettered elections be held soon—perhaps within a month—on the
basis of open suffrage and secret ballot; that émigré
leaders could take part in them. What was really at
stake, however, was not the general formula but how
much opportunity London and Washington would have,

in fact, to influence the reorganization of the government, and to monitor the conduct of the elections. Even on this score Stalin conceded that the American and British ambassadors to the Soviets could consult with Lublin and non-Lublin leaders in Moscow, but the specific arrangements for holding and policing the elections were left obscure.

"Mr. President," said Admiral Leahy when he saw the compromise formula, "this is so elastic that the Russians can stretch it all the way from Yalta to Washington without even technically breaking it."

"I know, Bill—I know it. But it's the best I can do for Poland at this time."

The best he could do. Roosevelt was not ill at Yalta, or befuddled, or weak, or unpatriotic. As a realist, he saw that he had reached the limit of his bargaining power. He simply did not hold the cards. He wanted far more from Stalin than Stalin wanted from him. This fact dominated settlement of the other crucial question at Yalta: the Far East.

Roosevelt had no illusions about what Stalin wanted in the Far East, for the Russians had long made this clear—chiefly the return of the Kuriles and southern Sakhalin to Russia; and special railroad and port concessions in Port Arthur, Dairen, and Harbin. The Russians had also made clear that they would enter the war against Japan some time after Germany was beaten. Some Americans naïvely wondered whether Stalin would make good on this promise; actually, there had never been any question whether Stalin would be in on the Far Eastern kill. The American military was desperately anxious that the Soviets share the burden of the final conquest of Japan. It was expected to be very costly. One million Anglo-American casualties were forecast—and many more if the Russians did not come into the war on the continent.

But Stalin—and probably Roosevelt, too—knew that what was crucial was not the fact of Soviet participation but its timing and strength. And here Stalin was in the delicious situation of having Roosevelt and Churchill in just the position that they had had him for three long years. He could delay his Far East attack until London and Washington had suffered terrible losses in overcoming the home islands—and then he could march on the mainland against the collapsing Japanese forces there. In Europe, his allies had made the Red Army take the bloodbath; now he could let the Americans and British carry the burden of battle, and he could take his share of the spoils. It was Roosevelt's task at Yalta to induce Stalin to come into the Far Eastern war at a time that would be advantageous to the British and Americans, not just the Russians. This Stalin agreed to do—but for his price in territory and concessions.

Instead of "bribing" Russia to come into the Far Eastern war, why did Roosevelt not rely on the atom bomb to defeat Japan? Was this proof of his ebbing health? Actually, the President kept in close touch with the Manhattan Project; at the end of 1944, Secretary of War Henry L. Stimson had told him that the first bomb (but without previous full-scale testing) would be ready about August 1, 1945. There was little indication, however, that the A-bomb, even if operative, would be effective against the military situation the Allies most feared—millions of Japanese soldiers (and civilians) fanatically resisting in caves and entrenchments along hundreds of miles of Japan's coasts and mountain ranges.

So in the Far East as well as in Poland there was an imbalance between what Stalin was asking of Roosevelt and what Roosevelt wanted from Stalin. All the Marshal really sought was legitimacy for dominating territory most of which he had the military power to control anyway. A third issue at Yalta, the nature of the new United Nations organization, was another case of imbalance; Roosevelt wanted a Soviet commitment to the United States, and Stalin was playing cool. In general, Roosevelt did the best he could with the strategic resources he had.

But we cannot leave the matter there. Why was Roosevelt's bargaining position so poor? The answers to this question are multifold: the Soviets' stupendous counterattack against Hitler, the weaknesses of a coalition divided by history and ideology, and simple geography and military power. But if we ask to what extent Roosevelt was responsible for his own strategic plight during his last year, the answer lies in part in his brilliance as Commander-in-Chief as compared with his failures as grand strategist. As Commander-in-Chief he conserved the lives of American soldiers in Europe and made a deal with Stalin to conserve them in the Pacific; he presided over a series of stunning military victories after 1942; but he bought these military victories at a political price. That price was exacted at Yalta.

Yet we cannot leave the matter even there. Roosevelt was not a mere military opportunist or improviser. He had exalted political goals; few leaders in history have defined them with such eloquence and persistence. But he was a deeply divided man. His major failing was that he acted out the parts of both improviser and man of principle without always seeing the interrelation of the two. He was a practical man who proceeded now boldly, now cautiously, step by step toward immediate ends. He was also a dreamer and a sermonizer who spelled out lofty goals. He was both a Soldier of the Faith, battling with his warrior comrades for an ideology of peace and freedom, and a Prince of the State, protecting the interests of his nation in a threatening world. The fact that his faith was more a set of attitudes than a firmly grounded moral code, that it embraced hope verging on utopianism and sentiment bordering on sentimentality—all this made his credo evocative but also soft and pasty, so that it crumbled easily under the press of harsh political alternatives and strategic decisions.

For a quarter-century now, Roosevelt has been under attack for his lack of "realism" during that last year. Perhaps a new generation of scholars and students is coming along that will pay more attention to Roosevelt the idealist. Without question he acted in large part on the basis of faith rather than realpolitik. At the final banquet at Yalta, he spoke of the time in 1933 when Eleanor Roosevelt had gone to a country town to open a school and had found on a classroom wall there a map of the world with a large, empty, unnamed blank space for the Soviet Union. Roosevelt felt that great progress had been made since his recognition of the Soviet Union in 1933; he had faith that more progress would be made. He was trying always to lift people out of their narrow and short-sighted ways and attitudes, at the risk of being called a utopian, an appeaser, or a dupe.

He picked up Woodrow Wilson's fallen banner, fashioned new symbols and programs to realize old ideals of peace and democracy, overcame his enemies with sword and pen, and died in a final exhausting effort to build a world citadel of freedom. In a day when we are trying to find out where we went wrong, how we can find our way again, how we can reestablish a principled and even idealistic foreign policy —in this day Roosevelt the idealist as well as Roosevelt the Machiavellian must be brought back before the bar of history.

The War Novel: From Mailer to Vonnegut

By Alfred Kazin

February 6, 1971

Norman Mailer's *The Naked and the Dead*, published in 1948 with enormous success of every kind, was the first "important"—and is probably still the best—novel about Americans at war, 1941–1945. Mailer at twenty-five was so thoroughly launched by his first book—it was exactly what people brought up on novels and films about the First World War expected of the "new war" novelists—that many of his later efforts were discon-

certing to his admirers. But even jealous older novelists
—Hemingway called the book "poor cheese, preten-
tiously wrapped"—understood the book in terms of
their own expectations. The moment was still ripe for
a novel that would honor war as a test of the literary
imagination.

Like everyone who has written well about war,
Mailer was palpably excited by it. The 1941–1945
war, "*the* war" as we used to call it, was a chance to
prove his "courage"—always a pressing subject with
Mailer—and a way of getting away from the Brooklyn
Jewishness that he found provincial and uninteresting.
War was a chance to meet head on the endurance, the
solidarity, the suffering that have always been the epic
stuff of war. ("It is well that war is so terrible," Robert
E. Lee said after Fredericksburg, "else we should grow
too fond of it.") Mailer is supposed even to have
insisted on his being sent to the Pacific because Europe
was such familiar literary territory. Having been interested in aeronautics and engineering at Harvard, he
also had a certain vanity about his ability to handle
the many technical problems that are created by war.

All these personal ambitions for war—his unmistakable delight in its dangers and tests, and his liking
for the Texans and the rednecks in his outfit—were
given shape by Mailer's intellectual fascination with
the unprecedented power that Americans could sum-
mon up for war. Mailer was at once excited by this
power and deeply suspicious of its over-reaching. He
was to write with excitement about the extreme physical exertion of soldiers, the violence done to the living
and the dead; his "political" sense of the possible
menace to the world in so much American power was
represented by a figure out of the "anti-Fascist" novels
of the 1930s: the sinister, epicene, arrogant General
Cummings. The "Fascist" mentality of General Cummings is a characterization typical of World War II
novels produced soon after the war; Mailer's was a
generation that had gone to war recognizing it as part
of the same social crisis that had produced Hitler. But
unlike the "progressive," more simple-minded novelists
of the immediate postwar period, Mailer saw the gen-

eral as also a victim of the military machine that absorbs everything—even generals—into itself.

At the end of *The Naked and the Dead*, General Cummings's intellectual vanity—he has been a prophet of the "totalitarian century"—becomes a joke on himself; but the "liberal" professions of his aide, Lieutenant Hearn, are equally shown up when the young officer's efforts to demonstrate solidarity with the enlisted men result in his death. Sergeant Croft, who really runs the platoon, hates Hearn for stepping out of place and tricks the lieutenant into exposing himself to enemy fire; the decisive victory of the American forces invading "Anopopei Island" is secured by the mechanical decision of a staff bureaucrat when the general is away from the island trying to get the Navy's help. These ironies are important items in Mailer's respect for the bludgeoning organization of the military machine. He is not sentimental about the GIs, hard-luck types who were as pathetic in South Boston and San Antonio as they are in the Army. The whole book works for Mailer as a highly organized effort to show war as the ultimate expression of our society. Although his book owes some of its appeal to the shared experiences that so many readers bring to it, the urgently effective quality behind *The Naked and the Dead* is respect for war as the systematized deployment of technical skills.

"You and I, Rinaldi," said the Hemingway hero in that other far-off war, "we've made a separate peace." Nobody in novels about World War II "makes" a separate peace. Nowadays we are far removed indeed from the literary detachment of those ambulance volunteers who wrote *In Our Time, 1919*, and *The Enormous Room*. Mailer writes as a soldier from the ranks and from hard-won knowledge, both in the field and after the "peace," of what World War II did to hammer America into a militarized, bureaucratized "superpower." Hemingway, Cummings, even Dos Passos in his "Left" days, never saw war as the inevitable extension of our super-power. There are no free agents in Mailer's work. Truly a child of the Second World War, Mailer owes his easy handling of the composite sides of war to his political understanding of America the colossus at mid-century. The enlisted men in his novel are always in friction—battling, pushing, swearing—and this personal emotion has not the slightest effect on the actual course of the fighting. What interests Mailer about war is what follows from so much relentless, organized, sanctioned violence. He loves the psychic extremes, the hysteria of soldiers drunkenly stumbling around Japanese corpses looking for "souvenirs" and of soldiers in the jungle pushing themselves unconscious with exhaustion. Dread, extreme fatigue, killing and getting killed become forms of intoxication that lift people out of their usual selves—always a prime motive in Mailer. War is still the one "big" experience that the common man will have in his life. War frees each man to realize his most intimate fantasy before it obliterates him. D. H. Lawrence said of the First World War that it was "sensational delight posing as pious idealism." Mailer, in his first book, still accepts the "sensational delight" of war. *The Naked and the Dead* is now a very old-fashioned novel.

World War II has turned into a very different war during the twenty-five years in which we have been forced to think of Hiroshima, Auschwitz, Dresden, the thirty million dead, the threat of universal nuclear destruction. Of *this* war, as opposed to our restricted image of it during the 1940s, one can say that no individual experience, as reported in literature, has done justice to it or can, and that the most atrocious individual experiences still seem unreal when we read about them. When the British liberated Belsen on April 15, 1945, they came upon 40,000 sick, starving, and dying prisoners, and more than 10,000 corpses stacked in heaps. Belsen was not the worst Nazi concentration camp, merely the first to be exposed to the world. The London *Times* correspondent began his dispatch: "It is my duty to describe something beyond the imagination of mankind." This reaction became part of every serious and honest view of World War II so that, by the 1950s, it blended into so many uncovered horrors, so many possible future wars, such a continuous general ominousness that "*the* war" soon became War anywhere, anytime—War that has never ended.

Realism, observation, even one's own experience could no longer express "War" as it did "*the* war." War as an actuality, bound by space and time, an event that literature could "do justice" to, has yielded to an apocalyptic sense of the possible destruction of mankind, of the boundlessness of man's enmities. Above all, we have had the sense of a world made totally absurd; war has become the normal, omnipresent condition of daily living, dominating a whole generation by the terror of its own weapons, and by the visible undoing, in its preparations for war, of all those human loyalties and common values in the name of which war used to be fought.

The essence of such novels as Joseph Heller's *Catch-22* and Kurt Vonnegut's *Slaughterhouse-Five, or the Children's Crusade* is that though both are ostensibly about the 1941–1945 war, in which both writers served, they are really about The Next War, and thus about a war that will be without limits and without meaning, a war that will end only when no one is alive to fight it. The theme of *Catch-22* in particular is the total craziness of war, the craziness of all those who submit to it, and the struggle for sanity by one man, Yossarian, who wants just to survive. But how can one construct fictional meaning, narrative logic, out of a system in which virtually everyone but the hero assents to madness and willingly poses as mad? The answer is that *Catch-22* is about the hypothesis of a totally insane world, a difficult subject for anyone not a Jonathan Swift, a Lewis Carroll, or a Franz Kafka; so Heller, who combines the bitterness of a total pacifist with the mocking pseudo-rationality of traditional Jewish humor, has to fetch up one gag after another. "The dead man in Yossarian's tent was simply not easy to live with." "General Dreedle was incensed by General Peckem's recent directive requiring all tents in the Mediterranean theater of operations to be pitched along parallel lines with entrances facing back proudly toward the Washington Monument." The book proceeds by Yossarian's asking sensible, human, logical questions about war, to which the answers are madly inconsequent. Heller himself is the straight man on this lunatic stage, Yossarian the one human being in this farcically anti-human setup. The jokes are variations on the classic Yiddish story of the totally innocent recruit who pokes his head over the trench, discovers that everyone is firing away, and cries out in wonder, "One can get killed here!"

Yet, the impressive emotion in *Catch-22* is not "black humor," the totally absurd, but horror. Whenever the book veers back to its primal scene, a bombardier's evisceration in a plane being smashed by flak, which is described directly and piteously, we recognize that what makes *Catch-22* disturbing is this: The gags are a strained effort to articulate the imminence now of *anyone's* death by violence, and it is just this that makes it impossible to "describe war" in traditional literary ways. Despite the running gags, the telltale quality of *Catch-22* is that it doesn't move; it can't. The buried-alive feeling of being caught in a plane under attack, of seeing one's partner eviscerated, produces total impotence, the feeling of being unable to move, to escape. And this horror-cold immobility is reproduced both in the static, self-conscious distortion of the gags and in the violence of the straight, "serious" passages.

> The forward bombardier would have liked to be a ball turret gunner. That was where he wanted to be if he had to be there at all, instead of hung out there in front like some goddamned cantilevered goldfish in some goddamn cantilevered goldfish bowl while the goddamn foul black towers of flak were bursting and booming and billowing all around and above and below him in a climbing, cracking, staggered, banging, phantasmagorical, cosmological wickedness that jarred and tossed and shivered, clattered and pierced, and threatened to annihilate them all in one splinter of a second in one vast flash of fire.

Thus, the urgent emotion in Heller's book is every individual's sense today of being directly in the line of fire, of being trapped, of war not as an affair of groups in which *we* may escape but as my and your nemesis. The psychology in *Catch-22* is that of a man being led forth to execution, of a gallows humor in which the rope around one's neck feels all too real. This sense of oneself not as a soldier in a large protective group but as an isolated wretch doomed to die *unaccountably* is more and more a feature of literature about World War II. It haunts all fiction by Jewish writers about the war, even novels that do not deal directly with the war, such as Saul Bellow's *Mr. Sammler's Planet.* More and more, every account of the holocaust turns into one man's war, one man's account of insupportable and inexplicable evil, into the fantasy of a world coming down on the single witness who is telling the story. There is no politics in our contemporary war novels, for it is impossible to posit any aim to destruction on such a scale as the thirty million who died in World War II. Destruction was wreaked on Hiroshima, Nagasaki, and Dresden because the weapons were available, because these cities were on the timetable.

Kurt Vonnegut's books are haunted by the fact that he was an American prisoner of war in Dresden when the city, in the worst single episode of bombing during the war, was firebombed by the U.S. Army Air Corps. Vonnegut and other Allied prisoners were saved because they were being kept in a powerfully built slaughterhouse. Everything Vonnegut has written about this experience is "true" with the same preposterous irony; after the bombing was over, one of the Americans was tried and shot for "stealing" a teapot from amidst the rubble. All this has given *Slaughterhouse-Five, or the Children's Crusade* an impishly sentimental humor based on the sheer helplessness, the total ineffectuality, of *anyone* caught up in such a massacre. The novel starts on the pseudo-breezy, bitterly quiescent note of a man who cannot forget the terror, but at the same time cannot put it into a novel—and is not sure that anyone should.

When I came home from the Second World War twenty-three years ago, I thought it would be easy for

me to write about the destruction of Dresden, since
all I would have to do would be to report what I had
seen. And I thought, too, that it would be a masterpiece or at least make me a lot of money, since the
subject was so big. . . .

The book . . . is so short and jumbled and jangled
. . . because there is nothing to say about a massacre.
Everybody is supposed to be dead, to never say anything or want anything ever again. Everything is
supposed to be very quiet after a massacre, and it
always is, except for the birds.

And what do the birds say? All there is to say about
a massacre, things like, *"Poo-tee-weet."*

This belittling of his book is typical of Vonnegut's
way of fading out on his subjects, of posing as the little
man who can never do anything about things. Billy
Pilgrim, the little businessman from Indianapolis who
was another prisoner in Dresden, is a figure of entirely
unreproachful innocence; he *never* knows what is happening to him, especially when he is taken off by some
of Vonnegut's usual visitors from outer space. Yet, he
is a solid, good citizen of Mid-America, able to succeed
in business. Billy in wartime, as a prisoner of war, inspired the German guards to look at him "owlishly,"
to coo "calmingly. They had never dealt with Americans before, but they surely understood this general sort
of freight. They knew that it was essentially a liquid
which could be induced to flow slowly toward cooing
and light."

Vonnegut is always at home with characters who are
not with it in our kind of world, people whose total
helplessness and inability to explain *anything* have
indeed made them unworldly, extraterrestrial, open to
mischief from outer space. Vonnegut's use of space
fiction is always too droll for my taste, a boy's fantasy
of more rational creatures than ourselves. Just as there
is "nothing to say about a massacre," so there is nothing to explain or protest. The "Tralfamadorian" who
takes Billy Pilgrim off explains condescendingly that
"Earthlings are the great explainers, explaining why
this event is structured as it is, telling how other events

may be achieved or avoided. I am a Tralfamadorian, seeing all time as you might see a stretch of the Rocky Mountains. All time is all time. It does not change. It does not lend itself to warnings and explanations. It simply *is*. . . . Only on Earth is there any talk of free will." In the same spirit, Vonnegut deprecates any attempt to see tragedy that day in the Dresden massacre. It is simply viewed as too much for all of us, whether to remember, record, or understand. Noting one horror after another, he likes to say with arch fatalism, "So it goes."

Vonnegut is at his best not in *Slaughterhouse-Five* but in such satires of the American scene as *God Bless You, Mr. Rosewater*. In these, his authentic bitterness at the souring of so many American hopes takes on the wildly comic quality natural to him. In *Slaughter-house-Five* he seems, all too understandably, subdued by his material and plays it dumb. The book is short, loose, and somehow helpless. But Vonnegut's total horror of war has endeared him to the young, who find it hard to believe that even World War II had a purpose, and who see themselves as belonging to the universe at large rather than to the country that sends them to fight in Asia. Vonnegut's fixed social idea, especially in *Slaughterhouse-Five*, is a human vulnerability too innocent in the face of war to offer any political explanation or protest; Vonnegut's amiable self-deprecation finally becomes a picture of the whole human race. Thus, all evil is eliminated from the war that Hitler started but that, as Vonnegut says over and again, certainly made everyone "very tough." By now we are morally perishing of so much toughness, and think longingly of E. E. Cummings's "There's a hell of a better universe next door. Let's go."

The gifted, morbid French novelist Louis-Ferdinand Céline was a Fascist, served the Vichy regime, and finally fled to Germany with other French Fascists and collaborators. In his remarkable account of being cooped up in Germany, *Castle to Castle*, Céline, on the basis of information given him by the Vichy consul in Dresden, tells us more what the Dresden fire-bombing was like than does Vonnegut, who was there:

. . . the tactic of total squashing and frying in phosphorus . . . American invention! really perfected the last "new look" before the A-bomb . . . first the suburbs, the periphery, with liquid sulphur and avalanches of torpedoes . . . then general roasting . . . the whole center! Act II . . . churches, parks, museums . . . no survivors wanted. . . .

Why does the American who was there avoid such strong, plain language? Céline's bluntness, his graphic power, incorporates his willingness to take sides, his deep political outrage at the specific American "tactic of total squashing and frying in phosphorus." Vonnegut's evasion of any realistic description seems typical of the purely moral, unpolitical, widespread American sense of futility about our government's having made war in and on Indochina for an entire decade. Vietnam now colors all our thinking about earlier wars. Until Vietnam, Americans did not fully take in that theirs was a permanent war economy, totally bureaucratized for war, prepared to make war endlessly. In retrospect, even the fiction of the "separate peace" about the First World War, based on aristocratic disdain for politicians and humanist protest against the slaughter of a whole generation, seems more political than those American stories and reports of Vietnam that made a veteran correspondent there, once a hawk, finally say that "the war—or wars—has become as unreal and macabre as a bad trip in the East Village."

But, of course, the Vietnam War is not "a bad trip." Our disgust with the interminable killing may no longer be a strong enough emotion to write books with. Still, the disgust is all too understandable. The Vietnam War has been so sickeningly "covered" by television, by dogged journalists still looking for a "fresh angle" on the war, that the serious novelist trying to describe Vietnam finds himself outdone by the manic plenitude of American destructiveness there. There have been films on TV of American soldiers aboard boats pouring an unceasing fire into the forest as if they were spraying insecticide. The factory methods of Americans making war in Asia seem to defeat the most unreconstructed literary imagination. Even so strong and astringent a novel about the war in Vietnam as William Eastlake's *The Bamboo Bed* (and there haven't been many serious novels about Vietnam at all) finally seems to defeat itself. In Eastlake's book the Americans fight the Vietnamese as Americans once fought the Indians. The book is an indictment of our historic American ferocity, and is finally not about Vietnam but about all of America's wars. As in a nightmare, the Americans in this endless pageant-play of war no longer seem to know where they are or whom they are fighting, and the same war takes place over and again.

More than anything else, it is the American bad conscience over Vietnam that robs *The Bamboo Bed* of every effective quality but scorn. Eastlake is an excellent novelist, but with such a subject *nobody* comes off right in a novel—everyone is touched with the same guilt, just as the Asian forest absorbs and outlasts all the death we pour into it. The death of Captain Clancy, a brave, traditional American warrior, represents nothing but his own death, which means, in effect, the end of civilization. A single man's death in Vietnam has become a biological episode important only to his dwindling sensations. Nobody cares, for a dead man frightens us with the reality of *our* death.

Yet, meanwhile, in the "bamboo bed" itself, a helicopter on a search-and-rescue operation, a lieutenant and a nurse make love 10,000 feet above the battle. The helicopter, on automatic pilot, swoops and rises merrily through the air like a wild bird released. Most important, *The Bamboo Bed* is a satire on Hemingway's style and the Hemingway hero, for Captain Clancy is an old-fashioned American male devoted to the honor of his maleness. But what to do when the wars are no longer worthy of us, when we cannot exercise our maleness as true warriors the way Captain Clancy once did? Vietnam is the wrong place and time for those who still believe in war. Captain Clancy experiences total futility at everything in war but dying. No wonder General Westmoreland anticipates a time when war will be completely automated.

The Return of the Case
of Ezra Pound

By Irving Howe

October 24, 1972

The case of Ezra Pound, it begins to seem, will be with us forever. Like a bad dream, it keeps coming back, prodding us to struggle with difficult, perhaps insoluble problems: the relation of art to morality; the terms of aesthetic judgment when confronting literary works with a heavy ideological freight; the reasons a good many major twentieth-century writers succumbed to totalitarianism. Painful as it may be, this return to old issues has a positive value: It forces us to remember what might be more pleasant to forget.

Twenty-three years ago, in 1949, the Bollingen Award was given to Ezra Pound. The jury included such distinguished writers as T. S. Eliot, Robert Lowell, W. H. Auden, and Allen Tate. There followed a harsh dispute, in *Partisan Review* and elsewhere, concerning the ethical propriety of honoring a poet who, only a few years earlier, had been making wartime speeches on Mussolini's radio in praise of fascism and anti-Semitism. Now, this past summer, we have had a replay. The American Academy of Arts and Sciences decided to reject a subcommittee's recommendation that Pound be given its Emerson-Thoreau Award, whereupon followed a spate of resignations, statements, and letters to the editor almost as heated as those of 1949. Clearly this issue presses on a sensitive nerve, and just as clearly, neither side has succeeded in persuading the other of its rightness.

In 1949 I played a very small part in the Pound dispute, as one of those arguing against the award. While still of the same opinion, I hope now to avoid passionate declamations and instead try to elucidate the social and aesthetic issues entangled in this controversy. For quite apart from Pound himself, the issues in this dispute remain with us, bedeviling our judgments in any number of ways.

When the Bollingen Award to Pound was announced in 1949, he was a mental patient at St. Elizabeth's Hospital in Washington, D.C. At the end of the war Pound had fallen into the hands of the U.S. Army in Italy and by all accounts been badly mistreated; the result was a nervous breakdown. Brought back to the United States, he faced a possible charge of treason for his wartime broadcasts.

In 1949 he was put on trial and judged to be of "unsound mind." He was then confined to St. Elizabeth's, where he would remain in benign captivity for twelve years. Though cruelly prolonged, this sentence was perhaps a desirable evasion of what might otherwise have been the excruciating spectacle of a great or once-great poet being tried for conduct that could have brought far more severe punishment.

Some of Pound's defenders would later use the juridical verdict of "unsound mind" to dismiss or minimize the significance of his wartime broadcasts. Rarely, however, were they prepared to accept the consequences of their argument—first, that his speeches on the Italian radio were consistent with, if more extreme than, what he had been saying earlier, especially in his book *Guide to Kulchur*; and second, that if the verdict of "unsound mind" is to be seen as relevant to Pound's wartime activities (Prof. Harry Levin says that the "psychiatrists would seem to have absolved him" from "responsibility for antisocial behavior"), then that same verdict becomes embarrassingly relevant to the writings composed directly after the war and for which the Bollingen Award was honoring him. For how, one wonders, could a man of "unsound mind" have written a considerable quantity of verse without imprinting on it the marks of his condition?

Historical memory is painfully short; new horrors pile up on the old ones; younger generations prefer not to remember. So it may be useful to cite a few passages from Pound's wartime broadcasts:

[April 23, 1942] Any man who submits to Roosevelt's treason to the public commits a breach of citizen's duty. . . . Had you the sense to eliminate Roosevelt and his Jews . . . at the last election, you would not now be at war.

[May 10, 1942] England will certainly have nothing whatever to say about the terms [of the next peace]. Neither, I think, will simplehearted Joe Stalin, not wholly trusted by the kikery which is his master.

[May 26, 1942] Every sane act you commit is committed in homage to Mussolini and Hitler. . . . They are your leaders, however much you think you are conducted by Roosevelt or told up by Churchill. You follow Mussolini and Hitler in every constructive act of your government.

"Sound mind" or not, Pound was here repeating the standard line of the Hitler-Mussolini axis. If there was any doubt as to his sentiments, he put it to rest with an interview on May 25, 1945, in which he told a reporter that Hitler was "a Jeanne d'Arc, a saint . . . a martyr."

What makes the Pound case especially complicated is that in his long poem, *The Cantos*, to which he has kept adding over the years, Pound included some decidedly similar sentiments, ranging from a number of anti-Semitic passages to expressions of tenderness for Mussolini to such sickening lines as "Pétain defended Verdun while Blum/was defending a bidet." It therefore becomes difficult to make a clear-cut distinction of the kind urged by his supporters between the man who spoke in behalf of the Fascist powers and the poet who is to be judged solely on literary grounds.

The first major anti-Semitic passages occur in "Canto XXXV," published in the Thirties:

The tale of the perfect schnorrer: a peautiful chewisch poy
wit a vo-ice dot woult
meldt dh heart offa schtone
and wit a likeing for to make arhtvoiks
and ven dh oldt ladty wasn't dhere any more

and dey didn't know why, tdhere ee woss in the
oldt antique schop and nobodty knew how he got dhere

I suppose there are people who find this sort of
thing amusing and perhaps deaf-mutes who praise the
accuracy of the poet's ear. But in my judgment, even
if we grant that Pound's intentions may not have been
vicious, this passage shows that a highly cultured man
can be as sensitive as a street bum. "There is no point
in denying," writes Prof. Donald Davie in his sympathetic study of Pound, that such material in "Canto
XXXV" is anti-Semitic; indeed, there is a point in
asserting it. By the *Pisan Cantos*, published after the
war and the immediate occasion for the Bollingen
Award, the anti-Semitism is blunter and the intent
behind it utterly vicious:

the yidd is a stimulant, and the goyim are cattle in
gt / proportion and go to saleable slaughter with the
maximum of docility.

There are other anti-Semitic passages in *The Cantos*,
including a statement fraudulently attributed to Benjamin Franklin by an American Fascist newspaper, which
in 1934 Pound picked up without checking and threw
into his poem:

Remarked Ben: better keep out the jews or yr/ grand
children will curse you

How important, one may ask, are these anti-Semitic
passages in *The Cantos?* Are they central to the whole
thrust of the work or mere incidental blemishes? It
is hard to answer this question with complete as-
surance, since *The Cantos*, at least in my reading, are
a chaos of reflections, diatribes, vignettes, reminis-
cences, arguments, visions, and self-contained lyrics,
a grab bag of incoherence in which the mind of the
poet reveals itself without the benefit of disciplined
form. Quantitatively the percentage of anti-Semitic
passages is small, but thematically they are closely related to the whole political drift of the poem, which

at some points is explicitly Fascist and at other points supportive of the Fascist myth. In any case, how many outbursts of anti-Semitic venom would be required for Pound's defenders to acknowledge that they constituted more than an "incidental blemish"?

That Pound was a major force in the development of modern poetry; that he performed wonders in the chastening of the English language; that he often displayed a gift for metrical innovation; that he showed himself a teacher and colleague remarkably kind and helpful—all this, attested to in numerous memoirs and histories, is beyond challenge. But it does not tell us very much about the nature and quality of his major work.

Here I would call upon the testimony of Allen Tate, a poet who voted for giving the Bollingen Award to Pound in 1949 and who then passionately defended his position:

> As a result of observing Pound's use of language in the past thirty years, I had become convinced that he had done more than any other living man to regenerate the language, if not the imaginative forms, of English verse. I had to face the disagreeable fact that he had done this even in passages of verse in which the opinions expressed ranged from the childish to the detestable.

Now it seems to me possible to accept Tate's judgment while still disagreeing with him as to the propriety of the award—but of that more later. Let me quote from Tate what is, I believe, a crucial statement about *The Cantos*:

> The work for which I voted is formless, eccentric, and personal. *The Cantos* are . . . "about nothing at all." They have a voice but no subject. . . . Pound is incapable of sustained thought in either prose or verse. His acute verbal sensibility is thus at the mercy of random flights of "angelic insight," an Icarian self-

indulgence of prejudice which is not checked by a total view. . . .

And still more cogent:

> I have little sympathy with the view that holds that Pound's irresponsible opinions merely lie alongside the poetry, which thus remains uncontaminated by them. The disagreeable opinions are right in the middle of the poetry. And they have got to be seen for what they are . . . unrelated to a mature and coherent conception of life.

This seems to me an accurate description: "the disagreeable opinions are right in the middle of the poetry"—more accurate, I think, than Prof. Harry Levin's reference to "an artistic achievement flawed by certain problematic commitments."

Erza Pound summed up in his career the wrenching contradictions of modernist culture. He was a generous man committed to murderous ideology. A midwestern provincial let loose in the inferno of twentieth-century Europe, he pretended—with an arrogance too many other writers of his generation shared—to universal knowledge on everything from Chinese culture to economics and began to preach in verse and prose grandiose schemes for monetary reform that were marked by a simplistic illiteracy. His mind contained large amounts of historical information, but he had no ordered sense of European history—small wonder he could be taken in by a buffoon like Mussolini or suppose Stalin to be "simplehearted." *The Cantos*, with their linkage of Jefferson and Mussolini, their absurd celebration of Martin Van Buren, their rantings against the Rothschilds, are a junk shop of intellectual debris. (How morally bracing, by contrast, is James Joyce's sardonic remark in 1934, "I am afraid poor Mr. Hitler will soon have few friends in Europe apart from my nephews, Masters W. Lewis and E. Pound.") Yet there are also superb passages in *The Cantos*, brilliantly recorded dialogue, keen fragments of action, affecting lyrics. It is a work of that distinctly American type, the Crank as Genius—or near-Genius.

Here, for example, is a passage that brings together Pound's lyrical gifts with his obsession about usury—though it is important to note that "usura" figures here as a quite abstract category, so that one could easily substitute for it another term or concept, and what really matters is Pound's evocation of human dismay:

> With usura hath no man a house of good stone
> each block cut smooth and well fitting
> that design might cover their face,
> with usura
> hath no man a painted paradise on his church wall
>
> with usura, sin against nature,
> is thy bread ever more of stale rags
> is thy bread dry as paper,
> with no mountain wheat, no strong flour

And there is the single greatest passage in *The Cantos*, much quoted but not thereby any the less pleasurable:

> What thou lovest well remains, the rest is dross
> What thou lov'st well shall not be reft from thee
> What thou lov'st well is thy true heritage
>
> The ant's a centaur in his dragon world.
> Pull down thy vanity, it is not man
> Made courage, or made order, or made grace,
> Pull down thy vanity, I say pull down.

Written while Pound was a prisoner of the U.S. Army in Pisa, these lines reflect a softening of temper, the single boon of defeat. Toward individual persons Pound grew more merciful, his sufferings taught him that "No man who has passed a month in the death cell/believes in cages for beasts." And at the end:

> If the hoar frost grips thy tent
> Thou wilt give thanks when night is spent.

When the Bollingen judges announced their decision, they were aware that it might stir up a quantity of protest, and they therefore wrote: "To permit other considerations than that of poetic achievement to sway the decision would destroy the significance of the award and would in principle deny the validity of that objective perception of value on which any civilized society must rest."

Now, in principle, this is a statement with which anyone at all concerned for literature must surely be inclined to agree. The bitter experiences of our century have taught us that literary judgments should not be at the service of political movements or ideologies. Just as we are appalled at the Soviet government's persecution of Solzhenitsyn because of his anti-Communist opinions, so we should not allow, say, our distaste for Pablo Neruda's Communist opinions to impede our appreciation of his poetry or prejudice us against him in case he were being considered for an award. (But please notice a crucial difference: The issue in the Soviet Union is not whether the government should honor Solzhenitsyn but whether it should allow his books to be published; while in the Pound controversy the issue is not whether Pound should be censored, something that no responsible person has advocated, but whether he should be honored.)

We are all, or should all be, committed to the value of autonomous aesthetic judgment; but to say that is not yet to cope with the difficulties raised by a work like *The Cantos*. For in this case there can be no clear separation between the man and the poet, or his opinions and his creative work. Any effort to weigh Pound's "poetic achievement" must take into account the kinds of anti-Semitic passages I have quoted—passages that involve not only political beliefs with which one may or may not disagree but something far more fundamental in our moral life, emotions of hatred utterly repugnant. "How far is it possible," asked William Barrett in the Bollingen discussion, "for technical embellishments [or even, one might add, integral technical accomplishments—I. H.] to transform vicious and ugly matter into beautiful poetry?"

If we look at the anti-Semitic and Fascist passages in isolation, then there should be little difficulty in advancing a negative *literary* judgment, since they have no distinction of thought or language. If we ask what the weight of such passages may be in the work as a whole, then the problem becomes trickier: We must rely on our intelligence, our sense of tact, our view of the relation between the parts and the whole.

But perhaps I have gone too fast. There is a possible judgment suggested by Allen Tate, the most complicated of all, that might go like this: "Yes, these passages are indeed odious but even in them, as in *The Cantos* in their entirety, language is employed with such power and vividness that we have no choice but to overlook the detested content and praise the verbal achievement." This view, pushing the separation between form and content to an extreme, is one that I find hard to accept. Yet in honesty I must admit that it points to a fact in our experience of literature: the fact that we can at times find moving and significant a poem or novel that we may also find, in its controlling ideas, deplorable or offensive.

The question then becomes, how far can we push this kind of analysis? I confess that I have no general answer, only an appeal to a common experience of tact. Perhaps a few examples will help. I am greatly moved by John Donne's *Holy Sonnets*, even though I am not a Christian—but here it is simply a matter of grasping imaginatively the power of a religious outlook that is not mine yet has behind it an enormous penetrative grasp of human existence. I deeply admire Louis-Ferdinand Céline's novels, though I detest his fascism —but here it is simply a matter of making a neat distinction between his novels, authentic works of art almost entirely free of ideology, and his tracts, which are mere rubbish. I read with pleasure the poems of Bertolt Brecht, though I am repelled by his Stalinism— but here, not so simply, it is a matter of seeing how his subtlety of mind breaks past, complicates, and sometimes undercuts his ideological stance.

But—to turn to a writer of far less consequence— when I read LeRoi Jones calling for "dagger poems in the slimy bellies of the owner-jews" or urging black people to say "the magic words . . .: Up against the wall mother fucker this is a stick up!" to "Sears, Bambergers, Klein's, Hahnes', Chase, and the smaller joosh enterprises," then I know I am in the presence of a racist hoodlum inciting people to blood. And I am not going to be deflected from that perception by talk about rhythm, metaphor, and diction.

Erza Pound's *Cantos* fall somewhere between the two kinds of writing I have just noted, those in which intellectual disapproval does not significantly affect one's appreciation of a literary work and those in which the detestable matter is so gross, so ugly that there is nothing to appreciate. The truth is, then, that almost any literary statement about *The Cantos* is likely to have some validity and that the problem is to rank particular judgments into a proper discipline.

Let us therefore, if only for the sake of the argument but also for more than its sake, grant the "poetic achievement" of *The Cantos*. That still does not settle the problem of whether an award should have been given to its author. The argument put forward by Clement Greenberg in 1949 is a very serious one:

> I do not quarrel here with the aesthetic verdict, but I question its primacy in the affair at hand, a primacy that hints at an absolute acceptance of the autonomy not only of art but of every separate field of human activity. Does no hierarchy of value obtain among them? Would Mr. Eliot, for instance, approve of this for his "Christian society"?

It was considerations of this kind that led some of us to feel that even if the *Pisan Cantos* were indeed the best poetry of 1948, the award to Pound should still not have been given and that an appropriate response would have been: "Yes, Pound wrote the best poetry of this past year, but on those occasions when aesthetic standards and our central human values clash in fundamental ways, the latter can be more important. We do not wish in any way to harm Ezra Pound, but because of what he has done as both poet and man, we cannot extend to him that hand of admiration that a prize would signify."

Something, if only a word or two, needs to be said about "the autonomy of literature," the standard that has been raised as the main reason for favoring an award to Pound. The matter is very complicated, and all I wish to do here is to suggest that it is possible for a reasonable man to believe in the autonomy of literature while nevertheless holding to any one of several views on the Pound case.

By the autonomy of literature we mean, I would say, that a poem or novel has properties distinctive to itself; that such a work must be perceived, analyzed, and judged with categories distinctive to its kind; that it is an imaginative verbal composition, whch cannot be reduced to other kinds of communication since it involves a use of language different from the ways language may be used in exposition, argument, or exhortation. So far, with necessary verbal corrections, most critics would probably agree.

Difficulties arise when we try to discover the relations between this literary work and the external world of familiar experience. How are we to relate our experience of the literary work, an experience distinctive and irreducible, to the larger flow of human experience of which it is presumably a part?

Some critics, including myself, would say that even as they recognize that the work of literature constitutes a distinctive object, qualitatively different from any others, it also shares elements of valuation and perception with those employed both in our common experience and in our response to other kinds of verbal composition. The poem or novel is not a tract or a case study, but the materials it employs and the criteria by which it organizes them are drawn from experiences and perceptions that can also pertain to the tract or the case study. As a result, there cannot be a total discontinuity between the way we use precepts of morality and norms of social valuation in literary analysis and the way we use them in direct experience.

There is, however, another view, very powerful among literary people. This view insists that the work of literature is not merely autonomous in the sense of being distinctive but also, one might say, "separate" in kind, "self-sufficient" in its very being. It cannot really be understood by references back to external reality; it is not a mere imitation of the world we know; it inhabits a universe of its own. Consequently statements in a poem may not be understood or judged as if they had been made in direct speech, for the "aesthetic transaction" has its own norms and justifications.

Now, even this hurried description ought to suggest the ways in which contrasting aesthetic premises may lead to sharply varying responses to the Pound case— as it also suggests that a belief in the autonomy of literature does not automatically confirm any response. Granted that a poem is not, in any ordinary sense, a statement, what are we to make of the statements that occur within the poem? That is the question with which we end and it is perhaps just as well to leave it at that. I would only add that Pound himself has never taken shelter in any aestheticist defense, but has always insisted on the continuity of his life, his thought, and his work.

There remains one argument, a troubling argument, for granting Pound an award in 1972, though not in 1949: "It was right to refuse in 1949 to join in honoring Pound, but now time has passed, the old poet has endured enough suffering, so that we should be ready to forgive him. What is more, in a 1968 interview with Allen Ginsburg, Pound expressed his regret for having made anti-Semitic statements." This argument appeals to one's humane impulses—who would not like to think himself capable of forgiving those who have wronged him? But I wonder whether it is pertinent here.

Insofar as I am concerned, or anyone else involved in the Pound dispute, there is nothing to forgive. Pound has not wronged me in any direct way, and I am ready to suppose that if I had chanced to visit him a few decades ago, as a fledgling critic eager to talk to a master poet, he would have been as generous to me as he was to many others—even though I happen to be a Jew.

Yet that is precisely what makes one feel so complete a despair about literary anti-Semitism. Pound wished none of us personal harm; his rantings against the Jews were utterly *abstract*, a phantasm of ideology that is a major dimension of their terribleness. It was a theological hatred that he was releasing, a hatred that never sought a particular victim or even envisaged the consequences of its rhetoric; all one can charge him with— all!—is a blind complicity in the twentieth century's victimization of innocents.

We may then wonder: Does anyone have the right to forgive Ezra Pound? Who could grant me or any other person the right to speak for those millions who paid the final price for anti-Semitism? It might be said by way of reply that neither have I nor has anyone else been granted the right to refuse Pound forgiveness. And I would entirely agree with that, too.

But the question of whether to honor Pound involves neither the granting nor the refusal of forgiveness. It involves something else: I do not believe that we can yet close the books of twentieth-century history, certainly not as long as any of us remains alive who can remember the days of the mass murder. The wounds have not healed, and for some they never will. That is why the time has not come when Ezra Pound should be honored by his fellow writers. For it is not at all a matter of forgiving; it is a matter of remembering.

The Story of a Novel

By Thomas Wolfe

December 14, 1935

A great editor, who is also a good friend of mine, told me about six months ago that he was sorry he had not kept a diary about the work that both of us were doing, the whole stroke, catch, flow, stop, and ending, the ten thousand fittings, changings, triumphs, and surrenders that went into the making of a book. This editor remarked that some of it was fantastic, much incredible, all astonishing, and he was also kind enough to say that the whole experience was the most interesting he had known during the twenty-five years he had been a member of the publishing business.

I propose to tell about this experience. I cannot tell anyone how to write books; I cannot attempt to give anyone rules whereby he will be enabled to get his books published by publishers or his stories accepted by high-paying magazines. I am not a professional writer; I am not even a skilled writer; I am just a writer who is on the way to learning his profession and to discovering the line, the structure, and the articulation of the language which I must discover if I do the work I want to do. It is for just this reason, because I blunder, because every energy of my life and talent is still involved in this process of discovery, that I am speaking as I speak here. I am going to tell the way in which I wrote a book. It will be intensely personal. It was the most intense part of my life for several years. There is nothing very literary about it. It is a story of sweat and pain and despair and partial achievement. I don't know how to write a story yet. I don't know how to write a novel yet. But I have learned something about myself and about the work of writing, and if I can, I am going to try to tell what it is.

I don't know when it occurred to me first that I would be a writer. I suppose that like a great many other children in this country of my generation, I may have thought that it would be a fine thing because a writer was a man like Lord Byron or Lord Tennyson or Longfellow or Percy Bysshe Shelley. A writer was a man who was far away like these people I have mentioned, and since I was myself an American and an American not of the wealthy or university-going sort of people, it seemed to me that a writer was a man from a kind of remote people that I could never approach. I don't know how I became a writer, but I think it was because of a certain force in me that had to write and that finally burst through and found a channel. My people were of the working class of people. My father, a stonecutter, was a man with a great respect and veneration for literature. He had a tremendous memory, and he loved poetry, and the poetry that he loved best was naturally of the rhetorical kind that such a man would like. Nevertheless it was good poetry, Hamlet's Soliloquy, *Macbeth,* Mark Antony's Funeral Oration, Gray's "Elegy," and all the rest of it. I heard it all as a child; I memorized and learned it all.

He sent me to college to the state university. The desire to write which had been strong during all my days in high school, grew stronger still. I was editor of the college paper, the college magazine, etc., and in my last year or two I was a member of a course in playwriting which had just been established there. I wrote several little one-act plays, still thinking I would become a lawyer or a newspaper man, never daring to believe I could seriously become a writer. Then I went to Harvard, wrote some more plays there, became obsessed with the idea that I had to be a playwright, left Harvard, had my plays rejected, and finally in the autumn of 1926, how, why, or in what manner I have never exactly been able to determine, I began to write my first book in London. I was living all alone at that time. I had two rooms—a bedroom and a sitting room—in a little square in Chelsea in which all the houses had that familiar, smoked brick and cream-yellow-plaster look of London houses. They looked exactly alike.

As I say, I was living alone at that time and in a foreign country. I did not know why I was there or what the direction of my life should be, and that was the way I began to write my book. I think that is one of the hardest times a writer goes through. There is no standard, no outward judgment, by which he can measure what he has done. By day I would write for hours in big ledgers which I had bought for the purpose; then at night I would lie in bed and fold my hands behind my head and think of what I had done that day and hear the solid, leather footbeat of the London bobby as he came by my window, and remember that I was born in North Carolina and wonder why the hell I was now in London lying in the darkened bed, and thinking about words I had that day put down on paper. I would get a great, hollow, utterly futile feeling inside me, and then I would get up and switch on the light and read the words I had written that day, and then I would wonder: why am I here now? why have I come? I worked there every day with such feelings as I have described, and came back to America in the winter and worked here. I would teach all day and write all night, and finally about two and a half years after I had begun the book in London, I finished it in New York.

I should like to tell about this, too. I was very young at the time, and I had the kind of wild, exultant vigor which a man has at that period of his life. The book took hold of me and possessed me. In a way, I think it shaped itself. Like every young man, I was strongly under the influence of writers I admired. One of the chief writers at that time was Mr. James Joyce with his book *Ulysses*. The book that I was writing was much influenced, I believe, by his own book, and yet the powerful energy and fire of my own youth played over and, I think, possessed it all. Like Mr. Joyce, I wrote about things that I had known, the immediate life and experience that had been familiar to me in my childhood. Unlike Mr. Joyce, I had no literary experience. I had never had anything published before. My feeling toward writers, publishers, books, that whole fabulous faraway world, was almost as romantically unreal as when I was a child. And yet my book, the characters with which I had peopled it, the color and the weather of the universe which I had created, had possessed me, and so I wrote and wrote with that bright flame with which a young man writes who never has been published, and who yet is sure all will be good and must go well. This is a curious thing and hard to tell about, yet easy to understand in every writer's mind. I wanted fame, as every youth who ever wrote must want it, and yet fame was a shining, bright, and most uncertain thing.

The book was finished in my twenty-eighth year. I knew no publishers and no writers. A friend of mine took the huge manuscript—it was about 350,000 words long—and sent it to a publisher whom she knew. In a few days, a week or two, I received an answer from this man saying that the book could not be published. The gist of what he said was that his house had published several books like it the year before, that all of them had failed, and that, further, the book in its present form was so amateurish, autobiographical, and unskillful that a publisher could not risk a chance on it. I was, myself, so depressed and weary by this time, the illusion of creation which had sustained me for two and a half years had so far worn off, that I believed what the man said. At that time I was a teacher in one of New York's great universities, and when the year came to a close, I went abroad. It was only after I had been abroad almost six months that news came to me from another publisher in America that he had read my manuscript and would like to talk to me about it as soon as I came home.

I came home on New Year's Day that year. The next day I called up the publisher who had written me. He asked me if I would come to his office and talk to him. I went at once, and before I had left his office that morning, I had signed a contract and had a check for five hundred dollars in my hand.

It was the first time, so far as I can remember, that anyone had concretely suggested to me that anything I had written was worth as much as fifteen cents, and I know that I left the publisher's office that day and entered into the great swarm of men and women who passed constantly along Fifth Avenue at Forty-eighth

Street and that presently I found myself at a Hundred and Tenth Street, and from that day to this I have never known how I got there.

For the next six or eight months I taught at the university and worked upon the manuscript of my book with this great editor. The book appeared in the month of October, 1929. The whole experience still had elements of that dreamlike terror and unreality that writing had had for me when I had first begun it seriously and had lain in my room in London with my hands below my head and thought why am I here now? The awful, utter nakedness of print, that thing which is for all of us so namelessly akin to shame, came closer day by day. That I had wanted this exposure, I could not believe. It seemed to me that I had shamelessly exposed myself and yet that subtle drug of my desire and my creating held me with a serpent's eye, and I could do no other. I turned at last to this editor who had worked with me and found me, and I asked him if he could foretell the end and verdict of my labor. He said that he would rather tell me nothing, that he could not prophesy or know what profit I would have. He said, "All that I know is that they cannot let it go, they cannot ignore it. The book will find its way."

And that fairly describes what happened. I have read in recent months that this first book was received with what is called a "storm of critical applause," but this really did not happen. It got some wonderful reviews in some places; it got some unfavorable reviews in others, but it unquestionably did have a good reception for a first book, and what was best of all, as time went on, it continued to make friends among people who read books. It continued to sell over a period of four or five years in the publisher's edition, and later in a cheaper edition, The Modern Library, it renewed its life and began to sell again. The upshot of it was that after the publication of this book in the autumn of 1929, I found myself with a position as a writer. And here one of the first of my great lessons as a writer began.

Up to this time I had been a young man who wanted to be a writer more than anything on earth and who had created his first book in the great blaze of illusion which a young writer must feel when he has no evidence except his hope to drive him on. Now, in a certain measure, this had changed. I had been a writer in hope and in desire before and now I was a writer in fact. I would read about myself, for example, as one of the "younger American writers." I was a person who, some of the critics said, was to be watched. They were looking forward to my future book with interest and with a certain amount of apprehension. Here, too, my education as a writer was increasing all the time. Now, indeed, I could hear myself discussed, and somehow the fact was far more formidable than I had dreamed that it could be. It worried me, confused me, gave me a strange feeling of guilt and responsibility. I was a young American writer, and they had hopes and fears about my future, and what would I do, or would it be anything, nothing, much, or little? Would the faults which they had found in my work grow worse or would I conquer them? Was I another flash in the pan? Would I come through? What would happen to me?

I let it worry me. I would go home at night and look around my room and see that morning's coffee cup still unwashed and books on the floor and a shirt where I had thrown it the night before and great stacks of manuscript and everything so common and familiar-looking and so disorderly, and then I would think that I was now a young American writer; that somehow I was practicing an imposture on my readers and my critics because my shirt looked the way it did and my books and my bed—not, you understand, because they were disorderly, common, familiar, but just because they looked the way they did.

But now another fact began to gnaw a way into my consciousness.

The critics had begun to ask questions about the second book, and so now I had to think about the second one as well. I had always wanted to think about the second one and the thirty-second one and the fifty-second one. I had been sure that I had a hundred books in me, that all of them would be good, that each of them would make me famous. But here again was a strange and jolting transition from wild hope and exultant conviction; and plain, blazing fact remained. Now that I had actually written one book and THEY, the actual readers and the critics who had read it, were looking for a second, I was up against it. I was not up against it the way I dreaded, I was just up against it cold and hard as one comes up against a wall. I was a writer. I had made the writer's life my life; there was no going back; I had to go on. What could I do? After the first book there had to be a second book. What was the second book to be about? Where would it come from?

This inexorable fact, although it became more and more pressing, did not bother me so much at first. Rather I was concerned with many other things that had to do with the publication of that first book, and, as before, I had foreseen none of them. In the first place, I had not foreseen one fact which becomes absolutely plain after a man has written a book, but which he cannot foresee until he has written one. This fact is that one writes a book not in order to remember it, but in order to forget it, and now this fact was evident. As soon as the book was in print, I began to forget about it, I wanted to forget about it, I didn't want people to talk to me or question me about it. I just wanted them to leave me alone and shut up about it. And yet I longed desperately for my book's success. I wanted it to have the position of proud esteem and honor in the world that I longed for it to have—I wanted, in short, to be a successful and a famous man, and I wanted to lead the same kind of obscure and private life I'd always had and not to be told about my fame and success.

From this problem, another painful and difficult situation was produced. I had written my book, more or less, directly from the experience of my own life, and, furthermore, I now think that I may have written it with a certain naked intensity of spirit which is likely to characterize the earliest work of a young writer. At any rate, I can honestly say that I did not foresee what was to happen. I was surprised not only by the kind of response my book had with the critics and the general public, I was most of all surprised with the response it had in my native town. I had thought there might be a hundred people in that town who would read the book, but if there were a hundred outside of the Negro population, the blind, and the positively illiterate who did not read it, I do not know where they are. For months the town seethed with a fury of resentment which I had not believed possible. The book was denounced from the pulpit by the ministers of the leading churches. Men collected on street corners to denounce it. For weeks the women's clubs, bridge parties, teas, receptions, book clubs, the whole complex fabric of a small town's social life was absorbed by an outraged clamor. I received anonymous letters full of vilification and abuse, one which threatened to kill me if I came back home, others which were merely obscene. One venerable old lady, whom I had known all my life, wrote me that although she had never believed in lynch law, she would do nothing to prevent a mob from dragging my "big overgroan karkus" across the public square. She informed me further, that my mother had taken to her bed "as white as a ghost" and would "never rise from it again."

There were many other venomous attacks from my home town and for the first time I learned another lesson which every young writer has got to learn. And that lesson is the naked, blazing power of print. At that time it was for me a bewildering and almost overwhelming situation. My joy at the success my book had won mixed with bitter chagrin at its reception in my native town. And yet I think I learned something from that experience, too. For the first time I was forced to consider squarely this problem: where does the material of an artist come from? What are the proper uses of that material, and how far must his freedom in the use of that material be controlled by his responsibility as a member of society? This is a difficult problem, and I have by no means come to the bottom of it yet. Perhaps I never will, but as a result of all the distress which I suffered at that time and which others may have suffered on account of me, I have done much thinking and arrived at certain conclusions.

My book was what is often referred to as an autobiographical novel. I protested against this term in a preface to the book upon the grounds that any serious work of creation is of necessity autobiographical and that few more autobiographical works than *Gulliver's Travels* have ever been written. I added that Dr. Johnson had remarked that a man might turn over half the volumes in his library to make a single book, and that in a similar way, a novelist might turn over half the characters in his native town to make a single figure for his novel. In spite of this the people in my native town were not persuaded or appeased, and the charge of autobiography was brought against me in many other places.

As I have said, my conviction is that all serious creative work must be at bottom autobiographical, and that a man must use the material and experience of his own life if he is to create anything that has substantial value. But I also believe now that the young writer is often led through inexperience to a use of the materials of life which are, perhaps, somewhat too naked and direct for the purpose of a work of art. The thing a young writer is likely to do is to confuse the limits between actuality and reality. He tends unconsciously to describe an event in such a way because it actually happened that way, and from an artistic point of view, I can now see that this is wrong. It is not, for example, important that one remembers a beautiful woman of easy virtue as having come from the state of Kentucky in the year 1907. She could perfectly well have come from Idaho or Texas or Nova Scotia. The important thing really is only to express as well as possible the character and quality of the beautiful woman of easy virtue. But the young writer, chained to fact and to his own inexperience, as yet unliberated by maturity, is likely to argue, "she must be described as coming from Kentucky because that is where she actually did come from."

In spite of this, it is impossible for a man who has the stuff of creation in him to make a literal transcription of his own experience. Everything in a work of art is changed and transfigured by the personality of the artist. And as far as my own first book is concerned, I can truthfully say that I do not believe that there is a single page of it that is true to fact. And from this circumstance, also, I learned another curious thing about writing. For although my book was not true to fact, it was true to the general experience of the town I came from and I hope, of course, to the general experience of all men living. The best way I can describe the situation is this: it was as if I were a sculptor who had found a certain kind of clay with which to model. Now a farmer who knew well the neighborhood from which this clay had come might pass by and find the sculptor at his work and say to him, "I know the farm from which you got that clay." But it would be unfair of him to say, "I know the figure, too." Now I think what happened in my native town is that having seen the clay, they became immediately convinced that they recognized the figure, too, and the results of this misconception were so painful and ludicrous that the telling of it is almost past belief.

It was my experience to be assured by people from my native town not only that they remembered incidents and characters in my first book, which may have had some basis in actuality, but also that they remembered incidents which so far as I know had no historical basis whatever. For example, there was one scene in the book in which a stonecutter is represented as selling to a notorious woman of the town a statue of a marble angel which he has treasured for many years. So far as I know, there was no basis in fact for this story, and yet I was informed by several people later that they not only remembered the incident perfectly, but had actually been witnesses to the transaction. Nor was this the end of the story. I heard that one of the newspapers sent a reporter and a photographer to the cemetery and a photograph was printed in the paper with a statement to the effect that the angel was the now famous angel which had stood upon the stonecutter's porch for so many years and had given the title to my book. The unfortunate part of this proceeding was that I had never seen or heard of this angel before, and that this angel was, in fact, erected over the grave of a well-known Methodist lady who had died a few years before and that her indignant family had immediately written the paper to demand a retraction of its story, saying that their mother had been in no way connected with the infamous book or the infamous angel which had given the infamous book its name. Such, then, were some of the unforeseen difficulties with which I was confronted after the publication of my first book.

Month was passing into month, I had had a success. The way was opened to me. There was only one thing for me to do and that was work, and I was spending my time consuming myself with anger, grief, and useless passion about the reception the book had had in my native town, or wasting myself again in exuberant elation because of the critics' and the readers' praise, or in anguish and bitterness because of their ridicule. For the first time, I realized the nature of one of the artist's greatest conflicts, and was faced with the need of meeting it. For the first time I saw not only that the artist must live and sweat and love and suffer and enjoy as other men, but that the artist must also work as other men and that furthermore, he must work even while these common events of life are going on. It seems a simple and banal assertion, but I learned it hardly, and in one of the worst moments of my life. There is no such thing as an artistic vacuum; there is no such thing as a time when the artist may work in a delightful atmosphere, free of agony that other men must know, or if the artist ever does find such a time, it is something not to be hoped for, something not to be sought for definitely.

At any rate, while my life and energy were absorbed in the emotional vortex which my first book had created, I was getting almost no work done on the second. And now I was faced with another fundamental problem which every young writer must meet squarely if he is to continue. How is a man to get his writing done? How long should he work at writing? and how often? What kind of method, if any, must he find in following his work? I suddenly found myself face to face with the grim necessity of constant, daily work. And as simple as this discovery may seem to everyone, I was not prepared for it. A young writer without a public does not feel the sense of necessity, the pressure of time, as does a writer who has been published and who must now begin to think of time schedules, publishing seasons, the completion of his next book. I realized suddenly with a sense of definite shock that I had let six months go by since the publication of my first book and that, save for a great many notes and fragments, I had done nothing. Meanwhile, the book continued to sell slowly but steadily, and in February 1930, about five months after its publication, I found it possible to resign from the faculty of New York University and devote my full time to the preparation of a second book. That spring I was also fortunate enough to be awarded the Guggenheim Fellowship which would enable me to live and work abroad for a year. And accordingly at the beginning of May, I went abroad again.

I was in Paris for a couple of months, until the middle of July, and although I now compelled myself to work for four or five hours a day, my effort at composition was still confused and broken, and there was nothing yet that had the structural form and unity of a book. The life of the great city fascinated me as it had always done, but also aroused all the old feelings of naked homelessness, rootlessness, and loneliness which I have always felt there. During that summer in Paris, I think I felt this great homesickness more than ever before, and I really believe that from this emotion, this constant and almost intolerable effort of memory and desire, the material and the structure of the books I now began to write were derived.

The quality of my memory is characterized, I believe, in a more than ordinary degree by the intensity of its sense impressions, its power to evoke and bring back the odors, sounds, colors, shapes, and feel of things with concrete vividness. Now my memory was at work night and day, in a way that I could at first neither check nor control and that swarmed unbidden in a stream of blazing pageantry across my mind, with the million forms and substances of the life that I had left, which was my own, America. I would be sitting, for example, on the terrace of a café watching the flash and play of life before me on the Avenue de l'Opéra and suddenly I would remember the iron railing that goes along the boardwalk at Atlantic City. I could see it instantly just the way it was, the heavy iron pipe; its raw galvanized look; the way the joints were fitted together. It was all so vivid and concrete that I could feel my hand upon it and know the exact dimensions, its size and weight and shape. And suddenly I would realize that I had never seen any railing that looked like this in Europe. And this utterly familiar, common thing would suddenly be revealed to me with all the wonder with which we discover a thing which we have seen all our life and yet have never known before. Or again, it would be a bridge, the look of an old iron bridge across an American river, the sound the train makes as it goes across it; the spoke-and-hollow rumble of the ties below; the look of the muddy banks; the slow, thick, yellow wash of an American river; an old flat-bottomed boat half filled with water stogged in the muddy bank. Or again, it would be an American street with all its jumble of a thousand ugly architectures. It would be Montague Street or Fulton Street in Brooklyn, or Eleventh Street in New York, or other streets where I had lived; and suddenly I would see the gaunt and savage webbing of the elevated structure along Fulton Street, and how the light swarmed through in dusty, broken bars, and I could remember the old, familiar rusty color, that incomparable rusty color that gets into so many things here in America. And this also would be like something I had seen a million times and lived with all my life.

I would sit there, looking out upon the Avenue de l'Opéra and my life would ache with the whole memory of it; the desire to see it again; somehow to find a word for it; a language that would tell its shape, its color, the way we have all known and felt and seen it. And when I understood this thing, I saw that I must find for myself the tongue to utter what I knew but could not say. And from the moment of that discovery, the line and purpose of my life was shaped. The end toward which every energy of my life and talent would be henceforth directed was in such a way as this defined. It was as if I had discovered a whole new universe of chemical elements and had begun to see certain relations between some of them but had by no means begun to organize the whole series into a harmonious and coherent union. From this time on, I think my efforts might be described as the effort to complete that organization, to discover that articulation for which I strove, to bring about that final coherent union. I know that I have failed thus far in doing so, but I believe I understand pretty thoroughly just where the nature of my failure lies, and of course my deepest and most earnest hope is that the time will come when I will not fail.

At any rate, from this time on the general progress of the three books which I was to write in the next four and a half years could be fairly described in somewhat this way. It was a progress that began in a whirling vortex and a creative chaos and that proceeded slowly at the expense of infinite confusion, toil, and error toward clarification and the articulation of an ordered and formal structure. An extraordinary image remains to me from that year, the year I spent abroad when the material of these books first began to take on an articulate form. It seemed that I had inside me, swelling and gathering all the time, a huge black cloud, and that this cloud was loaded with electricity, pregnant, crested, with a kind of hurricane violence that could not be held in check much longer; that the moment was approaching fast when it must break. Well, all I can say is that the storm did break. It broke that summer while I was in Switzerland. It came in torrents, and it is not over yet.

I cannot really say the book was written. It was something that took hold of me and possessed me, and before I was done with it—that is, before I finally emerged with the first completed part—it seemed to me that it had done for me. It was exactly as if this great black storm cloud I have spoken of had opened up and, mid flashes of lightning, was pouring from its depth a torrential and ungovernable flood. Upon that flood everything was swept and borne along as by a great river. And I was borne along with it.

There was nothing at first which could be called a novel. I wrote about night and darkness in America, and the faces of the sleepers in ten thousand little towns; and of the tides of sleep and how the rivers flowed forever in the darkness. I wrote about the hissing glut of tides upon ten thousand miles of coast; of how the moonlight blazed down on the wilderness and filled the cat's cold eye with blazing yellow. I wrote about death and sleep, and of that enfabled rock of life we call the city. I wrote about October, of great trains that thundered through the night, of ships and stations in the morning; of men in harbors and the traffic of the ships.

I spent the winter of that year in England from October until March, and here perhaps because of the homely familiarity of the English life, the sense of order and repose which such a life can give one, my work moved forward still another step from this flood tide chaos of creation. For the first time the work began to take on the lineaments of design. These lineaments were still confused and broken, sometimes utterly lost, but now I really did get the sense at last that I was working on a great block of marble, shaping a figure which no one but its maker could as yet define, but which was emerging more and more into the sinewy lines of composition.

From the beginning—and this was one fact that in all my times of hopelessness returned to fortify my faith in my conviction—the idea, the central legend that I wished my book to express had not changed. And this central idea was this: the deepest search in life, it seemed to me, the thing that in one way or another was central to all living was man's search to find a father, not merely the father of his flesh, not merely the lost father of his youth, but the image of a strength and wisdom external to his need and superior to his hunger, to which the belief and power of his own life could be united.

Yet I was terribly far away from the actual accomplishment of a book—how far away I could not at that time foresee. But four more years would have to pass before the first of the series of books on which I was now embarked would be ready for the press, and if I could have known that in those next four years there would be packed a hundred lives of birth and death, despair, defeat, and triumph and the sheer exhaustion of a brute fatigue, I do not know whether or not I could have found the power within myself to continue. But I was still sustained by the exuberant optimism of youth. My temperament, which is pessimistic about many things, has always been a curiously sanguine one concerning time, and although more than a year had now gone by and I had done no more than write great chants on death and sleep, prepare countless notes and trace here and there the first dim outlines of a formal pattern, I was confident that by the spring or the fall of the next year my book would somehow miraculously be ready.

So far as I can describe with any accuracy, the progress of that winter's work in England was not along the lines of planned design, but along this line that I have mentioned—writing some of the sections which I knew would have to be in the book. Meanwhile what was really going on in my whole creative consciousness, during all this time, although I did not realize it at the moment, was this: What I was really doing, what I had been doing all the time since my discovery of my America in Paris the summer before, was to explore day by day and month by month with a fanatic intensity, the whole material domain of my resources as a man and as a writer. This exploration went on for a period which I can estimate conservatively as two years and a half. It is still going on, although not with the same all-absorbing and fanatical intensity, because the work it led to, the work that after infinite waste and labor it helped me wonderfully to define, that work has reached such a state of final definition that the immediate task of finishing it is the one that now occupies my energy and interest.

In a way, during that period of my life, I think I was like the Ancient Mariner who told the Wedding Guest that his frame was wrenched by the woeful agony which forced him to begin his tale before it left him free. In my own experience, my wedding guests were the great ledgers in which I wrote, and the tale which I told to them would have seemed, I am afraid, completely incoherent, as meaningless as Chinese characters, had any reader seen them. I could by no means hope to give a comprehensive idea of its whole extent because three years of work and perhaps a million and a half words went into these books. It included everything from gigantic and staggering lists of the towns, cities, counties, states, and countries I had been in, to minutely thorough, desperately evocative descriptions of the undercarriage, the springs, wheels, flanges, axle rods, color, weight, and quality of the day coach of an American railway train. There were lists of the rooms and houses in which I had lived or in which I had slept for at least a night, together with the most accurate and evocative descriptions of those rooms that I could write—their size, their shape, the color and design of the wallpaper, the way a towel hung down, the way a chair creaked, a streak of water rust upon the ceiling. There were countless charts, catalogues, descriptions that I can only classify here under the general heading of Amount and Number. What were the total combined populations of all the countries in Europe and America? In how many of those countries had I had some personal and vital experience? In the course of my twenty-nine or thirty years of living, how many people had I seen? How many had I passed by on the streets? How many had I seen on trains and subways, in theaters, at baseball or football games? With how many had I actually had some vital and illuminating experience, whether of joy, pain, anger, pity, love, or simple casual companionship, however brief?

In addition, one might come upon other sections under some such cryptic heading as "Where now?" Under such a heading as this, there would be brief notations of those thousands of things which all of us have seen for just a flash, a moment in our lives, which seem to be of no consequence whatever at the moment that we see them, and which live in our minds and hearts forever, which are somehow pregnant with all the joy and sorrow of the human destiny, and which we know, somehow, are therefore more important than many things of more apparent consequence. "Where now?" Some quiet steps that came and passed along a leafy nighttime street in summer in a little town down South long years ago; a woman's voice, her sudden burst of low and tender laughter; then the voices and the footsteps going, silence, the leafy rustle of the trees. "Where now?" Two trains that met and paused at a little station at some little town at some unknown moment upon the huge body of the continent; a girl who looked and smiled from the window of the other train; another passing in a motorcar on the streets of Norfolk; the winter boarders in a little boardinghouse down South twenty years ago; Miss Florrie Mangle, the trained nurse; Miss Jessie Rimmer, the cashier at Reed's drugstore; Dr. Richards, the clairvoyant; the pretty girl who cracked the whip and thrust her head into the lion's mouth with Johnny J. Jones Carnival and Combined Shows.

"Where now?" It went beyond the limits of man's actual memory. It went back to the farthest adytum of his childhood before conscious memory had begun, the way he thought he must have felt the sun one day and heard Peagram's cow next door wrenching the coarse grass against the fence, or heard the streetcar stop upon the hill above his father's house at noon; and Earnest Peagram coming home to lunch, his hearty voice in midday greeting; and then the streetcar going, the sudden lonely green-gold silence of the streetcar's absence and an iron gate slamming, then the light of that lost day fades out. "Where now?" He can recall no more and does not know if what he has recalled is fact or fable or a fusion of the two. Where now—in these great ledger books, month after month, I wrote such things as this. Not only the concrete, material record of man's ordered memory, but all the things he scarcely dares to think he has remembered; all the flicks and darts and haunting lights that flash across the mind of man that will return unbidden at an unexpected moment; a voice once heard; a face that vanished; the way the sunlight came and went; the rustling of a leaf upon a bough; a stone, a leaf, a door.

It may be objected, it has been objected already by certain critics, that in such research as I have here attempted to describe there is a quality of intemperate excess, an almost insane hunger to devour the entire body of human experience, to attempt to include more, experience more, than the measure of one life can hold, or than the limits of a single work of art can well define. I readily admit the validity of this criticism. I think I realize as well as anyone the fatal dangers that are consequent to such a ravenous desire, the damage it may wreak upon one's life and on one's work. But having had this thing within me, it was in no way possible for me to reason it out of me, no matter how cogently my reason worked against it. The only way I could meet it was to meet it squarely not with reason, but with life.

It was part of my life; for many years it was my life; and the only way I could get it out of me was to live it out of me. And that is what I did. I have not wholly succeeded in that purpose yet, but I have succeeded better than I at one time dared to hope. And now I really believe that so far as the artist is concerned, the unlimited extent of human experience is not so important for him as the depth and intensity with which he experiences things. I also know now that it is a great deal more important to have known one hundred living men and women in New York, to have understood their lives, to have got, somehow, at the root and source from which their natures came than to have seen or passed or talked with 7,000,000 people upon the city streets. And what finally I should most like to say about this research which I have attempted to describe is this: That foolish and mistaken as much of it may seem, the total quality, end, and impact of that whole experience was not useless or excessive. And from my own point of view, at least, it is in its whole implication the one thing I may have to tell about my experience as a writer which may be of some concrete value to other people. I consider this experience on the whole the most valuable and practical in my whole life thus far as a writer. With all the waste and error and confusion it led me into, it brought me closer to a concrete definition of my resources, a true estimate of my talents at this period of my life, and, most of all, toward a rudimentary, a just-beginning, but a living apprehension of the articulation I am looking for, the language I have got to have if, as an artist, my life is to proceed and grow, than any other thing that has ever happened to me.

I know the door is not yet open. I know the tongue, the speech, the language that I seek is not yet found, but I believe with all my heart that I have found the way, have made a channel, am started on my first beginning. And I believe with all my heart, also, that each man for himself and in his own way, each man who ever hopes to make a living thing out of the substances of his one life, must find that way, that language, and that door—must find it for himself as I have tried to do.

When I returned to America in the spring of 1931, although I had three or four hundred thousand words of material, I had nothing that could be published as a novel. Almost a year and a half had elapsed since the publication of my first book and already people had begun to ask that question which is so well meant, but which as year followed year was to become more intolerable to my ears than the most deliberate mockery: "Have you finished your next book yet?" "When is it going to be published?"

At this time I was sure that a few months of steady work would bring the book to completion. I found a place, a little basement flat in the Assyrian quarter in South Brooklyn, and there I went about my task.

The spring passed into the summer; the summer, into autumn. I was working hard, day after day, and still nothing that had the unity and design of a single work appeared. October came and with it a second full year since the publication of my first book. And now, for the first time, I was irrevocably committed so far as the publication of my book was concerned. I began to feel the sensation of pressure, and of naked desperation which was to become almost maddeningly intolerable in the next three years. For the first time I began to realize that my project was much larger than I thought it was. I had still believed at the time of my return from Europe that I was writing a single book, which would be comprised within the limits of about 200,000 words.

Now as scene followed scene, as character after character came into being, as my understanding of my material became more comprehensive, I discovered that it would be impossible to write the book I had planned within the limits I had thought would be sufficient.

All of this time I was being baffled by a certain time element in the book, by a time relation which could not be escaped, and for which I was now desperately seeking some structural channel. There were three time elements inherent in the material. The first and most obvious was an element of actual present time, an element which carried the narrative forward, which represented characters and events as living in the present and moving forward into an immediate future. The second time element was of past time, one which represented these same characters as acting and as being acted upon by all the accumulated impact of man's experience so that each moment of their life was conditioned not only by what they experienced in that moment, but by all that they had experienced up to that moment. In addition to these two time elements, there was a third which I conceived as being time immutable, the time of rivers, mountains, oceans, and the earth; a kind of eternal and unchanging universe of time against which would be projected the transience of man's life, the bitter briefness of his day. It was the tremendous problem of these three time elements that almost defeated me and that cost me countless hours of anguish in the years that were to follow.

As I began to realize the true nature of the task I had set for myself, the image of the river began to haunt my mind. I actually felt that I had a great river thrusting for release inside of me and that I had to find a channel into which its floodlike power could pour. I knew I had to find it or I would be destroyed in the flood of my own creation, and I am sure that every artist who ever lived has had the same experience.

Meanwhile, I was being baffled by a fixed and impossible idea whose error at the time I did not fully apprehend. I was convinced at that time that this whole gigantic plan had to be realized within the limits of a single book which would be called "The October

Fair." It was not until more than a year had passed, when I realized finally that what I had to deal with was material which covered almost 150 years in history, demanded the action of more than 2,000 characters, and would in its final design include almost every racial type and social class of American life, that I realized that even the pages of a book of 200,000 words were wholly inadequate for the purpose.

How did I finally arrive at this conclusion? I think it is not too much to say that I simply wrote myself into it. During all that year, I was writing furiously, feeling now the full pressure of inexorable time, the necessity to finish something. I wrote like mad; I finished scene after scene, chapter after chapter. The characters began to come to life, to grow and multiply until they were numbered by the hundreds, but so huge was the extent of my design, as I now desperately realized, that I can liken these chapters only to a row of lights which one sometimes sees at night from the windows of a speeding train, strung out across a dark and lonely countryside.

I would work furiously day after day until my creative energies were utterly exhausted, and although at the end of such a period I would have written perhaps as much as 200,000 words, enough in itself to make a very long book, I would realize with a feeling of horrible despair that what I had completed was only one small section of a single book.

During this time I reached that state of naked need and utter isolation which every artist has got to meet and conquer if he is to survive at all. Before this I had been sustained by that delightful illusion of success which we all have when we dream about the books we are going to write instead of actually doing them. Now I was face to face with it, and suddenly I realized that I had committed my life and my integrity so irrevocably to this struggle that I must conquer now or be destroyed. I was alone with my own work, and suddenly I knew that I had to be alone with it, that no one could help me with it now no matter how anyone might wish to help. For the first time I realized another naked fact which every artist must know, and that is that in a man's work there are contained not only the seeds of life, but the seeds of death, and that that power of creation which sustains us will also destroy us like a leprosy if we let it rot stillborn in our vitals. I had to get it out of me somehow. I saw that now. And now for the first time a terrible doubt began to creep into my mind that I might not live long enough to get it out of me, that I had created a labor so large and so impossible that the energy of a dozen lifetimes would not suffice for its accomplishment.

During this time, however, I was sustained by one piece of inestimable good fortune. I had for a friend a man who is, I believe, not only the greatest editor of his time, but a man of immense and patient wisdom and a gentle but unyielding fortitude. I think that if I was not destroyed at this time by the sense of hopelessness which these gigantic labors had awakened in me, it was largely because of the courage and patience of this man. I did not give in because he would not let me give in, and I think it is also true that at this particular time he had the advantage of being in the position of a skilled observer at a battle. I was myself engaged in that battle, covered by its dust and sweat and exhausted by its struggle, and I understood far less clearly than my friend the nature and the progress of the struggle in which I was engaged. At this time there was little that this man could do except observe, and in one way or another keep me at my task, and in many quiet and marvelous ways he succeeded in doing this.

I was now at the place where I must produce, and even the greatest editor can do little for a writer until he has brought from the secret darkness of his own spirit into the common light of day the completed concrete accomplishment of his imagining. My friend, the editor, has likened his own function at this painful time to that of a man who is trying to hang on to the fin of a plunging whale, but hang on he did, and it is to his tenacity that I owe my final release. Meanwhile, my creative power was functioning at the highest intensity it had ever known. I wrote at times without belief that I would ever finish, with nothing in me but black despair, and yet I wrote and wrote and could not give up writing. And it seemed that despair itself was the very goad that urged me on, that made me write even when I had no belief that I would ever finish. It seemed to me that my life in Brooklyn, although I had been there only two and a half years, went back through centuries of time, through ocean depths of black and bottomless experience which no ordinary scale of hours would ever measure. People have sometimes asked me what happened to my life during these years. They have asked me how I ever found time to know anything that was going on in the world about me when my life was so completely absorbed by this world of writing. Well, it may seem to be an extraordinary fact, but the truth is that never in my whole life have I lived so fully, have I shared so richly in the common life of man as I did during these three years when I was struggling with the giant problem of my own work.

For one thing, my whole sensory and creative equipment, my powers of feeling and reflection—even the sense of hearing, and above all, my powers of memory, had reached the greatest degree of sharpness that they had ever known. At the end of the day of savage labor, my mind was still blazing with its effort, could by no opiate of reading, poetry, music, alcohol, or any other pleasure, be put at rest. I was unable to sleep, unable to subdue the tumult of these creative energies, and as a result of this condition, for three years I prowled the streets, explored the swarming web of the million-footed city and came to know it as I had never done before. It was a black time in the history of the nation, a black time in my own life and, I suppose, it is but natural that my own memory of it now should be a pretty grim and painful one.

Everywhere around me, during these years, I saw the evidence of an incalculable ruin and suffering. And the staggering impact of this black picture of man's inhumanity to his fellow-man, the unending repercussions of these scenes of suffering, violence, oppression, hunger, cold, and filth and poverty going on unheeded in a world in which the rich were still rotten with their wealth left a scar upon my life, a conviction in my soul which I shall never lose.

And from it all, there has come as the final deposit,

a burning memory, a certain evidence of the fortitude of man, his ability to suffer and somehow to survive. And it is for this reason now that I think I shall always remember this black period with a kind of joy that I could not at that time have believed possible, for it was during this time that I lived my life through to a first completion, and through the suffering and labor of my own life came to share those qualities in the lives of people all around me. And that is another thing which the making of a book has done for me. It has given my life that kind of growth which I think the fulfillment of each work does give the artist's life, and insofar as I have known these things, I think that they have added to my stature.

The early winter of 1933 arrived and with it, it seemed to me, the final doom of an abysmal failure. I still wrote and wrote, but blindly, hopelessly, like an old horse who trots around in the unending circle of a treadmill and knows no other end nor purpose for his life than this. If I slept at night, it was to sleep an unceasing nightmare of blazing visions that swept across my fevered and unresting mind. And when I woke, it was to wake exhausted, not knowing anything but work, lashing myself on into a hopeless labor, and so furiously at it through the day and then night again, a frenzied prowling of a thousand streets, and so to bed and sleepless sleep again, the nightmare pageantry to which my consciousness lay chained a spectator.

Such was the state my life had come to in the early winter of 1933, and even at that moment, although I could not see it, the end of my huge labor was in sight. In the middle of December of that year the great editor, of whom I have spoken, and who, during all this tormented period, had kept a quiet watch upon me, called me to his home and calmly informed me that my book was finished. I could only look at him with stunned surprise, and finally I only could tell him out of the depth of my own hopelessness, that he was mistaken, that the book was not finished, that it could never be completed, that I could write no more. He answered with the same quiet finality that the book was finished whether I knew it or not, and then he told me to go to my room and spend the next week in collecting in its proper order the manuscript which had accumulated during the last two years.

I followed his instructions, still without hope and without belief. I worked for six days sitting in the middle of the floor surrounded by mountainous stacks of typed manuscript on every side. At the end of a week I had the first part of it together, and just two days before Christmas, 1933, I delivered to him the manuscript of "The October Fair," and a few days later, the manuscript of "The Hills Beyond Pentland." The manuscript of "The Fair" was, at that time, something over 1,000,000 words in length. He had seen most of it in its dismembered fragments during the three preceding years, but now, for the first time, he was seeing them in their sequential order, and once again his marvelous intuition was right; he had told me the truth when he said that I had finished the book.

It was not finished in any way that was publishable or readable. It was really not a book so much as it was the skeleton of a book, but for the first time in four years the skeleton was all there. An enormous labor of revision, weaving together, shaping, and, above all, cutting remained, but I had the book now so that nothing, not even the despair of my own spirit, could take it from me. He told me so, and suddenly I saw that he was right.

I was like a man who is drowning and who suddenly, at the last gasp of his dying effort, feels earth beneath his feet again. My spirit was overwhelmed by the greatest triumph it had ever known, and although my mind was tired, my body exhausted, from that moment on I felt equal to anything on earth.

It was evident that many problems were before us, but now we had the thing, and we welcomed the labor before us with happy confidence. In the first place there was the problem of the book's gigantic length. Even in this skeletonized form the manuscript of "The October Fair" was over a million words in length, which is about twelve times the length of the average novel or twice the length of *War and Peace*. It was manifest, therefore, that it would not only be utterly impossible to publish such a manuscript in a single volume, but that even if it were published in several volumes, the tremendous length of such a manuscript would practically annihilate its chances of ever finding a public which would read it.

This problem now faced us, and the editor grappled with it immediately. As his examination of the manuscript of "The October Fair" proceeded, he found that the book did describe two complete and separate cycles. The first of these was a movement which described the period of wandering and hunger in a man's youth. The second cycle described the period of greater certitude, and was dominated by the unity of a single passion. It was obvious, therefore, that what we had in the two cyclic movements of this book was really the material of two completely different chronicles, and although the second of the two was by far the more finished, the first cycle, of course, was the one which logically we ought to complete and publish first, and we decided on this course.

We took the first part. I immediately prepared a minutely thorough synopsis which described not only the course of the book from the first to last, but which also included an analysis of those chapters which had been completed in their entirety, of those which were completed only in part, and of those which had not been written at all, and with this synopsis before us, we set to work immediately to prepare the book for press. This work occupied me throughout the whole of the year 1934. The book was completed at the beginning of 1935, and was published in March of that year under the title of *Of Time and the River*.

In the first place, the manuscript, even in its unfinished form, called for the most radical cutting, and because of the way in which the book had been written, as well as the fatigue which I now felt, I was not well prepared to do by myself the task that lay ahead of us.

Cutting had always been the most difficult and distasteful part of writing to me; my tendency had always been to write rather than to cut. Moreover, whatever critical faculty I may have had concerning my own work had been seriously impaired, for the time being at least, by the frenzied labor of the past four years. When a man's work has poured from him for almost five years like burning lava from a volcano; when all of it, however superfluous, has been given fire and passion by the white heat of his own creative energy, it is very difficult suddenly to become coldly surgical, ruthlessly detached.

To give a few concrete illustrations of the difficulties that now confronted us: The opening section of the book describes the journey of a train across the state of Virginia at night. Its function in the book is simply to introduce some of the chief characters, to indicate a central situation, to give something of the background from which the book proceeds, and perhaps through the movement of the train across the stillness of the earth to establish a certain beat, evoke a certain emotion which is inherent to the nature of the book. Such a section, therefore, undoubtedly serves an important function, but in proportion to the whole purport of the book, its function is a secondary one and must be related to the whole book in a proportionate way.

Now in the original version, the manuscript which described the journey of the train across Virginia at night was considerably longer than the average novel. What was needed was just an introductory chapter or two, and what I had written was over 100,000 words in length, and this same difficulty, this lack of proportion, was also evident in other parts of the manuscript.

What I had written about the great train was really good. But what I had to face, the very bitter lesson that every one who wants to write has got to learn, was that a thing may in itself be the finest piece of writing one has ever done, and yet have absolutely no place in the manuscript one hopes to publish. This is a hard thing, but it must be faced, and so we faced it.

My spirit quivered at the bloody execution. My soul recoiled before the carnage of so many lovely things cut out upon which my heart was set. But it had to be done, and we did it. And so it went all up and down the line. Chapters 50,000 words long were reduced to ten or fifteen thousand words, and having faced this inevitable necessity, I finally acquired a kind of ruthlessness of my own, and once or twice, myself, did more cutting than my editor was willing to allow.

Such, then, were some of our major difficulties with the manuscript we had in hand, and although since its publication there have been many declarations to the effect that the book would have benefited by a much more radical cutting, the cutting we did do was much more drastic than I had dreamed was possible.

Meanwhile I was proceeding at full speed with the work of completing my design, finishing the unfinished parts and filling in the transition links which were essential.

This in itself was an enormous job and kept me writing all day long as hard as I could go for a full year. Here again the nature of my chief fault was manifest. I wrote too much again. I not only wrote what was essential, but time and time again my enthusiasm for a good scene, one of those enchanting vistas which can open up so magically to a man in the full flow of his creation would overpower me, and I would write thousands of words upon a scene which contributed nothing of vital importance to a book whose greatest need already was ruthless condensation.

During the course of this year, I must have written well over a half million words of additional manuscript, of which, of course, only a small part was finally used.

The nature of my method, the desire fully to explore my material, had led me into another error. The whole effect of those five years in incessant writing had been to make me feel not only that everything had to be used, but that everything had to be told, that nothing could be implied. Therefore, at the end, there were at least a dozen additional chapters which I felt had to be completed to give the book its final value. A thousand times I debated this question desperately with my editor. I told him that these chapters had to go in simply because I felt the book would not be complete without them, and with every argument he had, he tried to show me that I was wrong. I see now that on the whole he was right about it, but at the time I was so inextricably involved in my work, that I did not have the detachment necessary for a true appraisal.

The end came suddenly—the end of those five years of torment and incessant productivity. In October I took a trip to Chicago, a two weeks' vacation, my first in over a year. When I returned I found that my editor had quietly and decisively sent the manuscript to the press, the printers were already at work on it, the proof was beginning to come in. I had not foreseen it; I was desperate, bewildered. "You can't do it," I told him, "the book is not yet finished. I must have six months more on it."

To this he answered that the book was not only finished, but that if I took six months more on it, I would then demand another six months and six months more beyond that, and that I might very well become so obsessed with this one work that I would never get it published. He went on to say, and I think with complete justice, that such a course was wrong for me. I was not, he said, a Flaubert kind of writer. I was not a perfectionist. I had twenty, thirty, almost any number of books in me, and the important thing was to get them produced and not to spend the rest of my life in perfecting one book. He agreed that with six months' additional work upon the book, I might achieve a certain finish and completeness, but he did not think that the benefit would be nearly as great as I thought it would be, and his own deep conviction was that the book should be published at once without further delay, that I should get it out of me, forget about it, turn my life to the final completion of the work which was already prepared and ready, waiting for me. He told me, furthermore, exactly what the nature of the criticism would be, the criticism of its length, its adjectives, its overabundance, but he told me not to despair.

He told me finally that I would go on and do better work, that I would learn to work without so much confusion, waste, and useless torment, that my future books would more and more achieve the unity, sureness, and finality that every artist wants his work to have, but that I had to learn in the way I had learned, groping, struggling, finding my own way for myself, that this was the only way to learn.

In January 1935, I finished the last of my revisions

on the proof; the first printed copies came from the press in February. The book was released for final publication early in March. I was not here when it came out. I had taken a ship for Europe the week before, and as the ship got farther and farther from the American shores, my spirits sank lower and lower, reaching, I think, the lowest state of hopeless depression they had ever known. This, I believe, was largely a physical reaction, the inevitable effect of relaxation upon a human organism which had for five years been strained to its utmost limit. My life seemed to me to be like a great spring which had been taut for years and which was now slowly uncoiling from its tension. I had the most extraordinary sense of desolation I had ever known when I thought about my book. I had never realized until now how close I had been to it, how much a part of me it had become, and now that it had been taken away from me, my life felt utterly futile, hollow as a shell. And now that the book was gone, now that there was nothing more that I could do about it, I felt the most abysmal sensation of failure. I have always been somewhat afraid of print, although print is a thing I have tried so hard to achieve. Yet it is literally true that with everything I have ever written, I have felt when the hour of naked print drew nigh a kind of desperation and have even entreated my publisher not only to defer the publication of my book until another season, but have asked the editors of magazines to put off the publication of a story for another month or two until I had a chance to work on it some more, do something to it, I was not always sure what.

Now I had an overwhelming sense of shame greater than any I have felt before. I felt as if I had ruinously exposed myself as a pitiable fool who had no talent and who once and for all had completely vindicated the prophecies of the critics who had felt the first book was just a flash in the pan. It was in this frame of mind that I arrived in Paris on March 8, the day the book was to be published in America. I had come away to forget about it, and yet I thought about it all the time. I prowled the streets from night to morning, at least a dozen times in two short weeks I heard the celebration of Mass at Sacré Coeur, and then would walk the streets again and come back to my hotel at ten o'clock and lie upon the bed, and still I could not sleep.

After several days of this, I steeled myself to go to the office of the travel agency where a message might be waiting for me. I found a cablegram there. It was from my publisher, and it said simply: "Magnificent reviews somewhat critical in ways expected, full of greatest praise." I read it the first time with a feeling of almost intolerable joy but as I continued to read and reread it, the old dark doubt began to creep across my mind and by the time night had come I was convinced that this wonderful cable was just a sentence of doom, and that my editor, out of the infinite compassion of his spirit, had taken this means of breaking the news to me that my book was a colossal failure.

Three days passed in which I prowled the streets of Paris like a maddened animal, and of those three days I could later remember almost nothing. At the end of that time I sent a frenzied cablegram to that editor in which I told him I could stand anything better than this state of damnable uncertainty and pleaded with him to give me the blunt truth no matter how bitter it might be. His answer to this cable was such that I could no longer doubt him or the reception which the book had had at home.

This completes, as far as I can remember it, the story of the making of a book and what happened to its maker. I know it is too long a story; I know, also, that it must seem to be a story filled with the record of a man's blunders and ludicrous mistakes, but simply because it is that kind of story, I hope that it may have some value. It is a story of the artist as a man and as a worker. It is a story of the artist as a man who is derived out of the common family of earth and who knows all the anguish, error, and frustration that any man alive can know.

The life of the artist at any epoch of man's history has not been an easy one. And here in America, it has often seemed to me, it may well be the hardest life that man has ever known. I am not speaking of some frustration in our native life, some barrenness of spirit, some arid Philistinism which contends against the artist's life and which prevents his growth. I do not speak of these things because I do not put the same belief in them that I once did. I am speaking as I have tried to speak from first to last in the concrete terms of the artist's actual experience, the nature of the physical task before him. It seems to me that that task is one whose physical proportions are vaster and more difficult here than in any other nation on the earth. It is not merely that in the cultures of Europe and of the Orient the American artist can find no antecedent scheme, no structural plan, no body of tradition that can give his own work the validity and truth that it must have. It is not merely that he must make somehow a new tradition for himself, derived from his own life and from the enormous space and energy of American life, the structure of his own design; it is not merely that he is confronted by these problems; it is even more than this, that the labor of a complete and whole articulation, the discovery of an entire universe and of a complete language, is the task that lies before him.

Such is the nature of the struggle to which henceforth our lives must be devoted. Out of the billion forms of America, out of the savage violence and the dense complexity of all its swarming, million-footed life; from the unique and single substance of this land and life of ours, must we draw the power and energy of our own life, the articulation of our speech, the substance of our art.

For here it seems to me in hard and honest ways like these we may find the tongue, the language, and the conscience that as men and artists we have got to have. Here, too, perhaps, must we who have no more than what we have, who know no more than what we know, who are no more than what we are, find our America. Here, at this present hour and moment of my life, I seek for mine.

Memories of A. E. Housman

By Laurence Housman

September 19, 1936

Of the early years of an eldest brother, six years my senior, I know little except on hearsay from himself and others. In a brief autobiographical note, which he supplied to a French translator of some of his poems, he gave the following account of himself:

> I was born in Worcestershire, not Shropshire, where I have never spent much time. My father and mother were respectively Lancashire and Cornish. I had a sentimental feeling for Shropshire because its hills were our western horizon. My topographical details—Hughley, Abdon-under-Clee, etc., are sometimes quite wrong: but I know Ludlow and Wenlock.
>
> I took an interest in astronomy almost as early as I can remember: the cause, I think, was a little book we had in the house.
>
> I was brought up in the Church of England and in the High Church party, which is much the best religion I have ever come across. But Lemprière's *Classical Dictionary,* read when I was eight, made me prefer paganism to Christianity; I abandoned Christianity at thirteen, and became an atheist at twenty-one.
>
> I never had any scientific education. I wrote verse at eight or earlier, but very little until I was thirty-five.

That last statement needs qualification. He had a great facility for verse-writing, and not only wrote poems of a serious character but was prolific in *vers d'occasion.* In early years his compositions so much exceeded his own use for them that he sometimes palmed them off on others, and my first sonnet, written

247

when I was about six and before I knew what constituted a sonnet, was dragged out of me, or squeezed
into me, by a process of hypnotic suggestion which left
me entirely convinced at the time that the poem was
mine, though I know better now.

Under his leadership, in a family of seven, we all
wrote poems, even the unpoetic ones: lyrics, ballads,
sonnets, narrative poems, nonsense-rhymes, and compositions to which each contributed a verse (not always
in the same meter) which occupied almost as much of
our playtime as the more active games of childhood, in
which also, as often as not, he led and we followed.

His early education was first under a governess, then
at a small dame-school, where a slipper was the regular
instrument used for corporal punishment; at the age of
eleven he was elected to a Foundation Scholarship at
Bromsgrove School, where he remained to the end of
his schooldays.

Having gained an open scholarship at St. John's
College, Oxford, in 1877, he went up in the autumn
of that year. There was no particular reason, except
the need for a good scholarship, why that college
should have been chosen. Unfortunately there were
parental reasons against two others which might have
suited him better. His father would not allow him to
try for a Balliol Scholarship from disapproval of the
theological views of Dr. Jowett, the Master; Cambridge was ruled out unless he could obtain a scholarship at the college (St. John's) where uncles and
grandparents had graduated, and where one had become Dean.

It is probable that Cambridge, with its Classical
Tripos, would have opened for him a better course
of study than Oxford, where after gaining a First in
"Moderations" in 1879, he failed in "Greats" two years
later—so bringing his university career to a catastrophic end, which, for the time at any rate, destroyed
all chance of a scholastic appointment at Oxford or
Cambridge, and compelled him to accept as an alternative the uncongenial work of a civil servant in H. M.
Patent Office, where he remained for ten years.

An explanation of his failure in "Greats" has recently

been given by one of his friends and contemporaries at Oxford. Finding himself unable to deal to his full, honest satisfaction with certain of the set papers, he gave no answers at all, thus, as he himself declared, leaving the examiners no alternative to the course they took. But to the best of my recollection, for home consumption (where the disappointment was naturally very great) he gave no explanation at all.

On leaving Oxford he remained a member of the university, and having in a subsequent year passed the necessary examination, took his B.A. and his M.A. together in 1892, when, on the strength of the reputation which he had built up for himself, by his classical contributions to the learned journals, he was appointed Professor of Latin at University College, London.

In the autobiographical note from which I have already quoted, "Oxford" wrote Alfred, "had not much effect upon me, except that I there met my greatest friend." A statement which can hardly be as true as he would have liked it to be; since this, at any rate, can be said for certain—he came back from Oxford a changed character. It was probably the blow of his failure which caused him from that time on to withdraw so completely into himself, and he became a silent and impenetrable recluse in the midst of his own family, during the year which elapsed before he left home to take up his Civil Service appointment in London. Up to the beginning of his university career he had been our social and intellectual leader, the inventor of our games, the composer and producer of our plays (impromptus devised only on the day of their performance), the editor and chief contributor to our *Family Magazine*, and the instigator of all our attempts in prose and poetry. When he came back, and for a good many years afterward, we ceased to know him—mainly, if not entirely, because he was determined not to be known. If sympathy was what he feared to receive on his return from Oxford, he took the best means to deprive himself of it; and only very occasionally at first, and then gradually as the years went on, did he allow a breaking-down of the barrier.

But in those first years while up at Oxford, his correspondence with members of the family was lively and amusing; and during vacation there was no diminution of his social affability. It must have been during those intervals of college life that he delighted us with some of his best pieces of nonsense-verse. Our evening diversions, almost as long as I can remember, had often been of a semi-literary character. One of these was the writing of short poems, containing a collection of nouns, each member of the company supplying one. Here is a sample of the sort of thing which Alfred was able to turn out in the course of fifteen or twenty minutes. The nouns were: hat, novel, banker, cucumber, yacht, and abridgment. Obviously the last was the crux; and this is how Alfred tackled it:

> *At the door of my own little hovel,*
> *Reading a novel I sat;*
> *And as I was reading the novel*
> *A gnat flew away with my hat.*
> *As fast as a fraudulent banker*
> *Away with my hat it fled,*
> *And calmly came to an anchor*
> *In the midst of the cucumber bed.*
>
> *I went and purchased a yacht,*
> *And traversed the garden tank,*
> *And I gave it that insect hot*
> *When I got to the other bank;*
> *Of its life I made an abridgment*
> *By squeezing it somewhat flat,*
> *And I cannot think what that midge meant*
> *By flying away with my hat.*

One Christmas (1879, I think), we attempted something more ambitious, which produced a memorable result. Each wrote a story, and on Christmas Eve, or thereabouts, the stories were read out to the assembled family. Alfred's contribution was a domestic sketch in verse and prose entitled "A Morning with the Royal Family," the opening sentence of which ran: " 'Pigs on the front lawn!' cried the King, 'Lend me a cannon, somebody!' Nobody lent him a cannon, so seizing a teaspoon from the breakfast table he rushed from the apartment." The whole story—the only complete work of fiction, I think, which he ever produced—was published a year or two later, without his permission, in the school magazine, of which at that time another brother was editor: and it has remained ever since a prized but rather private family possession, republication having been strictly forbidden by the author.

While at University College, Alfred contributed occasional nonsense-rhymes to the *College Magazine*, three of which (though not his best) he allowed to be privately reprinted in 1935. He also gave, about once a year, a written paper on one of the British poets, before the College Literary Society; his chosen poets were: Tennyson, Matthew Arnold, Burns, Campbell, Erasmus, Darwin, Swinburne, and "The Spasmodic School." He was only quite kind to two of them— Matthew Arnold and Campbell; all the others were subjected to varying degrees of satirical criticism—so severe, in the case of Burns, that a Scottish professor, rising in wrath, declared he would never forgive the lecturer for what he had said of him. It would be unkind on my part to excite the interest of my readers any further in material which I am under orders to destroy. These papers have to share the fate of a very much better one—the Inaugural Lecture which my brother gave on his appointment, in 1911, to the Kennedy Professorship of Latin at Cambridge University, and which he would not allow to be published because of his inability to retrace his authority for a statement which he had made concerning a Shelley manuscript; as to which later investigation has gone rather against him.

In the autobiographical note from which I have already quoted, Alfred writes of his years in London as follows:

> While I was at the Patent Office I read a great deal of Greek and Latin at the British Museum of an evening. While at University College, which is not residential, I lived alone in lodgings in the environs of London.
>
> *A Shropshire Lad* was written in Byron Cottage, 17

North Road, Highgate, where I lived from 1886 to 1905.

A Shropshire Lad was offered to Macmillan, and declined by them on the advice, I have been told, of Mr. John Morley, who was their reader. Then a friend introduced me to Kegan Paul; but the book was published at my own expense.

It was to this friend (Alfred W. Pollard) that he owed a change in the proposed title of the book, which must have had a considerable effect on its fortunes. He had intended to call it *Poems of Terence Hearsay*. Pollard suggested *A Shropshire Lad* as better, a piece of good advice which the author was luckily not above taking.

The *Shropshire Lad* [the note goes on to say] is an imaginary character, with something of my temper and view of life. Very little in the book is biographical.

As regards the influences affecting his poems, he added:

"Reader of the Greek Anthology" is not a good name for me. Of course I have read it, or most of it, but with no special heed; and my favorite Greek poet is Aeschylus. No doubt I have unconsciously been influenced by the Greeks and Latins, but I was surprised when critics spoke of my poetry as "classical." Its chief sources of which I am conscious are Shakespeare's songs, the Scottish Border Ballads, and Heine.

In answer to an inquiry whether *A Shropshire Lad* had been the product of "a crisis of pessimism" he replied that he had never had any such crisis.

In the first place I am not a pessimist but a pejorist (as George Eliot said she was not an optimist but a meliorist); and that philosophy is founded on my observation of the world, not on anything so trivial and irrelevant as personal history. Secondly, I did not begin to write poetry in earnest until the really emotional part of my life was over; and my poetry, so far as I could make out, sprang chiefly from physical causes, such as a relaxed sore throat during my most prolific period, the first five months of 1895.

Finally, to the same correspondent, he writes:

> I respect the Epicureans more than the Stoics, but my man is Aristippus of Cyrene, who was not afraid of words. Of the writers you mention, the only two I have read and admired much are Pascal and Leopardi. For Hardy I had a great affection, and admiration for some of his novels and a little of his poetry.
>
> As some of the questions which you ask in your flattering curiosity may possibly be asked by future generations, and as most of them can only be answered by me, I make this reply.

The one English novelist whom Alfred preferred to Hardy was Jane Austen. When he told Hardy so, Hardy replied, "Well, of course it's the greater thing." "What he meant by that," said Alfred, "I'm sure I don't know."

Another of his rather unexpected admirations was Christina Rossetti, of whom he said that posterity would probably place her above Swinburne. It was an admiration which we shared; twice I had the pleasure of introducing him to poems by her which he did not know; of one he asked me to send him a copy; of the other (a poem called "The River of Life") he said, "Yes, it's the sort of nonsense that is worth writing": a remark which somewhat consoled me for his having described certain devotional poems of my own as "nonsense-poems." Some years later he said he thought they were the "cleverest" I had ever written; from which I gathered that with him "nonsense" as applied to poetry was not a word of opprobrium.

During the years preceding his appointment at University College, London, Alfred remained for most of the members of his family a somewhat distant acquaintance, and neither from our occasional meetings, nor from our quite formal correspondence, have I anything to record that seems now worth telling. Indeed it was not until after *A Shropshire Lad* was published that our correspondence became fairly frequent, and that his letters began once more to be individual and amusing. The astonished exclamation of a member of the family, after reading the first six or seven of the *Shropshire Lad* poems, "Alfred has a heart!" is sufficient indication of the pains he had taken to conceal it during the years of his bitter disappointment over the finish of his university career. But even while he lived so far removed from the familiar association of early days, he still had his eye on us, as regards our literary activities, and when any of them pleased him, he let us know it. When his sister Clemence's story "The Were Wolf" appeared in the Christmas number of *Atalanta* in 1889 she got from him a letter of warm appreciation beginning "Capital, capital, capital!" And quite early, with my own stories, poems, and plays, I was conscious of more regard for what Alfred would think and say of them than for what any other critic or the general public might think or say.

It so happened that I sent him the manuscript of my first book of poems for criticism, at the very time when, without my knowing it, he was preparing his own for publication; and I got from him two long letters of detailed criticism—sometimes scathing in its terms, but also considerate and kind where it seemed to him that kindness was deserved. Shortly after our two books had been published, I received a letter from him, the terms of which will be better understood if I explain beforehand that I had designed for the cover of my own book *Green Arras* a very elaborate and as I thought beautiful cover of gold scrollwork. "The other day," wrote Alfred,

I was sitting at dinner next to a man who thought to interest me by talking about *you* and *your* poems. He said he liked *Green Arras;* he added that *A Shropshire Lad* had a pretty cover. I am your affectionate brother, A.E.H. P.S. He did not say that *Green Arras* had a pretty cover; nor has it! P.P.S. I was just licking the envelope when the following envenomed remark occurred to me: I had far far rather have my poems mistaken as yours than your poems mistaken as mine.

This was the sort of thing which he enjoyed writing; and to me it was done less maliciously than to others, because he knew that I also enjoyed it, having reason to know that sometimes he said kinder things about me behind my back than he wrote to my face. But there can be no doubt that he did greatly enjoy writing and saying bitter and contemptuous things about people who seemed to him to deserve them; and he had in his notebook pages stocked with phrases which were apparently waiting a suitable victim to whom they might be applied. Many of these found a place in his critical writings—the introductions to his own editions of the classics and his reviews of books by other scholars whose claim to that term he would not admit; and one does not doubt that the more highly established their reputations, the more did he enjoy bringing them down into the dust.

Without naming names I give here just a few samples of the gentle ferocity with which he put into their places certain people of supposed importance in the scholastic world, in order that those who are not readers of the edited classics may here get an idea of that gift for invective which made him the most feared, and perhaps also the most hated, among the pedants (his own pet phrase) of his day.

I can easily understand why Mr. —— should not tell the truth about other people. He fears reprisals: he apprehends that they may tell the truth about *him*.

If Mr. —— were a postage stamp he would be a very good postage stamp; but adhesiveness is not the virtue of a critic. A critic is free and detached.

To put a finish to this pillorying of unnamed victims, here is one more pronouncement which would miss its point were its subject left nameless:

Swinburne was as good a critic as a rhinoceros can possibly be—a much better critic than his fellow rhinoceros Macaulay. But to be a good critic you must be more sensitive to pain than either of these illustrious pachyderms. . . . Swinburne reading Shakespeare was like a bear rifling a bees' nest; he eats and enjoys the honey, and the bees cannot sting him through his hide.

What all this goes mainly to show is that while Alfred considered truth the first duty of a critic and a scholar, he enjoyed telling the truth provocatively. Illustrative of which (on a matter not of literature but of morals) was his remark that the rarest of sexual aberrations is chastity! It is quite true, but it could hardly be said in a more provocative way.

Alfred's minute insistence on accuracy is well exemplified in his reply to a friend who regretted that she had been unable to obtain a first edition of *Last Poems* and had been obliged to content herself with the second. "In that case," he wrote, "you have got the more valuable edition. In the first a comma is missing."

People seem to have got the impression that Alfred disliked being questioned about his poems. That was not my own experience; if the question had any interest in it he liked answering it. I asked him once whether as a rule, his so-happily-chosen adjectives had come to him spontaneously or after labor and with difficulty; and I gave as an instance "colored counties," a phrase which has become famous. "Now that you should have picked that out," he said, "is interesting. When I wrote the poem I put down a quite ordinary adjective, just to fill up for the time, which didn't satisfy me. Then with the poem in my head, I went to bed and dreamed, and in my dream I hit on the word 'painted'; when I woke up I saw that 'painted' wouldn't do, but it gave me 'colored' as the right word."

This is confirmed in the first draft of the poem, which I found in one of his notebooks where the alternatives run: sunny, pleasant, checkered, patterned; "painted" is left out; it was not necessary for that to be written down.

I have given, in the preceding pages, instances of Alfred's ruthless treatment of intellectual foolishness, more especially of foolishness which gave itself the airs of learning. In that direction he could be cruel with relish: but toward moral foolishness, especially toward the foolishness of troubled youth, his inclination was all the other way. Even deflections from rectitude which he would not have tolerated in himself caused no withdrawal of aid when once it had been proffered; and in a case known to me, conduct which he described as nefarious did not alter relations of real personal friendship between him and the offender, though the offense was to himself. Certain "laws of God and man," with their socially imposed sanctions, he disliked heartily, and with recognition of human nature's imperfect material, made a wide allowance for its failures. This is shown clearly in many of his published poems.

Two years ago, when we were taking a holiday together, I found Alfred more communicative than I had ever known him before. Of the poem called "New Year's Eve" which he published in a magazine while at Oxford, he wrote it, he said, in his twentieth year. "I was then a deist." "And now," I asked, "what do you call yourself—agnostic?" "No, I am an atheist," he said, decisively. He then went on to say that he thought the Church of England the best religion ever invented; it was less disturbing than other forms, and eliminated "so much Christian nonsense." Christianity, he added, was most harmful in its social application.

Belief in immortality was quite unnecessary, he said, for good morals. The Hebrews had a higher code of morals than the Egyptians, and did not allow themselves to be perverted from the nonbelief in a future life by Egyptian superstition.

Of certain things published under a pseudonym during his undergraduate days he said he would be very much obliged to me if I would let them rest in oblivion; they were less good than his home-productions because they were written to order, not for pleasure.

Of the reputation which his poems won for him he wrote to an American correspondent: "Though it gives me no lively pleasure, it is something like a mattress interposed between me and the hard ground."

Those words were written when life was ceasing to have any comfort for him.

For several years he had persistently declined all the academic honors offered him by various universities, at home and abroad. The proposal from his own University of Oxford to confer on him the honorary degree of Doctor of Letters he had twice refused, in 1928 and 1934.

It was about five years ago that he admitted to me another refusal, which, till then, he had kept secret. I had for some time felt a brotherly concern that the one honor which I thought he would be willing to accept, the Order of Merit, had not been offered him. Since others were feeling as I did, I broached the question— would he accept it? He replied that he would not, and when, disappointed, I asked why, he said that, though he had always known that it would be offered him if he lived to the age of eighty, he had decided against accepting any honor, and against this particular one because it was not always given to the right persons. He had condoled, he said, with Robert Bridges for having had to receive the honor at the same time as John Galsworthy, whose writing they both disliked, and Bridges had admitted that the circumstance had not given him pleasure.

I suppose I pressed him further, for suddenly he blushed (an unexpected gift which he had retained from the days of his youth) and said:

Well, as a matter of fact, Mr. Baldwin did write to me not long ago to say that the King was ready to offer it; and I believe it was offered at the same time to Bernard Shaw. But for the reason I have already stated, and because I could not have the trouble of going to be received by the King, I declined. But [he added] I don't want it to be known: it wouldn't be fair to the King.

Who first gave away the secret I do not know. It was only after my brother's death that I found that others knew of it, and that word of it had gone to the press.

Three years ago his health began rapidly to decline, and his walking powers, which all his life had given that quiet companionship of nature which suited him best, had considerably diminished.

Early in January 1936, his condition became so serious that he was not expected to live more than another week; but when term approached, he announced his intention of leaving the Nursing Home and returning to his rooms to give his lectures. His doctor told him that this was impossible. "It is my duty and my pleasure," he replied, "and I shall do it." At the end of term, writing to a member of the family, he said that he had never lectured better in his life. But the effort sent him back to the Nursing Home, from which he went, at the commencement of the Easter Term, and gave two lectures, sitting down. That was the end.

Over the grave, where his ashes have been laid under the north wall of the parish church at Ludlow, is a tablet bearing these words:

In Memory of Alfred Edward Housman, M.A. Oxon. Kennedy Professor of Latin and Fellow of Trinity College in the University of Cambridge.
Author of "A Shropshire Lad."
Born 26 March 1859. Died 30 April 1936.

Good night. Ensured release.
Imperishable peace:
Have these for yours.

E. B. W.

By James Thurber

October 15, 1938

Three—no, six years ago (how the time flies!) a gentleman came to the offices of *The New Yorker* and asked for E. B. White. He was shown into the reception room and Mr. White was told that someone was waiting for him there. White's customary practice in those days, if he couldn't place a caller's name, was to slip moodily out of the building by way of the fire escape and hide in the coolness of Schrafft's until the visitor went away. He is not afraid of process servers, blackmailers, borrowers, or cranks; he is afraid of the smiling stranger who tramples the inviolable flowers of your privacy bearing a letter of introduction from an old Phi Gam brother now in the real-estate game in Duluth. White knows that the Man in the Reception Room may not be so easy to get rid of as a process server—or even a blackmailer: he may grab great handfuls of your fairest hours, he may even appropriate a sizable chunk of your life, for no better reason than that he was anchor man on your brother's high-school relay team, or married the sister of your old girl, or met an aunt of yours on a West Indies cruise. Most of us, out of a politeness made up of faint curiosity and profound resignation, go out to meet the smiling stranger with a gesture of surrender and a fixed grin, but White has always taken to the fire escape. He has avoided the Man in the Reception Room as he has avoided the interviewer, the photographer, the microphone, the rostrum, the literary tea, and the Stork Club. His life is his own. He is the only writer of prominence I know of who could walk through the Algonquin lobby or between the tables at Jack and Charlie's and be recognized only by his friends.

But to get back to the particular caller of six years ago whom we left waiting in the reception room. On that occasion, out of some obscure compulsion, White decided to go out and confront the man and see what he wanted. "I'm White," he told the stranger he found sitting alone in the room. The man rose, stared for a long moment at the audacious fellow in front of him, and then said, with grim certainty, "You are not E. B. White." White admits that his hair leaped up, but it is my fond contention that his heart did, too. I like to think that he was a little disappointed when he realized, as he was bound to, that the man was wrong. I like to insist that he resumed his burden of identity with a small sigh. (Where the remarkable interview got to from the tense point to which I have brought it here I shall leave it to my memoirs to tell.)

In the early days of *The New Yorker* the object of this searching examination signed his first few stories and poems with his full name: Elwyn (as God is my judge) Brooks White. I cannot imagine what spark of abandon, what youthful spirit of devil-may-care prompted a poet who loves to live half hidden from the eye to come out thus boldly into the open. He didn't keep it up long; he couldn't stand the fierce glare of polysyllabic self-acknowledgment. For the past twelve years he has signed his casuals and his verses merely with his initials, E. B. W. To his friends he is Andy. It was a lucky break that saved him from Elly or Wynnie or whatever else one might make out of Elwyn in the diminutive. He went to Cornell and it seems that every White who goes there is nicknamed Andy for the simple if rather faraway reason that the first president of the university was named Andrew White.

It used to be (indeed I believe it still is) a wonder and a worry to White's boss, Mr. Harold Ross, the mystic and wonderful editor of *The New Yorker*, that his favorite and most invaluable assistant avoided people, lived along the untrodden ways, hid by mossy stones, and behaved generally in what Ross was pleased to call an antisocial manner. For a restlessly gregarious man who consorts with ten thousand people from Groucho Marx to Lord Dalhousie it is difficult to comprehend the spirit of Walden Pond. As long ago as the late nineteen twenties there were hundreds of people who implored Ross to introduce them to the man who wrote, on the already famous first page of *The New Yorker*, those silver and crystal sentences which have a ring like the ring of nobody else's sentences in the world. White declined to be taken to literary parties, or to any other kind of parties, but one day Ross lured him to the house of a certain literary lady who, White was persuaded to believe, would be found alone.

When the door of her house was opened to them, Ross pushed White into a hallway loud with the chatter of voices proceeding from a crowded living room, the unmistakably assertive voices of writers and artists. Ross made the serious mistake of entering the living room first. When he looked around for White, that shy young man had quietly disappeared. He had proceeded deviously through the house, to the disciplined dismay of the servants, out the back door, and over trees and fences, or whatever else may have been in his way, to the freedom he so greatly cherishes, leaving the curtsy, the compliment, and the booksy chat to writers who go in for that sort of thing.

"Isn't there," Ross demanded of him one time, "*any*-body you would like to meet?" White gave this difficult question his grave consideration and said, at what Alexander Woollcott would call long last, "Yes. Willie Stevens and Helen Hayes." It is a proof of the reckless zeal and the devoted energy of Harold Ross that he instantly set about trying to get hold of Willie Stevens for the purpose of inviting him to dinner in New York at which White and Miss Hayes were to be the only other guests. I am desolated to report that this little coming together could not be accomplished: Willie apparently knew too many people the way it was and declined the invitation with that gentle old-world courtesy of which he was so consummate a master. Ross did manage finally to bring White face to face with Helen Hayes. Our hero, I am informed, was discontented and tongue-tied during their brief, jumpy conversation and was glad when it was all over. I suppose Miss Hayes was, too.

E. B. W. was born in Mount Vernon, N. Y., and will be forty next year. He had an ordinary, normal childhood, monkeying with an old Oliver typewriter, shooting with an air gun at the weather vane on his father's barn. At Cornell he charmed and astonished his English professors with a prose style so far above Cayuga's ordinary run of literary talent as to be considered something of a miracle. The *Cornell Sun* under White's editorship must have been the best-written college newspaper in the country. After Cornell he drove a model T Ford across the country with a friend named Howard Cushman. When they ran out of money, they played for their supper—and their gasoline—on a fascinating musical instrument that White had made out of some pieces of wire and an old shoe or something. In Seattle the young explorer got a job as reporter on the *Times*, the kind of newspaper that did not allow you to use the verb "to mangle." Accurately reporting, one day, the anguished cry of a poor husband who had found the body of his wife in the municipal morgue, White wrote, "My God, it's her!" and when the city editor changed this to "My God, it is she!" our wanderer moved sadly on to where they had a better understanding of people and a proper feeling for the finer usages of the English tongue. He became mess boy on a ship bound for Alaska, commanded by an old whaling captain, and manned by a crew who knew that a man says it's her when he finds her dead.

Shortly after *The New Yorker* was founded, its editors began to get occasionally manuscripts from an unknown young man named E. B. White who was a production assistant in an advertising agency. Harold Ross and Katharine Angell, his literary editor, were not slow to perceive that here were the perfect eye and ear, the authentic voice and accent for their struggling magazine. It tooks months, however, to trap the elusive writer into a conference and weeks to persuade him to come to work in the office; he finally agreed to give them his Thursdays. It is not too much to say that Andy White was the most valuable person on the magazine. His delicate tinkering with the works of *The New Yorker* caused it to move with a new ease and grace. His tag lines for those little newsbreaks which the magazine uses at the bottom of columns were soon being read joyfully aloud around town. His contributions to the Talk of the Town, particularly his Notes and Comment on the first page, struck the shining note that Ross had dreamed of striking. He has written a great many of the most memorable picture captions, including the famous one that has passed (usually misquoted) into song and legend, editorial and, I daresay, sermon: "I say it's spinach and I say the hell with it."

He had a hand in everything: he even painted a cover and wrote a few advertisements. One day nine years ago he decided that some pencil drawings I had absently made and thrown on the floor should be published in *The New Yorker*, so he picked them up, inked in the lines, and, to the surprise of us all, including Ross, got them published in *The New Yorker*.

Andy White understands begonias and children, canaries and goldfish, dachshunds and Scottish terriers, men and motives. His ear not only notes the louder cosmic rhythms but catches the faintest ticking sounds. He plays a fair ping-pong, a good piano, and a terrible poker (once, holding four natural jacks, he dropped out of the betting under the delusion that there were eight jacks in the deck and all he had was half of them). He has steadfastly refused to learn to play bridge or to take out life insurance. Once he offered an airplane pilot a thousand dollars to take him through a stormy dawn from Roosevelt Field to Chicago because a mysterious phone call had made him believe a friend was in great distress. The pilot had to make a forced landing in Pittsburgh, so that all White had to pay to see for himself that all was quiet along Lake Michigan was eight hundred dollars and his railroad fare from Pittsburgh. When a band of desperadoes stole his Buick sedan out of a quiet Turtle Bay garage and used it in the robbery of an upstate bank, White was suspected by the New York police of being the "brain guy" who devised the operations of a large and dangerous mob. For days detectives shrewdly infested his office, peering under tables, asking questions, staring in suspicious bewilderment at the preposterous array of scrawls, dentist's dates, symbols, phone numbers, photographs, and maps that littered his walls. Eventually they went shrewdly away, but every time I hear the sirens scream, I think they are coming for White. The former suspect is a good man with ax, rifle, and canoe (for several years he was part owner of a boys' camp in darkest Canada), and he sails a thirty-foot boat expertly. Two of his favorite books are Van Zanten's *Happy Days* and Alain-Fournier's *The Wanderer*. In the country he is afflicted with hay fever and in the city with a dizziness that resembles ordinary dizziness only as the mist resembles the rain. He expects every day of his life that something will kill him: a bit of mold, a small bug, a piece of huckleberry pie.

Some years ago White bought a farm in Maine and he now lives there the year around with his wife, who was Katharine Angell, and their son. He spends most of his time delousing turkeys, gathering bantam eggs, building mice-proof closets, and ripping out old fireplaces and putting in new ones. There is in him not a little of the spirit of Thoreau, who believed "that the world crowds round the individual, leaving him no vista, and shuts out the beauty of the earth; and that the wholesome wants of man are few." Now and then, between sunup and milking time, Andy White manages to write a casual or a poem for *The New Yorker*, and he does a monthly department for *Harper's* magazine. Many of the things he writes seem to me as lovely as a tree—say a maple after the first frost, or the cherry hung with snow. What he will go on to do in his forties and fifties I have no idea. If he simply continues to do what he has always done, it will be all right with me.

Memories of Oscar Wilde

By Ford Madox Ford

May 27, 1939

In December of the year before the trial of Oscar Wilde, the writer's uncle called the male children of his family together and solemnly informed them that if any older man made to us "proposals or advances of a certain nature," we were morally and legally at liberty to kill him "with any weapon that offered itself." The person speaking thus was not merely the brother of Dante Gabriel Rossetti, the pre-Raphaelite poet, but also her Majesty's Secretary of the Inland Revenue; one of the most weighty and responsible of Great Britain's permanent officials, and the most reasonable human being ever sent on this earth.

From that you may understand that London parents of adolescent male children of the end of '94 saw "perverters" lurking in all the shadows; and Wilde and Oscarisms, in their several kinds, were the preoccupation of that metropolis almost to the exclusion of all other intellectual pabula. And, beneath the comfortable strata of Society, growled the immense, frightening quicksand of the Lower Classes and the underworld, with ears all pricked up to hear details of the encounters of their own Fighting Marquis, a toff called Wilde, and the riffraff of the Mews. Every two or three days, inspired by the generous port of his lunch, the Home Secretary issued a warrant against Mr. Wilde; but in the mists of before-dinner indigestion ordered it withdrawn. The Queen and Mr. Gladstone, then retired, were mercifully shielded from these whisperings—or Heaven knows what they would not have done!

The writer, however, was conscious of none of these things . . . until the first night of *The Importance of Being Earnest*. Instances—or indeed knowledge—of what was called "perversion" had never come his way; even Mr. Rossetti's exhortation had seemed nearly unmeaning. And that any blame could attach to Mr. Wilde would have seemed fantastic. Mr. Wilde was a quiet individual who came every Saturday, for years, to tea with the writer's grandfather—Ford Madox Brown. Wilde would sit in a high-backed armchair, stretching out one hand a little toward the blaze of the wood fire on the hearth and talking of the dullest possible things to Ford Madox Brown, who, with his healthy colored cheeks and white hair cut like the King of Hearts, sat on the other side of the fire in another high-backed chair and, stretching out toward the flames his other hand, disagreed usually with Mr. Wilde on subjects like that of the Home Rule for Ireland Bill or the Conversion of the Consolidated Debt.

Mr. Wilde was, in fact, for the writer and, as far as he knows, for his cousins, the younger Rossettis, what we should have called one of the common objects of the countryside. Like Ford Madox Brown's other old friends or protégés and poor relations he had his weekly day on which to pay his respects to the Father of the pre-Raphaelites. He had begun the practice during a long period of very serious illness on the part of the older man and he continued it, as he said later, out of liking for the only house in London where he did not have to stand on his head.

Certainly, there, he could be as quiet as he liked, for, as often as not, he and Madox Brown would sit silent for minutes on end in the twilight. So that the painter was accustomed to deny that the young poet who sat at his feet possessed any wit at all, and, since Madox Brown died the year before the Wilde-Queensberry trial, he went to his death without any knowledge at all of the singular nature of the bird of paradise who had nestled on Saturday afternoons in the high-backed *bergère* beside the fire. Thus the only utterance of that date that comes back to the writer as at all weighty on the part of Mr. Wilde, the private gentleman, was an admission that he had been mistaken in a political prophecy. The Tory Government of that day had decided to reduce the rate of interest on Consols. Mr. Wilde had prophesied that that "conversion" would be disastrous to the finances of the country. The rate was, however, reduced from 3 to 2¾ per cent without any panic on the Stock Exchange. The Government had triumphed, and the writer still remembers very vividly the by then extremely bulky figure of Wilde as he entered the studio in a Saturday dusk, came to a standstill, loosened his great overcoat, removed his gloves and in the fashion of the day, smacked them against his left-hand palm, and exclaimed in a voice of unusual sonority: "I see I was wrong, Brown, about Consols!"

And the writer might add that the last poem of Christina Rossetti—the manuscript of which he happens to possess—is written on the back of a used envelope on the front of which the poetess had made a number of jottings—as to fluctuations in the price of Consols. So much did that day resemble our own!

Thus, the first intimation of what, whether it were irresponsible or sinister, Wilde meant to London and later to the world came with Lord Queensberry's presentation of his bouquet to Wilde on the first night of *The Importance of Being Earnest*. That was an occasion! The writer may have been obtuse or may have been merely inexperienced. But it was impossible during the performance of the play not to feel that both the audience and the quality of that audience's emotions were something different from those of any other first night he had attended. That audience was almost infinitely "smart." It consisted, presumably, one half of "decadents" more or less reckless and irresponsible, and of rich, more or less cultured and titled people who were, at least, in the know and presumably did not disapprove of what Wilde represented. What exactly Wilde represented at that moment it would be too complicated here to analyze.

On the fall of the curtain, Wilde appeared, rather pallid, blinking against the glare of the footlights and singularly prophetic of what Mr. Morley looked like in *Oscar Wilde* at the Fulton Theater the other day. He said some words, in the voice of Mr. Morley, that singular mixture of Balliol and brogue. Then unrest in the audience made him hesitate. His eyes, always uneasy, roved more uneasily than usual over the whole audience from gallery to pit. An immense pink and white bouquet was being carried down the gangway between the stalls.

That alone was sufficient to cause tittering emotion —because bouquets were only handed to women. But when the bouquet reached that solitary black figure with the pallid face and the audience could realize of what it consisted, then an extraordinarily black undertone of panic surged right through that semi-oval bowl. You saw men starting to their feet and women pulling their ermine cloaks hastily up over their shoulders—as if they felt they must incontinently flee from a scene on which violence was about to burst out.

For that bouquet consisted, plain to the view, of carrots and turnips framed in a foam of coarse lace paper. The panic in the face of Wilde exceeded the final panic that came over him under the cross-examination of Sir Edward Carson in *Wilde vs. Queensberry*. He shook and his lips bubbled. During the trial his break-down was very gradual; there behind the footlights he was struck by a thunderbolt. For he and all the hundreds in the theater had realized within a second that this was Queensberry's final insult to the author of that play. The whole matter *could* no longer keep under ground. And the hurried exit of all that audience from the theater was like a public desertion of that unfortunate idol of the unthinking. You saw people running to get out and the cries of encouragement of the few decadents who had the courage to take it were completely drowned in the voices of those departing who were explaining to each other what it all meant. And next day all whispering London heard that the Marquis had left in the hall of Wilde's club a card of his own bearing an unmistakable insult.

Thus, the libel action of Wilde against the Marquis was a really horrible occasion. It was not so much Wilde as the spirit of irresponsibility that was on trial and so many of us all—all London that in the remotest degree counted—had been guilty of sympathizing with the spirit of irresponsibility.

And there was another feature. It should be remembered that for the first and last time in the whole history of London the Arts, at least of painting and poetry, had really for a year or so counted as one of the important attributes of the metropolis. We, the poets and painters of London, had for the first time in the history of the world, become front-page news. Our hearths, our bookshelves, our favorite dogs, our back yards, were photographed for publication with all the honors of flashlights. Yes, the very pen of this writer here writing was reproduced in the shiny papers of the capital's weeklies and his inkpot, too.

This accounted for the hesitation of the Home Secretary in issuing and withdrawing his warrant. People who then used the pen in London were a clan with whom one must very seriously take account. And the same fact accounted for the final downfall of Wilde. He could not believe that the Victorian state would dare to measure itself against the chief pre-Raphaelite poet and the foremost playwright of the day.

His breakdown at the Queensberry trial came very slowly and was, therefore, the more agonizing. The cross-examination at the hands of Carson lasted at least as long as the whole play of *Oscar Wilde* at the Fulton. And it was obviously impossible that our sympathies should not go out to that doomed rat in that rat pit without issue. Every time that he got back on Carson—as when he said: "No, it is not poetry when you read it"—one breathed with relief as if a sorry hero had achieved the impossible. For in the arid panoply of English law procedure the dice are so weighted in favor of the cross-examiner that one would doubt if the archangel Michael or in the alternative Machiavelli could ever finally get back on learned counsel. Wilde, however, came very near it once or twice.

No, your sympathies were bound to be with Wilde in that place and on that occasion. It is a detail that is by no means a criticism of the art displayed on the Fulton stage that the cross-examination there shown in no way duplicated the process of the London law courts. There was none of the shouting and parading about the court by counsel that the Fulton stage showed. Sir Edward Carson spoke from a sort of a box, at some distance from the plaintiff and in a quite low if very clear voice. It made it the more horrible when suddenly you saw that pallid man's left hand begin to quiver along the lower edge of his waistcoat. And then a long time afterward his right hand, holding his gloves, quivering on the lapel of his coat. You just waited and waited for the next sign of discomfiture until finally it came with his throwing his gloves hysterically into the well of the court, his lips bubbling with undistinguishable words until they ended in silence. The whole three stages of breakdown took perhaps an hour and a half to accomplish.

Yes, Wilde overestimated the position in the Victorian hierarchy of a poet-playwright who was the cynosure of two continents. He felt behind him all the reckless and unthinking of London, Paris, New York, and why not the boundless prairies of the Middle West? Chicago had given him a king's reception.

Thus, immediately after the end of the Queensberry trial, the Home Secretary let it be signified to Robert Humphreys, who was Wilde's lawyer—and happened also to be the writer's—that a warrant would be issued for the arrest of Wilde at 6:51 that evening. That was a word to the wise, its significance being that the boat train for Paris left Victoria station at 6:50. There was a sufficient crowd of the smart that left by that train but Wilde unfortunately was not one of them. He came into Humphreys' office about two o'clock that afternoon and before Humphreys could get words spoken, he had sunk into a chair, covered his face with his hands, and sobbingly deplored the excesses of his youth, his wasted talent, and his abhorred manhood. He spread himself in Biblical lamentation. But when Humphreys, coming round his table, was intent on patting him on the shoulder and telling him to cheer up and be a man and cut his stick for Paris, Wilde suddenly took his hands down from his face, winked jovially at Bob, and exclaimed: "Got you there, old fellow."

And no persuasions of Humphreys could make him leave for Paris. No. He drew himself up, assumed his air of an autocrat and exclaimed: "Do you think they dare touch me! The author of *Lady Windermere's Fan!* I tell you the Government must fall if they did it. Why, the French would declare war. Even America!" He really believed it.

He was, by the bye, much more erect in figure than Mr. Morley made him. The writer remembers seeing him in the sunlight at the Bishop of London's garden party at Fulham in a white top hat and a gray frock coat with black buttons and braiding, much too tight across him. And he seemed, as we have said, very erect, a rather virile figure, if much too stout. The writer has very strongly the vision of Mr. Wilde, who was a common object of the countryside, who sat in a high-backed chair, consuming tea and muffins with the luxury of a great Persian cat coiled up before the fire. And wasn't that in all probability the real Wilde? The man who sighed with relief to find himself in the one house in London where he did not have to stand on his head?

Even today, the writer or painter who is to secure even the modicum of thin oatmeal that will keep the skin over his bones has to perform a sufficiency of antics in the securing of publicity for himself. But in Victorian days those antics must be still more fantastic because press agents did not yet exist and the public was even more indifferent to the Arts. Almost no Victorian great poet or painter did not owe at least half of the impress that he made on the public to one singularity or another of costume or one or another eccentricity of behavior in public. The process was called alternately *épater les bourgeois,* or "touching the philistine on the raw." And since Wilde was determined and was successful in keeping himself monstrously in the center of the picture, it would seem to have been inevitable that he should have landed where he did whether on account of his personal taste or the remorseless logic of publicity.

The writer is hardened in his half conviction that Wilde *péchait par snobisme* by the nature of his few contacts with Wilde in Paris during the latter days. Certainly Wilde, weeping and slobbering and surrounded by teasing students, was a sufficiently lamentable spectacle of indigence, solitude, and alcoholism. The students carried on with him an almost nightly comedy. Those were the days of the great Apache scares. Wilde possessed only one thing of value and that he treasured excessively. It was a heavy black ebony cane with a crook for a handle, inlaid with numerous little pinpoints of ivory. The students would come up to his table and would say, "You see Bibi la Touche, the King of the Apaches, there? He has taken a fancy to your fine stick. You must give it to him or your life will not be worth a moment's purchase."

And after they had kept this up for a long time, Wilde, weeping still more copiously, would surrender his stick. The students would take the trouble to take it home to his hotel in the Rue Jacob and next morning, Wilde, who was presumed to have forgotten the overnight incident, would find his stick, sally forth to Montmartre, and the whole thing would begin all over again.

And one may be quite uncertain as to whether the whole thing was not one last, or nearly last attempt to *épater les bourgeois*. Wilde was so obviously—so almost melodramatically—degenerated, deserted, and soaked in alcohol that one was apt to suspect that that lamentable *mise en scène* was put up for the benefit of the bystander. The writer's contacts with him at that date limited themselves solely to buying him rather rare drinks, or, if the hour were very late and Wilde quite alone, to taking him to the Rue Jacob in a *fiacre*.

One doesn't, of course, know to what extent Wilde was really deserted by his friends. He did, perhaps, tire out the patience of people. But it pleases the writer to consider that, perhaps, Wilde, in all this, was really scoring a world at which he had consistently mocked.

At any rate, one night very late, the writer found Wilde, hopelessly drunk, sprawled over a table outside of one Montmartre bistro or another. The writer was in the embarrassing position of having at the moment only exactly two francs. Wilde might be presumed to be completely penniless. It was, therefore, necessary to walk him quite a long way before arriving at a place that would be a reasonable two-franc cab fare from his hotel. It was at first very difficult to rouse the poet; but when he realized who was talking to him he came to himself rather suddenly, exclaiming, "Hey, oh yes, I'll come without resistance." He staggered for some yards, true to character, and then threw back his shoulders and we walked quite a distance side by side down the dark Rue Pigalle, he talking with quite sensible regret of the writer's grandfather and the great old house in Fitzroy Square. He seemed to retain even then quite an affection for the memory of Madox Brown, who was by that time dead. The walk comes back to this writer as having been excruciatingly painful. He was very young at the time, and that the quiet gentleman of Madox Brown's Saturdays should have fallen so low seemed to him terribly a part of the tears of things. Suddenly Wilde exclaimed, "Hello, what is all this? Why are we walking? Man was not made to walk when there are wheels on the streets."

I said, "I'm very sorry, Mr. Wilde; I haven't got the money to pay for a cab."

He said, "Oh, is that all?" And thrusting his right hand deep into his trouser pocket produced quite a respectable roll of small notes. He waved to a cab, got into it and drove off, like any other English gentleman, leaving the writer planted there on the curb.

So one may take it as one likes. And as far as this writer is concerned he likes to take it that Wilde did in the end get a little of his own back—out of this writer and all us other imbeciles—and that he died as he lived, not beyond his means, but keeping, as the phrase is, his eyes quite consummately in his own boat. It is at least pleasant to think of him winking at St. Peter as before he winked at Bob Humphreys and exclaiming, "Had you there, old fellow."

D. H. Lawrence

By Richard Aldington

June 24, 1939

Nearly ten years have passed since the death of D. H. Lawrence; and more than ten years since I last said goodbye to him, with no suspicion that I should never see him again. True, during the eight or nine weeks we had been together, he had been seriously ill; but then he had been ill so often, yet had always recovered. It seemed as if some mysterious inner vitality triumphed over sickness. Actually there was a physical basis for this. Recently I talked with the doctor who attended Lawrence in his last illness. From him I learned that, although the lungs were badly scarred, there was still plenty of resistance, and he would have survived even then but for the psychological defeat which had destroyed his will to live.

I propose here only to relate the outline of this tragedy—the inner complexities need a long essay. Lawrence, it must be remembered, was a striking personality. The books published about him show the almost fanatical devotion he aroused in his own inner group. I have never been able to see why this was the occasion for so much sneering. On the other hand, little or nothing is said about the equally fanatical and far more extensive hatred developed against him. I have often been astonished by it, and still am. People who had never even seen Lawrence, to whom he had done no harm, who had merely listened to gossip and given a prejudiced glance to one or two of his books, united to disparage and thwart him in a way which virtually amounted to persecution. It is to Lawrence's credit that he never developed persecution mania, though he was aware of this hatred, deeply wounded by it, and naturally rather resentful.

It is a peculiar situation. Here was the son of a workingman who, through his mother's determination and self-sacrifice, received enough education to become an elementary-school teacher in a London suburb. Since his father could barely read and write, that was already an achievement. But from that he went on to make a world reputation as an imaginative writer, with no resources beyond what he could earn with his pen, and in spite of ever-growing opposition. Nothing very criminal in this, one would suppose.

From the beginning an odious class snobbery came into action. Lawrence was condescendingly patronized by the London intelligentsia as a worthy sort of inferior who ought to be glad to receive their superior instruction. His early books were handled pretty roughly by the London journalists while they praised forgotten mediocrities. There was some Pecksniffian grumbling about what was called his "eroticism," and this became virulent when he eloped with a married woman, who subsequently became his wife. In spite of or perhaps because of malicious gossip, his third book was a success. But in September 1915, a year after the outbreak of war, his fourth novel, *The Rainbow,* was successfully prosecuted for obscenity and ordered to be destroyed. The book contains one paragraph with a faint suggestion of female homosexuality (so faint that I didn't see it until it was pointed out to me) and several chapters expressing disapproval of war. British magistrates love to insult authors and artists, and the defendant never has the ghost of a chance. The so-called "trial" is invariably a farce, as the judge refuses to admit any witnesses for the defense.

A few weeks after this trial I was surprised to receive a copy of a report issued by the London "Public Morality Council," which among other activities sends old women to previews of films to shorten the kisses and cut out the underclothes. The Bishop of London was an active supporter. My subscription to this association of sex-starved spinsters was demanded on the grounds that they had been responsible for getting *The Rainbow* suppressed. These people know nothing about literature and are nothing more than smut-hounds, but they still continue to function.

The Lawrences were ruined at a stroke by this. No royalties, naturally; and then no British publisher dared issue a novel by Lawrence until after the war. It would have been unpatriotic. The Lawrences took refuge in a tiny cottage on the north coast of Cornwall, for which they paid about a dollar a week and even then nearly starved. You would think they were harmless enough.

Lawrence was rejected by the army as totally unfit, and by way of doing what he could, worked on a farm. But Mrs. Lawrence was a German by birth; and sitting by the fire at night they sometimes sang German folk songs. Suddenly the military descended and searched the house, carrying off Lawrence's papers. All the papers were subsequently returned as harmless; but the

Lawrences were ordered to leave Cornwall. Apparently they had been accused of showing lights to guide non-existent German submarines into the Bristol Channel! Lawrence, who of course was utterly and entirely innocent, could never be made to see that mistakes like this do occur in wartime. Nor did he realize that the French at that moment had the jitters about spies, and had insisted that the British government take action against all suspicious characters.

Things did not rest here. Toward the end of 1917 the Lawrences stayed at the same house in London that I used. I had been back some months from the front and had just passed my final examinations as an officer-cadet. I came into the house alone at dusk one evening and found a strange man on the stairs. I asked him what he wanted, and to my amazement I found he was a detective sent to spy on Lawrence and probably to arrest him. I spent over an hour with this sinister dumb-bell trying to persuade him of the absurdity of his suspicions. Thanks chiefly to the fact that I was in uniform, I think I succeeded for the moment. Naturally, I didn't tell Lawrence about it—with his capacity for moral indignation he might have done something rash. So far as I know, he was not further troubled by spy-hunters during the war.

Curiously enough, at exactly this time another Lawrence was actively employed as a British agent in Arabia—a strange coincidence.

In 1919 D. H. Lawrence left England and never returned except on brief visits. The official and unofficial persecution did not disappear, however. In 1922 the Lawrences were in Australia, and he wrote an auto-biographical novel of their experiences called *Kangaroo*. In one chapter of that novel is a vivid description of Lawrence's fury and disgust when a hitherto friendly Australian turned up to inform him sneeringly that he was—a spy! Where had the man got this interesting information?

For the next three or four years the Lawrences were in America, and in no way troubled by this sort of thing. In 1926 on their return to Europe I saw them again, when they stayed in their home near Florence. In

1928 *Lady Chatterley's Lover* was printed in Florence and was immediately prosecuted. Opinions may differ as to the merit of that work, but I think any decent person would have been revolted by the columns and columns of swinish abuse of Lawrence published in the British press. I happened to be with Lawrence when these cuttings arrived and saw how outraged he was. The truth is that he never had the least intention of writing a pornographic book. He had lived so long away from ordinary people that he had half forgotten their prejudices. He felt he would soon die and wanted to leave a testament of beauty—he rewrote that book three times. With his narrowly passionate puritan nature and incredible naïveté, he saw himself as a crusader for a saner sex life. The foul abuse of the English press was as unexpected by him as it was shocking. I have a feeling that something died in him that night when we sat reading that malevolent trash before a log fire on the island of Port-Cros.

And this wasn't all. An exhibition of his pictures was closed by the police and several of them seized as obscene. Americans who have looked at the volume of colored reproductions will know how harmless they were—practically any modern art show has equally wicked examples of painting. The incredible thing is this. A few years later, long after Lawrence was dead, I happened to pick up a copy of an obscure and short-lived periodical containing an interview with Mr. Ernest Thesiger. In this interview he boasted that he and Sir John Squire had acted as common informers, and thus compelled the police to take action. I may add that this was not under the Bodkin regime. There was a Labor government in power, and Clynes was Home Secretary.

That makes the next stage even more amazing. As I have said, Lawrence was living with me in an old fort on the island of Port-Cros, which lies about twenty-five miles from the naval base of Toulon. The fort had been lent to me for two or three months by a French friend. It had a superb view, and French tourists occasionally asked to be allowed to see it. I invariably accompanied them, as Lawrence was very ill in bed—he had a terrible cough, and his lung had started to bleed again. One afternoon three French staff officers arrived and very politely made the usual request. I took them to the best viewpoint, and by the merest accident mentioned on the way that I had served in the war. We had the usual veterans' get-together, and then they began asking about Lawrence. I explained that he was a very talented English author, but that the British didn't like him because he had published a book of a sexual nature. This tickled the Gallic sense of humor, and they laughed heartily, while we all got in some cracks about British prudery and hypocrisy.

Still they insisted politely but firmly that they must see Lawrence. I explained how ill he was. They went on insisting, and suddenly the ghastly truth came to me—somebody had been pitching that idiotic spy story to the French naval authorities in Toulon! Luckily, Mrs. Lawrence then arrived on the scene and talked in her frank, open way, which I am certain reassured them. At last they went away. It would have been fatal for Lawrence to see them at that moment. He hated men in uniform, and with his extreme quickness would have seen at once what they were after. His anger over the *Lady Chatterley* press clippings had started his lung bleeding again; and the shock of that interview might have killed him. The intention seems to have been to get him deported from France, and as soon as he reached England he would probably have been prosecuted for "uttering an obscene libel."

In any case mail from him to England was being opened by the police, which is quite contrary to law. An envelope containing the manuscript of *Pansies* was confiscated by the police during transit through the mails, and certain poems destroyed by them.

As a rule, when a man dies, his obituary notices are not stones thrown on his grave. Such was not the case with Lawrence. An obscure journalistic clown named Jimmie Douglas published two columns of illiterate abuse under the title *The End of Filth,* and Jack Squire contributed a stupid and venomous insult to the dead. There were a good many others.

This disparagement by England of one of the most original English authors of this century still continues.

Every book about him has been sneered at. When Mrs. Lawrence published her memoirs, the newspapers quoted—with insulting banner headlines—anything which seemed to belittle him, but not a single word of the many passages showing the beauty and happiness of their lives together. Even his widow had to be insulted. More recently, the word has gone forth that Lawrence never amounted to anything and will soon be forgotten. It almost looks as if certain people *want* him to be forgotten. There is not even a birth plaque or memorial of any kind to him in his native town.

Meanwhile the other Lawrence has bloomed into a national hero and is commemorated by a public monument in St. Paul's Cathedral, London; and there is no end to the skillful publicity. It would be unfortunate if either of the two Lawrences were disparaged for the benefit of the other. . . .

The origins of the "spy" nonsense are easier to understand than the persistence of the delusion in the official mind. Imagine a harassed Military Authority in 1917; the growing submarine campaign against merchantmen; the French insistence on stringent action against spy activities in England; a man with a German wife, who sings German songs, who is disliked by the suspicious Cornish, who is alleged to be an author of obscene and subversive tendencies. . . . In wartime there is no time to investigate queer exceptions. But after the war, it should have been obvious even to the official mind that the whole charge was a grotesque error. Yet so persistent was the official prejudice against him that until recently the British Broadcasting Company would not allow his name to be mentioned. There was a rumor at one time that a well-known English author resigned his position as book commentator rather than submit to this restriction on his liberty of speech. Since then I have listened to an attack on Lawrence's prose style by that master of creative and imaginative prose, Mr. Desmond MacCarthy; and I have heard Lawrence quoted in a broadcast without acknowledgment.

There seem to be many Americans who believe that Lawrence's work is on the way to oblivion, the fate so

ardently desired for it in his own country. I don't believe it. The curve of every writer's reputation and
influence fluctuates, and usually falls to a low before
it begins gradually to rise to its true permanent level.
For various reasons the Lawrence curve is low and may
fall lower, but he will not be forgotten. His personality
is too remarkable; his work, though uneven, too original
and vivid, for such a fate. But it is a fact that nobody
can form an accurate judgment of Lawrence's achievement by reading a few of his books at hazard. The only
way to do that is to read the whole lot in chronological
order with constant reference to the Letters. Only thus
can a reader become fully acquainted with the strange
and sometimes very beautiful spirit of the last of the
individualists.

So You Want to be a Writer?

By Sherwood Anderson

December 9, 1939

In any group of young writers you will inevitably find
those who want to write and those who merely want to
be writers. They want, it seems, what they think of as
a kind of distinction that they believe comes with being
a writer. It's an odd thing. I daresay a kind of distinction, always I fear a bit synthetic, does come to a few,
but really there are so many writers nowadays. You
meet them everywhere. You can't escape them.

Let us say you are a writer. You write and write and
finally you get a book published and then another and
another. You get your picture in the book section of

The New York Times and in *The Saturday Review of Literature.*

So you go about. You meet people. You are probably thinking to yourself that everyone knows who you are. You forget that to be what is called famous as a writer only about one out of every 100,000 people need have ever even heard your name. The chances are that you have been associating a lot with others a good deal like yourself.

You have been seeking such people out and they have sought you out. You go about with so-called intellectuals. When your last book was published, your publisher, thinking it would boost your sales, has sent an advance copy of your book to a lot of other writers. He has said, "We are sending you by this mail an advance copy of Mr. Musgrave's new novel. We think it a great book. If you agree with us, please write." Or it may be a new novel by Miss Ethel Longshoreman. It seems women are nowadays writing our novels more and more. I guess they do it instead of getting married. It may be because of unemployment among the men. I don't know. Anyway it's a fact.

When it is put up to you, you do it. You think, "If I don't puff his or her book she or he won't puff mine." Very likely, however, you don't read the book. You get your mother-in-law to read it. Anyway that's my system.

The point is that you get to thinking everyone must know you. You have been about with other writers and they have said that your book is "just fine." They have said you have "a wonderful style" or something like that and you have paid them back by saying something nice about their last book and you have got rather to expecting it—I mean, you know, being something special, attracting attention wherever you go.

Then you get a jolt. Just when you want to be known, no one knows a thing about you. You have gone somewhere and have been introduced as an author. I knew a man, a manufacturer in Ohio. I was always meeting him in New York. He always had a blonde with him and always introduced her as a cousin. "Cousin Alice, meet my friend Sherwood Anderson, the author."

She always thought I was Maxwell Anderson or Robert Sherwood. She put me in the theater. She wasn't the kind that reads books.

"I just loved your last play."

Once I promised one of the man's cousins a part in one of my plays.

"I have just written a new play. You are just the type for it," I said.

His cousin became excited. I gave her Maxwell Anderson's address.

"You come to see me this afternoon."

It happens that I have never met Maxwell Anderson. I wonder if he is a strong man.

You are introduced as an author and at once someone is on the spot. You are introduced let's say to a doctor. He doesn't go about with a certain queer expectant light in his eyes, thinking that people who don't know all about him aren't cultured. He doesn't think that just because you haven't been to his office to get some medicine for your indigestion you are an ignoramus. He may even, up to the moment when he is introduced to you, have led an honorable, upright life. Like George Washington, he has never told a lie, but he tells one now. He thinks that, being an author, you are expecting it. He is like his wife who, when you once were invited to his house to dinner, rushed downtown and bought one of your books and put it on a table right in the middle of the living room, where no one could miss seeing it.

He says, "Oh yes. I have so enjoyed your books."

In a case like this, a man caught like this, in the company of an author he has never read, may try to get out of it by pretending he is a little deaf and hasn't heard when told you are an author, but he can't get away with that. It may be that you would let him get away with it, would be glad to, but someone is sure to pop up.

Let us say your name is Smith.

"How do you do, Mr. Smith. Glad to meet you," he says, and tries to make a getaway, but he is stopped.

"But this is Mr. Smith, the author," someone insists.

He gets a kind of hunted look on his face. There is

a pleading look in his eyes. Please, if any of you who read this happen to become writers, when a thing like this happens to you, be kind. Don't press the man. Don't compel him to say, as he must say if you crowd him, that something happened just as he was becoming absolutely absorbed in your last book when his wife took it away from him and every time he tried to get it back she cried.

It is a good idea in such a case to help the man out. Don't force him to tell too many lies. Let's say you have written a novel about a banker. Of course, I know none of you, if you ever become writers, will be that foolish. No one ever writes novels about bankers. Writers can't even borrow money from bankers. You all know, or should know, that nowadays it isn't worth while writing novels about any class other than the proletariat. If you write novels about people of any other class the Communists will get you. They'll call you a bourgeois, and then where are you?

So you are face to face with the man who has not read your novel about the banker and who has made the mistake of pretending that he has. You should bear this in mind. The man who has made the bluff about reading your book, when he has only some five minutes earlier heard of you for the first time, really made the bluff out of kindness of heart. You ought to try in turn to be kind to him. Help the man out. Give him a lead. Say something like this, say, "I think the banker in my novel was a most unusual man, don't you?" That will let him know that the book is about a banker.

Then go a little further. Mention the name of the town in which the banker had his bank. That will be a help. And then, if your banker ran away with the wife of the cashier of the bank, mention that. Try to drag it in. You will find it worth while. Authors should occasionally do these little deeds of kindness. Oh, the glad look that will come into such a man or woman's eyes.

I remember once being at a party with Mr. Ring Lardner. It was down in the city of New Orleans. Ring had come down there with Grantland Rice and Grantland was afraid the people of New Orleans might not know Ring was there. So Rice had done a lot of free publicity for Ring. He had called up the Mayor, the president of the Chamber of Commerce, the Kiwanis Club, the Rotary Club, the Lions Club. There was a big party at some rich person's house, and Ring took me along. He said, "Come on, Sherwood, let's give them two authors. Let's see if they know which is which."

So we did go and they knew we were authors. Grantland had told them. He got there ahead of us. He pointed us out. "There they are. There they come," he said.

He did everything but tell them what books we had written. He slipped up on that. That was what raised the devil with them. A kind of dark shadow came over the assembly. People went about with troubled eyes. They gathered in little groups whispering to each other but finally, out of one of the groups, a woman emerged. She was, I remember, very determined-looking. She had that kind of jaw, that kind of eyes. She was a rather big woman, strong and muscular, who, had she been a man, might well have been a professional wrestler.

She came up to us. She had this do or die look on her face. She tackled me first. Someone had given her my name.

"Oh, Mr. Anderson," she said, "I'm so glad you are here. I have been so longing to meet you." She said that she felt she already knew me through my books. She got that off, and there was a pause.

"Oh that last book of yours," she said. She thought it was very, very beautiful and suddenly I had a vicious impulse.

"And what book do you mean? Name it. I dare you to," I wanted to say but I didn't say it. I kept still and there was another pause. It was the kind of pause that, if it had been pregnant, should have brought forth triplets. There was this terrible waiting time and then Ring, out of the fullness of his heart, helped her out.

"You mean of course *The Great Gatsby*," he said, and there was a look of joy and gratitude on that woman's face that I'll never forget. It was the kind of good deed on Ring's part that inspired other good deeds. It inspired me and I told the woman that Ring was the author of *Sister Carrie* and of course she ran about and told all the others. It made everything all right. It made an evening that had started to be a complete flop a great success.

A few years ago I was living in a certain town down in Virginia and I bought and ran for a time a country newspaper in the town. I don't know just why I did it. I guess I didn't want the people of the town to think of me as a writer. I figured that if they thought of me as a writer they would be afraid of me as they had a right to be. So I thought I'd get around them by being a newspaper publisher. And people have a right to be afraid. We writers, in certain moods, will use anyone we can. We say to ourselves that we are after truth.

Once I did an unfair mean thing to a certain man in Ohio. He was my friend and I rather sold him out. He was angry. My name began to get up in the world and he threatened me. He said he was going to write telling just what kind of man I was.

"Please do," I said. "Rough it up. Send the whole story to me. I've half forgotten." I pointed out that I could do the job better than he could. I meant it too. I was a story-teller and I knew I could beat him telling the story.

There are certain men who are what I call "feeders." The story-teller loves such men. They go about telling little things that have happened to them. They cannot write the stories but they can tell them. Put pens into their hands and away fly the stories.

A man who worked for me on my farm was such a story-teller. What tales he told! There is a certain naïveté in such men. They look out upon life with clear eyes. They tell you the most wonderful tales of things they feel, things they have done, things that have been done to them. They tell everything very clearly. The man worked for me one summer and I cleaned up on him. I got several fine stories, heard them from his lips, while we worked together, or rather while he worked and I sat watching him, rushed at once into the house, put down the stories just as he had told them. Then I was a fool. At the end of the summer I told him what I had been doing and he grew afraid of me.

Or he thought I was getting too much for nothing. I should have kept my mouth shut. I lost a good feeder. Now the stories he might tell to many people through me are lost.

So there we are, we writers. We go about among people. We are presumed to be reading people as a man reads the pages of a book but most of the time we are doing nothing.

People keep coming up to a writer. "What are you at work on now?" they ask. He isn't working on anything. He has a tooth that needs filling and it hurts. He is wondering where he will get the money to buy a new car. He isn't at work on anything but he knows what is expected of him. It is expected that he will be at work on some big serious task. If he is wise he gives them what they expect. I do.

"I am at work on a history of the American Civil War," I say. It sounds dignified and scholarly. A look of awe and respect comes into the people's eyes.

"What a man!" they are thinking. It is wonderful. At times I almost convince myself that I am at some such great task.

We become self-conscious. That is what we have to fight against and it is sometimes a hard and bitter struggle. If we get up a little in the world people write about us. They put our pictures in newspapers and magazines. What we do about that is to send one taken when we were thirty, when our hair was thick yet, when our teeth were sound, when we had a fresh, cheerful look on our face.

Occasionally someone tells us that we are great.

It is so difficult not to believe and if you do convince yourself that it is all bunk you are miserable about that too.

So you want to be a writer?

Isn't it wonderful?

Heywood Broun

By Bennett Cerf

December 19, 1942

Heywood Broun has been dead now for three full years. The multitude of friends who loved and admired him from the bottom of their hearts find it hard to believe that it's as long as that since they saw him shambling into his favorite haunts, sloppily attired, tardy for appointments, but welcomed with shouts of joy wherever he appeared. His name bobs up in conversations as frequently as though he were still alive, turning in his daily columns. And what columns the doings of these past three years would have inspired in him! By a stroke of cruel irony, the space they once occupied is now devoted to the outpourings of Westbrook Pegler, who represents everything Broun detested most. "The trouble with Peg," he explained once, "is that he was bitten early in life by an income tax."

Broun's classmates at Harvard included John Reed, Walter Lippmann, and Hamilton Fish—an omen, possibly, of the later conflicts between his political convictions and his sybaritic personal habits. Foreign languages were his nemesis. An irate German professor shied an inkwell at him, but missed. His habit of fulfilling assignments at the last possible moment, if at all, failed to enchant the Harvard authorities, and he did not graduate. His classmates watched in awe while he threw all of his belongings helter-skelter into a trunk, and then climbed in himself and trampled them down after the fashion of a Burgundy grape presser.

Broun got a job with the *Tribune* and turned in some of the greatest baseball and football stories that ever have been written. Then he was transferred to the drama department. The day of the transfer, he acted as official scorer at a Giant-Cub ball game in the afternoon and covered Ethel Barrymore's opening in an Edna Ferber play called *Our Mrs. McChesney* in the evening. At the ball game, he scored a close play as an error for the visiting shortstop, thereby depriving the Giant batter of a base hit in the records. That evening, he roasted Miss Barrymore's performance to a fare-thee-well. The next day the *Tribune's* managing editor received two indignant communications. One, from the Giant batman, read, "What's the big idea of sending a lousy dramatic critic up here to be official scorer?" The other, signed by Miss Barrymore, concluded, "How dare you assign a cheap baseball reporter to cover the opening of a Barrymore play?"

Broun loved the theater, and the majority of his reviews were gentle and encouraging. One evening, however, an actor named Geoffrey Steyne gave a performance that displeased him. Broun allowed that Mr. Steyne was the worst actor on the American stage. Mr. Steyne sued. The whole principle of dramatic criticism was at stake in this suit; if the actor won it, obviously, a dangerous precedent would have been established. The case was dismissed, and it remained only to see what Heywood would say about Mr. Steyne on the occasion of his next New York appearance. The big night finally arrived, and the next morning initiates turned eagerly to Broun's review. He did not so much as mention Geoffrey Steyne until the last sentence of his last paragraph. This read simply, "Mr. Steyne's performance was not up to his usual standard."

Heywood was a war correspondent in France in 1918. General Pershing saw him in uniform and asked him if he had fallen into a ditch. A fellow worker once dubbed him "Six Characters in Search of a Laundry." Heywood usually forgot to put laces in his shoes. When he took them off for bowling—which he loved—he disclosed socks with such enormous holes that they looked like ankle supporters. His first wife, Ruth Hale, was just as careless as Heywood. The first time I visited their home, a step in the back staircase was broken; three years later it had not been repaired. Everybody just hopped over it, while Ruth would remark placidly, "Somebody's going to break his neck on that step someday!" I had come to collect an introduction for a

Modern Library book that Heywood had promised to deliver some two months previous. He wrote it while I waited. Then we lunched together in his kitchen. We vaulted the broken step and found that the icebox contained a single can of peaches. Heywood punctured the lid with a beer opener and emptied the peaches into two saucers that he salvaged from a pile of dirty dishes in the sink. We ate standing up.

When Dorothy Parker and Beatrice Kaufman visited the Broun Home Front, Mrs. K. is reported to have discovered a couple of deep brown, bedraggled old toothbrushes hanging in the bathroom. "Good heavens," she cried, "what are those things?" "Don't you recognize them?" said the ever helpful Miss Parker. "Those are the broomsticks witches ride on every Hallowe'en!" The last tenant of the Brouns was Ed McNamara, who plays every Irish cop role in Hollywood. "Mac," Heywood told him, "it's a shame that with a rich, resonant voice like yours, you don't ever know what the Hell you're talking about!" One night Mac came home to discover his trunk on the doorstep, and a note from Heywood written on the tag. "Dear Mac," it read, "I forgot to tell you that I sold the house!"

In 1921, Heywood joined the staff of the morning *World*, where he became scared to death of the editor, Herbert Bayard Swope. Years later, although they now were close friends and met night after night at various peoples' houses, he still held Swope—not to mention Swope's wife, Margaret—in something like awe. When Winston Churchill's son, Randolph, wangled a job on the *World* at the tender age of eighteen and called Swope "Herbert" the day he joined the staff, Heywood practically dropped in his tracks. A story he loved to tell about the Swopes concerned the day when the editor collected thirty-five men—including Broun—at the Belmont Race Track and invited them all to drop in for a drink at his Long Island home on their way back to New York. In the midst of the festivities, Broun was dumfounded when Swope turned to his guests and asked, "Why don't you all stay for dinner?" Without waiting for a reply, he turned to his wife and said,

"They're staying for dinner, my dear." Mrs. Swope rang for the maid, remarked calmly, "Mary, there will be thirty-five extra for dinner this evening," and sailed majestically out of the room. "It was terrific," whooped Heywood. Later he was dispatched in the Swope station wagon to fetch six dozen lamb chops from the Manhasset butcher shop.

Some of Heywood's quips at this time are still quoted and collected in anthologies. The depression had not yet come along to toughen our fiber and sharpen our consciousness of social inequalities; everybody drifted along in a happy haze of bathtub gin and Wall Street profits. Heywood lost more money at poker games and the race track in a single day than he had had to his name a few years previous. He labeled Woollcott "the smartest of Alecs." At a Bankhead opening, he whispered into the star's ear, "Don't look now, Tallulah, but your show's slipping!" Invited to a poker game by Ring Lardner, he reported over the telephone, "I can't come, Ring. It's my son Woodie's night out, and I've got to stay home with the nurse!" He made a disparaging statement about a fight manager in Syracuse. "You wouldn't dare come up here and repeat that," taunted the Upstater. Broun answered, "I'll be up there and say it next Friday at half past five!" "And did you?" asked the man to whom Broun was telling the story. "Of course not!" he replied. At the Baer-Carnera fight, Grantland Rice remarked, "Golly, that big fellow sure can take it." "Yeah," answered Broun, "but he doesn't seem to know what to do with it!" On the day that Babe Ruth smacked out two home runs in a world series game, and contributed a couple of sparkling catches as well, Broun's account began, "The Ruth is mighty and shall prevail!"

Heywood's dawning preoccupation with the class struggle manifested itself clearly in the Sacco-Vanzetti case in 1927. He regarded the execution of these two men as a flagrant miscarriage of justice and he wrote two burning and devastating columns about the case that belong with the great pieces of invective of all time. Ralph Pulitzer of the *World* asked him to write no more on this controversial subject, and Broun staged a one-man strike. Swope patched up the quarrel, but two years later, the wound still rankled, and Heywood accepted a fabulous offer from Roy Howard of the *Telegram*. This was when Broun first began to tell us, "You can't sit on the fence much longer. It's time to choose your side for keeps." Events of recent years have been his vindication. Referring to one fence-straddling commentator, Heywood remarked, "His mind is so open that the wind whistles through it. Nothing sticks. He's afraid to stay on any side if self-aggrandizement beckons to the other!" Heywood knew an appeaser when he saw one—years before any of us had occasion to use the word.

The last years of Heywood's life were devoted principally to the organization and promotion of the American Newspaper Guild. His customary carelessness disappeared like magic when he embraced this cause; newspapermen will never forget what he did to improve their pay and working conditions. Heywood respected all labor unions. It was against his principles to cross a picket line. One noon, however, the waiters at his favorite hangout were out on strike, and Heywood, lost in thought, passed the pickets. "Mr. Broun," said one of the waiters reproachfully, "we're on strike." "Tell me who your favorite customer is," said Broun contritely, "and I'll write him a letter and tell him to stay away." The waiter replied, "Why, you are, Mr. Broun." Heywood stormed into the restaurant, sent out luncheon to the pickets, and effected a settlement of the strike on the spot. He didn't know until much later that the proprietors had been dying to settle for days and awaited only some face-saving device to get them out of an embarrassing situation. At the height of the celebration, Broun cried, "My God, I'm due at a meeting of the Book-of-the-Month Club judges!" and rushed out, leaving behind, as usual, the galleys that were to be the subject of discussion that day. The other judges can't remember one occasion when Heywood arrived at a meeting in time. When he died, however, the directors couldn't bring themselves to appoint another judge in his place. The post is vacant to this day.

Over Thanksgiving weekend in 1938, the Averell Harrimans were hosts to a gathering of sixty at their estate in Arden. The house is located at the top of a steep hill. Heywood looked down from the summit and recalled that the year the house was built, he had eluded the guards at the outer gate, and crawled up the hill, intent on getting an exclusive interview with the ailing Edward H. Harriman, of the Union Pacific. He was caught the moment he emerged from the shrubbery, however, and hustled down to the bottom again. "Today," said Heywood, ruefully considering his build, "it's all I can do to get up the hill in an automobile." That evening, Heywood was very late to dinner. "I was down in the kitchen," he explained cheerfully to Averell Harriman, "trying to persuade the butler to strike for higher wages!"

This was the weekend that Broun and Swope decided to cross-examine Duff Cooper, another of the distinguished guests. We all gathered round expectantly, and Swope asked the first question, which Broun promptly answered—at considerable length. Then Broun essayed a query, which Swope answered. It gradually dawned on us that the interview was destined to be an exclusive dialogue between Swope and Broun. Their rhetoric flowed on, while Duff Cooper sat blinking in complete silence, like a tortoise with lumbago. Later he confided to a friend that we were the rudest people he had ever met. Of course, this was three years before he galloped off to Singapore to do nothing so magnificently while a great bastion of empire was crumbling over his head.

Two years later, we all spent another Thanksgiving with the Harrimans in Arden—all, that is, but Heywood, who was dead, and Quent Reynolds, who was reporting the Blitz from London. Swope proposed a toast that night to the two who were absent. "One," he said, "is in heaven, and the other is in hell."

Heywood had a genius for discovering strange methods to throw his money away. Once he ran for Congress on the Socialist ticket. Another time he edited a local newspaper called the *Connecticut Nutmeg*. His greatest extravagance was a play called *Shoot the*

Works, which he wrote, financed, and appeared in personally. Indirectly, this play provided him with the greatest happiness in his life. One of the girls in the chorus was named Connie Madison, and Heywood adored her at sight. They were married in 1935. She called him "The Commodore," and spruced him up almost beyond recognition. Heywood's friends accepted Connie without qualification the first time they met her. George Kaufman gave her a part in *Merrily We Roll Along*. She crossed the stage once and had a single line, which read, "I wouldn't dare bob my hair. My father would throw me out!" Broun, in his review, remarked, "Miss Madison was adequate." We hope that Connie will read this piece, and accept it as evidence that besides herself, there are a thousand and more old friends of Heywood Broun's who wish he were with us in this good fight, and who will never forget him as long as they live.

In Memory of George Gershwin

By Bennett Cerf

July 17, 1943

On an oppressively hot Sunday evening six years ago, a group of people was gathered in a Bucks County remodeled farmhouse, engaged in various desultory pastimes. A spiritless bridge game was in progress in one corner of the room; a bout of cribbage in another. The host was tinkering aimlessly with the radio dials. Some of the guests were splashing about in the pool outside, although there was no moon, and the night was pitch black. The heat had everybody down. Suddenly the clear voice of a news commentator came over the air: "The man who said he had more tunes in his head than he could put down on paper in a hundred years is dead tonight in Hollywood. George Gershwin succumbed today at the age of thirty-eight."

Everybody at that party was a close personal friend of George. Two of them had collaborated with him on his brightest Broadway hits. We had seen him within the month—joshed him on his complaint of recurring headaches (he had been telling us details of his symptoms and disorders for years; nobody took them seriously) and on a front-page report that a little French picture cutie had entrusted him with a gold key to her front door. His unbelievable energy and vitality had astounded us for so long that we sat speechless at the thought that he was dead. Now, six years later, his music is played so incessantly, stories about him spring so readily to mind, it is still somehow unbelievable that he is gone. Because he graduated from Tin Pan Alley, it has taken all these years to convince some critics that George Gershwin was a great composer—one of the greatest we have produced in America. Because his monumental but strangely unobjectionable conceit encouraged his friends to circulate hilarious anecdotes about him, some of them did not realize until he was dead how deeply they liked and admired him. The stories that I have gathered for this piece are set down in loving memory. George laughed at all of them himself.

George Gershwin was born in Brooklyn on September 26, 1898. He was the second of four children. Ira, whose sparkling lyrics were so perfectly attuned to George's music, was the oldest. Another brother, Arthur, followed George. The youngest was their sister Frances, happily married today to Leopold Godowsky. The family moved as a unit, a mutual admiration society that was completely unaffected by temporary failure or dizzying success. Mrs. Gershwin was adored by everybody. "You must meet my mother," George would tell anybody who called. "She's the most wonderful mother in the world." On further reflection, he would frequently add "and so modest about *me!*" The father, Morris, was one of those restless souls who embarked upon a new business career every year or so; the family was always ready to pull up stakes cheerfully at a moment's notice. George once figured that he lived in twenty-seven different houses before he finished school. Gershwin père was a lovable and loquacious soul whose accent lost none of its rich and indescribable flavor as the family fortunes rose. His son "Judge" was the apple of his eye. One day after the boys had hit the jackpot he was driving down Broadway in a roadster they had given him, when a cop flagged him for ignoring a red light. "But you can't do this to me!" he expostulated. "I'm Judge Gershwin's father!" "Oh, Judge Gershwin," said the copper, visibly impressed. "Pardon me for holding you up, sir!" New gadgets fascinated him. In the early days of radio, he came to George with an excited report about a new set that he wanted to order immediately. "Judge," he declared, "on this machine you could hear Havana, London, and China clear like a bell!" "London? China?" echoed George unbelievingly. "I'll settle for Havana," replied Mr. Gershwin hastily. When Professor Einstein published his paper on the theory of relativity, George commented, "Imagine being able to put the result of twenty years' study and research into three pages!" "But I'll bet it was very small print," said Mr. Gershwin.

When George was twelve, his mother bought a piano. The idea was for Ira to take lessons, but it didn't take long to discover that George was the one with music in his soul. At the High School of Commerce, he was pianist for the morning assembly exercises. At fifteen, he was a song plugger for the music publishing house of Jerome Remick. One of his chores took him to Atlantic City, where he pounded out Remick melodies at the local five and ten. Down the Boardwalk, Harry Ruby was doing a similar job for a rival outfit. At night the boys would dine together at Childs and dream of writing songs of their own.

His first song was published in 1916. It was called "When You Want 'Em You Can't Get 'Em," and it earned him an advance of five dollars. His next few numbers began to carry lyrics by Arthur Francis. That was brother Ira making his debut as a lyricist, using the first names of his older brother and kid sister as a pseudonym. His first real clicks came in 1919, when he did his first complete score for *La La Lucille* (remember "Nobody But You": "Billie Burke—Alice Joyce—none of them were my choice"?) and wrote a couple of numbers for the opening bill of Broadway's biggest movie palace of its time, the Capitol. One of the numbers was "Swanee," and I've heard it twice on the radio this very week.

Beginning in 1920, George wrote the music for *George White's Scandals* for five consecutive years. A few of the hits of these scores were "Drifting Along with the Tide," "I'll Build a Stairway to Paradise," and "Somebody Loves Me." Most of the lyrics were contributed by Buddy De Sylva, now head man at the Paramount Studios. In those days, White was the great Ziegfeld's only serious rival. Gershwin didn't meet up with Ziegfeld himself until 1929, when he wrote the score of *Show Girl*. Working with Ziegfeld was perfect training for a siege on Guadalcanal, but that's another story. After the contract with Gershwin was signed, Ziegfeld went to Carnegie Hall to hear *An American in Paris*. At the symphony's completion, Otto Kahn rose and made a brief speech in which he declared that George was well-nigh a genius. "In fact," said Kahn, "some day he will be a genius, but geniuses must suffer, and George hasn't suffered yet." Ziegfeld turned to Larry Hart, who was sitting next to him and said to him, with a sly wink, "He'll suffer!"

George became internationally famous in 1924, when Paul Whiteman introduced his *Rhapsody in Blue* at a concert in Aeolian Hall. By now the family was located in a private house on West 103rd Street, where George worked imperturbably amidst a hubbub that suggested Grand Central Station on the eve of a Fourth of July weekend. The *Rhapsody* was written there in exactly three weeks; George had to meet a deadline! That year saw, too, the first of seven musical comedies produced by Aarons and Freedley, with music by George and lyrics by Ira. Five of them made Broadway history. They were, in order, *Lady Be Good, Tip Toes,*

Oh, Kay, Funny Face, and *Girl Crazy.* They made stars of Fred and Adele Astaire, Gertrude Lawrence, Ethel Merman, and Ginger Rogers. "Fascinating Rhythm," "Do, Do, Do," "Sweet and Low Down," "Embraceable You," "I Got Rhythm," and a dozen other wonderful songs followed one another in dizzy succession. In addition, *Of Thee I Sing,* written with George Kaufman and Morrie Ryskind, won the Pulitzer Prize in 1932. George moved to a Riverside Drive penthouse, which became headquarters for a series of wondrous Sunday evening delicatessen suppers that featured Barney Greengrass' sturgeon and attracted the greatest wits and socialites of the town. That's when the Gershwin saga really started. George, who loved to play the piano for hours on end, and naïvely—also justifiably —took it for granted that nobody wanted to hear anything but his own music, would finally suspend operations to seek refreshments. His place would be taken by a surly young man who played George's music just as well as the composer. His name was Oscar Levant.

Oscar likes to tell the story of the night he and George journeyed to Pittsburgh to play with the symphony orchestra there. George took it for granted that the lower berth of the compartment was his proper due. Before turning out the light, Oscar peered over the edges of the upper to see George sprawled complacently below, puffing on a huge cigar. "Do you know what this picture represents?" said George pleasantly, when he spied Oscar's face. "It's the difference between talent and genius!" One day, Oscar, George, Ira, and I journeyed up to Baker Field to see a Columbia-Navy football game. We were late, and I weaved in and out of the trolley poles on Sedgwick Avenue rather recklessly. "For God's sake, be careful!" cautioned George. "You've got *Gershwin* in the car!"

George loved to go to parties, and thought nothing of playing the entire score of a forthcoming musical for his friends. This practice irked his canny collaborator, George Kaufman. "If you play that score one more time before we open," Kaufman once told him, "people are going to think it's a revival." Kaufman also de-

plored Gershwin's genial habit of inviting everybody
he met to sit in on rehearsals. Kaufman left one run-
through with a deep scowl. "It's going to be a prize
flop," he predicted. "What makes you say that? I
thought it went beautifully," protested Gershwin. "Not
at all," grumbled Kaufman. "The balcony was only
half filled!"

I accompanied George on some wonderful vacation
trips. They were a succession of hilarious adventures
and beautiful girls. He banged out the Rhapsody once
in the parlor of the Colonial Hotel in Nassau at seven
in the morning to please a girl he had met on the boat,
and was indignant when the manager made him stop.
"I guess he didn't know I was Gershwin," he consoled
himself. In Havana, a sixteen-piece rumba band
serenaded him en masse at four in the morning outside
his room at the old Almendares Hotel. Several outraged patrons left the next morning. George was so
flattered that he promised to write a rumba of his own.
He did, too. His "Cuban Overture" was played for
the first time at the Lewisohn Stadium in August 1932.
In Havana George reached his greatest height of indignation. A lovely Cuban miss failed to keep a luncheon
date with him. Later that afternoon he spied her on
the Yacht Club terrace, and exclaimed, "Hey, do you
know that you stood me up today?" "Oh, I meant to
phone and tell you I couldn't meet you," said the
contrite maiden, "but do you know something? I simply
couldn't think of your name!" George didn't recover
for days. . . . He reserved one unpublished little waltz
tune for affairs of the heart. "You're the kind of girl
who makes me feel like composing a song," he would
tell the enraptured lady of the moment, and lead her
off to his suite. We would follow on tiptoe to hear him
compose the familiar tune for her. "It will be dedicated
to you," he would conclude soulfully. One day, I happened to remark that the score of one of his infrequent
failures, *Pardon My English*, was below par. George
demurred. All of us were sun-bathing in the nude;
George insisted that we all go inside while he proved
his point by going through the score from opening

chorus to finale. I can still see him sitting at the piano, stark naked, playing the songs and singing them, too, at the top of his voice. George belonged at a piano. I have never seen a man happier, more bursting with the sheer joy of living, than George when he was playing his songs. He would improvise and introduce subtle variations, and chuckle with childlike delight when his audience exclaimed over them.

The work that George Gershwin loved best was *Porgy and Bess.* He composed it in eleven months and orchestrated it in nine. Its initial production by the Guild in 1935, a bit too stuffy and pretentious, was only moderately successful. When it was revived seven years later, it really came into its own, and its songs seem destined to become part of America's richest musical heritage; the tragedy is that George wasn't living to see that come to pass.

George moved to Hollywood in 1936. He wrote the music for the Fred Astaire-Ginger Rogers picture *Shall We Dance?*, which included one of his best songs ("Oh, No, You Can't Take That Away from Me") and "A Damsel in Distress." He was working on the Goldwyn Follies when he was stricken by a brain tumor.

The last years of Gershwin's life were almost equally divided between composing and painting. George took his painting very seriously, and indeed had a genuine talent for it. At a memorable dinner one evening he said, "A man told me today that I need never write another note; I could make a fortune with my palette and brush!" "Isn't it amazing," said one awed lady, "that one man should possess a genius for two of the arts!" "Oh, I don't know," said George modestly. "Look at Leonardo da Vinci!" At another dinner, apropos of nothing, George suddenly said, "Has anybody here seen my new cigarette case?" It was solid gold, and inscribed thereon were facsimile signatures of a score of famous men. It had been presented to him after a performance of his Concerto in F. The case was passed clear around the table. As George was putting it back into his pocket, his brother Ira produced a crumpled pack of Camels. "Anybody want a cigarette?" he inquired pleasantly.

But Ira, like everybody else who knew him well, adored George Gershwin. After his death, Ira wrote practically nothing for years. That he had lost none of his talent he proved, however, with the lyrics for *Lady in the Dark*. Now he is going to work on the screen biography of George Gershwin. The title role has not yet been filled, but Oscar Levant will play himself in the film.

George Gershwin expressed his credo in these words: "My people are American, my time is today. Music must repeat the thought and aspirations of the times." Six years after his death, his exciting songs are played more frequently than they were during his lifetime. One critic recently remarked, "George Gershwin brought to serious consideration a new idiom in American music, and forever changed its future direction." Last Tuesday twenty thousand people gathered in New York to hear a program dedicated to his memory. As the first familiar strains of the *Rhapsody in Blue* hushed the expectant audience, it was hard to believe that the composer had been dead for over six years. It seemed like yesterday that he had sat beside me in Cuba, listening to the same composition on the radio, and saying, "It *is* great, isn't it? But wait till you hear the one I'm working on now!"

Genius in the Madhouse

By Harrison Smith

March 31, 1945

Once upon a time the New York *Tribune* decided to brighten its pages with colorful reporting of local events, so Mr. Reid bought himself a young reporter or two whom he might otherwise have kept off the payroll. I never saw Mr. Reid, but in the end he knew I was there all right. The city editor was a nice, sarcastic, swearing gentleman who was always asking me, what the hell kind of a place did I think the *Tribune* was?

One Monday I got in on time, while most of the boys were busy with hangovers, or catching up on their sleep, and was summoned to the throne. "For God's sake, find out what this woman wants, I don't know what the hell she is trying to say." I was introduced to a middle-aged woman with glittering eyes and a fine neckpiece of rat's fur around her throat. Her name was Mrs. Adams, and she said, "I want to talk to someone about Ralph Blakelock."

I was just the man for Mrs. Adams. It so happened that I knew about Ralph Albert Blakelock, born in 1847. He was one of our greatest landscape painters, he had an immense canvas in the Met with trees against a yellow sky and another one of a moonlit tree that I thought had the edge on Corot's trees and moons. I seemed to recall that Blakelock had died ages ago of whatever people die of, or maybe of poverty. But I learned from this jumpy woman with some kind of facial twitch that Blakelock was only artistically dead, that his living remains were incarcerated in an insane asylum, where his wife had placed him after he had burned up a hundred dollars in the kitchen stove, because that was all he got for a painting for which he had been promised a thousand.

So Blakelock was alive, after all! In those days I had, or thought I had, a scent for a front-page story. If I had been a bird dog, I would have pointed at her, but, being only a reporter, prickles ran up my backbone. I looked in our morgue, where Ralph Blakelock's newspaper biography had ended years ago, though his paintings had come to life all over the country and had been sold for tens of thousands of dollars. He was a dead man to all intents and purposes, but he had never been officially buried. I poured all this in one long sentence into the ear of the city editor who looked at me as if I was offering him a dose of poison. But he scooped up a phone and called Middletown State Insane Asylum, still glaring at me.

Well, Blakelock was in Middletown all right, and I was on my way to him before the city editor put down the phone. They took me in to see him. Blakelock was in a room that might have belonged to one of the nicer cell blocks in Sing Sing. He had been sitting there, or in other rooms like it, for almost twenty years. He began to talk in a mild voice. He told me about the blue diamond of the Emperor of Brazil that somebody had stolen from him. If he had it now, he said, he would sell it and go somewhere and paint. The asylum had known nothing about him or his career, except that his name was Blakelock, and that he was mad. The reason why he jumped up from his chair as if someone had stuck a pin in him when I mentioned his canvases in the Metropolitan was because he was afraid he would be hydropathically punished if he talked about it. I looked at his frightened eyes, and I could hear a warden saying, "Blakelock, in 418, is talking about the Metropolitan Art Museum again, sir," and the director saying, "Take his temperature and give him a bath."

I stayed in the Middletown Asylum for four hectic and fascinating days. I had never been in an asylum before, and I made up my mind right then to maintain an appearance of sanity for the rest of my days. I was aflame with a kind of youthful ardor to make this old man's agony the story of the year, and, somehow, to make up for his neglect by the American people.

Middletown's director was of course charmed to discover that for all these years he and his predecessors had been sheltering a genius. It seems that he had had other geniuses there, nice quiet people, who were a credit to his institution. He thought that geniuses were naturally attracted to insane asylums. I liked him, all right, but he had a young daughter whom I liked a lot better, and I used to sit up with her in the kitchen after midnight when Pa had gone to bed. She had some lovely childhood recollections and one of the nicest was her remembrance of a night when she was chased around the very table I had my feet on by a lunatic, brandishing a carving knife. There was a dance one night and some female screwball who was skipping around took a fancy to the pink-striped shirt I wore and wanted me to take it off and give it to her. It was a good shirt so I kept it on.

One day the city editor phoned me at Middletown and asked me why the hell I didn't come home, and what the devil did I think I was writing, a front-page story? I said, Yes, I was going to write a front-page story, and I wanted two or three columns on the front page for Thursday night. He said, bitterly, "Are you crazy?" I said that I was, but that I was going to bring Ralph Blakelock back with me to New York with the director of the Asylum Thursday afternoon, that I wanted a suite for them at a grade-A hotel, and an unlimited expense account for myself for our lunch. "What in God's name is happening?" he screamed. "Look at your art page," I said, coldly, "and you will find a notice of a loan exhibition of Blakelock's paintings on Fifth Avenue near Forty-second Street."

There was a long deadly silence, but when he said, "Christ!" as if I had set fire to his coattails, I knew that I had him, that I had put it over. If I live to be a thousand, I will never experience a moment like that again.

Then he said bitterly, "But you can't write it yourself! I'll give you your two columns and a rewrite man." I said, "I will take the columns and shoot your rewrite man." There was another silence; then, "All right, but I don't believe you can do it." As a matter of fact, I didn't either.

Before we started for New York, I had a long talk with old Blakelock, who still looked nervous when he spoke about his own work. His mind was as clear as a bell about it, until the diamond of the Emperor of Brazil crept in. We talked about the Asylum as if it was a rest home in the country to which he had voluntarily retired. The warden sat beside me, smiling patronizingly at us, as if I were carrying on a conversation with one of his patients who thought he was Jesus or Napoleon. I asked Blakelock a silly question. Had he been able to do any painting in Middletown? He said that five years ago he had been given a child's paint-box, but it had been taken away from him, and that a long time ago he had discovered how to paint with ink. He showed me the brushes that he used. Brushes! They were made out of matchsticks, with the white hairs that he had pulled out of his head secured to the ends by rubber bands. I will swear on the Bible that this is true. And he diluted the ink, so that he could get, as he said, an almost infinite gradation of blue colors.

And so Blakelock, who seemed when we were finally on the train, to be less and less of a man, and more like a pale, long-fingered leprechaun, and the director, still inflated with this discovery of a genius who had been under his eyes for years, and my humble and frightened self rode to New York.

When Blakelock had left New York, it was a flat, brownstone city. He looked at the towering buildings on Fifth Avenue, and said mildly, "My, my!"

By this time I was really scared to death. I felt that I had made a damn fool of myself, that I had made the gesture of a D'Artagnan, without having any more courage than a rabbit, that I had put the boss and the whole noble outfit that was the *Tribune,* including Mr. Reid, in a spot they couldn't get out of. Also I knew that I was done for, and I could probably look forward to going back to Middletown—alone.

Well, we arrived at the big art gallery where Blakelock's work was on exhibition. It had been swept clear of visitors. A suave and nervous gentleman in a morning coat and a Van Dyke beard was there; also an experienced reporter from the *Tribune,* to take over in case I fainted, or something. Oh, no, the *Tribune* wasn't taking any chances on me! The gallery walls were lined with Blakelock's paintings, brought there from all over the country, a million dollar's worth, maybe. The effect on Blakelock was prodigious. He seemed to have gained a foot in height. Then I stopped looking at him because I didn't think I could take it any longer.

It turned into quite a story when I got downtown. I wrote it in a daze; it literally ran out of the typewriter by itself. The *Tribune* gave it the works, front page and all, and some weeks later a fund was raised to get the old painter out of the Asylum and put him in charge of the very Mrs. Adams who told me the story that morning in the office. Of course, Blakelock was graduated from Middletown, cum laude and all. He went to live in the Adirondacks. Four years later he died. Mrs. Adams came to see me after his death, twitching worse than ever and as mad as a hatter, I thought. She said that Blakelock had been murdered by the gang who had been forging his paintings. Maybe he had been. Certainly that afternoon in the gallery he had twice seized my arm and whispered in his precise voice, "I didn't paint that one." And then later, across the room, before another large canvas, "This one I had only started to paint." But that story was never printed. After all, Blakelock was supposed to be insane, wasn't he?

This, then, is the true story of the rediscovery of a great American painter. Even the Dictionary of American Biography omits the fact that he had been neglected and that his fate was known to only a few. It says mildly, "His health improved so distinctly that he left the asylum where his return to New York created much interest, not only owing to the signal appreciation of his pictures shown by high prices but because of sympathy for a man of attractive personality who had been overtaken by disaster at the high tide of his career." This is streamlined biography with a vengeance. It skips lightly over seventeen years of incarceration and forgets that he was not released because "his health improved" but because an aroused public restored him to life.

There used to be several ways of disposing of painters who were a nuisance while they were alive, but prospectively valuable ten years after they were dead. They could be starved in garret studios, knocked flat by critics, and neglected by commercial galleries who, nevertheless, kept stocks of their forgotten canvases in storage. Today, if another Ralph Blakelock sprang into prominence, his work would be reproduced in six colors in *Life* and written up in *Time* and *Newsweek*. His mind would not be unhinged by lack of money. He would not be a dead genius while he was still alive.

Newspaper anecdotes do not need any point, but

this yarn of the exhuming of Ralph Blakelock has one. It is good to know how far we have come in our willingness to recognize and reward the talents of artists in the last quarter of a century, a period about which so many calumnies have been written.

Adventures in Starting a Literary Magazine

By Henry Seidel Canby

October 13, 1945

I began my career as a literary journalist in old downtown New York. From my window in an office building on Vesey Street I looked down on the ancient churchyard and across to the eighteenth-century belfry of St. Paul's, then ringed about with towers still the highest in New York. Broadway roared a block away, and to mingle in the sidewalk crowds of bankers' clerks, financiers, and journalists brushed off the scholar's cobwebs and gave a useful sense of responsibility to a large and indifferent world.

North a little way were the offices of all the great newspapers, except the *Times,* which had already gone uptown, and down toward the North River were narrow dirty streets under the elevated viaducts, with hole-in-the-wall restaurants, incongruous slums under million-dollar office buildings, and tiny shops for everything from ship models, trout flies, typewriter ribbons, patent medicine, old books to betting on the races. The ancient publishing house of Harper's was not far off, entered into by a broad flight of iron steps to a great semicircle of desks, from which cold eyes seemed to be looking down at the nervous contributor as he carried up his manuscript. Over by the East River was Walt Whitman's favorite eating place, and if the masts were all gone from the waterfront, the sea mist still blew in our windows, and the mournful blasts of liners' whistles were the undertones for the newsboys' shouts of extra, and the clatter of the elevators.

I had come to New York in 1920 to establish a literary supplement of high quality worthy of a long tradition for the old New York *Evening Post,* dean of American newspapers, but frequently regarded as a dean *emeritus.* Alexander Hamilton had founded the *Post* to represent conservative interests in the young republic, and his ghost still walked the corridors, though it had a curious way of looking more like Thomas Jefferson. For the *Post* became what the English call a conservative radical. It represented the vested interests when they behaved themselves, and was proud of having the best financial section in New York. It was liberal, and progressive up to the point where the existing order seemed to be threatened. It was probably the best written, certainly the most scholarly paper in America, and in its subconscious was an impulse deeper than thought to oppose the majority whenever and however it came to power. The *Post,* under a different ownership, had been antiwar up to 1917. We were still anti to most of the current political and economic movements except world order and the League of Nations. It was a magnificent, a high-minded, a deeply responsible paper, but it was about as popular as the president of the antisaloon league. There could have been no better foundation on which to erect an independent, scholarly, and responsible review of literature and current books.

The *Evening Post* gave me my only experience of newspaper journalism, and taught me more about cooperative endeavor than I had ever learned in a university. For an established newspaper, with a tradition behind it, is a corporate being in which a dozen trades, professions, skills are inseparably bound together in a common enterprise. The editorial writer, whose specialties may be pure milk, municipal politics, or the

Missouri Valley, becomes conscious of his dependence upon the hard-knuckled thugs who get the paper distributed. The head of a literary section must learn a good deal about printing or be helpless when he is told that type lice have eaten up his overset.

I found a newspaper as rich in eccentrics as a university, and stuffed with personalities. We had an absorbed editor who never knew that he was to become a father until they telephoned him from the hospital. We had a temperamental typesetter who burst into tears whenever there was too much copy at the last moment, and had to be comforted by the lady assistants. There were the series of promotion men, all big-fisted, high-hearted fellows, who banged on the table and then went out to spend $100,000 on promotion, with no appreciable results. The wise and humorous Simeon Strunsky was at the head of our editorial council. At the darkest moments he could make us believe in the inevitable survival of virtue. These were the boom days, when Thomas W. Lamont, who had taken over the paper and many of the staff from Oswald Garrison Villard, was abroad on affairs of the Peace, leaving his purse strings behind. He was a backer of good will and good works, never seeking his own advantage, and leaving us complete independence. I wish that before he left, he had taught us a little more about practical finance. There was too much belief on our staff in Tennyson's aphorism, "We needs must love the highest when we see it." The larger public simply couldn't see the *Post,* even if it was bristling with high standards. So those bad times came when everyone from the editor, Edwin F. Gay, an honest and able man, though not newspaper-minded, down to the office boys, was made to feel that the *Post* was an institution more important than private welfare, and that we must save it—and for a while we did.

My job in 1920 began in the boom days, but I was so accustomed to the parsimony of a university that it never occurred to me to ask for my share of the promotion money being spent so lavishly. My task was to organize a *Literary Review* to be published with the Saturday paper as a supplement—and when we came to the first printing, that was what we called it. Both time and place were propitious.

Before our regime, the *Nation* had been an organ of the *Post,* but it had declined into stodginess relieved only by occasional critical essays of great worth, written by the old guard, where erudition, however, did not always make up for their lack of contact with the on-coming age. It used to be told of the *Nation* of that day that it reviewed the Christmas gift books of one year in the following November. I doubt whether it mattered. The *Times* and the *Tribune* had fallen into the same rut together. Their leading articles on important books were competent and well written, but too often were designed to show how much more the critic knew about the subject than did the author. The book itself was buried by the review, and sometimes had no resurrection. The rest of the columns were entrusted to reviewers who could be expected not to say anything unpleasant. I hoped to kindle a new fire in these dry logs and brush heaps of criticism, and in addition I had my own private desire, which was to bring to the interpretation of new books for the intelligent reader the service of the erudition and trained thinking of scholarship in the univer-sities.

And so I sharpened my pencil (a tool much more dear to me than pen or typewriter), organized my edi-torial staff, and set to work. Miss Amy Loveman, one of the ablest, certainly the kindest, assuredly one of the most useful women in New York, was my associate. William Rose Benét, poet and critic, was my literary adviser, a man of mingled fire and honey, whose con-cern was every human interest except his own. In a cubicle next door to my office, puffing pipe smoke at the hinges, was the columnist of the *Post,* Christopher Morley—a rusher in and out, bubbling ideas like a soda fountain, a wit, a wagster, an Elizabethan philosopher, with one of the few minds I have ever known that seemed to be continuously enjoying itself. Then I settled down to the first office job I had ever held, and though I could never learn to work happily in shirt sleeves and suspenders, and so was clearly not a congenital newspaperman, I spent engrossed and happy days.

Perhaps it is only in a small periodical in its formative years that one gets the sense of a gathering of a family of minds, so that when the magazine comes to maturity it has a personality of its own. Such a magazine was *Time* in its earliest years, when, for a while, our family group was associated with it. Such a magazine was this *Literary Review* of ours, which, if conceived in my brain, owed its vitality, and also its longevity (for the present *Saturday Review of Literature*** is the same child grown up under another name) to a diverse group of like-minded editors. And it would seem that these earliest 1920s were by some literary astrology the right time for a corporate literary personality to be born. As I have said elsewhere, the columnists had been preparing an audience ready to support vitality and competence in either creative literature or in criticism. The success of a magazine like *The New Yorker* (born 1921) would have been impossible in, say, 1910. Whatever the cause, an editor who wished to give new books a chance to be read by the right people in the right way got plenty of support of the kind that cannot be bought.

This support came from the writers as well as from the audience. I was sure from past experience that if we gave good writers a chance to do what they wanted we should not (as indeed we could not) have to pay more than modest sums for their work. It is a fact that literary writing done for nothing is seldom good for much. Apparently the author who does not expect to be paid for his work loses his sense of audience and becomes too self-regarding. He writes just to please himself, which is a form of dilettantism. But if a payment is established, the amount has little relation to the excellence of the product provided it is all the editor can afford to pay. The editor's problem is to get the writer to work for him on subjects possible for his periodical or publishing house. The professional author will not write better for twice the money for he cannot.

---

* In 1952 the name of *The Saturday Review of Literature* was shortened to *The Saturday Review* and its scope was accordingly broadened to include the subjects of music, science, travel, and other not strictly literary content.

A fat purse is useful to an editor only in buying talent away from other editors or in priming the pump of a lazy mind. But a fat purse means a large circulation behind it, which means that the writer gets more money but a diluted audience, for whom often, though not always, it is impossible for him to write on the themes that interest him most. That is the vicious—but inevitable—circle. Fortunately, we were not seeking fiction or sensational news articles—the most expensive varieties of magazine literature—and yet we got, with a few exceptions, what we wanted for what we were able to pay. What we lacked in cash, however, had to be made up by double duty in the search for the right man for an appealing opportunity.

We believed that a literary supplement of a newspaper, which, however excellent, was local to one city, should have a subscription which was national even though small, and got permission to circularize among the right people, and soon had 8,000 to 10,000 subscribers strategically distributed all over the country. We believed that a literary magazine should be as carefully composed as was good literature itself. Carl P. Rollins, the typographer, helped us with our layout, in which we began by breaking two journalistic traditions. The leading article had only a one-column head, balancing the editorial essay on the other side, leaving the middle of the first page for a poem.

It was an audacious shifting of emphasis from the timely to attempts to present aspects of the eternal; and probably unwise, for there was often as much, or as little, of the eternal in the leading article as in an editorial. But I still like to look at that old first page. And it did represent something deep in my mind, which was that criticism written for the general intelligent reader should be liberal in its definition. It should include humor and wisdom and beauty also, as well as fact-finding and theory. The review was supposed to revolve around two planetary centers, with orbits interweaving in a harmony: the one, books under review for which the leading article beat the big drum; the other literary, in which creative comment on aspects of life and literature, interspersed with cartoon, caricature, and enlightened gossip about the authors who made the books, would relate our estimates of success or failure in the bookshops, with the long vistas of literary history.

We spent three months recruiting, balancing what we got, arranging a first number where everything was to swing into place like toy stars and planets in a model for a class in astronomy. The result was farcical, since it pleased everyone but the editor, who was still too inexperienced to be anything but a perfectionist. This outline so interested the publishers that an actual storm of last-minute advertising swept away the further reaches of our orbits with their nice adjustments of minor constellations of criticism and comment intended to complete the harmony of the whole. To change the figure, the rear of the magazine became a billboard; and to change it again, to my eyes, though fortunately not to others, the first number of the *Literary Review* looked like a man in a dress suit, with the tails cut off, and patches visible on the seat of his trousers.

My colleagues developed abilities which they scarcely knew that they possessed. Amy Loveman was soon more knowledgeable about books and authors than anyone else in town. She had been trained as an assistant on an encyclopedia, and heartily enjoyed escaping from the dead to the living. William Rose Benét, already a poet of distinction, proved to be a congenial columnist, and his wise and witty comments on the human comedy of literary creation were soon being widely quoted. His neighbor in the next cubicle, Christopher Morley, and he soon borrowed a name from the half legendary figure of Sir Kenelm Digby, which they shifted back and forth as a shield behind which to shoot at all and sundry, including each other. I was not only editor, but contact man in a large way. It was my job to herd the great in name and experience into our little clearing and milk them of what they could be persuaded to let down of critical wisdom or scholarly erudition. It was surprising how many came.

A magazine, I decided, must have either a policy or an idea, or both, in which case the emphasis would be sure to fall on one or the other. I had no objection to

the policy magazine, as long as the policy did not interfere with the job of making a good magazine. The *New
Republic,* once so brilliant, had been left sprawling by
the war and was seeking a line by which to pull itself
together again. The old, rather pedantic, *Nation* was
turning leftward, with new blood in its veins. The *New
Masses,* a portent of the fanatic ideologies and brutal
politics in the storm clouds ahead, was all policy, so
much so that in the reviewing pages you could predict
in advance what they would say of any controversial
book. It was a valuable irritant, but bitterly unfair,
and often stupidly ignorant of any values not in its own
ten commandments. Being a Quaker in mood, tolerant,
but passionately concerned for a more intelligent world,
I was better pleased by magazines with ideas rather
than dogmatisms behind them. I liked *The New Yorker*
because it was aware of the new sophistication of
urban society, and made its own very real idealism
articulate by good-humored irony, whose cutting edge
just emerged like a safety-razor blade. I respected,
though I did not always like, *Time,* because in an ac-
celerating world it made the escape from provincialism
easier.

My own idea was not original. Indeed it was only the
Jeffersonian belief in the necessity of education for a
successful democracy. I wanted to go in for adult education in the values of books—all kinds of books,
foreign as well as native, but particularly the current
books of our country. I wanted criticism to be first of
all a teaching job. And, indeed, whether running a
Freshman class, or editing the *Saturday Review,* or
chairmaning the Book-of-the-Month Club, the inner
impulse with me, and probably the chief value, has been
the same, to teach.

Teaching is a delicate affair—a real art—and has to
be separated from the more obvious tasks of critics,
such as making and breaking reputations. I did some
of that, but chose for my main task a series of weekly
editorial essays whose purpose was a commentary on the
ups and downs and ins and outs of the life of books,
interpreting, prophesying when I dared, summarizing
when I could, and never hesitating to swing from critical

theory into nature descriptions (which I liked to write) if I felt that the cockneys were getting too far away from earth. They were true "assays," that is experiments in the search for values, leaving the working out of what I suggested to others, often to later and more ambitious efforts of my own.

And so the *Literary Review,* the parent of the *Saturday Review,* began to slide weekly from the presses. I took opinions as to its merits and demerits wherever I could get them, but the management of the *Evening Post,* on which, for all our independence, we were dependent for our existence, naturally looked to the publishers, whose support, or lack of it, could make or break us. They supported us, but they were by no means enthusiastic. I had thrown my nets widely for contributions, but most widely in the academic pool which I knew best. The magazine, so the trade thought, was unnecessarily erudite. And indeed it soon became more authoritative in its reviews of serious books than any other medium in America. It was the literary supplement of the *London Times,* and no periodical on this side of the water, which was held up to us as an example of a dignity and a scope to which we had not yet attained, and indeed I could well understand that publishers' salesmen and booksellers were at first inclined to regard the *Review* as just one more burden in their difficult business.

The inevitable day came when the *Evening Post,* staggering under its debts, was swallowed in one expensive gulp by the Curtis family organization, then at the height of its affluence. Henceforth, and for a little while our *Post* was to become a New York edition of a Philadelphia paper.

I came back from a brief Southern vacation to find a brisk managerial person in charge, who regarded our practical idealism (for our book section had made money) and our national circulation and influence as a string quartet playing irrelevantly in the corner of his three-ring circus. And so I wrote a final editorial headed, "And Twitched His Mantle Blue," guessing that the new proprietors would not know what was the following line in "Lycidas"—"Tomorrow to fresh woods, and pastures new."

The *Literary Review* itself became, first a hodge-podge, then a heading with a few reviews beneath it. But our friends would not let us die. With the support of Thomas W. Lamont and the co-operation of the editors of *Time,* two of whom had been students of mine at Yale, we migrated en masse—editors, columnists, poets, reviewers, critics, and commentators, with a baggage of ideas, and a somewhat dubiously acquired subscription list—left Vesey Street for good and all, and in three months launched the *Saturday Review of Literature,* which was the old *Literary Review* come of age, more humorous, more literary, broader in scope, better looking, but with the same will to further the cause of good thinking, good feeling, good writing, and good books.

New York and American literature were growing fast. The real end of the nineteenth-century era was close at hand. We were fortunate in our nearly five years of existence to have learned the hard way in financial restriction and by youthful experiment what could and could not be done before the new age brought new conflicts and new kinds of literature. I had shaken off some pedantic academicism, and no longer yearned to publish articles that only scholars could understand but almost no one, not even scholars, bothered to read. Much more important, our team had found their way to attics, studios, newspaper desks, Connecticut hilltops, and Greenwich Village hideouts, to libraries and universities, to selected minds in England, Ireland, France, and Germany, and recruited knowledge, perception, and good writing, often where no critical writing had been done before. Our friends came with us. I do not suppose that the Saturday edition of the *Post* in the New York area, which carried with it the *Literary Review,* ever had more than fifty or sixty thousand circulation, to which we added eight to ten thousand from our national, independent distribution. But we seemed to have found the right minds for our appeal, and they followed us to our new office uptown, above a factory, with floors reverberating from the machinery below in a new rhythm of a new age.

But most important and most interesting of all, we had lived intensely in what I have called a brief golden age of American writing before the boom and the burst and the preliminaries of war. We had become part of that literary scene which I still think was the first classical pausing moment of perfected art and summary achievements since the great days of the 1850s. And we had experienced what never can happen twice with the same excitement, an initiation into the curious swirl of the literary life around a young and creative magazine.

They Think They Know Joyce

By Oliver St. John Gogarty

March 18, 1950

We were young, we were merry in our salad days in Dublin. There were James Joyce, John Elwood (we called him "the Citizen," an ebullient, tangential fellow with quizzical, dancing eyes and a lovely mouth, whose favorite adjective was "terrific!"), and myself.

Opposite the National Library, where we met, was the National Museum with a curved colonnade. Its hall was circular and decorated by nude plaster casts, somewhat larger than life, of the famous statues of antiquity. One afternoon Joyce confronted Elwood as we gathered at our usual meeting place. He assumed an air of very great gravity as he was wont to do when about to perpetrate a joke.

"It has come to my notice, Citizen," he said solemnly, "that this morning between the hours of ten-thirty and eleven you inscribed your name in lead pencil on the backside of the Venus of Cnidus. Are there any extenuating reasons that may be cited in your defense?"

"He's terrific," said the Citizen when we talked about it afterward. "He's a great artist. Terrific."

In the Dublin use of the word *artist* lies the key to James Joyce: the explanation of how this contradictory character, who in his early days knew beauty so well, became chief of the apostles of confusion and ugliness, the leader of the decadents.

In Dublin *artist* does not denote one who is devoted to painting or any of the arts. In Dublin an artist is a merry droll, a player of hoaxes. In Dublin if you went to a fancy-dress ball attired as a bird and laid an egg that exploded, you would be an artist; if you bought a ham in the morning, paid for it, left it hanging outside the store until the rush hour, and then ran off, carrying it under your arm, with the police in hot pursuit, you would be an artist of the first category.

I wonder what all the worshipers of Joyce would say if they realized that they had become the victims of a gigantic hoax, of one of the most enormous leg-pulls in history.

Floods of nonsense have been poured on James Joyce by those who know nothing about Dublin. The authors of these learned treatises see significances and palimpsests, connections with the nine months' gestation of the human embryo and the development of the earth, as well as parodies of authors appropriate to the theme.

I think with sorrow of the Joyce worshipers. Perhaps when we consider that their enthusiasm is the measure of their ignorance it would be folly to try to enlighten them. But when they pretend that Joyce and they are inventors of something new and unprecedented in literature, "a new speech dimension," as one gentleman, C. Giedion-Welcker, calls it, our indulgence ceases. Here is a specimen of what Mr. Giedion-Welcker so admires in Joyce: "He had already woven various word jokes about Zurich into the section concerning 'Anna Livia Plurabelle.' 'Well, that's the Limmat' (for limit), 'You don't say the silly-post?' (for Sihlpost), and 'legging a jig or so on the sihl. . . . There's the bell for Sexaloitez. . . .' " A new speech dimension? It is infantile. Mairzy Doats! As Jung put it:

> [I] read it [*Ulysses*] from the end backwards. This proved to be as good a way as the usual one, for it has no forwards and no backwards, no top and no bottom. Everything could as well have been so before, or might easily still become so in the future . . . the entire work reminds us of the bisected worm that can grow a new tail and a new head where they are needed. We are in doubt whether we are dealing with a physical or with a transcendental tapeworm. In itself the tapeworm is a whole living cosmos—and it is fabulously procreative. This, it seems to me, is an unbeautiful though hardly an unfitting comparison for Joyce's chapters. It is true that the tapeworm can produce nothing but other tapeworms, yet it can produce them in inexhaustive quantities.

When we think of anyone's hailing *Ulysses* and *Finnegans Wake* as all the world's erudition in disguise, the question of the sanity, or even of the literacy, of the Joyce enthusiast arises. It is said that there are only 600 in a generation whom Nature has equipped with the necessary apparatus for perceiving the beauty of poetry. Joyce was pre-eminently equipped. He had a "nose like a rhinoceros for literature," as Juvenal said about the long-haired boys in Rome. His repertory was prodigious; he was familiar with every line of the masters of English poetry and prose. His love of beauty, his capability, and his unerring taste resulted in his little book of poems *Chamber Music,* composed when he was about nineteen, which contains all that he wished to keep of his visions of youth and loveliness.

What happened to cause him to produce *Ulysses,* a triumph of ugliness and chaos and ineffectuality?

There was a small publishing firm in Dublin whose manager burned a whole edition of *Dubliners*—all but one copy, which he allowed Joyce to take with him to the Continent. He claimed that *Dubliners* contained an offensive reference to the King, which was unlikely, seeing that Joyce received a grant from the King's Privy Purse long before he established a place for himself in literature. This was the unkindest cut of all, coming on the top of failure to obtain employment or even food. The persecution complex was supplied. Something broke in Joyce: to Maunsell's firm and to the slum-stricken town he said, "A pox on both your houses." He fled to Flushing in Holland, whence he sent two abusive poems to his acquaintants. He admitted no one to his friendship. Henceforth it was to be James Augustine Joyce against the world.

He had come to consider all Dubliners his enemies. The last time he visited that city he called on me in Ely Place. He looked out at my garden, which was in all the beauty of blossom.

"Is this your revenge?" he asked.

"Revenge on whom?" I inquired.

"The public, of course," he said.

He was the most predamned soul I have ever encountered.

From Flushing I received a post card with a photograph of Joyce dressed to resemble Arthur Rimbaud. Rimbaud's revolution against established canons made him a god to Joyce. We must not leave Rimbaud out of the reckoning; if we do, we will fail to understand the influences that fashioned Joyce. Rimbaud, disgusted with mankind, had withdrawn from the world. The logical end was for him to withdraw from all authorship because his kind of private writing would lead only to talking to himself. Joyce did not withdraw, so he ended by listening to himself talking in his sleep— *Finnegans Wake*. The Greeks have a name for such private persons—*idiotes*.

Dublin had proved itself to be sterile: his publishing ventures had been disastrous. With his persecution complex now uppermost, he decided he would put down all that he felt about the futility of life, the meaningless days of Everyman, all the ugliness of human existence. Above all, he would record the boredom of life in the cracked mirror of *Ulysses*, with its preposterous and factitious parallel to Homer's fairy tale. He would depict a world open at both ends wherein nothing happened, though everything was just about to happen, and all would hurry on in a senseless, chaotic cataract. He would hold up a mirror to a Dublin that had come to nothing.

In future he would give the world the obverse side of the medal, the gargoyle and the grotesque, instead of anything that might exalt and beautify life. He would write so that all who run might read all that Dublin offered to him. On the backside of beauty he would inscribe his name. If the writing proved to be indelible, all the better.

About this time the obscene bulk of Gertrude Stein appeared. She began making nonsense of the language and presenting the potpourri to a public which could be reached by people of her sort who controlled the avenues of publicity. *A Portrait of Mabel Dodge at the Villa Curona* appeared about 1907. It stated among other messages that "blankets are warmer in the summer: the explicit visit: there has been William."

Joyce moved to Trieste. Here for a dozen years he labored at *Ulysses* without any hope of its ever seeing the light. From what used to be thieves' argot—"elephant's trunk" for "drunk" and then for "drunk" simply "elephants"—he evolved the extraordinary amalgam of correlatives, echoes, parodies, and caricatures which is one of the most depressing things that has ever come out of literature: *Ulysses*.

Joyce was educated as a "Schoolman." According to his brother, who has written the most presentable account of him, he very nearly became a Jesuit. He never could be said to have left the order, for he was never received in it. But he never left the Middle Ages. He was "trained in the school of old Aquinas," he once said of himself.

Therefore it should not come as a surprise when we read that the Schoolmen of the Middle Ages, the very early Middle Ages, were in the habit of playing tricks with words. Here is a quotation from *The Gateway of the Middle Ages,* by Eleanor Shipley Duckett, with reference to *The Hesperica Famina, the Western Sayings:* "This is a collection of texts on various subjects composed in a bizarre and artificial style that seems to have been a vogue among cultured writers of Britain and Ireland in the fifth, sixth, and seventh centuries. . . . It seems as if the devotees of some literary cult had used all their ingenuity to pick out from the glossaries and all recondite and mysterious sources a language of their own foreign to the writing of the time."

Joyce had taught for a time at the Berlitz language school in Paris. What greater glossary could he have at hand than all the languages of the Berlitz schools?

I, who knew Joyce and the Dublin in which he lived and the way it treated him, find amusement here and there in *Ulysses,* even in the fact that Ulysses never comes into the book. Ulysses is the author, Joyce himself, seeking his true home in gaunt Ithaca. I personally can find here and there some pay dirt in *Ulysses,* for there are sparks to be glimpsed of bawdiness and argot. But these must pass completely unrecognized by anyone not well informed about the randy songs of the old city, with its despairing degradation of human life.

Ulysses was published at last. I have once been called "an accessory before the act" of Joyce's *Ulysses.* The United States may be called with more justice "an accessory after the act." Had it not been for Sylvia Beach, who published *Ulysses,* and Miss Wearing, who endowed Joyce with a liberal allowance, which enabled him to live in comfort for the first time in his life, there might have been neither *Ulysses* nor what followed.

Suddenly Joyce found that his leg-pull had acquired an international audience. Suddenly he discovered that to write his name on the backside of beauty was the most significant action of his life. He dared not retract; money and fame were at stake. He dared not let anyone into a joke that had gone too far and had been taken too seriously. I wonder what he thought when he found himself taken seriously so far from the only place where he could count on understanding. He could not let down his followers or his fans. His thin lips could not for one moment relax in a grim smile. The seriousness which he assumed when perpetrating a joke had overwhelmed him. Mockery was catching. What an "artist" he had become!

We must not blame Joyce's admirers too much if they are unaware of what happened in the monasteries and the schools of Ireland in the fifth and sixth centuries. In large part his admirers are internationalists whose mother tongue is any language but English. How should they know of this medieval gibberish?

But a stern protest becomes due when tribes of the inept but intellectually arrogant failures in literature, such as Gertrude Stein, seize on the opportunity of imitating *Ulysses* in presenting boredom, dirt, and despair as fitting subjects for poetry and prose. They ask us to bow down before all followers of "The Master," to hail them as innovators and immortal geniuses. The only thing about them that is immortal is their ineptitude. They ask us to join them in hailing the loss of human dignity, the degradation and disgrace of Man.

In the Polynesian group are certain islands where the demented are worshiped, and there is an island where to be happy is taboo. Joyce was far from demented. He had deliberation, persistence, and fortitude; *Ulysses,* his stink bomb for Dublin, had long, careful preparation. Like the unfortunate Polynesians, the Joyce worshipers reverence the topsy-turvy; by dwelling on the ugliness and misery of things they make themselves miserable and then expect us to share their wretchedness. In literature as in life their practice is the same. False contrasts, strangulated adjectives, pettiness, and rhythmless platitudes are all they can offer in the place of poetry. *Ulysses* was an example of making ineffectuality the subject of a novel. What a chance this presented for cashing in on their incompetence. Beards for the chinless!

Joyce's power of construction was weak, hence the obscene conjunction of *Ulysses* with the Homeric poem. As in the case of the so-called modern poets, Joyce's inheritors, a dislocated world demands a dislocated poem to describe it. But the business of the poet is to build anew and magnify, not to photograph or to hold a cracked mirror up to nature. It would be as logical to submit that you must talk broken English if you have a broken leg.

This mere conglomeration without sequence has

been excused by reviewers calling it the adventures of the subconscious or, contradictorily, the stream of consciousness. All an effort to give significance where there is none, and where none was intended. The fatuousness of life was what Joyce wished to convey and this he accomplished. We are told that Mrs. Bloom, for instance, means the blossoming earth. If so, why not say it, and sweetly without stench?

This decadence might have been all harmless if it had remained on the Left Bank of the Seine. But, unfortunately, it has become in its most pronounced phases associated with America. Decadence and America! One would think they were antipodes. Whatever excuse there might be for the failure of the vital spirit in Europe, there is none for it in the New World. In England no one takes Joyce as a Colossus. In Dublin there are many unfamed (I will not say "infamous") "artists" of his ilk.

According to the *James Joyce Year Book*, the following is from the pen of a London critic:

> The reader who returns to *Ulysses* today finds it, first and foremost, a child of its age. The tens of thousands of capital letters and punctuation marks massacred on the Left Bank of the Seine by earnest disciples bear witness to the novel's effect on American expatriates. France and Germany have produced commentaries on it. But even in America itself, where Joyce's momentum was felt far more strongly than in England, one would say that the Joycean influence has been chiefly on writers not of the first rank.

Notice the "not of the first rank." Could there be a better example of understatement?

When I read those who although they have never been in Dublin set themselves up as "guides to Joyce" or as masters of "The Master," I feel sorrow for their ignorance and then anger at their presumption. I know how Joyce, who used a grim attitude long sustained when he was acting rather than "making" a joke, would laugh at these "fans" of his—and his dupes.

How does it happen that America should have become the chief infirmary for Joyceans? The answer is because America is the country *par excellence* of the detective story, the crossword puzzle, and the smoke signal. All these are supplied by *Ulysses*. Here, too, where mental homes are numerous, are to be found that unique class who think that the unraveling of an enigma or a puzzle is the height of poetry. The snake pits have become vocal.

Are we to take our values from the insane no matter how atrophied their taste has become, and no matter how arrogant their claim to be arbiters? When they can prove to us that poetry can be without rhythm and prose can be without sense, I will be happy to join them. Meanwhile, I think that poetry is powerful enough to survive even as Gulliver survived all the indignities of Lilliput, though even there the king issued no edicts on matters of taste. Joyce is said to have told a reader that he expected him to devote his whole life to the study of *Finnegans Wake*. What a puzzle that would be.

Language is meant to convey ideas, emotions, and messages. If a messenger boy spent his time in handsprings, wheels, and back somersaults instead of delivering the message, and defended himself with the plea that he had superseded and enhanced it, we would have a parallel to what Joyce has done with the language. He has (to change the metaphor) substituted the lampshade for the light.

Two catastrophic wars have destroyed our values. The world is filled with the rubble of these wars, until rubble seems to the slum-dwellers of literature to be more normal than a city. Hence the cult of fragments in vogue today. Loot was everywhere; the art dealers' stores became junk shops until the trash took the place of the art. Bad artists were promoted; the taste, the discrimination of the public was deliberately debauched.

Lately an art dealer (notice the "dealer") said, "Thank God we have got rid of beauty."

Men as robust and as creative as Aeschylus, Cervantes, Ben Jonson, and a host of others were off at the wars. During their absence the toads crept up the stairs and began to croak. The atmosphere turned miasmic, and "brek-e-kek-kek-kek-kek-kek-koax" became the sole medium of intellectual exchange.

But all this is nothing new. The islander Greeks suffered from trespassers on Parnassus. I have faith in the intelligence of the human race, in the necessity for beauty and poetry to light and lighten our days. There is no need for violence to cleanse the literary stables; all we need do is to turn into them the stream of decency and sense. And healthy laughter. For when laughter comes it is a sign of a return of sanity. And impostors must run away.

Henry L. Mencken

By Gerald W. Johnson

February 11, 1956

H. L. Mencken's *Prejudices,* especially the first three volumes, his *American Mercury* 1924–1934, his *American Language* with its supplements, and his *Days,* in form an autobiography but in fact a social history of extraordinary color and texture, constitute a body of work commanding the respectful attention of the literary world. As critic, as editor, as philologist, and as historian the man made original and arresting contributions to the national letters; and a writer who has scored in four separate fields is sufficiently unusual to deserve careful scrutiny and analysis. His passing may be relied on to draw all pundits to their typewriters or dictaphones.

But there was also a character known as Henry Mencken to a relatively small circle in Baltimore and to an even smaller group outside the city; and he was, at least in the opinion of this writer, more remarkable than the H. L. Mencken known to everybody. His passing on January 29 also deserves notice, not in the style of literary analysis, but in the plain speech of the unschooled, in which he was as expert as he was in the language of the Academy.

This man was conspicuously kindly and polite. The information may come as a stunning surprise to those who are familiar only with the roaring invective of which H. L. Mencken was master and the acid wit in which he barbecued heroes and demigods of all sects and fashions; but I refer, not to H. L. Mencken, the public figure, but to Henry Mencken, citizen of Baltimore. He was fully aware of this distinction and drew it sharply himself; as far as he could, he screened Henry Mencken from the observation of press and public, while thrusting H. L. Mencken to the fore.

He once told a friend that when he went into the Stork Club in New York and the diners stared and then turned to whisper to each other, he thought it was swell; but when the same thing happened in Miller's Baltimore restaurant he found himself perspiring and acutely uncomfortable. For that reason he commonly avoided the big places, especially when dining alone. What café society calls "a celebrity" appeared to his realistic eye merely as a curiosity, and he hated the idea of being a curiosity in his home town.

But he was, of course. No such vivid personality could live anywhere without being something of a curiosity, no matter how sedulously he might avoid outward eccentricity. Mencken avoided it. He was of medium height, five feet eight or nine, but stocky enough to look shorter. Clean-shaved and conservatively dressed, with no oddities of posture or gait, he should have merged imperceptibly into a street crowd. But he didn't. He stuck out, for reasons almost impossible to capture and fix in words. The best one can say is that he stood and walked and talked like other men, only more so. He was conspicuously normal.

Into that medium-sized body was packed the vitality of twenty ordinary men. He was surcharged, and the fact was evident in whatever he did, even in the way he put his foot down in walking, or the flip of a hand when he returned a greeting. It was revealed in an immense capacity for work, and in a correspondingly immense capacity for enjoyment. This enraged ascetics, of course, and they called him a sensualist, which, in the way they meant it, was nonsense.

But in another way, a quite extraordinary way, perhaps the charge had something in it. Henry Mencken's perceptions were keen, as are those of any man who is intensely alive; to observers it seemed that he could extract more, and more profound, pleasure out of one seidel of beer than most men could from a gallon; certainly he could extract energy and encouragement from apparent defeat; and certainly he could detect and savor lusty humors in situations which to most men meant only tragedy and despair. In seventy-five years he not only outlived the rest of us, he lived far longer; one is tempted to assert that he lived like Noah and Seth and Enoch, those Old Testament ancients.

This gave him a towering advantage over the majority of those with whom he came in contact, and as a rule the man who enjoys a towering advantage is a hateful fellow. The marvel of Henry Mencken is that he was nothing of the sort. H. L. Mencken was hated. Every opprobrious term in the vocabulary of billingsgate was hurled at him, and even honorable terms were applied to him with the force of epithets; he was called a Jew, a Catholic, and a Communist, but never by a Jew, a Catholic, or a Communist, always by their enemies. It would be difficult, indeed, to identify a man who didn't hate H. L. Mencken at one time or another and for one reason or another.

But I have yet to encounter man, woman, child, or beast of burden who knew Henry Mencken and hated him. He was too expansive, too free of envy, too obviously void of any disposition to grasp at personal advantage. Even those most captious of critics, writers who knew that he could out-write them, once they came within the magnetic field of his personality lost the capacity to hate. They could be exasperated by him, they could denounce him with fire and fury; but they had trouble doing it with a straight face.

The explanation is that Henry Mencken was an

intellectual philanthropist. Occasionally he would follow some deliverance with the warning, "Now don't you write that. I mean to use it myself"; but as a rule he scattered ideas with the grand abandon, so astonishing to Darwin, of the fir tree in scattering pollen.

Incidentally, the writers who knew Henry Mencken were few. Every semi-literate scribbler in the country knew H. L. Mencken, of course, and those who had met him in the flesh must have numbered thousands; but in Baltimore his intimates, outside the group closely associated with him on the Baltimore *Sun*, included relatively few writers. True, he married the novelist, Sara Haardt, but there was a touch of the Pygmalion complex in that. Mencken had done a great deal toward pruning and strengthening her literary style when she was an aspiring youngster and he was probably a bit in love with his own creation. But this factor was only a touch; the charming lady from Alabama had plenty to account for the romance without seeking explanations in the subconscious. One of her charms was her extraordinary wisdom in being not merely tolerant but gracious to any odd fish that Henry chose to bring to the house.

And odd they certainly were! All the human flotsam and jetsam of the seven seas of literature eventually washed up on the big brownstone steps of the Cathedral Street house—this was during Mencken's married life, tragically brief, as Sara died within a few years—and it included, as H.L.M. once said of the lady drys, "some specimens so dreadful that one wonders how a self-respecting God could have made them." But these were at most friends of H. L. Mencken's, more often mere acquaintances, and all too often complete strangers brazen enough to walk in uninvited.

The friends of Henry Mencken's were odd, but in a different sense—odd in that they didn't match, could not be listed in any one category. Status of any sort, social, economic, intellectual, or other, was irrelevant. They were so different that one can think of but a single characteristic that they possessed in common— they were all vibrantly alive. Whether it was Max Broedel, the anatomical artist, who rarely had a cent, or Harry C. Black, principal owner of the *Sun*, who had dollars and some millions of them; whether it was Raymond Pearl, the biologist and one of the great brains of Johns Hopkins, or William Woollcott, the mucilage manufacturer, who loudly proclaimed that he had no brain at all (although he was a finer wit than his famous brother, Alexander); whether it was a barber or a governor, any man to whom Henry Mencken took a liking was one who savored life, sometimes with a wry face, but definitely.

In the office of the *Sun* H. L. Mencken could work with anybody, although there were some who tried him to the limit. But Henry Mencken's close associates again were various: Paul Patterson, the publisher, diplomatic but as refractory as basalt; Henry Hyde, veteran star reporter, as stately as Mencken was ebullient; the two Eds, Murphy, managing editor, and Duffy, cartoonist, explosive Irishmen; and the Owens pair, John and Hamilton, chief editors, distant cousins and distantly Welshmen. They were all experts, but there were other experts around the place who maintained polite relations with H. L. Mencken, yet never caught a glimpse of Henry. Those who did had something more than *expertise*; they had zest and a fine appreciation of the flavor of life even when—perhaps especially when—it displeased them.

To us smaller fry in the organization he was consistently genial and consistently helpful, although he could be sardonic. To me one day he observed, blandly, "He is a great cartoonist, but in politics, of course, Duffy is an idiot." Since Duffy's politics and mine were identical I got it, all right.

The newspaperman, however, was not Baltimore's Henry Mencken. That character was never to be found in public places, but only in private houses, or semi-private apartments such as the upper room over Schellhäse's restaurant, where he led the Saturday Night Club in wild forays in the realm of music, sometimes murderous enterprises such as playing the nine symphonies of Beethoven in succession—they finished at dawn—sometimes elaborate buffooneries such as orchestrating for ninety instruments Willie Woollcott's ribald ditty about the 100 per cent American; or alone at home devising preposterous communications and mementos. I had on my desk for years a three-pound chunk of rock sent through the mails at terrific expense with a preternaturally solemn document certifying it as an authentic madstone.

But the unforgettable Henry Mencken, the man who really altered the lives of the relatively few who knew him, was Mencken sitting at ease after the day's work was over, with a cigar in his mouth, a seidel in his hand, and around him a small group who were equal to the rapier play of his wit—Woollcott, Pearl, Gilbert Chinard, a very few others. In such surroundings Henry Mencken talked better than H. L. Mencken ever wrote—lightly, ironically, extravagantly, but with a flashing perception that illuminated whatever it touched, and it touched everything. A display of intellectual pyrotechnics it was, certainly, but like any fine fireworks display it created in an ordinary place on an ordinary night a glittering illusion; momentarily, at least, life sparkled and blazed, and the knowledge that it can ever sparkle and blaze is worth having. In fact, it is one of the best things a man can have.

It was not optimism. Henry Mencken, like H. L. Mencken, was a pessimist; but his pessimism was more invigorating than the gurgling of any male Pollyanna. "The trouble about fighting for human freedom," he remarked once, "is that you have to spend much of your life defending sons-of-bitches; for oppressive laws are always aimed at them originally, and oppression must be stopped in the beginning if it is to be stopped at all." It is hard to imagine anything more dismal, but I do not believe it will sap the courage of any fighting character.

Mencken would have disliked being compared to pietistic Samuel Johnson, but he played a very similar role in his own city. The difference was that Johnson always and Mencken never took himself too seriously; nevertheless, each was not only witty, "but the cause that wit is in other men." Nor did it stop with wit. They caused a zest for life to be renewed in other men; they touched the dull fabric of our days and gave it a silken sheen. Boswell, greatest of biographers, recognized but never could translate into words the quality that made contact with his hero a milestone in every man's life; and if Boswell could not do it for Johnson, what hope is there that any lesser person can do it for Mencken? One may only record the fact and pass on.

Nevertheless, it is true that when Mencken died there were those in Baltimore who were not much interested in what the world had lost—the incomparable reporter, the critic, the philologist, the social historian, H. L. Mencken. They were too much occupied in lamenting their own loss—Henry Mencken, the unique, who, deriding them exalted them, in threatening them encouraged them, in prophesying death and doom gave them a new, strong grip on life. The man who really knew him will do far more living in the same number of days than he would have done without that contact. If there is a finer gift that a man can bestow upon his friends, I cannot name it. They mourn with cause.

The Literary Churchill

By J. H. Plumb

February 6, 1965

Winston Churchill was many things during the ninety years of his life, but in all of them he remained a man of letters. Few public figures have valued the written and spoken word as he did, and few have used it with such versatility or to such effect. To consider him as a literary man, therefore, is to come very close to one of the central aspects of his life. Churchill himself once remarked, in fact, that he regarded himself as a writer who had been only momentarily interrupted by two world wars.

Sir Winston Churchill was born at Blenheim Palace, not a house or a home but a monument, built to glorify his ancestor, John Duke of Marlborough, and his battles. His father was Lord Randolph Churchill, a Duke's son, gifted, flamboyant, reckless, an orator who could hold the Victorian House of Commons spellbound. He died early, a failure, crushed and defeated by the inexorable men of small mind who are the bone and sinew of politics. His mother was Jennie Jerome, the gay, pleasure-loving daughter of a tough American millionaire. Although she loved English social life, she always stood a little apart, conscious of other places, other people. Sir Winston's education followed the pattern of the English aristocracy: governess, preparatory school, public school (Harrow), the Royal Military College, Sandhurst, a remorseless emphasis on Latin, Greek, mathematics; for exercise, the horse and the gun; for the molding of character, the officers' training corps. There was a little history and geography, and bits and pieces of literature—Macaulay's *Lays of Ancient Rome*, Stevenson's tales—as solace for the imagination. It was a life—bright, rich, ordinary for its class—yet shadowed in strange places with tragedy and discontent.

Nor were his parents rich by the standards of their friends. They lived high—parties, dinners, balls, the lavish gaiety of the Victorian social round. Large houses, a drove of servants, and extravagant clothes ate away their smallish income and sharpened the anxieties that Lord Randolph's political life engendered. The brilliant father, cheated of his ambition, died a difficult death. By then Churchill, who had done abysmally badly at school, was a young subaltern, about to join the Fourth Hussars, an expensive regiment for a man without any means worth talking about. For the next four years Churchill careered about the world, using his social influence, tasting excitement— guerilla warfare in Cuba and fighting tribesmen on the northwestern frontier of India. This was a spirited time interlaced with danger. Churchill next witnessed the bloody affair of the Mahdi that culminated in the Battle of Omdurman. Then came a time as a war correspondent in South Africa for the Boer War. This led to capture and imprisonment. All of this was the stuff of history as well as war. During these years, principally at Bangalore in India between bouts of polo, Churchill began to read serious history, Gibbon, Macaulay, J. R. Green, and even more serious political philosophy—Plato, Aristotle, Schopenhauer, Malthus. The life of action had proved insufficient for this small, restless, red-headed young aristocrat; his creative energies were too great, his need for expression was too insistent.

And so Churchill began to write contemporary military and imperial history, describing his campaigns as if they were Caesar's: first came *The Malakand Field Force*, then *The River War*. These brought quick fame for Churchill, followed by invitations to lecture, to write articles, to undertake books. America welcomed him as ardently as Britain. The historian was launched. And so was the politician, for enough money to live on enabled him to quit the army and finally, after initial defeat, to enter the House of Commons. For the next fifty years the historian and the statesman worked together, molding each other's ideas and subtly influencing decisions about the present and the past. Very rarely in the history of mankind have great statesmen been historians. Even rarer has it been for the great historians to be statesmen. Yet Churchill was undeniably both. And both the historian and the statesman were tied to a special, an almost personal past— to Blenheim, to the tough world of Victorian politics where a commonplace Cecil had stifled a Churchill genius, to the exotic, glamorous life of a cavalry officer in the India of the British Raj. It was a world of privilege and tradition. These were the influences and forces that were to mold not only the choice of subjects that Churchill the historian wrote about but also the way he was to write his books.

His works were, however, the result of his character as well as his environment. As with most great statesmen, Churchill's temperament was not a subtle one. His private life was straightforward. He married late, but married happily. There was no complexity. Friend-ship did not come easily; most men distrusted his vivid imagination and his obvious thirst for power. Those ties that he did form with Beaverbrook, Cherwell, and Brendan Bracken were marked by a tenacious, obsti-nate loyalty. Many thought him rash because Churchill took decisions easily—not only about actions but also about people and about principles. Once made, they were difficult to change. He enjoyed being obstinate. His compulsive desire for decisive acts led him to prefer military and political history, to delight in the trenchant delineation of character, and to love pungent historical judgments.

Although simple and somewhat inflexible, Churchill's character bubbled with passion. He obviously enjoyed anger and ferocity, yet he was also warmhearted, quickly moved to tears, and could indulge a generosity that is rare in political life. He responded directly to a sense of occasion with something of the unawareness of a child. This is as true of his histories as of his life. Time and time again, one is reminded of one of his great models in the writing of history—Macaulay. He, too, was a man of straightforward feeling and judg-ment, quick to praise, quick to condemn, resolute, forthright, blinkered to subtlety, and like Churchill he lacked doubt. No wonder Churchill read and reread him. Certainty, simplicity, warm feeling, these are all qualities which, when transferred into the language of literature, make for a mastery of narrative, a clarity of exposition, and a universality of appeal that most historians can never hope to possess.

These advantageous gifts had, however, their corol-lary of weakness. Churchill was not a clever man. He possessed a good memory and a splendid capacity for self-expression but he was no intellectual. One looks almost in vain in his *History of the English Speaking Peoples* for the complexities of economic, intellectual, scientific, or technological history. True, the reason for this partly lay in his social origins, date of birth, and education, but it was also partly due to the limitations imposed on him by his very moderate intelligence. His lack of high intellectual powers made it easy for him

to accept without question the historical traditions of
his class. This was the grand whiggery of his Spencer
ancestors—English history was the slow growth of law
and liberty, via Magna Carta, reformation, civil war,
and so on to the triumph of Parliament and of Cabinet;
these liberties the English planted overseas, carried to
alien races, and conferred on the lower orders. The
unity of the empire was brought about by kingship
and by an ever-abiding sense of the destiny of the
English-speaking peoples that embodied God's will.

This was the kernel of his historical belief, as it was
the mainspring of his political attitude. There were
times when his concept of the English historical tradition gave to his statesmanship a sense of destiny, as
when he stood four-square for resistance to Hitler after
the appalling defeats of 1940. Yet there were other
occasions when this attachment to the past blinded his
vision of the future. His attitude to India was deeply
historic and deeply absurd. He realized that India had
been a prey to invasion for centuries; he knew that
Russia's interest, over a century old by 1945, had not
waned; he had experienced the ferocity of tribal warfare on India's frontiers and the weakness of her peas-
antry; he had lived long enough in India to appreciate
the slowness of her progress, and the terrible inertia
of her caste-ridden society. And his memory dwelt on
the countless Englishmen who had lived and fought and
died for English supremacy. None of these things
should have mattered against the concept of a future
India—free, industrialized, struggling by itself and for
itself, escaping from its dingy history. This he could
not perceive; lacking all capacity for historical analysis,
his intellect could not lead him to conclusions at
variance with his beliefs. The future, except in war,
was never in Churchill's bones.

In many ways his best books deal with contemporary
military history. His two great books on World War I
and World War II will remain masterpieces. They
possess vital information, magnificent writing, and
Churchill's point of view. They cannot yet be ade-
quately criticized, for not enough material has been
published. Churchill was conscious of being a historian

who would write of the events even as he enacted them. This conscious knowledge that everything he wrote was a historical document will make the task of the suspicious historian doubly difficult. To unravel the true course of events, to analyze the exact interplay of character or to weigh the importance of decisions will require a profound knowledge of Churchill and the way he worked as a historian. Decades must pass, and thousands of documents become available, before a proper criticism of these books can be made. Whatever the final evaluation may be, they will remain as the most remarkable historical survey ever made by a statesman of world stature. The qualities that make these books so readable—the exceptional mastery of complex events, the rapid narrative pace sustained for hundreds of thousands of words, the splendor of the language that rises, as so few writers of this century have made it rise, to the grandeur of man's destiny whether for triumph or tragedy—are to be found, in embryo, in his earlier books. *The Malakand Field Force* is, true enough, overwritten and untidy in detail, yet it was, and is, immensely readable—the first quality required in any book.

And *The River War* is an excellent piece of military history. Without their author's fame to sustain them, however, both books might have died early deaths. The same cannot be said of the three books by which Churchill must be judged as a historian in its accepted sense: the life of his father, *Lord Randolph Churchill*, the monumental biography of his ancestor, *John Duke of Marlborough*, and his four-volume *History of the English Speaking Peoples*.

Both of his historical biographies possess one quality that should ensure their survival, whatever their merits; they contain, as indeed do all the Churchillian volumes on contemporary history, a vast collection of documents not obtainable elsewhere. Churchill liked to print the documents on which he based his judgments. The life of his father, too, contains a great quantity of information derived from Lord Randolph's friends, colleagues, and enemies that is obtainable nowhere else. And this book will remain, for these facts alone, fundamental to the study of late nineteenth-century politics. The same is true to a lesser extent of *Marlborough*. Churchill was able to ransack the Blenheim archives, which scarcely anyone had used for well over 100 years. Furthermore, he was rich enough by the 1930s to be able to afford first-class scholars to work for him in the great collections of European archives at The Hague, Vienna, Paris, and elsewhere. His quick, sure eye for the relevant dispatch and memorandum rarely failed him, and these, too, went pretty well verbatim into his *Marlborough*. The standard of transcription was high and so, irrespective of its other qualities, the *Marlborough* is a rich quarry of source material. And of course both books have other qualities. Both are essentially about men in action—Lord Randolph in politics, Marlborough in war—and Churchill understood, better than most historians, the way decisions in these matters were arrived at. Lord Randolph's political campaigns are as real and exciting as Marlborough's battles. So long as Churchill is dealing with the question "how" rather than the question "why" he reaches the very highest class of historical writing. And of course the lives of men of action are more concerned with "how" than "why." Finally, both books aim to be literature. Churchill understood history to be a part of a nation's culture like its poetry or drama or music. His two acknowledged masters—Gibbon and Macaulay—had written for all who love literature, not for their professional colleagues. So Churchill always tried not only to write well but also to link what he had to say about history with common human experience. In this his success was betwixt and between. So long as the events or the human reactions were on a bold scale—dealing with courage, endurance, misery, or defeat—he wrote with authority and with deep understanding, and often his words clothed his feeling in majestic and memorable phrases. If the human or political situation became complex—a mixture of conscious and unconscious motives, of good and evil, of treachery and patriotism existing side by side—then he tended to stumble or to evade the issues. That is why the over-all picture both of Marlborough and Lord

Randolph is too simple, too direct. There is a total absence of any comprehension of the deeper motivations at work in these characters or of those with whom they worked or against whom they struggled. Churchill's characters are pre-Freudian as his history is pre-Marxian.

The faults of Churchill as a historian tend to outweigh his qualities in his last book, *History of the English Speaking Peoples*. Of course, this is a remarkable book, remarkable because Churchill wrote it and remarkable, too, for the quality of his writing. As might be expected, the political and military history in this book is well told. The narrative rattles along, the comments are vivid, and human achievement and suffering in war are expressed in eloquent and moving prose. And the book is as accurate as first-class scholarship could make it, for Churchill commandeered a small army of professional historians to weed out his errors of fact and interpretation. It is in many ways an elegy for the generous view of English history and institutions that lay at the core of the Whig aristocratic tradition. Nor was this tradition all nonsense. The English acquired and maintained political liberty, and the history of Europe and of the world demonstrates that this was no mean achievement; certainly the Whig aristocracy played a significant part in acquiring it.

The trouble is that the book belongs to the nineteenth, not the twentieth, century. One looks in vain for so much that has conferred distinction on the English-speaking peoples—its literature, its science, its philosophy, and its industrial technology. There is scarcely a word on Shakespeare, on Hobbes or Locke, and hardly anything at all on Newton, Boyle, Faraday, Maxwell, or Rutherford; the Industrial Revolution and all the political and social change that it has produced is brushed aside in a few pages. And these serious omissions are indicative of the great fault of Churchill, both as a historian and as a statesman: he lacked a sense of the deeper motives that control human society and make it change, just as he lacked in the same way an interest in the deeper human motives. The past is comprehensible only in terms of the future, but Churchill's mind was immersed in tradition. It made him a splendid symbol for a nation in torment but inhibited his vision when he came to survey the broad sweep of English history. The influence of its exceptionally intricate class structure and the problems created by the even more remarkable tenacity of its feudal continuum in an industrial society eluded him. The pageantry of a coronation superimposed on the steel mills of Sheffield or the sprawling suburbia of Manchester never struck him as mildly odd; for him the right things were in the right places. In spite of his generosity and the warmth of his devotion to the English land and its people, he could not see its future, so his vision of its past was clouded, limited to the past of his ancestors, of Lord Randolph, of Marlborough, of Blenheim.

In a way the *History of the English Speaking Peoples* is a historical document rather than a history, an epitaph of a class, of its strong traditions and intellectual shortcomings. Yet it possesses rare qualities; the narrative dances along, the prose rises and falls from simplicity to majesty as occasion requires, the judgments of men and affairs are decisive, the standard of accuracy is remarkably high. Criticism of the book cannot easily fasten on what it contains, but only on what it omits.

It would be fruitless to attempt to assess Churchill's ability as a historian, divorced from the rest of his career; the fact of who he was must add dimensions to his work that would have been absent had it been written by another. And yet his books will not live merely because he wrote them. They possess what all great literature must possess, whether imaginative or historical: a view of life that is at the same time deeply personal yet a revelation to other men of the nature of human experience. In his books as in statesmanship there is a sense of the grandeur of mankind, its capacity to endure and to triumph. A sense of greatness informed all that he did or wrote. He was perhaps a brontosaurus, but in a world of minnows.

The Worlds of Robert E. Sherwood

By John Mason Brown

August 14, 1965

You cease living your own life when you start writing someone else's. You want to. You have to. But neither your having to nor wanting to is the true cause for the change that occurs. Without your being aware of it, you are no longer alone within yourself. Your mind and heart have a new tenant. Once he has moved in, you find that he requires more and more space, space which you are delighted to let him have. His every concern becomes yours, as does everything that concerns him. Day and night he is in the background of your thoughts even when he is not, as he most often is, in the foreground of your thinking. I have lived happily with this knowledge for the past nine years, during which, in spite of unavoidable interruptions, I have been living with the life of Robert Emmet Sherwood.

I confess I did not realize how far the subway was to carry me beyond the stop at which I got off when, one September morning in 1956, I went down to Wall Street to take my first glance at Sherwood's letters and papers stored at the United States Trust Company of New York. I made the trip at the suggestion of Harper's Cass Canfield and with the permission of Sherwood's widow, Madeline, and of John Wharton, the lawyer for his estate.

Cass Canfield had in mind a collection of Sherwood's correspondence and wondered if I would be interested in editing it and writing a commentary. To help me, he had asked Marguerite Hoyle, an able editor of his (who, incidentally, had worked on Sherwood's *Roosevelt and Hopkins*), to go through the files and extract a sampling from the thirty thousand items with which they bulged.

I had planned to spend a few days going over this material before deciding. Almost at once, however, as I dipped into Sherwood's letters to and from Woollcott, the Lunts, Edna Ferber, the Garson Kanins, Geoffrey Kerr, Samuel Goldwyn, S. N. Behrman, and Maxwell Anderson, or William Allen White, Elmer Davis, Felix Frankfurter, Franklin D. Roosevelt, Winston Churchill, Averell Harriman, Adlai Stevenson, Truman, and Eisenhower (to mention only a few), I knew I was the captive of what was before me. Within hours I was taxiing uptown to Harper's to admit this to Cass Canfield.

Soon thereafter Sherwood's files began to arrive, one by one, at my apartment and to rise like a cluster of green office buildings in my already hopelessly overcrowded study. The new tenant had moved in, although I could not then guess, welcome as he was, the length of his stay or the extent to which he would take over.

As the weeks and months slipped by and I dug deeper into the files, the more certain I became of one thing. I did not want to stop with editing the letters. There was too much else that tempted me. Those files soon ceased for me to be repositories of crumbling clippings, fading photographs, thousands of old letters, the drafts of speeches long since delivered, and manuscripts abandoned or completed. Increasingly I came to realize that very much alive in them was an exceptional man who had touched his times in many ways.

The whole man was not in the files. But the search for as much of the whole Sherwood as I could track down, understand, and assemble from these fragments of his thinking and living became for me an absorption that quickly swelled into an obsession. The more I knew about Sherwood the more I wanted to know. The files had pushed me into the unanticipated role of biographer. Shaw once described a dramatic critic as a man who leaves no turn unstoned. A biographer is different. He cannot live with himself if he leaves one pebble unexamined or unweighed, and he is haunted by the fear that another pebble will come to light after he has combed the beach.

Few of our contemporaries have lived so many lives with such abundance as Sherwood. Few have so reflected the changing decades with their changing issues, interests, and climates as this skyscraper of a man, mournful of face, gay at heart, slow in talk, fluent with pen, and serious of purpose, who could seem solitary even in company. Bob Sherwood, though he had close friends and an army of distant close friends, was a man easy to admire and hard to know. Many who loved and admired him and knew him long and intimately have told me this. Their experience, I admit, was mine. I did not know him as a friend until the war years in London, when he was Overseas Director of the OWI and I a transient in the Navy. I had known about him, of course, since his *Barnum Was Right* was produced by the Hasty Pudding in 1920 when I was a freshman at Harvard, and had followed his work since, in the Twenties, I read his movie reviews in *Life*. From 1927 and *The Road to Rome* on, I had reviewed all his plays that were done professionally in New York, damning some, praising others.

We had corresponded about a few of these, and had our emphatic disagreements in print. We had met two or three times stiffly and self-consciously, because a dramatist and a critic are apt to have a Montague and Capulet relationship. It took a war to bring about an armistice between us. Even when I saw him in London and much more intimately thereafter in New York, and had come to love him, I cannot say that I knew him. I mean really knew him on the easy terms that we know most friends.

Naturally, I know him much better now, this longtime tenant of my interest. Biography is by obligation an invasion of privacy. This is its privilege and its point. Bob Sherwood's papers have given me insights into him that I could never have hoped to gain when he was alive, and a chance to know him at closer range than I do friends whom I think and feel I know best. They have also given me insights into people and events which I had observed from the outside. He was only four years older than I; hence his times were mine. The difference was that, though we shared many interests, he had lived through the altering decades importantly as a participant, often near or at the center of many worlds which I had followed from the sidelines.

When Sherwood died, he was not only a playwright who had written about Lincoln but a person who in the public mind had wrapped around his shoulders a portion of Abe Lincoln's shawl. He was an individual who had become a myth, a personage in addition to a dramatist, a literary figure who had emerged as a delegate-at-large for the American conscience. Like the rest of us, he was not one man but many men. He, however, was a bigger man than most and his contradictions therefore seem the larger and are the more interesting. "History," Garson Kanin once wrote him lovingly, "will surely remember you as a soldier, author, monstrosity, playwright, lover, songwriter, wit." This was before he had turned biographer with *Roosevelt and Hopkins*.

Bob Sherwood in Illinois: Why Abe Lincoln? Had Sherwood been a small man, he said he might, instead, have written a play about Napoleon. But Lincoln was a tall man outside and a giant within, and Sherwood a taller man who was growing inside year by year. This inner growth readied him for *Abe*—this plus the fact that, with the challenges to freedom multiplying throughout the world, Lincoln moved into the present with a new timeliness as "a man of peace who had had to face the issue of appeasement or war."

We say much about ourselves in our choice of heroes. They are the mirrors not only of what we would like to be but a reflection in part of what we are. From his youth Lincoln had occupied a special place among Sherwood's idols. He saw Lincoln then and for many years thereafter through the usual fog of reverence, saw him as the myth, not the man, as a statue that had somehow been alive. No other hero in our history reached so deep into Sherwood's heart as this figure of sadness, suffering, homely humor, and compassion. There was a kinship between them of temperament and beliefs, of bafflement and courage, and loneliness and eloquence.

For some fifteen years Sherwood had talked vaguely of writing a play about Lincoln's early life. *The Prairie Years* (1926), which he reread again and again during the next decade, eventually strengthened his determination to do so ("Can't open this wonderful book without feeling a rush of emotion to the imagination"). Sandburg gave him an understanding he had not had before of the intricacies and contradictions of Lincoln's character and served as an invaluable guide to "the main sources of Lincoln lore."

This copious lore cracked for him the marble of Lincoln as a public statue, thereby permitting the man to emerge, flesh, blood, and fallibility, and all the greater for being human. Sherwood came to see, and state conqueringly in his episodic drama, the importance of Lincoln's frailties to his virtues. More and more he realized that, however heretical any admission of Lincoln's faults might seem, these faults were a part of his size. As he put it, the doubts and fears that tormented Lincoln "could not have occurred to a lesser man" and his ultimate triumph over them was "in many ways the supreme achievement of his life."

In the winter of 1936 Sherwood began to write a play on Lincoln. At a Child's Restaurant on 48th Street he wrote the prayer for the recovery of a sick boy (really a prayer for America) which Lincoln speaks in the seventh scene. But he could get no further. His play had not formed in his mind nor his Lincoln come into focus. He needed more time in which to brood and plan and absorb. And greater and more intimate knowledge, too. Accordingly, led by Sandburg, he went to work in earnest.

Earnest in his case meant furious application. Never a decent student at school or college, Sherwood was always a painstaking researcher when, as a writer, he dealt with history. Before taking the license to which he was entitled as a dramatist, he had to know the facts from which he was departing. He had no desire in his notes to set himself up as a "learned biographer." But he was learned about Lincoln, drawn to his knowledge not only by the instinctive understanding he felt for him but by his theory of what a play about Lincoln should be. No one was more aware than Sherwood that "the playwright's chief stock in trade is feelings, not facts." A dramatist, he believed, was "at best an interpreter, with a certain facility for translating all that he has heard in a manner sufficiently dramatic to attract a crowd." He felt, however, that in a play about the development of Lincoln's character a strict regard for the plain truth was both obligatory and desirable. "His life as he lived it was a work of art, forming a veritable allegory of the growth of the democratic spirit, with its humble origins, its inward struggles, its seemingly timid policy of 'live and let live' and 'mind your own business,' its slow awakening to the dreadful problems of reality, and its battles with and conquest of those problems."

His conviction was that, just as Lincoln's life needed no adornments to make it pertinent, his character needed "no romanticizing, no sentimentalizing, no dramatizing." To a reporter he said that, before he began, he made up his mind "not to have a line of hokum in the play. I love hoke in the theater," he went on, "but this time I decided that, while they might say the play was dull, they couldn't say it was 'theater.' "

To his Aunt Lydia he confided that he was "not concerned with Abraham Lincoln's position in history—because no one needs to elaborate on that. It was his remarkable character. It seems to me that all the contrasted qualities of the human race—the hopes and fears, the doubts and convictions, the mortal frailty and super-human endurance, the prescience and the neuroses, the desire for escape from reality, and the fundamental, unshakable nobility—were concentrated and magnified in him as they were in Oedipus Rex and in Hamlet. Except that he was no creation of the poetic imagination. He was a living American, and in his living words are the answers—or the only conceivable answers—to all the questions that distract the world today."

Sherwood's shadowing of Lincoln when he was pondering his play did not stop with history or biography. Language, Lincoln's language public and private, the language of his period and of the authors who, having fed the hungers of his mind, helped to shape his style, became Sherwood's natural concern. To give authenticity to the dialogue in his scenes about the young Lincoln, he bought an English grammar of 1816. For period flavor he savored the *Pickwick Papers* and, to catch the swing and phraseology of common speech along the Mississippi, he reread *Huckleberry Finn*. Again and again he searched the Bible, Shakespeare, Jefferson, and Whitman for an appropriately somber passage with which the student Lincoln could conclude the opening scene. Finding none, he used Keats's "On Death" as being right in spirit even if there was no record of Lincoln's having read it. The poem contained a phrase in "his rugged path" which stuck in Sherwood's mind. For a while he considered *The Rugged Path* for the title of his Lincoln play, which earlier he had thought of calling *The First American,* then *An American.*

In the midst of the activities at Great Enton, his summer place in England, Sherwood made another try at Lincoln in June, 1937. Again he found he was not ready and, after a few unsuccessful attempts, he put the project aside. But he was haunted by the play and continued to read for it and think about it. Not until the beginning of November did he actually settle down to writing. "Get to work on *Abe,* you lazy bastard," his diary exhorts, followed by "Got to work on Scene 2. Not too greatly pleased with progress." Once started, he wrote rapidly, finishing the first draft in eighteen days.

Abe Lincoln in Illinois was a turning point in Sherwood's career. So were the happenings of an afternoon soon after he had finished that first draft. Sherwood presided then for the first time as president at a meeting of the council of the Dramatists' Guild. The day was dull, as Elmer Rice remembered it in *Minority Report,* and so was the meeting. The discussion of movie money in the theater dragged on for three hours. Little was accomplished, and to Sherwood the afternoon seemed "a terrible ordeal."

When it was at last over, he, Rice, and Maxwell Anderson found themselves on the same elevator. They were tired men, and depressed. To raise their spirits, they went to a nearby bar where, over their drinks, they shared their grievances against the American theater in general and producers in particular. As Rice recalled, Sherwood and Anderson spoke with special vehemence against the Theatre Guild with which they both, while in the process of having successes, had had painful experiences.

The Guild's committee system, which had irked Sherwood when *Reunion in Vienna* and *Idiot's Delight* were being done, was attacked by him and by Anderson. The two of them objected strenuously to the fact that at the Guild they had been "harassed by disagreements about casting, revisions, and the disposition of subsidiary rights." They both expressed the wish that "their plays could be done as they wanted them done, without interference!"

In a spirit of fraternal revolt they revived a dream that for some years had come no nearer to reality than talk. This was a group of playwrights who, dispensing with the middlemen who were managers, would produce their own plays. Rice had long been a champion of such an idea, notwithstanding the failure of a previous association known as the Dramatists' Theatre, which, after producing only one success among too many attempts, had died of dissension. Shortly after the hit of *Street Scene* (1929) he had suggested another project of the same kind to Anderson, Philip Barry, and George Kelly, without arousing their interest. This time the idea took root. Anderson and Sherwood committed themselves to it at once and asked Rice to join them, which he did with enthusiasm. Sidney Howard, whose *They Knew What They Wanted, Ned McCobb's Daughter,* and *The Silver Cord* had had hugely successful Theatre Guild productions, was also invited to be one of them, an invitation which he, as an ever-ready champion of new ideas, welcomed.

They had made a promising start. Then Thanksgiving intervened. This one was spent by the Sherwoods with the Averell Harrimans at Arden. During it Sherwood, while considering revisions for *Abe* and thinking about the newly conceived Playwrights' Company, spent his time bowling, playing badminton, parlor games and, in general, seeming to loaf. The Harrimans' guests included among others the Heywood Brouns, the William Paleys, the Donald Klopfers, Alice Duer Miller, Charles Lederer, Oscar Levant, Rosamond Pinchot, the George Backers, Peggy Pulitzer, the Harold Rosses, the George Kaufmans, and the Herbert Bayard Swopes. Someone said, "What a play this gathering would make," to which Kaufman replied, "Yes, the title would be *The Upper Depths.*"

Early the next week the four men, all quite excited by then, met at the Plaza's Oak Room to discuss definite plans. They decided to add another dramatist, feeling, according to Rice, "that five playwrights could presumably be expected to turn in three plays a year. If only one was even a moderate success, we would be on safe ground; a big hit every three years or so would provide a wide margin of safety." The candidate they tapped was S. N. Behrman, who, in the Guild's productions of *The Second Man, Meteor, Biography, Rain from Heaven,* and *Amphitryon 38,* had long since established himself as a comic dramatist. He took persuading, not wanting to involve himself actively in play production, but he accepted.

The problems of management now descended on the five dramatists themselves. They named their organization the Playwrights' Company at the suggestion of Anderson, who had the medieval guilds in mind, and overnight it began to take shape. Money, of course, was a necessity. They thought that they could operate with a capital of $100,000, each investing $10,000 and with $50,000 more to be raised among their friends. Sherwood proved to be the most successful fund raiser, attracting on Long Island weekends such investors as Harriman, Dorothy Schiff, George Backer, Harold Guinzburg, Howard Cullman, Alicia Patterson, and Raymond Massey.

The agreement among the playwrights was that the company would produce any script written by a member so long as the production budget was not in excess of $25,000, an amount then considered ample. According to Rice, "Plays calling for a greater expenditure required majority approval. Each playwright was to be in complete charge of his own production, calling upon his colleagues whenever he chose for script criticism, casting suggestions, comments at rehearsals and tryouts." All the plays to be submitted were to be new ones, unretrieved from trunks and dresser drawers. Each member, in Sherwood's words, "would get a straight ten per cent royalty on his play and sixty per cent of a picture sale. A dramatist would abandon hope for a play of his if his fellows all voted against it." In the years ahead all of them submitted scripts to the Playwrights' Company which were not produced by it. In such cases they were free to turn to other managements.

While writing *Abe,* Sherwood had been torn between exaltation and despair. He had had days of being unable to start and days of being unable to stop. There had been nights when he experienced "such excitement" that it interfered with sleep. These were followed by periods of black melancholy. At times he felt "perfectly wonderful," convinced that "I've done at last what I most wanted to do with my work—express America." Then would come hours of torturing doubts when, laid low by attacks of *tic douloureux,* he found himself harassed by the episodic form he had chosen. "I'm geared to drive through an act, & so many starts, spurts & stops make it difficult for me to know whether I'm sustaining the interest."

One thing was plain. Even before his first meeting with Rice and Anderson, Sherwood had reached the climax of loneliness and uncertainty when a writer needs to discover whether all the effort and agony he has poured into his work have justified themselves. Early in December he retyped a lot of *Abe,* read it all through, and felt "terribly depressed. . . . It seems awfully, awfully dull. Fussed with it and stewed over it until suddenly I decided I should go nuts if it remained in the house another minute. So I packed it up and took it to Miss Simone to be typed. Lord—I hope this feeling of despair about it is only nervous reaction or something & that it's better than I fear it is now—a hell of a lot better." When the text came back, his wife Madeline read it and, while she was doing so, Sherwood experienced the anxieties of an opening night. "Thank God she liked it & made some very good criticisms and suggestions which I shall act upon immediately."

Encouraged, he took a copy to his mother on her eighty-first birthday, read the play to Ned Sheldon, and sent copies to the other Playwrights, and to Edna Ferber, and Raymond Massey. The latter, who was in England, shared his with Goeffrey Kerr. The jailbound days of waiting for a verdict were mercifully short and all the responses fulfillments of Sherwood's highest hopes. The Playwrights were so enthusiastic that they decided to overlook the fact that the production costs would exceed the allotted $25,000. Anderson voiced their group reaction when he telephoned to say that *Abe* had given him "a lifting of the heart." Sheldon hailed it as "a noble portrait painted with a noble art." Miss Ferber thought it "an amazing characterization, touching, real, and done with a masterly simplicity." Massey, whom Sherwood had had in mind for Lincoln since seeing him in *Ethan Frome,* cabled that he was "too moved for words" by *Abe.* Kerr was confident that he could see the play acted even as it then was and "have as good an evening in the theatre as I have ever had."

Some nine months were to creep by before the Playwrights inaugurated their first season. One of the reasons for delaying the production of *Abe* was that Massey had to complete his London run of *Idiot's Delight.* Soon after this, on one of the most beautiful mornings he had ever seen, with New York at its best and his hopes high, Sherwood sailed down the bay on a revenue cutter at 6:45 A.M. to meet Massey on the *Queen Mary.* The rehearsals for *Abe* started the next day and to Sherwood the play sounded fine. Two weeks later came the run-through—a challenge, which had been an ordeal when the Theatre Guild's directors met as a group to sit in judgment on one of his plays. This time, with the Playwrights as audience, it was no ordeal at all. After another two weeks of arduous rehearsing, which on one occasion lasted from 7 P.M. to 5 A.M., *Abe* opened in Washington to "superb" notices, "a triumph" for the play and for Massey, which was repeated the next week in Baltimore.

The gauntlet of the New York opening was still to be run. It was faced on October 15, a Saturday night, which meant an apprehensive Sunday spent waiting for Monday's reviews. Sherwood and Madeline watched the performance from the light balcony of the Plymouth Theatre with Rice and Anderson. All of them were nervous; all had much at stake. The first two acts seemed dull to Sherwood—"too many coughs." Rice, as the director, was relieved to see that the performance was dynamic and the mechanics smooth. But later, in *Minority Reports,* he confessed he was disturbed by his feeling that the audience, though attentive, lacked warmth and excitement. He saw that Sherwood was worried, too.

With the beginning of the first scene in the third act the atmosphere changed. There was, to be sure, a woman in the front row who created momentary consternation by talking as audibly as if she were one of the speakers in the Lincoln-Douglas Debate. She turned out to be Sherwood's mother, Rosina, proud and approving but so deaf that she was unaware that she could be heard. In spite of her, Rice remembered the scene "evoked a great round of applause" and "from then on the intensity of response increased." The evening's end, according to Sherwood, was "really thrilling —tremendous cheers—twenty-six curtain calls."

The Sherwoods gave a large party at the Barberry Room after the opening. It was one of those theatrical parties which can be either a launching or a wake. Although the mood was jubilant, the congratulations flowed like the champagne, and the party lasted until five in the morning, Sherwood was dubious. From long experience he knew that the spoken enthusiasm of friends can be very different from the printed opinions of critics. Pleased as he was, he was impatient for Monday's papers and the reviews. The long, the unnerving watch lay ahead. He got through the blue Sunday as best he could. After dining with Madeline at home, the two of them went to Rice's apartment to wait for the early editions which were on the streets by midnight. The raves in the *Times* and *Tribune* put an end to the agony. By the next afternoon all the daily notices were in, and Sherwood summarized them in his diary by saying, *"Times, Tribune, World-Telegram*—fine. *Mirror, News, Sun, Journal*—fair. *Post* (John Mason Brown) —rotten."

I was decidedly in the minority with almost everyone against me, certainly everyone whose opinion I respected. I have come to know from his diary that what I challenged in *Abe* was what in part bothered Sherwood in his despairing moments while writing it. This was too much reading, too much homework, and too little playwriting by Sherwood himself.

In successive scenes Sherwood showed the young Lincoln as a student, a postmaster, the suitor of Ann Rutledge, a small-town lawyer, the reluctant husband of Mary Todd, a negligible Congressman, and a hater of war who long avoided the issue that might bring it about. Exciting and noble as the final episodes are, I still think there is a shadowy, pageant-like quality about these earlier scenes during which Lincoln emerges, in spite of himself, as the great, sad man who leaves Springfield to shape the nation's course in Washington. What I failed to sense on that opening night was the true dimension of Sherwood's play, his rightness in letting history speak for itself, and the skill with which he, aided by Raymond Massey's superbly moving performance, restated the American dream at a moment in the world when this restatement was dramatically needed.

During the writing of *Abe,* Sherwood had had many dreams in which Lincoln appeared telling him he had done a good job. Although less authoritative, the critics and the public were of the same opinion. Few plays in our time have been greeted with such notices as *Abe* received.

Abe Lincoln in Illinois did not win the Critics Award —no play did that season—but it did win him his second Pulitzer Prize. It did achieve a resounding run of 472 performances, and collect a cozy $225,000 when the film rights were sold to RKO and Max Gordon. Moreover the public found in Raymond Massey an Abe who still haunts the memory as the embodiment of the bumbling, humorous, tragic Lincoln, illumined by an inner light, who was summoned to greatness by events.

It did more than that. It marked, as I was too blind to realize at the time, a tremendous development in Sherwood himself and a reversal of the negative attitude which had been his during the years of disillusionment after the First World War. "It seems to me," he wrote when he was working on *Abe,* "there's one fundamental subject with which I am most concerned—*growth.* My own growth, and that of the characters I write about, and the ideas they express. No play seems worth writing if, at its end, its principal characters have failed to attain during its two hours greater stature. Of course, *Abe* is the supreme manifestation of that purpose so far."

The growth that Sherwood marveled at in Lincoln had in its own way occurred within him. Lincoln, opposed to slavery, was at first even more opposed to the idea of going to war to end it. He hated war with Sherwood's fervor, but in the end was forced to admit that the moment comes when men must fight for what they believe in. This moment was not to overtake Sherwood until after months of soul-searching during which he hoped and despaired, and finally recognized the inevitable was at hand.

As the New York first night of *Abe* approached, events clutched increasingly at Sherwood's conscience. That he, long articulate as a pacifist, chose to write about a man who was forced to wage a war which would cost thousands of lives, including his own, was in itself a change, a change in attitude as marked as the change in the form he used and the tone of his writing. Busy as he was rewriting his play, attending rehearsals and out-of-town tryouts, or following the fortunes of *Knickerbocker Holiday* on the road, he could not tether his interest to the make-believe of the theater. The headlines preyed increasingly on his mind. More and more they pointed to the coming of that war the outbreak of which he had dramatized in *Idiot's Delight.*

Sherwood wrote *Abe* from basic beliefs that had changed, and it changed his career. From then on, more than being a playwright, he emerged in the public mind as a public man. As surely as it took years for Massey to escape from the part of Abe, Sherwood in the future was associated with the dimensions of his play about Lincoln. Having presented Abe as the embodiment of all that was challenged in democratic values, he himself came to be considered as a spokesman for those values. He did not carry Lincoln to the White House in his play, but his play was to bring Sherwood there, and in time make him a member of Roosevelt's inner circle.

Although they had never met, five days after the Washington opening Eleanor Roosevelt wrote him a longhand letter from the White House. "Dear Mr. Sherwood: I am just back from seeing your play and must tell you not only that I enjoyed it but that it moved me deeply. Mr. Massey acts beautifully a difficult part, and the audience was more enthusiastic than I have ever heard them here. I hope the play has a long run. Strange, how fundamentally people seem to have fought on much the same issues throughout our history! My congratulations to you." Mrs. Roosevelt, whom Sherwood had long admired, did not stop there. In her syndicated column "My Day" she wrote the first of her glowing tributes to *Abe*. Her generous enthusiasm was the beginning of a long and close friendship.

The person who did most to open the White House door to Sherwood was Harry Hopkins. Sherwood met this bright-eyed, intrepid, deeply loathed and deeply loved man early in September when *Abe* had just gone into rehearsal. Their first meeting took place on a Long Island weekend "under the hospitable roof of Herbert and Margaret Swope." He seemed taller than he was because of his ravished body. Plainly he was "a master of the naked insult," and no less plainly his fervor shone out in spite of his frailty. His laugh was "high and sharp and seemed to have an exclamation point in it."

In his diary Sherwood noted, "Long talk at breakfast with Harry Hopkins, the WPA Administrator, a profoundly shrewd and faintly ominous man." This was all he put down, but he remembered that on that occasion

Hopkins talked to him "very agreeably, revealing a considerable knowledge of and enthusiasm for the theater. He took obvious pride in the achievements of WPA in the Federal Theatre and Arts Projects," and Sherwood believed he had every right to be proud.

But, he added, "I did not quite like him. He used such phrases as, 'We've got to crack down on the bastards.' I could not disagree with his estimate of the targets in question but I did not like the idea of cracking down. I had the characteristically American suspicion of anyone who appeared to be getting 'too big for his breeches.' "

Nonetheless Sherwood was interested in Hopkins and Hopkins in him, though neither of them had the slightest notion that their acquaintance would lead to the closest friendship and bring Sherwood into intimate association with Roosevelt as one of his ghostwriters. This interest showed itself on the day when a nervous Sherwood was awaiting the opening of *Abe* in Washington. Hopkins considerately asked Sherwood to lunch with him. Then he took him to the White House where he showed him Lincoln's bedroom. "Furniture perfect. A great thrill," noted Sherwood.

He did not realize that in the years ahead he would on occasion sleep in that bed himself or the great thrills which were to be his at the White House. Hopkins, it might be added, was at the party at the Barberry Room after the New York first night of *Abe*. No one was more responsible than he for choosing Sherwood for the role he was to play at the heart of great events— and on a larger stage.

PART IV
The Sound of Laughter

Top of My Head

By Goodman Ace

March 21, 1970

Somberly

As it must to everyone, it fell to my lot some months ago to be appointed, for the first time, the "arranger" of a funeral. A close and cherished member of the family had died.

He had not passed on, or passed over, or departed, or left us. He died. Years before his span. Suddenly.

The shock absorbed, replaced by the usual and unreasonable bitterness and the asking of why, I entered the funeral parlor. Black-suited, black-tied attendants directed me softly to the man in charge of such details. He sat behind a desk spotlessly clean of all clutter. I resented him for that. But I realized here was a man who knew where everything, and everybody, belonged.

"This won't take long, will it?" I asked.

"No," he replied, drawing a long printed form from his desk, "only about thirty minutes." An eternity.

With pen poised, he asked the first startling question. "What was his Social Security number?"

I shook my head. He could see I didn't know. He could also see how inept an arranger I was going to be. Other questions followed, and he was helpful in leading me to answers. I don't remember all the questions, but I have total recall of the last four:

"Now what about flowers?" he asked.

"We have asked that flowers be omitted," I replied.

"No, I mean the spray on the casket. Do you want a spray?"

"Well, I guess so."

"They come in three sizes. There's the small piece placed in the center, or the three-quarter length, or the blanket of flowers that covers the entire casket."

"Well, I don't know. What would you think?"

"May I suggest the three-quarter length?"

I nodded.

He made the entry as he said, "Flowers, seventy-nine dollars. Now, what about music? Something classical?"

"I suppose so."

"Bach? Beethoven? Mozart?"

"Yes," I replied, as I felt myself disintegrating.

"Which one?"

"I don't know," I said rising, unreasonably disturbed at my own inadequacy to answer a few simple questions.

As I paced, he remained calm and made a note on the form, and asked the next question.

"Now, what about clothes?"

I sat again in utter bewilderment. This was to be a cremation. Did it matter? I gathered it did from his next remark.

"We can furnish a suit, if you like. Or some prefer a robe or even pajamas."

He waited for my answer while I sat there thinking, "This too shall pass." But it didn't.

"I suggest pajamas," he offered.

I nodded.

He wrote, as he said, "Pajamas, twelve dollars and sixty cents." And then he added, "That includes the sales tax."

And there you have it—the two irrevocables, death and taxes.

As I was about to leave, he asked the fourth question, almost in passing. "By the way," he said, "have you signed the paper for the release of the deceased from the hospital?"

I hadn't. He said I should. He was right. All my other arrangements would have been rather flat without it.

He was quite helpful here. He phoned the hospital to tell them I was coming down to sign. Then he wrote down the window and the name of the doctor I was to ask for.

When I arrived at the hospital, the doctor I was to see was out to lunch. There was some scurrying around to find him, and finally I was rescued by a courteous young man in an office who benevolently suggested that

I sign the paper and he would have the doctor fill out the details later. I signed.

"I will mail you a copy," he said.

I thanked him for his help.

"Glad to be of service," he replied. He put out his hand, "Good-by, and I hope the next time we meet it will be under more pleasant circumstances." We shook on it.

In the cab on the way back I thought that over. "The next time we meet?" When? Where? When were we going to meet again? Socially? Hardly. Did he mean as a bereaved or as a client?

A day to remember. Thinking back on it, I have the feeling that the man for whom I made the arrangements would have laughed at my discomfiture and joined with me in my disapprobation of this "civilized" ritual.

What it amounts to is we go into a funeral shop to buy a man something that he wouldn't get for himself, and that he has never had before.

Curmudgeon-at-Large

By Cleveland Amory

February 23, 1974

The latest in children's books is something called Me-Books—from Hollywood.

All you have to do to get one, we noticed in an advertisement, is to fill out a coupon containing what's called your "Personalized Story Data." This includes such matters as boy/girl—check one—your first name; your address; your birthday; the names of "up to three friends, brothers, or sisters," and finally your dog's name and/or your cat's name.

You do this, the advertisement claimed, and then, "a Magic Computer does the rest." And, in short order, you will receive a whole book—all about just you. Well, not *just* you—but still, you're the big cheese in it. You have, at present, four choices—*My Birthday Land Adventure*, *My Special Christmas*, *My Jungle Holiday*, and *My Friendly Giraffe*.

It was a tough choice, all right—things like this are never easy—but we finally crossed the Rubicon with *My Friendly Giraffe*. For one thing the advertisement for this one said—and we quote—"Personalized in Over 70 places." We weren't quite sure what this meant —whether there were going to be that many references to us throughout the book, or whether we were going to be a big man all over the map—but anyway, that was the one we picked. And we even included our childhood nickname, "Clip"—one that we have been fairly successfully burying for forty years. It's not that we had any particular big thing about "Clip," you understand; it was just that nobody got it right. They called us either "Cliff" or, sometimes, "Kip"—and Cleveland Fadiman already had that one.

Well, sir, when our Me-Book arrived, what do you think the first sentence was? You'll never guess. "Once upon a time," it read, "in a place called New York, there lived a little boy named Chip Amory."

Chip, for God's sake. And what do you think was the name of the damned giraffe? *Pihc!* No, we're *not* kidding. It *was* Pihc. And it turned out, if you can bear it, that Pihc was named that because it was *Chip* spelled backwards. Honest to Pete, we'd have been better off with Cliff. Even a computer might have balked at Ffilc.

Well, no matter—we suppose it takes all kinds. But the more we thought about the idea of these books, the more we wondered if these Me-Boys weren't on to a pretty big thing. After all, these aren't the most modest of times. The way we see it, there's no reason to waste as good an idea as this one on mere children.

Take us, for example. Sure, we got a kick out of being in *My Friendly Giraffe,* but now that we've been bitten, so to speak, we can see no reason not to move on. We would like, for instance, *My Gone With the Wind,* or even *My War and Peace.* And we think other book buyers would feel the same way. After all, there should be no difficulty getting enough of these books written—Norman Mailer, to use just one name, has been writing Me-Books for years. And the field is a broad one. Some readers might prefer *My Joy of Cooking;* others, *My Joy of Sex.* There's something for everyone. And no need anymore to read a book like *Seven Who Shaped Our Destiny.* Make it, we say, *Eight.* And there'll be an end to all those tiresome guessing games you have to play, say, with an author like Jacqueline Susann, to know whom she's writing about. Hell, you don't have to play any games anymore—the ball, so to speak, is in your court. And finally, the whole Me-Book thing is certainly the answer for giving books as presents. Imagine the thrill of giving your godfather not just *The Godfather* but *My Godfather.*

Notice Department—as found by Jean and Howard Albano of Los Angeles, in the Weiser (Idaho) *American*:

NOTICE TO ALL CITY ASPIRANTS
FOR MAYOR AND CITY COUNCIL

We, of the Weiser Coffee Committee, are very much concerned about the behavior of our elected officials in high government offices. We further realize that these men grew up in towns such as ours and must have gone astray in their younger lives. We feel that a much closer check must be made of the behavior of men at the grass roots.

Therefore, we urgently request all aspirants who are running for city office this coming election to reveal to the public a written report in detail of all their behavior from the time they were five years old.

Respectfully,
Weiser Coffee Committee

We say make it four—these days, you can't be too careful.

Critics' Choice—as spotted by Sharon Gaiser of Independence, Missouri, in John O'Connor's TV review in *The New York Times*:

The Rockefellers prevail. And, as the documentary makes clear, they prevail a gold course dotted with rather awesomely. The 3,500-acre Rockefeller estate on the Hudson River contains eleven homes, one a fifty-room mansion, and such amenities as a stable of twenty-five horses and remarked, "It's what God sculptures by Picasso, Calder, Henry Moore, et al. As George S. Kaufman once reportedly would have done if He had the money.

Gee. And we always thought God said it—about Moss Hart.

Through History with J. Wesley Smith

Cartoons by Burr Shafer

"I'm afraid little Nero will never set the world on fire."

"Never mind why—we're moving to Florence and changing the name of the firm."

"Why don't we form a democracy? Then we'd only have to satisfy 51 per cent of the people."

"And if you're not out by 12 o'clock, General Washington, I'll have to charge you for another day!"

Classified Ads

Important Notice: If you are one of the hundreds of parachuting enthusiasts who bought our course entitled "Easy Sky Diving in One Fell Swoop," please make the following correction: On page 8, line 7, change "state zip code" to "pull rip cord."

•

Available: Catalogue of carefully selected dervishes for instant whirling. WM, Box CL.

•

If You're Allergic to Dogs and still want to protect your hearth and home, we have the perfect solution. Our trained snapping turtles don't shed, bark, or beg to be petted, but will strike fear in the heart of any thug. Our little guardians are trained to lunge for the ankles. Heavy boots also available for members of your household. Write for information. *Watchturtles*, Inc., WM, Box SK2.

•

Why Not Retire and raise hackles? Many choice locations available, urban, suburban areas. Write Box W-K.

•

24-Hour Emergency Service. Electrical and plumbing problems our specialty. Staff of qualified technicians ready to serve you day and night. Write (airmail): Habibullah, 1 East Amanullah Strasse, Kandahar, Afghanistan.

•

To all Users of Denture Sticktite: We regret that our product exceeded our most optimistic expectations. Our chemists are working around the clock to develop a tasty and effective release solvent. In the meantime, we ask our friends to be patient. SR/W Box TR.

POSTSCRIPT

Musings on a Golden Anniversary

By Norman Cousins

August 10, 1974

The earliest Greek book of which there is a historical record, Hesiod's *Works and Days,* cried out for a return to the good old days, when life was less complicated and more trusting and when, presumably, one's illusions were intact. This is the way the remote but remembered past tends to appear to the present. Retrospect imparts a quality of innocence to bygone times.

The past sets up far fewer barriers to the understanding of causes and effects than does the present. You assemble your reference materials about the past; there they rest, accessible and obedient, waiting to be sorted out and judged. But the facts of the present won't sit still for a portrait; they are constantly vibrating, full of clutter and confusion.

Today's elusive and complicated facts, however, are apt to be viewed as simplicities a generation hence. And all the current sophistications will probably seem like a species of innocence. What happens, of course, is that people never lose their innocence; they just take on new perspectives. This is where nostalgia begins. It is also what makes the reading of history so engaging and the writing of it so precarious.

The founding editors of *SR* tried to maintain a constancy of attitude toward past and present. They tried to look beyond the events, the manners, and the aberrations that lent themselves all too easily to striking labels and catch phrases—catch phrases that were to become fixed totalities in the minds of later generations. The world of the 1920s that emerged from the pages of *SRL* was not just a world of rumrunners, spangled flappers, jazz, high-flying stocks, Teapot Domes, Gatsbys, Kennicotts, and Babbitts. It was a world which produced scholars and scientists who successfully challenged theories that had held for centuries; a world that was tooling up for great change; a world that was at least as interested in examining values as it was in experimenting with them; a world in which teachers such as Dewey, Kilpatrick, and Rugg were laying down new educational foundations; a world in which poets like A. E. Housman, W. B. Yeats, Robert Frost, Robinson Jeffers, and Edna St. Vincent Millay were finding responsive audiences; a world that relished the intellectual juxtaposition of George Bernard Shaw against H. G. Wells; a world that, for all its vaunted twitching, could sit still long enough to enjoy storytellers like Ellen Glasgow, Edith Wharton, Willa Cather, Thomas Hardy, Joseph Conrad, and E. M. Forster, and still notice new writers like Ernest Hemingway, Sinclair Lewis, and William Faulkner; a world which knew the enjoyment of laughter that men like Robert Benchley and Ring Lardner could provide.

The *Saturday Review,* through its changes in ownership and editorship over a half-century, has never departed from two fixed points in its basic purpose. One has been to avoid becoming a captive of chronology, neither being charmed by the submissiveness of materials dealing with the past nor intimidated by the complexities and loose ends of the present.

The second fixed point has been the resistance to cynicism. Complexities are the natural habitat of cynicism, if only because they set the stage for concealment and manipulation. Especially is this true of complexities that embrace manifest injustice or malevolence or special privilege or corruption or callousness. And the disillusion that is joined to cynicism breeds distrust. This is how societies begin to fall apart. John Middleton Murry, the English critic, in the August 29, 1925, issue of SRL, had this to say of the generation of his countrymen who emerged from the First World War:

If they had the luck not to die, their brothers had no such luck. From the very beginning, they had to face ultimate questions. The whole civilization which had been taken for granted by their elders was to them an object of suspicion and a cause of despair. ... They did not become revolutionaries, for revolution seemed to them as futile as war itself. They became nihilists; they touched the bottom of an abyss of despair. ... It is not easy to create out of despair. ... They are struggling to create for themselves a philosophy of life by which they may live; they are trying to discover for themselves a justification of their own activity. ...

The perennial academic question: What is the function of art? has suddenly taken on an almost agonized actuality. ... So long as this effort at criticism remains purely intellectual, a cynical pessimism is its inevitable conclusion, and the function of the writer is fixed as one of mere amusement. ... Certain things have to be accepted as beyond the scrutiny of the intellect; chief among them is life itself. The system or the society of which the individual is a member is profoundly mistrusted. The individual cannot trust the system; he must trust himself. So that the critical problem with which modern English literature is trying to grapple is twofold. Is there in the universe at large a general process man may trust? Has he a self he can trust?

What Murry was doing, a quarter of a century before Sartre, Camus, and Tillich, was posing the supreme existentialist questions. His description of the philosophical position of the young English writers following World War I was also prophetically true of the new generation of writers in France and Germany following World War II and, in a sense, of the American writers much later in their reaction to the Vietnam war. The significant difference between the Europeans and the Americans, of course, was that the Europeans manifested their opposition through bitterness and withdrawal, whereas the Americans turned to scorn and activism. Common to both, however, was the deep and corrosive distrust of established institutions and even, in a subliminal sense, of life itself.

Middleton Murry correctly identified the connection between cynicism and cold intellectuality. He didn't feel that a purely intellectual response was adequate to the challenge of life. He never explicitly defined intellectuality, but it must be assumed he was thinking of it in terms of sophisticated indifference or disdain. The intellectuality he criticizes has to be juxtaposed against the positivist attitudes—a belief in the perfectibility of the individual; the notion of an accountable society; confidence in the use of the rational intelligence; faith in the regenerative capacity. Murry felt that the ability to think created the obligation to define purpose: that is, the need to probe for, and constantly refine, the values by which humans add meaning to existence.

How did it happen that all four editors of *SR* during the half-century existence of the magazine were militantly opposed to cynicism—despite Teapot Domes, breadlines, gas chambers, social and racial injustices, four wars, air bombings, and Watergates? The answer is that they all shared substantially the same values. It is remarkable, now that I think back upon it, that all of us, despite widely different backgrounds and varying views on the place of literature in society, should have come off the same philosophical spool. Our mentors were men like Francis Bacon, Milton, John Stuart Mill, Jefferson, and the American transcendentalists. We were all deeply rooted on native grounds, though we had different centers of attraction. For Henry Canby it was the world of Thoreau, Emerson, and Whitman. For Bernard DeVoto, it was the early explorers of the American West. For George Stevens, it was the perception of America by such writers as John Steinbeck and Willa Cather. For me, it was the kinds of ideas that were ventilated in the Jefferson-Adams correspondence and, much later, in the Holmes-Pollock letters. All these separate interests and enthusiasms converged in giving the magazine continuity of primary character.

Our approach to the editing of the magazine represented perhaps our most striking differences. Henry Canby was less enamored of book reviewing than of

criticism. By criticism he meant the conditions of literature, the particular values of a writer and his lines of
literary connection, stylistic distinctions and comparative analysis, and, in general, the place of a specific
work in the natural history of books. He had no difficulty in accepting Matthew Arnold's statement that
the true object of criticism is to bring forward and make
known to all readers that which is best both in past
and present literature. DeVoto and Stevens put greater
emphasis on general reviewing and book coverage than
did Canby. They believed the magazine should search
out excitement in the literary arena, as when they made
front-page news by publishing an account of the "secret"
Lawrence papers. My own bias was to connect the
world of books to the world of ideas and to provide a
well-rounded magazine for people who made no separation between their cultural interests and their world
concerns.

DeVoto was perhaps the only one of the four who
not only did not shun personal feuds but seemed, indeed, to thrive on them. He had a free-swinging style,
and there was no ambiguity in his vocabulary or in his
soul. But, like the rest of us, he was energized by a
belief in the possibilities of a humane society. All of
us saw the connection between progress toward that
goal and the full exercise of the unfettered mind. We
shied away from debunking and cheap shots. We were
not easily pushed around by ideologies or dogma. We
avoided intellectual and literary cliques. We had no
"crowd" that we were especially eager to please or that
counted on us for support. We were more interested
in the meeting of minds than in establishing a watering-
hole for followers.

Is there a single theme or purpose that emerges from
the varied history of the magazine during these past
50 years? I believe there is. That theme or purpose has
to do with the conditions of creativity. The editorial
page of *SR* from the start has seen creativity as an
aspect of human uniqueness that needs special tending.
Creativity can be stifled or throttled not just by political
juggernauts but also by brutality or wickedness or

squalor. It is folly, therefore, to assume that the editor or the writer or the artist has no obligation to the conditions that make creativity possible.

Arguments over the ivory tower versus the arena are usually a waste of time. They tend to juxtapose Art against Involvement. They assume that creativity never needs its champions, that there is no connection between the shape of the society and the condition of the arts, and that the world of ideas is somehow separate from the world in which great books are written or great music composed or canvases painted or great drama staged. What is the good society if not the creative society? The conditions of life are inseparable from the conditions of art. The truly creative writer or artist never has to choose between the ivory tower and the arena. He moves freely from one to the other according to his needs and his concerns.

Nothing is more vital for the creative artist than access to the arena. Repressive and insecure societies keep the artist under control not by forbidding him to write or paint but by separating him from his audience. What Solzhenitsyn protested was not that he was forbidden to write but that his writing was not available to his countrymen. And great audiences, as Walt Whitman reminded us, are necessary if we want to have great poets. For it is the audience that ultimately has to uphold the values of the ivory tower.

One of the prime characteristics of a monolithic society is not just that it tries to expunge the free and creative spirit but that it cuts off a free and creative response. When Nikita Khrushchev tried to release the Russian people from the paralyzing effects of Stalinism, one of the first things he did was to permit artists to exhibit works of their own choosing, as apart from those approved by political controllers. Paintings by the thousands came out of cellars. The dominant character of those paintings was not exactly what one might find in a showing of uninhibited abstractionism, but it was remarkably devoid of exhortation or "poster naturalism." What was most significant about that exhibition perhaps was that the audience seemed tentative in attitude, as though the people weren't quite sure it was really safe to see what the artist himself wanted them to see. The habit of selective encounters with art had become so strong that the great audience, in Whitman's phrase, was not ready.

The prime function of the *Saturday Review* over the years, therefore, has been to act as a bridge between artist and audience. Both have their needs; both have their rights. Neither exists in splendid isolation. Yet it has not been an easy time—the Fifties and Sixties especially—for creating a rapport between the two. In the fine arts, we have been passing through a period of estrangement between practitioner and public. The artist properly insists on his right to express himself and to experiment as fully as he wishes. He does not believe he shoud be asked to explain what he means or to justify his belief that what he has produced deserves to be exhibited. But the art-loving public, even more than the critic, holds the ultimate power. The empty galleries that greeted many of the showings of experimental art during the Sixties flashed the danger sign that people, almost as a Tolstoyan prophecy come true, insist on their own definition of art and cannot be pushed beyond certain limits. Today, the swing is back to realism and romanticism, but the heavily imitative and repetitious nature of much of the work may dim public enthusiasm.

If the audience seems detached from the arts today, then it is not a solitary phenomenon. There is evidence on every hand that the American people are in a general mood of withdrawal. The clamorous activism of the Sixties has given way to the distrust and disillusion of the Seventies. There is little disposition to rally around banners, whether new or old. It is a lean time for leaders.

The problem is not that persons of stature are vanishing. The problem is that the American people right now are not in a heroic mood. The face of their history has been disfigured by government itself. The deepest and most nourishing part of their tradition is the principle that government cannot make secret commitments which the people are then compelled to redeem. Yet through at least two presidencies, such commitments were made. The fact that the government would deliberately and consistently lie to the American people has cracked open the wall of confidence that they instinctively believed would never be breached. The endless horrors of Watergate have compounded that distrust and added to the disillusion.

We are back again, then, at the question Middleton Murry asked with reference to England 50 years ago: Is there anything or anyone people can trust? Can the individual trust himself?

Useful answers to those questions are not likely to come out of cynicism. The society cries out for regeneration and reintegration. Beyond that, the world has to be kept from sliding into a grotesque downward spiral. The nation has always been the ultimate form of human organization. Yet that institution is the principal factor in the downward spiral. It is no longer able to perform its historic function. It cannot protect the lives or property of its people; it cannot uphold their cultures or their values. The sudden compression of all the nations into a single geographic unit has produced no corresponding response in terms of an organization of the whole. Instead, there is virtual anarchy in the world arena.

The problems inside the arena demand a world view, a world philosophy, a world sensitivity to the dangers that now extend to the whole of the human race. One problem is the bulging stockpile of nuclear weapons that could produce a global holocaust. The stockpile has long since passed the point at which it has any relationship to any theoretical military need. Yet the nuclear explosives pile higher each year, as though the nations are determined that, if war should come, no leaf or grain of sand would escape the furnace nor any evidence remain of a world exquisitely suited to life in all its forms.

A world dimension applies to the other major problems as well—contamination of the total environment, squandered resources, limping societies, too little food and too many people, persistence of social injustices, shrinkage in the conditions of creative growth.

These problems call for the highest energies and keenest perceptions of which the human race is capable. Cynicism blocks off access to those energies and dulls those perceptions, if only because the cynic positions himself for defeat. Progress begins with the idea that progress is possible. Cynicism begins with acceptance of the impossible.

Nothing is more false historically or more dangerous than the notion of helplessness. The past half-century, perhaps more than any previous period in history, has demonstrated that history is not immutable and that existing forces are not inexorable. In our lifetime, we have witnessed a vast enlargement in the definition of human uniqueness. The human species is unique because it alone can do things for the first time.

The opportunity for a journal such as the *Saturday Review,* therefore, is to argue for the proposition that human beings are equal to their needs, that a problem can be resolved if it can be perceived, that progress is what is left over after the seemingly impossible has been retired, and that the crisis today in human affairs is represented not by the absence of human capacity but by the failure to recognize that the capacity exists.

Optimism versus pessimism, like the arena versus the ivory tower, is a false issue. Certainly we should not minimize or blink at our problems in all their complexity. Neither ought we blind ourselves to untapped potentialities of brain and spirit for meeting them.

ACKNOWLEDGMENTS

"What Is English?" from A CONTINUING JOURNEY by Archibald MacLeish: Copyright © 1967 by Archibald MacLeish. Reprinted by permission of Houghton Mifflin Company.

"The Historian's Opportunity" by Barbara W. Tuchman: Copyright © 1967 by Saturday Review. Reprinted by permission of Russell & Volkening, Inc. as agents for the author.

"Lessons of the Cuban Missile Crisis" from THIRTEEN DAYS, A Memoir of the Cuban Missile Crisis, by Robert F. Kennedy: Copyright © 1971, 1969 by W. W. Norton & Company, Inc. Copyright © 1968 by McCall Corporation. Reprinted by permission of W. W. Norton & Company, Inc.

"Why and How I Work" from EXPERIENCES by Arnold J. Toynbee: Copyright © 1969 by Oxford University Press. Reprinted by permission of the publisher.

"New Light on the Human Potential" by Herbert A. Otto: Copyright © 1969 by Saturday Review. Reprinted by permission of Gunther Stuhlmann as agent for the author.

"FDR: The Untold Story of His Last Year" by James MacGregor Burns: Copyright © 1970 by Saturday Review. Reprinted by permission of the author.

"The War Novel: From Mailer to Vonnegut" by Alfred Kazin: Copyright © 1971 by Saturday Review. Reprinted by permission of the author.

"The Return of the Case of Ezra Pound" from THE CRITICAL POINT: ON LITERATURE AND CULTURE by Irving Howe, 1973, Horizon Press. Reprinted by permission of the author.

"E.B.W." from CREDOS and CURIOS by James Thurber: Copyright © 1962 by Helen Thurber. Published by Harper & Row, Publishers, Inc. Reprinted by permission of Helen Thurber.

"Memories of A. E. Housman" by Laurence Housman: Copyright © 1936 by Saturday Review. Reprinted by permission of the Executors of the Laurence Housman Estate.

"D. H. Lawrence" by Richard Aldington: Copyright © 1939 by Saturday Review. Reprinted by permission of Ann Elmo Agency, Inc., as agent for Richard Aldington.

"So You Want to be a Writer?" by Sherwood Anderson: Copyright © 1939 by Saturday Review. Renewed 1967 by Eleanor Copenhaver Anderson. Reprinted by permission of Harold Ober Associates.

"Heywood Broun" by Bennett Cerf: Copyright © 1942 by Saturday Review. Reprinted by permission of Phyllis Cerf.

"In Memory of George Gershwin" by Bennett Cerf: Copyright © 1943 by Saturday Review. Reprinted by permission of Phyllis Cerf.

"The Literary Churchill" by J. H. Plumb: Copyright © 1965 by J. H. Plumb. Reprinted by permission of the author.

"The worlds of Robert E. Sherwood" appears as *"By Way of Introduction"* and *"Bob Sherwood in Illinois"* in THE WORLDS OF ROBERT E. SHERWOOD by John Mason Brown: Copyright © 1965 by John Mason Brown. Reprinted by permission of Harper & Row, Publishers, Inc.

"Through History with J. Wesley Smith", Cartoons by Burr Shafer: Copyright © by Evelyn Shafer. Reprinted by permission of Evelyn Shafer.